Naples, Pompeii & the Amalfi Coast

Naples, Pompeii & Around
p47

The Islands
p119

The Amalfi Coast
p157

Salerno & the Cilento
p195

Cristian Bonetto, Brendan Sainsbury

Contents

PLAN YOUR TRIP

ON THE ROAD

GELATERIA DAVID P166

MARK READ/LONELY PLANET ©

CIMITERO DELLE
FONTANELLE P79

MASSIMO LAMA/500PX ©

ANTONIO GRAVANTE/SHUTTERSTOCK ©

VIA PORT'ALBA P63

Contents

COVID-19

We have re-checked every business in this book
before publication to ensure that it is still open after
the COVID-19 outbreak. However, the economic and
social impacts of COVID-19 will continue to be felt
long after the outbreak has been contained, and
many businesses, services and events referenced
in this guide may experience ongoing restrictions.
Some businesses may be temporarily closed, have
changed their opening hours and services, or require
bookings; some unfortunately could have closed
permanently. We suggest you check with venues
before visiting for the latest information.

Right:
Amalfi Coast
(p157)

WELCOME TO

Naples, Pompeii & the Amalfi Coast

For me, Campania is Italy at its most authentic, where billowing clothes dry on dilapidated balconies and buzzing Vespas speed through animated streets. I love it for its vivid contrasts, the way in which grit and grandiosity coexist. It's as if you're living in an opera, tinged with the comedy of Rossini and the tragedy of Pompeii. I often catch a bus to Amalfi where rough stairways climb through ancient pastures to spectacular Mediterranean viewpoints. Up there on the terraced cliffsides, it is as calm as Naples is chaotic.

Brendan Sainsbury
🐦 @sainsburyb
For more about our writers, see p288

MARK READ/LONELY PLANET ©

Naples & the Amalfi Coast

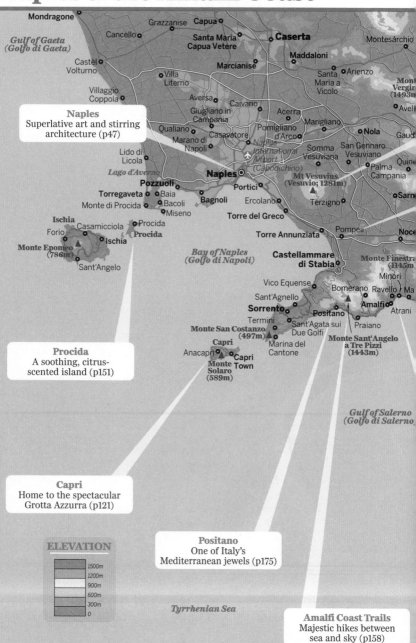

Naples
Superlative art and stirring architecture (p47)

Procida
A soothing, citrus-scented island (p151)

Capri
Home to the spectacular Grotta Azzurra (p121)

Positano
One of Italy's Mediterranean jewels (p175)

Amalfi Coast Trails
Majestic hikes between sea and sky (p158)

ELEVATION

1500m
1200m
900m
600m
300m
0

Mt Vesuvius
Climb a slumbering
menace (p110)

Pompeii
Step back in time in
ghostly Pompeii (p111)

Paestum
Glorious Greek temples
and treasures (p203)

Ravello
Heavenly views and a
summer arts festival (p187)

0 _____ 20 km
0 _____ 10 miles

PUGLIA

Melfi

Monticchio

Avellino

Montella
Bagnoli

CAMPANIA
Monte
Cervialto
(1808m)

Acerno

BASILICATA

Cava

Montecorvino

Salerno

Vietri
sul Mare
etara

Eboli

Battipaglia
Sele

Sicignano degli
Alburni
Postiglione
Auletta
Pertosa
Altavilla
Silentina
Monte
Alburno
(1742m)
Petina
Polla
Controne
Castelcivita

Sant'Angelo
a Fasanella

Capaccio
Scalo
Capaccio
Roccadaspide
Bellosguardo
Sala
Consilina
Paestum
Castel
San Lorenzo
Roscigno
Teggiano

Padula

Agropoli
Ogliastro
Parco Nazionale del Cilento,
Vallo di Diano e Alburni
(Cilento, Valley of Diano &
Alburni Mountains National Park)
Sassano

Santa Maria di
Castellabate
Laureana
Cilento
Monte Cervati
(1900m)
Castellabate
San Marco di
Castellabate
Perdifumo
Sanza

Marina
di Casal
Velino
Vallo della
Lucania
Pioppi
Ceraso
Acciaroli
Velia

Ascea

Pisciotta
Sapri

Centola
Camerota
San Giovanni
a Piro
Acquafredda
di Maratea
Palinuro
Marina di Camerota

Naples, Pompeii & the Amalfi Coast's Top Experiences

BALATE DORIN/SHUTTERSTOCK ©

1 HIKING THE COAST

When it comes to easy accessibility, gorgeous scenery and sheer number of trails, there's no better place to go hiking in Italy than the Amalfi. The coastline is handsomely endowed with footpaths, many dating back to medieval times when they served as the primary means of getting from village to village. These days local farmers still use the paths to access their terraced smallholdings, but the bulk of foot traffic is recreational walkers.

Above: Atrani (p187), Amalfi Coast

Sentiero degli Dei

Making a spectacular traverse high above the Mediterranean with heavenly views over terraced fields and hazy mountains, the 'path of the gods' crosses a typical Amalfi pastiche of dramatic natural landscapes modified by generations of human settlers. p158

Right: Walking the Sentiero degli Dei

MARK READ/LONELY PLANET ©

POLEUPHOTO/SHUTTERSTOCK ©

MAZERATH/SHUTTERSTOCK ©

Valle delle Ferriere

Often overshadowed by the Sentiero degli Dei, the damper, greener, more secluded Valle delle Ferriere inhabits a flora-rich valley north of Amalfi town that is still filled with the ghosts of a once vibrant milling industry. p160

Above: Overgrown ruin, Valle delle Ferriere

Sentiero dei Fortini

This 5km footpath along Capri's rocky western shore is practically the only place on the island where you can feel a genuine sense of history and solitude. It starts high above the Grotta Azzurra and finishes near a popular beach passing three Anglo-French ruined forts en route. p136

Above: Sentiero dei Fortini footpath

EKATERINA POKROVSKY/ SHUTTERSTOCK ©

2 TAKING A 'PAUSA'

No Campanian day is complete without at least one 'pausa', a brief sojourn to a cafe for a spirit-reviving dose of caffeine. But forget about takeaways. Hurry or no hurry, you'll be expected to prop up the bar or perch at a tiny table, and imbibe your coffee from a proper ceramic cup. Fortunately, numerous attractive cafes exist to make the 'pausa' a perfectly pleasant affair.

Above: Espresso with a view, Naples (p51)

La Zagara

Even if your budget won't stretch to a Michelin-starred meal in Positano, you can at least afford to stretch out your morning cappuccino on the pretty trellis-covered terrace of La Zagara while tuning in to the local grapevine. p179

Amalfi

Amalfi town's busy Piazza del Duomo is a wonderful place to flop down after a hilly hike or a tough session of sunbathing for an alfresco pastry and cappuccino served by an obliging *cameriere*. p185

Above top: Amalfi

Caffè Gambrinus

Every Italian city worth its salt has a storied coffee bar that's been in business for time immemorial. In Naples, the mantle is carried by the Gambrinus, which has been churning out potent espressos since the days of the Risorgimento. p90

Above: Caffè Gambrinus interior

3 ANALYZING ART

Art is everywhere in Campania: in churches and chapels, galleries and museums, streets and alleys, and, most famously, in the Neapolitan masterworks of the renaissance and baroque. In the golden era of the 17th and 18th centuries, Naples attracted a dubious collection of artistic mavericks, Caravaggio and Ribera among them, who seemed to reflect the dark energy of the city and its penchant for dramatic chiaroscuro art. Don't miss it.

Cappella Sansevero

Chapel it may be (and an exquisite one at that), but the Sansevero is as relevant to art lovers as religious worshippers courtesy of its hyper-realistic marble sculptures and vivid 18th-century frescoes. p55

Below: Ticket office, Cappella Sansevero

BONNIE ALBERTS/LONELY PLANET ©

BIGLIETTERIA
TICKET OFFICE

MUSEO | CAPPELLA
SANSEVERO

SAN
SEV
RO

SOLO
USCITA
EXIT ONLY

USCITA
EXIT

Palazzo Zevallos Stigliano

Exhibiting everything from religious epics to landscapes and portraits, the Zevallos will give you an important lesson in Neapolitan art history. p69

Above: Palazzo Zevallos Stigliano

MADRE

This contemporary gallery is a favourite of people who have overdosed on dark religious paintings and are craving a bit of Andy Warhol et al. p61

Right: MADRE courtyard

Image courtesy of the Donnaregina Foundation for the Contemporary Arts, Naples

AMEDEO BENESTANTE/MADRE · DONNAREGINA MUSEUM OF CONTEMPORARY ART

4 PERFECT PIZZA

CATHERINAUNGER/GETTY IMAGES ©

Above: Margherita pizza, Naples

People are often fastidious about how they make their pizza, but there's no debating about where it originated – Naples. The real deal – the practically holy margherita – has a thick-ish crust blistered at the edges, topped with a sauce made from San Marzano tomatoes grown on the volcanic soil of Mt Vesuvius, and *bufala* mozzarella produced from water buffalo reared on the marshlands of Campania and Lazio.

Concettina Ai Tre Santi

Best pizza in Naples = best pizza in the world. Could this be the one? Roll into the pizzeria of Ciro Oliva and cast your vote. p88

Antica Pizza Fritta da Zia Esterina Sorbillo

Visit 'Auntie' Esterina for that other little Neapolitan gift to the culinary world: the *pizza fritta* – deep-fried with pork lard, wrapped in paper and eaten take-out style. p88

Da Michele

In the heart of the *centro storico,* Da Michele has been serving up fast, simple, pizza with no ceremony since 1870. It's a two-way choice: margherita or marinara. Don't dilly-dally. p84

5 ITALIAN GARDENS

The Italians practically invented the modern notion of gardening, designing their multi-functional green spaces with an eye for art and aesthetics as much as plant production and horticulture. It's a line that can be traced back to the Romans and continued, through the Renaissance, to the majestic and often flamboyant sanctuaries that embellish the peninsula today.

Villa Rufolo

The grounds of this stunning villa in Ravello were once an operatic muse for Wagner. As picturesque as the plants are the views of the sea flanked by steep terraced fields. p187

Top left: Villa Rufolo gardens

Reggia di Caserta

When you're done ogling the giant baroque palace of Caserta, decamp to its equally colossal gardens with their statues, pools, fountains and waterfalls. p70

Bottom left: Reggia di Caserta

La Mortella

When British composer William Walton wasn't making music, he was searching for inspiration in his Ischia garden, a rich botanical beauty replete with tropical foliage. p148

Above: Pond, La Mortella

6 MONUMENTAL CATHEDRALS

PHOTOGOLFER/SHUTTERSTOCK ©

Naples

Built on top of Greek and Roman ruins and remodelled several times since, Naples' duomo is a wonderful hybrid stuffed with frescoes, mosaics, sculpture, and the remains of Naples' patron saint, Januarius. p51

Left: Duomo, Naples

Salerno

For an understated city, Salerno has a magnificent cathedral inaugurated in the 11th century and notable for its vivid medieval mosaics. p199

GLEN BERLIN / SHUTTERSTOCK ©

Amalfi

The over-sized Cattedrale di Sant'Andrea dominates the town of Amalfi. With its two-toned brickwork and grand staircase, it exhibits a mix of architectural styles from Arabic to Norman. p183

Left: Cattedrale di Sant'Andrea

Campania is overflowing with elaborate churches and multi-layered *duomos* (cathedrals), all of them architecturally, spiritually and atmospherically divine. Some double up as art galleries. Others rest on the remains of earlier churches. All resonate with fascinating stories of people who have sat, prayed, and preached in their hallowed interiors. The bigger cities provide the best examples, with architectural styles ranging from Gothic to baroque.

7 ISLAND ESCAPES

Under the beady eye of Mount Vesuvius, the three main islands in the Gulf of Naples come in three different flavours, like a block of sweet Neapolitan ice cream. Procida is unpretentious and urban, Capri is posh and pricey, while Ischia is bigger and more nuanced, with several small towns and its own distinct food culture. Which island you choose depends on your taste and budget.

Capri

Yes, it's crowded and expensive and teeming with tourists, but Capri still manages to exude a classy, refined beauty that is almost impossible not to fall in love with. p121

Below: Capri

Procida

The closest Gulf of Naples island to the mainland is also the most overlooked, yet tiny Procida has a weathered Southern Italian charm. p151

Above: Procida

Ischia

Lying somewhere between Capri's swank and Procida's authenticity, Ischia is a bigger more complex isle known for its thermal spas, manicured gardens, and rustic food. p136

Right: Ischia

8 GREEK & ROMAN RUINS

ANDREY LEBEDEV/SHUTTERSTOCK ©

Above: Tempio di Cerere (p204), Paestum

The Campania region does ancient ruins like Manhattan does modern skyscrapers. The name Pompeii is practically a synonym for Roman archaeological sites while, further south, the Doric temples of Paestum are testimony to the earlier civilisation of Magna Graecia. Together they provide the opening page of a story that resonates throughout the region from the mosaics of Herculaneum to the arches and tunnels of Cuma.

Pompeii

Like a freeze-frame photo of Roman life in 79 CE, Pompeii is one of the world's best-known ruins and astounding in its scale. An ongoing project, new discoveries are being brought to light all the time. p111

Paestum

While not as large or well-known as Pompeii, Paestum is older and, arguably, more atmospheric. Framed by wildflowers, its classical columns hark back to the pre-Roman colony of Magna Graecia. p203

Herculaneum

Pompeii's archaeological twin was a smaller wealthier town. Destroyed in the eruption of Vesuvius in 79 CE, it was rediscovered a little earlier than Pompeii, though excavations are still ongoing. p107

Need to Know

For more information, see Survival Guide (p259)

Currency
Euro (€)

Language
Italian

Visas
Generally not required for stays of up to 90 days (or at all for EU nationals); some nationalities need a Schengen visa.

Money
ATMs at Naples' Capodichino airport and major train stations; widely available in towns and cities. Credit cards accepted in most hotels and restaurants.

Mobile Phones
Local SIM cards can be used in European, Australian and some unlocked US phones. Other phones must be set to roaming.

Time
Central European Time (GMT/UTC plus one hour)

When to Go

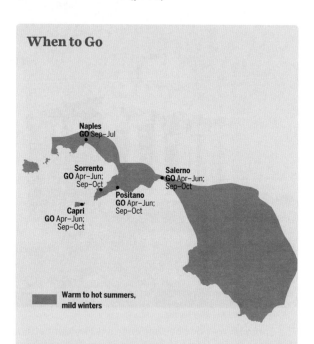

Naples
GO Sep–Jul

Sorrento
GO Apr–Jun;
Sep–Oct

Salerno
GO Apr–Jun;
Sep–Oct

Positano
GO Apr–Jun;
Sep–Oct

Capri
GO Apr–Jun;
Sep–Oct

Warm to hot summers,
mild winters

High Season
(Jul & Aug)

➡ Queues and crowds at big sights, beaches and on the road, especially August.

➡ Numerous restaurants and shops in Naples close for a few weeks in August.

➡ A good period for cultural events in tourist areas.

Shoulder
(Apr–Jun,
Sep & Oct)

➡ Good deals on accommodation.

➡ Spring is best for festivals, wildflowers and local produce.

➡ June and September generally deliver summer heat without the August crowds and traffic.

Low Season
(Nov–Mar)

➡ Prices at their lowest – up to 30% lower than high season.

➡ Many sights, hotels and restaurants closed in coastal and mountainous areas.

➡ Christmas feasting and colourful Carnevale celebrations.

Useful Websites

In Campania (www.incampania. com) Campania tourist-bureau website.

Napoli da Vivere (www.napoli davivere.it) Italian-language website listing upcoming festivals, special events and recent openings in Naples.

Positano (www.positano.com) Information on sights, activities, accommodation, transport and more along the Amalfi Coast.

Capri (www.capri.com) User-friendly site covering all aspects of Capri.

Trenitalia (www.trenitalia.com) Italian railways website.

Lonely Planet (www.lonely planet.com/italy/campania) Destination facts, hotel bookings, traveller forum and more.

Important Numbers

National and international phone numbers can be requested on ☏1254 (or online at www.1254.it).

Italy's country code	☏39
International access code	☏00
Ambulance	☏118
Fire	☏115
Police	☏112/☏113

Exchange Rates

Australia	A$1	€0.65
Canada	C$1	€0.65
Japan	¥100	€0.78
New Zealand	NZ$1	€0.60
UK	UK£1	€1.16
USA	US$1	€0.83

For current exchange rates, see www.xe.com.

Daily Costs

**Budget:
Less than €100**

➡ Dorm bed: €15–35

➡ Double room in a budget hotel: €50–110

➡ Lunch and dinner of pizza and pasta: €15

➡ Return Naples–Pompeii train fare: €5.60

**Midrange:
€100–200**

➡ Double room in a midrange hotel: €80–180

➡ Lunch and dinner in a local restaurant: €25–50

➡ Three-day Campania Artecard pass: €21

➡ One-way Naples–Capri hydrofoil ticket: €22.50

**Top end:
More than €200**

➡ Double room in a four- or five-star hotel: €150–450

➡ Top restaurant dinner: €50–120

➡ Car rental (five days): €260

Opening Hours

Opening hours vary throughout the year. We've provided high-season opening hours; hours will generally decrease in the shoulder and low seasons.

Banks 8.30am–1.30pm and 2.45–3.45pm Monday to Friday

Cafes 7.30am–8pm or later

Clubs 11pm–5am

Post offices 8am–6pm Monday to Friday, 8.30am–1pm Saturday; smaller branch offices close 1.30pm weekdays

Restaurants Noon–3pm and 7.30–11pm or midnight

Shops 9am–1pm and 3.30–7.30pm (or 4–8pm) Monday to Saturday, some close Monday morning and some open Sunday

Arriving in Naples & the Amalfi Coast

Naples International Airport
Alibus Airport Shuttle Bus runs to Napoli Centrale and the main ferry and hydrofoil terminal every 10 to 30 minutes from 6.30am to 11.40pm; tickets (€5) are available on board. Taxis are a €21 set fare to Piazza Municipio and adjoining Molo Beverello fast-ferry and hydrofoil terminal; journey time is 20 to 30 minutes.

Napoli Centrale Metro costs €1.10 (one-trip ANM ticket) from Naples' main station to Municipio (Piazza Municipio) every nine to 14 minutes, from around 6.20am to 11pm. Taxis are a €13 set fare to Piazza Municipio and Molo Beverello; journey time is 15 to 20 minutes.

Getting Around

Transport in the region is reasonably priced and relatively reliable in the main tourist areas.

Metro Line 1 connects Napoli Centrale (Garibaldi) to the ferry terminals (Municipio). Both lines skirt the city's *centro storico* (historic centre). Line 2 connects Naples to Pozzuoli in the Campi Flegrei.

Train Good for getting from Naples to Ercolano (Herculaneum), Pompeii, Sorrento, Salerno, Caserta and parts of the Campi Flegrei.

Bus Handy for travel along the Amalfi Coast and around Capri and Ischia. Some services reach sights in the Campi Flegrei. Others connect Naples to the Cilento.

Car Useful for reaching remote areas of the Cilento. Inadvisable in Naples year-round and along the Amalfi Coast in summer.

For much more on **getting around**, see p268

First Time Naples, Pompeii & the Amalfi Coast

For more information, see Survival Guide (p259)

Checklist

➡ Check the validity of your passport

➡ Check airline baggage restrictions

➡ Organise travel insurance

➡ Make bookings for accommodation, tours and entertainment

➡ Inform your credit-/debit-card company of your travel plans

➡ Check whether you can use your mobile (cell) phone

➡ Find out what you need to hire a car

What to Pack

➡ Passport (and a photocopy of it, kept separately)

➡ Credit cards and driving licence

➡ Phrasebook

➡ Italian electrical adapter

➡ Mobile (cell) phone charger

➡ Sunscreen, hat, sunglasses

➡ Waterproof jacket and comfy shoes

➡ A detailed driving map

Top Tips for Your Trip

➡ Visit in late spring, early summer or early autumn for gorgeous weather without the peak-season crowds.

➡ Speak at least a few Italian words. A little can go a long way.

➡ Queue jumping is common in Italy; be polite but assertive.

➡ Be mindful of your possessions, especially in crowds and on transport. Ignore touts, no matter how persistent they may be.

➡ Many museums close one day a week, usually on Tuesday or Wednesday. Plan ahead.

➡ Consider buying a Campania Artecard (p260) to save money.

➡ Avoid restaurants with touts and mediocre tourist menus.

What to Wear

The concept of *la bella figura* (making a good impression) encapsulates the Italian obsession with looking good. In general, trousers, jeans, shirts and polo shirts for men, and skirts or trousers for women, will serve you well in the city. Shorts, T-shirts and sandals are fine in summer and at the beach, but long sleeves are required for dining out. For the evening, think smart casual. A light sweater or waterproof jacket is useful in spring and autumn, and sturdy shoes are good for visiting archaeological sites. Dress modestly when visiting churches and religious sites, covering your torso, shoulders and thighs.

Tourist Information

Main tourist offices are generally open Monday to Friday; some also open on weekends, especially in urban areas or during the peak summer season. Affiliated information booths (at train stations and airports, for example) may keep slightly different hours. Be aware that in some popular tourist centres, private tour operators may style their business as a general 'tourist information' point. In reality, they are set up to sell their own tours and offerings.

Driving in Naples & the Amalfi Coast

➡ Much of central Naples is off limits to nonresident vehicles, and the combo of anarchic traffic and illegal parking attendants demanding tips will quickly ruin your holiday.

➡ Nonresident vehicles are prohibited on Capri for much of the year, and driving is largely discouraged on Ischia and Procida.

➡ Peak-season traffic can make driving along the Amalfi Coast stressful, though having your own vehicle here means ultimate flexibility.

➡ Driving is ideal in the Cilento region, allowing you to discover out-of-the-way towns and beaches.

➡ For information on traffic conditions, tolls and distances, see www.autostrade.it.

Bargaining

Gentle haggling is common in markets; in all other instances you're expected to pay the stated price.

Tipping

Tipping is generally optional.

Bars Neapolitans usually place a €0.10 coin on the bar when ordering their coffee; if drinks are brought to your table, leave a small tip.

Hotels Tip porters about €5 at high-end hotels.

Restaurants If *servizio* (service) is not included on your bill, leave a euro or two in pizzerias, or 10% of the bill in restaurants.

Taxis Most people round up to the nearest euro.

Language

Unlike in many other European countries, English is not widely spoken in Italy. Of course, in the main tourist centres you can get by, but in the countryside and off-the-tourist track you'll need to master a few basic phrases. This will improve your experience no end, especially when ordering in restaurants, some of which have no written menu. See the Language chapter (p273) of this book for all the phrases you need to get by.

 What's the local speciality?
Qual'è la specialità di questa regione?
kwa·le la spe·cha·lee·ta dee kwes·ta re·jo·ne

A bit like the rivalry between medieval Italian city-states, these days the country's regions compete in speciality foods and wines.

 Which combined tickets do you have?
Quali biglietti cumulativi avete?
kwa·lee bee·lye·tee koo·moo·la·tee·vee a·ve·te

Make the most of your euro by getting combined tickets to various sights; they are available in all major Italian cities.

 Where can I buy discount designer items?
C'è un outlet in zona? che oon owt·let in zo·na

Discount fashion outlets are big business in major cities – get bargain-priced seconds, samples and cast-offs for *la bella figura*.

 I'm here with my husband/boyfriend.
Sono qui con il mio marito/ragazzo.
so·no kwee kon eel mee·o ma·ree·to/ra·ga·tso

Solo women travellers may receive unwanted attention in some parts of Italy; if ignoring fails have a polite rejection ready.

5 **Let's meet at 6pm for pre-dinner drinks.**
Ci vediamo alle sei per un aperitivo.
chee ve·dya·mo a·le say per oon a·pe·ree·tee·vo

At dusk, watch the main piazza get crowded with people sipping colourful cocktails and snacking the evening away: join your new friends for this authentic Italian ritual!

Etiquette

Italy is a surprisingly formal society; the following tips will help you avoid any awkward moments.

Greetings Shake hands and say *buongiorno* (good day) or *buona-sera* (good evening) to strangers; kiss both cheeks and say *come stai?* (how are you?) for friends. Use *Lei* (you) in polite company; use *tu* (you) with friends and children. Only use first names if invited.

Asking for help Say *mi scusi* (excuse me) to attract attention; use *permesso* (permission) when you want to pass by in a crowded space.

Eating and drinking When dining in an Italian home, bring wine or a small gift of *dolci* (sweets) from a local *pasticceria* (pastry shop). Let your host lead when sitting and starting the meal.

Gestures Maintain eye contact during conversation and when toasting.

Accommodation

Naples' varied slumber options include frescoed palazzi, converted convents and the homes of local artists and intellectuals. Accommodation on the islands and the Amalfi Coast tends towards the higher end of the market and is generally seasonal.

Accommodation Types

Hotels All prices and levels of quality from bland city three-stars to chic boutique properties and luxury hotels in historic buildings.

B&Bs Often great value, ranging from rooms in family homes to self-catering studio apartments. A popular option on the Amalfi coast.

Agriturismi Perfect for families, *agriturismi* range from rustic farmhouses to luxe abodes with swimming pool.

Pensions Similar to hotels, though they're mostly of one- to three-star quality and family run.

Hostels You'll find both HI-affiliated and privately run *ostelli,* many also with private rooms, some with private bathrooms.

Convents & monasteries Some convents and monasteries let out cells or rooms as a modest revenue-making exercise and happily take in tourists. Many impose a fairly early curfew, but prices tend to be quite reasonable.

Camping Most campgrounds in Campania are major complexes with restaurants, swimming pools and supermarkets. Wild backcountry camping isn't the norm.

Where to Find the Best...

Hostels

Naples has an abundance of hostels, especially in the *centro storico,* and they're reasonably priced, with dorm beds starting at around €15. Most also offer private rooms for those more inclined to socially distance, from €50 to €85 for a basic double.

Elsewhere, hostel pickings are fairly slim outside the big towns – Sorrento hosts two good 'uns and Salerno's unique hostel is housed in a charming 16th-century convent.

Ironically, super-posh Positano on the Amalfi Coast is home to a decent hostel. It's a bit of a climb from the town centre and more expensive than your standard Naples joint, but beggars can't be choosers!

Agriturismi

Campania's best *agriturismi* are located in its more rural areas.

For proximity to Naples, try the Sorrento peninsula where you'll find farm stays with fabulous food in and around villages such as Sant'Agata sui Due Golfi.

Larger farm stays with swimming pools and rustic rooms can be found in the Parco Nazionale del Cilento, Vallo di Diano e Alburni further south. Many offer cooking courses, horse riding and plenty of opportunities to commune with nature. All grow at least some of their own food.

Historic Hotels

In a region soaked in history, why wouldn't you want recline in the erstwhile palaces and mansions that once hosted international conferences, feted European monarchs and provided inspiration for great writers. Naples is replete with historic hotels and there are plenty more on the Amalfi Coast, notably in Ravello.

Most have been lovingly restored to their former glory without compromising on modern 21st-century comforts.

Swimming pools are common, expensive linens and mattresses adorn beds and, if you're lucky, you might get to dine in an on-site Michelin-starred restaurant.

Tips for...

Budget Travellers

The main money drainer in Campania is the Amalfi Coast. Choose your town or village carefully here and you could bag a bargain. Positano is mega-expensive. Further east, villages such as Cetara hide better deals.

Cheap hostels are dotted here and there. There's even one in Positano! Apartment rentals with cooking facilities are also a good bet if you're on a budget and often offer more space than hotel rooms.

Families

There are some good family accommodation options on the Sorrento peninsula, including apartments, *agriturismi* and a campground (with on-site apartments), all within easy reach of the coast.

Italian families love the island of Ischia, which has some fine seaside hotels and campgrounds in among its famous spas.

While the Amalfi attracts rich romantics, Italian families tend to gravitate to the Cilento Coast and its unpretentious beach towns like Agropoli and Palinuro.

Solo Travellers

Naples has a wide selection of hostels with reasonable rates. These establishments usually have communal areas and group activities – a great way to meet other solo travellers.

The Amalfi is popular with couples seeking romantic escapes and not overflowing with cheap single rooms. Soloists might find a more informal and friendly environment in the smaller 'pension' hotels on the Cilento Coast.

Booking

The high season is July and August, with prices also peaking around Easter and Christmas. It's essential to book in

DALLAS STRIBLEY/GETTY IMAGES ©

Hotel Palazzo Murat (p24), Positano

advance during these periods. Conversely, prices drop between 30% and 50% in low season. In the winter months (November to Easter) many places, particularly on the coast and on the islands, completely shut down. In the cities and larger towns, accommodation tends to remain open all year. The relative lack of visitors in these down periods means you should have little trouble getting a room in those places that do stay open.

Lonely Planet (www.lonelyplanet.com/italy/campania/hotels) Recommendations and bookings.

Agriturismo.it (www.agriturismo.it) Wide range of *agriturismi* (farm stays).

SorrentoTourism.com (www.sorrentotourism.com) Basic list of hotels, hostels, B&Bs, apartments and more on the Sorrento Peninsula.

Capri.net (www.capri.net) User-friendly website with various accommodation categories.

Campeggi.com (www.campeggi.com) List of Italy's best campgrounds, including more than 150 in Campania.

Novasol.com (www.novasol.com) Easy to navigate website offering cottages and apartment stays across Europe.

BEST ACCOMMODATION IN NAPLES, POMPEII & THE AMALFI COAST

LOCATION	NAME	COST	CONTACT
Agropoli (p205), Salerno & the Cilento	B&B I Defini	s/d €40/75	www.idelfinibb.it
Amalfi (p183), The Amalfi Coast	DieciSedici	d from €145	www.diecisedici.it
Amalfi (p183), The Amalfi Coast	Hotel Santa Caterina	d €550-1300	www.hotelsantacaterina.it
Anacapri (p129), The Islands	Capri Palace	d/ste from €410/1070	www.capripalace.com
Capri Town (p123), The Islands	La Minerva	d €190-650	www.laminervacapri.com
Casal Velino, Salerno & the Cilento	Agriturismo i Moresani	d €90-110	www.agriturismoimoresani.com
Casal Velino, Salerno & the Cilento	Zio Cristoforo	d €150-200	www.agriturismoziocristoforo.com
Forio (p148), The Islands	Umberto a Mare	d €150-200	www.umbertoamare.it
Furore (p182), The Amalfi Coast	Agriturismo Serafina	s/d/tr €50/80/100	www.agriturismoserafina.it
Massa Lubrense (p173), The Amalfi Coast	Casale Villarena	2/4-person apt €120/220	www.casalevillarena.it
Naples (p51), Naples, Pompeii & Around	Dimora dei Giganti	s €40-60, d €55-80, tr €70-95, q €85-105	www.maisonsdecharme.it/dimoradeigiganti
Naples (p51), Naples, Pompeii & Around	Hostel of the Sun	dm €15-25, s €30-35, d €60-80	www.hostelnapoli.com
Naples (p51), Naples, Pompeii & Around	Hotel Piazza Bellini	d €90-190	www.hotelpiazzabellini.com
Naples (p51), Naples, Pompeii & Around	Schiara	d €50-100, tr €65-110, q €80-125	www.maisonsdecharme.it
Paestum (p203), Salerno & the Cilento	Casale Giancesare Villa Agricola	d €60-150, 4-person apt €80-185	www.casalegiancesare.com/en
Positano (p175), The Amalfi Coast	Hostel Brikette	dm €40-73, d €160-220	www.hostel-positano.com
Positano (p175), The Amalfi Coast	Hotel Palazzo Murat	d from €310	www.palazzomurat.it
Positano (p175), The Amalfi Coast	Villa Franca	d/ste €345/695	www.villafrancahotel.it
Procida (p151), The Islands	Hotel La Vigna	ste €160-230	www.albergolavigna.it
Ravello (p187), The Amalfi Coast	Belmond Hotel Caruso	d from €935	www.grandluxuryhotels.com
Ravello (p187), The Amalfi Coast	Palazzo Avino	d from €495	www.palazzoavino.com
Salerno (p199), Salerno & the Cilento	Ostello Ave Gratia Plena	dm/s/d €16/45/65	www.ostellodisalerno.it
Sorrento (p163), The Amalfi Coast	Palazzo Marziale	d/ste from €220/455	www.palazzomarziale.it

REVIEW	TYPE	GOOD FOR
Clean, economical and modern B&B close to the centre of Agropoli with an affable host	B&B	Solo travellers, budget travellers
The '1016' dresses up an old medieval palace using the style only the Italians can muster	B&B	Solo travelllers
Amalfi landmark and one of Italy's most famous hotels. Everything oozes luxury, from ultra-discreet service to fabulous gardens	Luxury hotel	Couples, luxury
Regal mix of chicness, opulence and unashamed luxury that takes the concept of 'dolce vita' to dizzying heights	Luxury hotel	Couples, romance
This gleaming establishment is a model of Capri style and considered one of the best hotels in Italy	Boutique hotel	Couples, luxury
This sprawling farm produces its own caprino goat's cheese, wine, olive oil and preserves for its notable restaurant	Agriturismo	Groups, families, self-catering
Zio feels more boutique hotel than farmstay and offers cooking classes in the winter; also rents three apartments	Agriturismo	Groups, families, self-catering
Eleven quiet rooms ooze understated chic with cool terracotta tiles, modern bathrooms and traditional shutters	Hotel	Couples
Seven spruce air-conditioned rooms in a farmhouse, each with its own small balcony and views over lush terraces below	Agriturismo	Families, budget travellers
Family-friendly apartments with good facilities, including shared pool, playground and beach within easy strolling distance	Apartments	Families, self-catering
Urbane B&B offering four colour-coordinated bedrooms with sculptural lamps, ethnic-inspired furnishings and designer bathrooms	B&B	Solo travellers, budget travellers, families
Ultra-friendly hostel near the hydrofoil terminal that's bright and sociable with multicoloured dorms and a casual in-house bar	Hostel	Solo travellers, budget travellers
Sharp, hip hotel in a 16th-century palazzo with pure-white spaces spiked with original majolica tiles and piperno-stone paving	Boutique hotel	Couples
Freshly minted B&B offering five contemporary rooms with bathrooms and playful artisan details inspired by southern Italian themes	B&B	Families, budget travellers, self-catering
Elegantly decorated 19th-century former farmhouse with seven farm-house-chic rooms and three apartments	B&B	Families, self-catering
A top-of-the-town building with wonderful views and range of sleeping options, from doubles to dorms	Hostel	Solo travellers, budget travellers
Magnificent hotel occupying the 18th-century palazzo that the one-time king of Naples used as his summer residence	Historic hotel	Couples
Posh even by Positano standards, the Franca is an operatic mix of stylish white minimalism and rich regal touches	Hotel	Couples, luxury
Enjoying a discreet cliffside location, this crenelated 18th-century villa comes complete with rambling garden, vines and swimming pool	Boutique hotel	Couples. retreat
Sublimely restored 11th-century palazzo with 15th-century vaulted ceil-ings, high-class ceramics and Moorish arches doubling as window frames	Historic hotel	Couples, luxury, romance
Inhabits a handsome, pale-pink 12th-century palace emboldened with fanciful Moorish touches	Historic hotel	Couples, luxury, romance
Housed in a 16th-century convent, Salerno's excellent HI hostel is right in the historic centre	Hostel	Solo travellers, budget travellers
Resplendent rooms with high ceilings, chaise longues and classy mattresses and linens	Boutique hotel	Couples, luxury

Month by Month

February

Short and accursed is how Italians describe February. It might still be chilly, but almond trees start to blossom and Carnevale season brightens things up with confetti, costumes and sugar-dusted treats.

☆☆ Carnevale

In the period leading up to Ash Wednesday, many southern Italian towns stage pre-Lenten carnivals. Kids don fancy costumes, and elaborate *carri* (floats) are paraded down the street. This is also the time for Carnevale treats like *chiacchiere* (fried pastry dough sprinkled with powdered sugar).

☆☆ Festa di Sant'Antonino

Sorrento's patron saint is celebrated on 14 February with street stalls, fireworks, and musical processions through the historic centre. Locals tuck into Sorrento's famous *torta di Sant'Antonino;* a chocolate- and cream-filled tart.

March

The weather in *marzo pazzo* (Crazy March) is temperamental. While the official start of spring is 21 March, things only really start to open up for the main season during the Easter Holy Week.

☆☆ Settimana Santa

Processions and passion plays mark Easter Holy Week across Campania. On Good Friday and the Thursday preceding it, hooded penitents walk through Sorrento. On tiny Procida, Good Friday sees wooden statues and life-size tableaux carted across the island.

☆ Festival MANN

For eight days in late March and early April, Naples' Museo Archeologico Nazionale serves up a feast of theatre, dance, concerts, art exhibitions, film screenings and panel discussions, both Italian and international (p83).

May

Roses and early summer produce make May a perfect time to travel, especially for walkers. The weather is warm but not too hot and prices are good value. It's also patron-saint season.

🍷 Wine & the City

A three-week celebration (p83) of regional vino in Naples, with free wine degustations, *aperitivo* sessions and cultural events in palaces, museums, boutiques and eateries across the city.

☆ Maggio dei Monumenti

As the weather warms up, Naples puts on a mammoth, month-long program of art exhibitions, concerts, performances and tours (p83). Many architectural and historical treasures usually off limits to the public are open and free to visit.

June

Summer kicks off: the temperature cranks up quickly, *lidi* (beaches) start to open in earnest and some of the big summer festivals commence. The Anniversary of the Republic on 2 June is a national holiday.

☆ Napoli Teatro Festival Italia

Naples' month-long theatre festival (p83) serves up Italian and foreign theatre, performance art, and exhibitions, both mainstream and fringe. Events take place across the city, from theatres to metro stations.

☆ Ravello Festival

Hilltop Ravello draws world-renowned artists during its summertime festival (p189). Spanning everything from music and dance to film and art exhibitions, several events take place in the exquisite Villa Rufolo gardens from late June to late August.

July

School is out and Italians everywhere are heading to the coast or mountains for their holidays. Prices and temperatures rise. The beaches are in full swing, as are several major cultural festivals.

☆ Giffoni Film Festival

Europe's biggest children's film festival livens up the town of Giffoni Valle Piana, east of Salerno (www.giffoni filmfestival.it). Attracting children and teens from across the world, the week-long event includes screenings, workshops, seminars and big-name guests such as Mark Ruffalo and Robert De Niro.

✕ Sagra del Tonno

Tiny Cetara plays host to this annual tuna festival (p192), held over four days in late July or early August. Tuna dishes aside, you can taste-test the town's celebrated anchovies, made famous thanks to its *colatura di alici* (anchovy paste).

🎆 Festa di Sant'Anna

Ischia celebrates the feast day of Sant'Anna to spectacular effect on 26 July (p154). The island's local councils build competing floats to sail in a flotilla, with fireworks and a symbolic 'burning' of Ischia Ponte's medieval Castello Aragonese.

August

August in Campania is hot, expensive and crowded. Everyone is on holiday and, while it may no longer be true that everything is shut, many businesses and restaurants do close for part of the month.

🎆 Ferragosto

After Christmas and Easter, Ferragosto (15 August) is Italy's biggest holiday. While it now marks the Feast of the Assumption, even the ancient Romans honoured their pagan gods on Feriae Augusti. The beaches are super crowded.

September

As summer waxes in autumn, the grape harvest begins. Adding to the culinary excitement are the many local *sagre* (food festivals) celebrating regional produce.

🎆 Festa di San Gennaro

On 19 September, San Gennaro's miracle takes place in Naples' Duomo. The event (p84) sees two phials of the saint's blood liquefy. If the miracle fails, the faithful consider it a bad omen for the city. The miracle also takes place in May and December.

☆ Festival Ethnos

Ethnos (www.festival ethnos.it) delivers over a week of world music in September and early October. Local and international acts play in venues across the Greater Naples region.

December

Despite the cooler days, looming Christmas festivities warm things up with festive street lights, nativity scenes and Yuletide specialities. Naples welcomes in the new year with free events and fireworks.

🎆 Natale

In the weeks preceding Christmas, many churches set up *presepi* (nativity scenes). People from across Italy hit Naples to buy *pastori* (nativity-scene figurines) on and around Via San Gregorio Armeno.

Itineraries

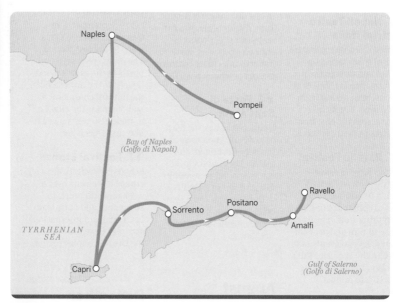

 Blockbuster Highlights

Campania's coastline is one of the world's most beautiful, inspiring countless artists, romantics and bon vivants. This itinerary takes in its most seductive highlights.

Start with two days in **Naples**, spending one day exploring its World Heritage–listed historic centre and another in nearby **Pompeii**. On day three, catch a morning ferry to **Capri**, giving yourself two days to fall madly in love with this fabled island. Glide into the dazzling Grotta Azzurra (Blue Grotto), ride up to Monte Solaro, and lose the hordes on bucolic walking trails. On day five, catch a ferry to **Sorrento**, from where buses and seasonal ferries continue to **Positano**. Base yourself here for your last nights, slipping on your Prada sandals and sauntering through its chic, labyrinthine laneways. Sup on fresh seafood, hire your own boat, or tie up your hiking boots and get a natural high on the Sentiero degli Dei (Path of the Gods). From Positano, **Amalfi** is an easy day trip, the deeply historic town famed for its eclectic, centuries-old cathedral and cloisters. From Amalfi, buses lead up to sky-high **Ravello**, whose world-famous panoramic gardens make for a breathtaking epilogue.

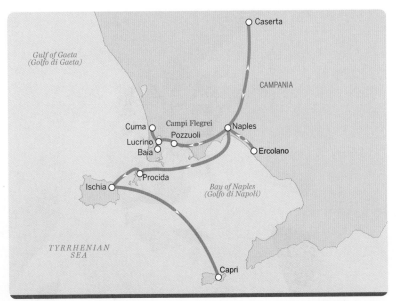

Palaces, Ruins & Islands

The greater Naples area is home to some of Italy's oldest and most impressive human achievements, not to mention some of its most outstanding natural scenery. Follow this route for an intoxicating mix of archaeology, artistry and soul-stirring beauty.

Base yourself in action-packed **Naples** for five days, savouring its World Heritage–status pizza and visceral street life. Make time for top-tier antiquities at the Museo Archeologico Nazionale and astounding 18th-century sculptures in the Capella Sansevero. Just leave time for a kayaking tour of the city's coastline, peppered with ancient ruins and anecdote-sparking villas.

Dedicate two days to day trips from the city. Options include **Caserta**, home to an epic, Unesco-lauded baroque palace that upstages Versailles, or **Ercolano**, home to the remarkably well-preserved ruins of Herculaneum. Another option is the underrated **Campi Flegrei**, a scattering of Graeco-Roman ruins and volcanic landscapes. Snoop around Italy's third-largest Roman amphitheatre in **Pozzuoli**, see where emperors soaked in **Baia**, or seek out the chamber inhabited by Aeneid's oracle at the ruins in **Cuma**. Alternatively, slip on a bathing suit and soak like the Romans in **Lucrino**.

Come day six, catch a ferry from Naples across to pastel-coloured **Procida** and spend a couple of days relaxing in stuck-in-time fishing villages and on secret beaches. From here, it's a short ferry ride across to the lush, verdant sprawl of **Ischia** on day eight. Take three days to explore the island's thermal springs, gardens, wineries and historic sites, among them a commanding Aragonese castle and an archaeological museum filled with local Hellenic finds.

From Ischia, high-season ferries offer direct connections to **Capri**. Outside this period, you will need to head back to Naples to catch a Capri-bound service. Either way, treat yourself to three days on the region's most fabled island. It's here that you'll find the scandal-riddled former retreats of Roman Emperor Tiberius and French poet Jacques d'Adelswärd-Fersen, not to mention some of Europe's most arresting coastal landscapes.

Top: Sea urchin dish, Santa Maria di Castellabate (p206)

Bottom: Medieval festival, Teggiano (p210)

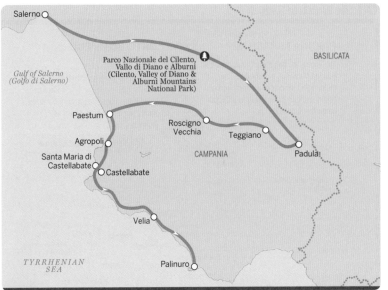

The Cilento Trail

While the lure of Naples, Capri and the Amalfi Coast are irresistible, Campania heaves with lesser-known marvels. From Hellenic temples and cave-studded mountains to one of Italy's largest monasteries, this route leads down less-trodden paths.

Start your adventure in the underrated city of **Salerno**, home to one of Italy's most captivating medieval cathedrals. Head up to the Castello di Arechi for sweeping views, and to the revamped waterfront for a late-afternoon *passeggiata* (stroll). After dark, join the *salernitani* (Salerno locals) in the city's vibrant medieval heart for a little bar-hopping and *movida* (partying). On day two, bid Salerno *arrivederci* and head inland for three days in the rugged beauty of the **Parco Nazionale del Cilento, Vallo di Diano e Alburni**, Italy's second-largest national park and a Unesco World Heritage site. Base yourself at one of the park's *agriturismi* and explore the area's famous grottoes, namely the Grotte di Castelcivita and Grotte di Pertosa-Auletta.

Make sure you spend a morning or afternoon in **Padula**, famous for its mammoth Carthusian monastery, the 14th-century Certosa di San Lorenzo. Not far from the Certosa is the fabled Valle delle Orchidee (Valley of the Orchids), whose 70-plus varieties of orchid create a spectacular blaze of springtime colour. Allow a few hours to explore the shamelessly charming medieval village of **Teggiano** and make a stop at **Roscigno Vecchia**. A veritable ghost town abandoned early last century, it's one of the national park's more curious sites.

Continue west towards the coast on day five to gasp at the mighty Greek temples of **Paestum**, the oldest of which dates back to the 6th century BC. Spend the evening and the following morning in **Agropoli**, wandering its atmospheric *centro storico* (historic centre) before heading south to **Santa Maria di Castellabate** for superlative seafood noshing. On day seven, head up to the beautiful medieval town of **Castellabate** and wander its shamelessly charming laneways, then spend the afternoon exploring the ancient ruins of **Velia**. End your Cilento travels with a couple of lazy beach days in **Palinuro**, which, like Capri, lays claim to a dazzling Grotta Azzurra (Blue Grotto).

Off the Beaten Track

PISCINA MIRABILIS

You'll need to call ahead to access the Piscina Mirabilis, a cathedral-like cistern and marvel of ancient Roman engineering, hidden away in a Bacoli backstreet. (p107)

ORTO BOTANICO DI NAPOLI

If you need a break from Naples' inexhaustible energy, find solace in this historic botanic garden, bursting with flora from as far afield as Australia. (p73)

Santa Maria O   O **Caserta**
Capua Vetere   **Maddaloni**

Castèl
Volturno O   O
                                                Arienzo
Gulf of Gaeta
(Golfo di Gaeta)   Villaggio   O Aversa
                     Coppola O   Acerra
                                 Giugliano in   O **Nola**
                     Qualiano O Campania O   O
Lido di   *Naples International*
Licola O   **Naples** *Airport (Capodichino)*
                    Pozzuoli   **Mt Vesuvius**
                              O **Portici** (Vesuvio; 1281m)
Torregaveta O   **Bagnoli**   O Ercolano ▲
           O Bacoli   O Pompeii
Procida   **Torre del Greco**
Casamicciola O   **Procida** **Torre Annunziata**
Monte Epomeo ▲ O Ischia   **Castellammare**
(786m)   *Bay of Naples* **di Stabia** O
         Ischia *(Golfo di Napoli)*
                              Vico Equense O Bomerano

MONTE EPOMEO & THE HINTERLAND

Beyond Ischia's beaches and spas is a rugged, lofty interior made for inspiring, contemplative hikes that reward with sensational vistas and natural beauty. (p145)

Sorrento O **Positano** O
                          Praiano
Anacapri O O **Capri**   **Monte Sant'Angelo**
        Capri Town   **a Tre Pizzi**
                             (1443m)

VINTAGE VILLAS

Pompeii and Herculaneum aren't the only Roman treasures flanking the Bay of Naples, with other survivors including a once-luxurious villa in ancient Oplontis. (p117)

Tyrrhenian Sea

PASSEGGIATA DEL PIZZOLUNGO

Escape the selfie sticks, shoppers and poseurs on one of Capri's most breathtaking walking trails, a manageable one-hour saunter that takes in spectacular west-coast sights. (p127)

VESUVIUS ON HORSEBACK

Mt Vesuvius is more than its panoramic crater, with slopes rich in flora and fauna. Explore its oft-overlooked wilderness on a horseback tour. (p110)

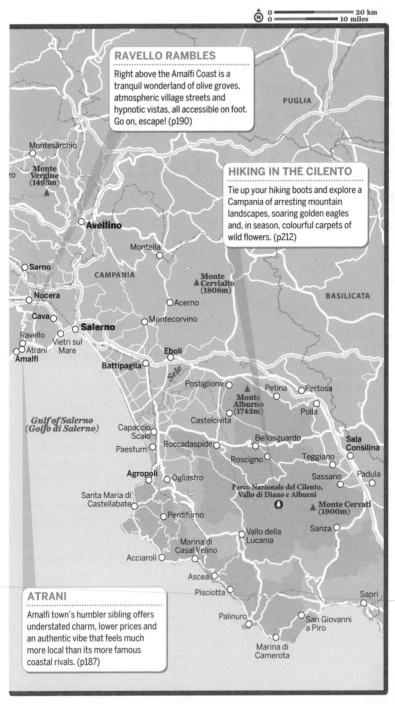

RAVELLO RAMBLES

Right above the Amalfi Coast is a tranquil wonderland of olive groves, atmospheric village streets and hypnotic vistas, all accessible on foot. Go on, escape! (p190)

HIKING IN THE CILENTO

Tie up your hiking boots and explore a Campania of arresting mountain landscapes, soaring golden eagles and, in season, colourful carpets of wild flowers. (p212)

ATRANI

Amalfi town's humbler sibling offers understated charm, lower prices and an authentic vibe that feels much more local than its more famous coastal rivals. (p187)

Plan Your Trip

Eat & Drink Like a Local

Campania is a culinary powerhouse, where impeccable produce and well-trained taste buds have created one of the world's most envied gastronomic landscapes. Some of the country's most celebrated edibles hail from this region, and nowhere else will they taste as good. So whet your appetite with the following food-trip essentials.

The Year in Food

There's never a bad time to raise your fork in Campania.

Spring (Mar–May)

Asparagus, artichokes and Easter specialities. Celebrate the region's vino at Naples' Wine & The City (p83).

Summer (Jun–Aug)

Aubergines, peppers, tomatoes and Cetara's Sagra del Tonno (p192). Bite into *albicocche vesuviane* (Vesuvian apricots) and *pere mastantuono* (Mastantuono pears).

Autumn (Sep–Nov)

Mushrooms, chestnuts, black truffles and *mele annurche* (Annurca apples). Plough through pasta at Minori food fest Gusta Minori (p191).

Winter (Dec–Feb)

Christmas and Carnevale treats, plus stalwarts like *zuppa di castagne e fagioli* (chestnut and bean soup). Dig into sausages at Sorrento's Sagra della Salsiccia e Ceppone (p166).

Food Experiences

So much produce, so many classics, so little time! Fine-tune your culinary radar with the following musts.

Meals of a Lifetime

Ristorante La Caravella, Amalfi Michelin-starred seafood and an incomparable wine list. (p186)

Il Focolare, Ischia A rustic Slow Food gem showcasing homegrown island produce. (p141)

President, Pompeii Confident, often playful takes on Campanian classics; worthy of its Michelin star. (p116)

La Palette, Capri Island produce and culinary creativity with a side of stirring bay views. (p126)

Cheap Treats

Pizza Both wood-fired and *fritta* (deep fried).

Fritture Deep-fried snacks including *crocchè* (potato croquettes), best bought from *friggitorie* (fried-food takeaway outlets).

Taralli Crunchy, usually savoury ring-shaped biscuits, sold plain or in variations like *taralli mandorlati* (with almonds).

Sfogliatella Cinnamon-scented ricotta pastries in *riccia* (filo) and *frolla* (shortcrust) varieties.

Gelato The best gelato uses seasonal ingredients and natural colours.

Local Specialities

Each corner of the region boasts its own edible staples. Some are well known, others more obscure. The following are some of the best.

Naples

While Naples is famous for its World Heritage–status pizza, it's only one of many local culinary protagonists. Fellow stars include *pizza fritta* – pizza dough stuffed with ingredients and gently bathed in boiling oil until golden. While the traditional filling consists of pork *cicoli* (dried lard cubes), *provola* (provolone cheese), ricotta and a dash of tomato, variations sometimes include the use of *salame* (salami), *prosciutto cotto* (ham) and *mozzarella di bufala* (buffalo-milk mozzarella).

Pasta classics include the simple yet seductive *spaghetti alle vongole,* spaghetti with clams, garlic, *peperoncino* (red chilli) and fresh parsley. Some prefer the dish *macchiato al pomodoro,* which adds fresh tomato.

Tomato is one of the main ingredients in *ragù napoletano,* an elaborately prepared, slowly simmered *sugo* (sauce) of tomato, onion and various types of meat. A Sunday lunch staple, the sauce is classically served with thicker pasta types (most commonly *ziti, rigatoni* or *maltagliati rigati*) as a *primo* (first course) while the cooked meat itself is set aside and served as the *secondo* (main course). Equally rich is *pasta alla genovese,* a slow-cooked sauce of beef and (copious amounts of) onion, also usually served with *ziti* pasta.

Like ragù, Naples' cake-like *sartù di riso* (rice timbale) also reflects the city's period of French rule. The dish's name reputedly hails from the French phrase *sur tout* (above all), a reference to the rice that covers its belt-busting filling of meatballs, sausage, mozzarella, peas and mushrooms.

The Islands

The trio of islands dotting the Gulf of Naples have their own culinary claims to fame. Capri's signature dish is *ravioli capresi,* ravioli filled with cheese (Parmesan and *caciotta*) and marjoram, then served with a fresh tomato *sugo.* Alternatively, it's tossed in melted butter and sage. The island's seafood shines in dishes like *totani e patate* (pasta with cuttlefish, potatoes, garlic and white wine) and *totani ripieni* (cuttlefish stuffed with caciotta cheese, Parmesan, fresh parsley and cuttlefish tentacles).

On Ischia, tackle *spaghetti alla puttanesca,* pasta served with tomato, black olives, capers, anchovies and (in some cases) a dash of *peperoncino.* The island's rugged interior inspires *coniglio all'ischitana,* a celebrated casserole of local rabbit cooked in a terracotta pot with cherry tomatoes, wild herbs (commonly rosemary, sage, thyme or marjoram), garlic, onion, chilli and aromatic white wine.

Tiny Procida is famous for its *limone di Procida,* a large, local variety of lemon distinguished by its thick albedo (the spongy white layer beneath the peel), its intense fragrance and its pleasant acidity. Locals commonly eat it sliced and sprinkled with sugar. It's also the hero ingredient in the island's *insalata di limoni* (lemon salad), a simple, refreshing melange of Procida lemons, onion, garlic, fresh mint, red chilli and olive oil.

Amalfi Coast

Sorrento's own lemon variety, the *limone di Sorrento,* enjoys IGP (Protected Geographical Indicaton) status. Known for its extreme juiciness and high levels of essential oils and mineral salts, the variety is used to make IGP-status *liquore di limone di Sorrento,* the area's premium *limoncello* liqueur. IGP appellation is also granted to the Amalfi Coast's local lemon, the *limone Costa d'Amalfi,* also used to make the ubiquitous lemon liqueur. Yet, the Amalfi Coast is known for more than *limoncello,* using local mountain herbs and plants to create classic *digestivi* like *finocchietto* (wild-fennel liqueur), *fragolino* (wild-strawberry liqueur) and *nocillo,* a liqueur made with walnuts traditionally harvested on the night of St John (June 24).

While Sorrento is famous for its *gnocchi alla sorrentina* (baked gnocchi with tomato and mozzarella), tiny Minori is home to *'ndunderi,* flour-and-ricotta dumplings said to be modern gnocchi's ancient precursor. The light, fluffy morsels are traditionally eaten on 13 July, the feast day of Minori's celestial patron, Santa Trofimena. Further east along the coast, Cetara is famed for its *colatura di alici,* an intense, salty anchovy sauce related to ancient *garum,* a popular condiment in Roman times.

For a blissful sugar hit, seek out the Amalfi Coast's *delizia di limone,* a zesty, decadent sponge cake filled with lemon cream and *limoncello,* coated in a lemon glaze and topped with whipped cream.

Salerno & the Cilento

This corner of Campania is famous for its *mozzarella di bufala,* produced in the area around Paestum and notably sweeter than its rival from Caserta. Also, look out for *cacioricotta di capra,* an intense-tasting goat's milk cheese. Milk from southern Italy's Podolica cow is used to create *caciocavallo podolico,* highly regarded cheese dubbed the *Grana Padano* of the South. While it can be eaten fresh, the variety improves with age so look for a version that is *stagionato* (mature). Some varieties are aged in tuff-stone caves. Another worthy addition to your local *tagliere* (platter) is *soppressata cilentana,* a local pork salami smoked using beech and oak.

How to Eat & Drink

When to Eat

Colazione (breakfast) Often little more than a pre-work espresso accompanied by a *cornetto* (Italian croissant) or a *sfogliatella* (sweet ricotta-filled pastry).

Pranzo (lunch) Traditionally the main meal of the day. Standard restaurant times are noon to 3pm; many locals don't lunch before 2pm.

Aperitivo Popular in Naples, post-work drinks sees numerous bars offer tasty morsels for the price of a *spritz* between 6pm and 9pm.

Cena (dinner) Traditionally lighter than lunch, though still a main meal. Standard restaurant hours are 7.30pm to 11pm (later in summer). Most locals don't dine before 8.30pm.

Where to Eat

Ristorante (restaurant) Formal service and refined dishes and wines; perfect for special occasions.

Trattoria A more casual version of a restaurant, with cheaper prices and regional specialities. Avoid places with 'tourist menus'.

Osteria Historically, a tavern focused on wine; the modern version is usually an intimate trattoria or wine bar offering a handful of dishes.

Enoteca Wine bars that often serve snacks to accompany your well-chosen tipple.

Agriturismo A working farmhouse offering accommodation, as well as food made with farm-grown produce.

Pizzeria Great for a cheap feed and cold beer.

Menu Decoder

Menù alla carta Choose whatever you like from the menu.

Menù di degustazione Degustation menu, usually consisting of six to eight 'tasting size' courses.

Menù turistico The 'tourist menu' usually signals mediocre fare for gullible tourists – steer clear!

Piatto del giorno Dish of the day.

Antipasto A hot or cold appetiser. For a tasting plate of different appetisers, request an *antipasto misto* (mixed antipasto).

Primo First course, usually a substantial pasta, rice or *zuppa* (soup) dish.

Secondo Second course, often *pesce* (fish) or *carne* (meat).

Contorno Side dish, usually *verdura* (vegetable).

Dolce Dessert, including *torta* (cake).

Frutta Fruit; usually the epilogue to a meal.

Nostra produzione Made in-house; used to describe anything from bread and pasta to *liquori* (liqueurs).

Surgelato Frozen; usually used to denote fish or seafood that has not been caught fresh.

Plan Your Trip
Activities

Campania lays claim to some of Italy's most dramatic and ruggedly walkable terrain – from paths worthy of gods on the Amalfi Coast to quiet, ancient woodlands in the Cilento. The sea is another feast of possibilities: surreally lit sea caves, self-drive boat rides to hidden coves, and marine parks perfect for diving.

Walking & Hiking

Campania's most renowned trail is called Sentiero degli Dei (Path of the Gods; p158) and it's no exaggeration: this is a heavenly place to stroll, walk or hike. Day-hiking is the modus operandi of most visitors, although some longer excursions are available in the wilder Cilento region.

Trails on the Amalfi coast and the Sorrento peninsula are generally well marked and well mapped. Most are equipped with paved steps to help walkers negotiate the steep cliffs and hillsides for which the area is famous. Although not technically difficult, the paths are often steep, hot (summer temperatures can hit 40°C;104°F) and – occasionally – mildly exposed. Enjoy them, but don't underestimate them.

Trails in the Parco Nazionale del Cilento, Vallo di Diano e Alburni are less well marked and, as result, far less utilised. The Gulf of Naples Islands are a mixed bag. Most visitors come here to engage in ambling strolls, but there are a handful of short, sharp climbs for those of a more adventurous nature.

Mt Vesuvius

Reaching the summit of Mt Vesuvius (p110) is easier than you may think, with regular shuttle buses connecting Ercolano–Scavi Circumvesuviana station to the summit car park. From here, it's a relatively easy 860m walk up to the summit, where your reward is a 360-degree

Best Outdoor Experiences

Best Things to Do
Coastal grottoes Sail into Campania's dazzling sea caves.

Amalfi Coast hikes See the fabled coast from high mountain paths.

Thermal therapy De-stress in Ischia's natural hot springs.

Mt Vesuvius Scale the slopes of the infamous volcano.

Punta Campanella Marine Reserve Dive down to meet some colourful local characters.

Grotte di Castelcivita Explore the caverns at Europe's oldest settlement.

Positano cruising Sail to a little-known archipelago for a sunset Campari.

Kayaking Circumnavigate the gentle shores of Procida.

Best Times to Go
April to June Walk among wildflowers.

July & September Water sports and warm-water diving without the August crowds.

panorama capturing Naples, its bay, and the distant Apennine mountains.

The volcano is part of the Parco Nazionale del Vesuvio (p110), a national park criss-crossed by nine nature *sentieri* (trails) of varying lengths and intensity. The most challenging and rewarding is the 6.7km Lungo la Strada Matrone (Rte 6). Starting from Via Cifelli, it heads up the volcano's southeastern slope to the summit. The park itself is a rich natural oasis, home to hedgehogs, moles, stone martens and foxes, as well as around 140 species of bird, including spotted woodpeckers, hawks and imperial ravens.

Gulf of Naples Islands

Of the three main Gulf of Naples islands, the surprise package for walkers is Capri. Indeed, walking in Capri is a good way to escape the tourist hordes. Most walks are on paved paths and all are unrelentingly spectacular. The longest and wildest sortie is the Sentiero dei Fortini (p136) along the west coast.

Ischia is less well endowed with clearly marked walking routes. The obligatory hike is the short jaunt to the summit of Monte Epomeo (p145). Guided walks of the thermally rich interior are offered by Geo-Ausfluge (p145), conducted by a local geologist.

Amalfi Coast

Despite its steep uncompromising terrain, the Amalfi Coast guards one of the best trail networks in Italy. Up above the busy tourist towns of Positano and Amalfi with their clattering cafes and bulging beaches lies a parallel universe of ancient footpaths and shady woodlands where hikers can find an inner calm.

The coast protects one of Italy's most iconic hikes, the Sentiero degli Dei (Path of the Gods; p158), plus numerous other circuits, point-to-points, mountain climbs and inter-village connections. The scenery is never less than glorious: terraced hillsides dotted with clusters of tumbling houses, air thick with the aroma of ripening lemons, and a backing track of church bells and braying goats interrupted occasionally by the distant honk of a bus klaxon. The Valle delle Ferriere circuit is a wonderful wooded hike in the hills behind Amalfi town, while the Valle del Sambuco

(p191) explores the lemon groves and oak forests north of Minori.

Most of the trails are well marked and well mapped. The only real drawback is the steps – there are lots of them and most hikes contain at least one energy-sapping climb. The bonus: the higher up you go, the more tranquil your surroundings become.

Parco Nazionale del Cilento, Vallo di Diano e Alburni

Southeast of the Amalfi Coast lies Parco Nazionale del Cilento, Vallo di Diano e Alburni (p209), Italy's second-largest national park. This remarkable wilderness area is home to around 3000 registered botanical species, as well as a number of rare birds, including the golden eagle and alpine chough. The potential for hiking here is enormous, but poor transportation links, fairly scant multilingual information and the area's sheer size (meaning trailheads are far apart and often hard to find), make this the preserve of a more adventurous type of walker.

Some of the more doable day-hikes lie closer to the coast. A good introduction to the latent joys of the Cilento can be sampled in the Trentova-Tresino nature reserve (p205) near Agropoli or around Capo Palinuro (p209).

Online, www.parks.it offers useful information on the region's national parks and trails.

Cycling

Cycling in Campania has its limitations, though they are by no means insurmountable. There is little flat land in these parts, the weather can be blisteringly hot, and roads are often narrow, serpentine and populated by fearless bus drivers.

The Amalfi coast road is regularly utilised by cyclists, but to join them you'll have to concentrate hard and be prepared to forsake the views for more urgent matters (eg cumbersome buses, speeding sports cars and steep dropoffs). Less trafficked and infinitely more bike-able roads cross the Parco Nazionale del Cilento, Vallo di Diano e Alburni (p209), and you can easily plan a DIY multiday excursion between small towns in this expansive national park (Italy's second largest).

Mountain biking isn't the done thing on the Amalfi, as most trails include steep stairs. Aspiring mountain bikers are better off heading to the quiet coastal trails in the Trentova-Tresino (p205) protected area just south of Agropoli.

Of the Gulf of Naples islands, Procida is the best place for a slow sedate cycle and has a bike rental outfit right on the ferry dock.

Beaches & Swimming

The region's best sandy beaches line the Cilento coast from Paestum down to Palinuro and are mainly frequented by Italian tourists. The area is celebrated for its Blue Flag beaches, meaning they are clean well-tended and crying out for a quick dip. Highlights include Castellabate's 4km stretch of yellow sand, the broad Spiaggia Grande di Acciaroli (p208) and the beaches around Palinuro. Not only are these beaches bigger than the coves closer to Naples, but they are also less crowded and more frequented by locals.

Ischia has some reasonable dark-sand beaches in close proximity to the island's famous spas and is the best place in the Gulf of Naples islands to lay down a towel. Procida's beaches are less impressive.

Both the Amalfi Coast and Capri lack broad sandy beache; rather. the 'beaches' in these regions are more likely to inhabit sheltered coves or rocky promontories. Some are only accessible by boat or steep staircases. This notwithstanding, the region is riotously popular and sports a celebrity cast of excellent (if expensive) beach clubs.

Swimming is perennially popular in the Campania region, with the water usually clean and warm enough for summer bathing. Popular beaches invariably support at least one beach club and often have safe roped-off areas for swimming. Beware of ocean currents on more isolated beaches. Campanians are rightly proud of their clean-and-green Blue Flag beaches, all ideal for a relaxing swim. Popular Blue Flags include Spiaggia del Fornillo (p177) in Positano, Spiaggia di Faro (p131) on Capri and Spiaggia Palinuro (p208) on the Cilento coast.

TOP BEACHES

Baia di Ieranto A spectacular beach at the tip of the Punta Penna peninsula south of Sorrento. (p172)

Spiaggia Grande di Acciaroli Acres of soft sand and clear waters on the Cilento coast. (p208)

Baia di Sorgeto Catch a water taxi to this toasty thermal beach on Ischia. (p150)

Spiaggia del Fornillo Crystal-clear water awaits at this in-the-know alternative to Positano's main beach. (p177)

Santa Maria di Castellabate Velvet-soft sand and powder-blue sea at a Cilento coast resort. (p206)

Spas & Springs

The Bay of Naples has been celebrated for its thermal waters for thousands of years, seducing everyone from Roman emperors to frazzled celebrities.

Volcanic Ischia is Italy's spa-island extraordinaire. Herein lies one of the world's richest, most diverse hydrothermal hotspots, with no fewer than 103 thermal springs, 67 fumaroles and 29 underground basins. The best spas, Negombo (p145) and Giardini Poseidon (p148), inhabit veritable parks that combine lush gardens and modern sculpture with a booty of mineral pools, massage treatments and private beaches. Less luxurious but more historic are the Terme Cavascura (p151), complete with old Roman baths. For those who object to paying to use what is, after all, natural hot water, head to the Baia di Sorgeto (p150), a free-access thermal bathing spot in the sea on the island's south coast.

Easily reached on the Cumana train from Naples, the Terme Stufe di Nerone (p106) is one of the most famous thermal spas in the Campi Flegrei, complete with indoor and outdoor pools, terraced gardens, and saunas carved out of the region's trademark tufa rock.

Kayaking & Canoeing

Water sports such as kayaking and canoeing seem to take second place to boating and yachting in Campania's ritzier resorts, although there's plenty of scope to engage in water-based exercise, if you know where to look.

Kayak Napoli (p82) runs day and evening tours of the city coast, which take in old *palazzi* and coastal caves. At **Marina Piccola** (Map p122; ☎ 081 837 02 21; Via Mulo 77; ⊙Jun-Sep) on Capri you can hire canoes if you're brave enough to pitch in amid the wasp's nest of pleasure boats in high summer. For a quieter paddle you're better off heading for Procida, probably the best place in the region to dip an oar. Kayaks can be hired next to the sheltered scimitar of Marina di Chiaiolella from where local company ASD Kayak Procida (p153) runs a wonderful circumnavigation of the island.

More chilled self-propelled water transport can be enjoyed on the Cilento coast. You'll find good kayak outfits in Agropoli (p206) and Palinuro (p209).

Diving

Diving is a popular pursuit in Campania and the underwater extravaganza is top notch by Mediterranean standards. Diving operators are active along most of the coast, offering guided immersions, equipment hire and courses for all levels. Good options are present in Ischia (p138), Agropoli (p206) and Marina di Praia (p182) on the Amalfi Coast.

If in doubt, head for the highlight, the Punta Campanella Marine Reserve (p175). Located at the tip of the Sorrento Peninsula, it's well known for its colourful marina fauna, small reefs and multicoloured seaweed. Nettuno Diving (p175) based at Marina del Cantone is one of the best dive operators in Campania and can organise special access to the marine reserve. Other favourite dive sites include the WWII wrecks at Agropoli, the turquoise waters around Capri and the underwater grottoes of Marina del Cantone.

Parco Sommerso di Gaiola (p81) is a marine reserve just below Posillipo near Naples with abundant marine life. Guided snorkelling and diving tours are offered here, as well as glass-bottom boat tours in the warmer months.

In general, avoid August, when much of Campania's coastline is besieged by holidaymakers and prices are at their highest. Information on diving schools and areas is available from local tourist offices and online at www.diveitaly.com (in Italian).

Plan Your Trip
Travel with Children

With a little planning and some background information on the region's gripping history, Naples and the Amalfi Coast are guaranteed to hook young, curious minds. After all, this is the land of giant gladiatorial arenas, mysterious catacombs, hissing craters and bubbling beaches. Jump in!

Naples & the Amalfi Coast for Kids

Children are adored in Campania and welcomed almost anywhere. On the downside, the region has few special amenities for junior travellers, and the combination of Naples' breathless pace, the Amalfi Coast's twisting coastal road, and the stroller-unfriendly cobbled stones at archaeological sites can prove challenging. With a little adaptation and an open mind, however, young families will find that Campania is a richly stimulating, rewarding destination.

Children's Highlights
Culture Vultures

MAV (Museo Archeologico Virtuale), Ercolano Campania's ancient ruins brought back to life with holograms and videos. (p201)

Museo della Carta, Amalfi Explore the region's proud papermaking tradition in an historic Amalfi paper mill. (p185)

Museo Virtuale della Scuola Medica Salernitana, Salerno An interactive museum dedicated to medieval medicine. (p201)

Giffoni Film Festival, Giffoni Valle Piana, Salerno Europe's biggest children's film festival. (p27)

Best By Region
Naples, Pompeii & Around

Capital attractions: step back in time at Pompeii, Herculaneum and Oplontis, explore ancient cisterns, passageways and ghoulish cemeteries below lively city streets, get experimental at a science museum and sidle up to a sizzling geological wonder.

The Islands

Water babies: seek your own perfect swimming cove on a private boat on Procida, sail into a sparkling, magical grotto on Capri, or pool-hop at a sprawling thermal-spa resort on lush, volcanic Ischia.

The Amalfi Coast

Surf and turf: chill out on a summertime boat trip, get splash-happy at a coveted beach, hike high above the coastline, and take in a little history at a quirky paper museum in Amalfi.

Salerno & the Cilento

Wild and cultured: learn about ancient medicine at a multimedia museum, attend a children's film festival, or run wild in wide open spaces, riding rivers, feeding farm animals and sorting out your stalactites from your stalagmites.

Thrills & Spills

Negombo, Ischia A thermal-springs park with mineral pools and thermal beach, plus massage and beauty treatments for frazzled parents (p145).

Grotta Azzurra, Capri Pixar has nothing on Capri's dazzling, other-worldly Blue Grotto (p134).

Parco Nazionale del Cilento, Vallo di Diano e Alburni Spooky caves, colourful sea-grottoes and *agriturismo* complete with furry friends (p209).

Monte Faito Spectacular cable-car ride up to the roof of the Lattari mountains (p173).

Time Travel

Pompeii Ancient theatres, houses, shops and even a stadium. The ancient brothel will no doubt bemuse teens (p111).

Herculaneum Smaller than Pompeii and better preserved, with carbonised furniture and ancient shop advertisements (p109).

Napoli Sotterranea, Naples Head down a secret porthole into a magical labyrinth of Graeco-Roman passageways and cisterns (p66).

Cimitero delle Fontanelle, Naples It's Halloween every day at the ghoulish Fontanelle Cemetery, neatly stacked with human skulls and bones (p77).

Planning

When to Go

May, June and September are generally warm and sunny, without the summer peak crowds. Colourful floats and costumes make Carnevale (February or March) another good bet, while the region's famous *presepi* (nativity scenes) can help make December magical.

Where to Stay

Book accommodation in advance whenever possible. In hotels, some double rooms can't accommodate an extra bed for kids, so check ahead. If the child is small enough to share your bed, some hoteliers will let you do this for free.

Hostels and apartments Good for multibed rooms, self-catering and lounge facilities.

Campgrounds Buzzing in high season (summer), with many offering activities for kids of all ages.

Farm stays Great for outdoor space; numerous *agriturismi* also come with cute, furry animals.

Where to Eat

➡ Most eateries, especially trattorias and pizzerias, welcome kids.

➡ If reserving a table, ask if they have a *seggiolone* (high chair).

➡ Children's menus are uncommon, though requesting a *mezzo piatto* (half plate) off the menu is usually fine.

Essentials

➡ Disposable nappies (diapers) are readily available at supermarkets and pharmacies. Pharmacies also stock baby formula in powder or liquid form, as well as sterilising solutions.

➡ Fresh cow's milk is sold in cartons in supermarkets and in bars with a 'Latteria' sign. UHT milk is popular, and in many out-of-the-way areas it's the only kind available.

Transport

➡ Cobbled streets, pot holes and crowded transport make travelling with a stroller cumbersome; consider investing in an ergonomic baby carrier instead.

➡ Public-transport operators offer free travel for one child aged up to six if accompanied by a paying adult. An adult accompanying more than one child must purchase one ticket per every two children.

➡ Most car-hire firms offer children's safety seats at a nominal cost, but book ahead.

Regions at a Glance

Naples, Pompeii & Around

History
Museums
Food

Ancient Sites

Neapolitans abide by the motto *carpe diem* (seize the day). All around them, at Pompeii, Ercolano, Pozzuoli, Baia and Cuma, they are reminded that life is short and unpredictable. Even beneath their feet lurk reminders of long-lost lives, from subterranean markets to macabre funerary frescoes.

Museums & Galleries

Naples explodes with art and antiquities, from colossal Roman statues at Museo Archeologico Nazionale to Caravaggio at Palazzo Reale di Capodimonte. Beyond them is a long list of lesser-known treasures, including Teatro San Carlo's own theatre museum, MeMus.

Pizza & Pasta

Naples' loud and lusty streets serve up some of the nation's most famous flavours: coffee, pizza, pasta, Vesuvian tomatoes, *sfogliatelle* (sweetened ricotta pastries), *babà* (rum-soaked sponge cake) and a panoply of seafood to be devoured every which way you can.

p47

The Islands

Food
Landscapes
Spas

Island Flavours

Whether you're enjoying *torta caprese* (almond-and-chocolate cake) on a Capri piazza, slow-cooked rabbit at a rustic Ischian trattoria or just-caught fish on a Procida beach, expect some long-lasting culinary memories.

Superlative Scenery

From Capri's vertiginous cliffs and electric-blue grotto to Ischia's luxe gardens and vine-clad hillsides to Procida's peeling, pastel villages, beautiful details define the Bay of Naples. So aim your camera and make the peeps back home turn a deeper shade of green.

Thermal Spas

Ischia's thermal springs have soothed weary muscles since ancient times. Find some zen at a bubbling beach, soak in an old Roman bath, then get wrapped and pummelled at a sprawling spa resort.

p119

The Amalfi Coast

Culture
Scenery
Activities

Art & Architecture

Contemporary painting and sculpture in Positano, medieval cloisters in Amalfi and classical overtures in Ravello: beyond the gleaming yachts, crowded beaches and Gucci-clad eye candy awaits a precious string of cultural riches.

Coastal Beauty

Cloud-scraping cliffs, terraced vineyards, tumbling fishing villages in mood-lifting hues, not to mention obscenely turquoise Tyrrhenian waters – views are at all angles on Italy's most stunning and celebrated coastline.

Natural Wonders

Above, below or at sea level, active types are spoilt for choice. Whether you fancy swimming or diving in crystal-clear seas, cove-hopping on a sailing boat or escaping the hordes on a hiking trail high above the sea, the Amalfi Coast will keep your heart rate up.

p157

Salerno & the Cilento

Food
Ruins
Nature

A Bountiful Larder

Luscious buffalo-milk mozzarella and peppery olive oil, perfect artichokes, velvety white figs, glistening seafood and plump, rum-soaked pastries – Salerno and the Cilento aren't short on lauded regional edibles.

Hellenic Ruins

Long before the Romans staked their claim, Greek sandals stamped around this turf. Pay tribute to the power and elegance of Magna Graecia (Greater Greece) at the stoic temples of Paestum and bucolic ruins of Velia.

Rugged Escapes

Deep, dark woods, exhilarating rapids and cathedral-like caves littered with evidence of early human history: the Parco Nazionale del Cilento, Vallo di Diano e Alburni is one of the country's biggest, wildest natural playgrounds and the ultimate spot for a back-to-nature adventure.

p195

On the Road

AT A GLANCE

★

POPULATION
966,145

PATRON SAINT
Januarius

**BEST
ANTIPASTI**
Capo Blu (p106)

**BEST
HANDMADE
GLOVES**
Omega (p95)

BEST FESTIVAL
Napoli Teatro Festival
Italia (p83)

📅

WHEN TO GO
May An especially
good month to
explore the Bay of
Naples, with mild
weather, good deals
on accommodation
and a month-long
culture-fest.

Jun-Sep Summer
means queues
and crowds at big
archaeological
sights.

Oct-Apr Quieter,
cooler and cheaper.
Naples is famous for
its *presepi* (nativity
scenes), drawing
Christmas crowds
from across Italy.

Architectural detail, Chiaia (p73), Naples
GREG ELMS/LONELY PLANET ©

Naples, Pompeii & Around

Naples is raw, high-octane energy, a place of soul-stirring art and panoramas, spontaneous conversations and unexpected, inimitable elegance. You'll find two royal palaces, three castles, and ancient ruins that include some of Christianity's oldest frescoes. The Naples region is also one of Italy's epicurean heavyweights: it's here that you'll find the country's best pizza, pasta and espresso, and its most appetising street markets.

Within easy day-tripping distance, the ruins of Pompeii and Herculaneum await. Towering over both, Mt Vesuvius offers rugged hiking trails and stunning views from its summit. To the west of Naples lie the sulphuric Campi Flegrei, speckled with evocative Greek ruins.

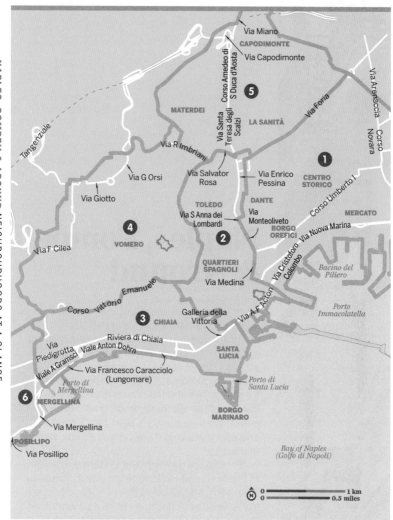

Via Miano
CAPODIMONTE
Via Capodimonte
Corso Amedeo di S Duca d'Aosta
Via Foria
Via Arenaccia
Corso Novara
MATERDEI
Via Santa Teresa degli Scalzi
LA SANITÀ
Tangenziale
Via R Imbriani
Via G Orsi
Via Salvator Rosa
Via Enrico Pessina
CENTRO STORICO
Corso Umberto I
Via Giotto
TOLEDO
Via S Anna dei Lombardi
DANTE
Via Monteoliveto
MERCATO
Via Nuova Marina
VOMERO
BORGO OREFICI
Via F Cilea
QUARTIERI SPAGNOLI
Via Medina
Via Cristoforo Colombo
Bacino del Piliero
Corso Vittorio Emanuele
Galleria della Vittoria
Via A F Acton
Porto Immacolatella
CHIAIA
Riviera di Chiaia
Via Piedigrotta
Viale Anton Dohrn
SANTA LUCIA
Viale A Gramsci
Via Francesco Caracciolo (Lungomare)
Porto di Santa Lucia
Porto di Mergellina
MERGELLINA
Via Mergellina
BORGO MARINARO
POSILLIPO
Via Posillipo
Bay of Naples (Golfo di Napoli)

N
0   1 km
0   0.5 miles

❶ Centro Storico (p51)

The *centro storico* (historic centre) is the loud, pounding heart of Naples, a dizzying rush of hip baristas, cultish shrines and operatic *palazzi* (mansions). Almost 3000 years old, its ancient warren of alleys and squares claim many of the city's most spectacular cultural assets, from frescoed chapels and cloisters to chariot-grooved subterranean streets. It's also where you'll find many of its top pizzerias and eateries, its most boho-spirited bars, and no shortage of artisan studios to browse and shop. Take a deep breath and dive right in.

❷ Toledo & Quartieri Spagnoli (p66)

Constructed by Spanish viceroy Pedro Álvarez de Toledo y Zúñiga in the 16th century, Via Toledo (aka Via Roma) heaves with window-shopping teens, besuited business folk and elegant *palazzi* that once housed worldly aristocrats. Skinny side streets lead west into the Quartieri Spagnoli, built for Don Pedro's Spanish troops and now an earthy, lived-in warren of dripping washing, renegade Vespas and old-school Neapolitan cooking. In sharp contrast, Via Toledo shoots south towards the gilded glories of Palazzo Reale and Teatro San Carlo, their own neighbour the one-time Angevin stronghold of Castel Nuovo (Maschio Angioino).

❸ Santa Lucia & Chiaia (p73)

Fin-de-siècle hotels, middle-class families and seaside promenading define Santa Lucia, a compact, respectable district anchored by eponymous Via Santa Lucia. This is the place for lazy waterfront *passeggiate* (strolls) and seafood feasts by bobbing boats. The latter are the order of the day on the petite islet of Borgo Marinaro, home to hulking Castel dell'Ovo and connected to the mainland by an artificial isthmus. Sprawling to the west of Santa Lucia is on-point Chiaia, home to high-end boutiques, bar-packed side streets, fashionable Neapolitans, and a former Rothschild villa.

❹ Vomero (p76)

All roads might lead to Rome, but three Neapolitan funiculars lead to Vomero, a hilltop neighbourhood where quasi-anarchy is replaced with mild-mannered professori, Liberty villas and the stunning Certosa di San Martino. Panoramic bay and city views,

not to mention one of Naples' best-loved public parks, make this neighbourhood an easily accessible antidote to the city centre's full-throttle intensity.

❺ La Sanità & Capodimonte (p78)

Located outside the city walls until the 18th century, La Sanità was for centuries where the city buried its dead. These days, its noisy, rough-and-tumble jumble of *bassi* (one-room, ground-floor houses), market stalls and baroque staircases pull an ever-growing number of resident artists and bohemians, drawn to the neighbourhood's rich textures and raw, authentic energy. Following in their lead is an ever-increasing number of plugged-in travellers, on the hunt for frescoed catacombs and secret artisan studios. To the north lies Capodimonte, a former royal hunting ground famed for its art-crammed palace.

❻ Mergellina & Posillipo (p81)

Located at the western end of the pedestrianised Lungomare (seafront), Mergellina exudes an air of faded grandeur with its Liberty palazzi and slightly scruffy seafront. Kitsch marina chalets sell gelato to lovestruck teens, while, close by, hydrofoils head out to the islands. Further west, on the headland dividing the Bay of Naples from the Bay of Pozzuoli, Posillipo is a verdant, blue-ribbon neighbourhood of sprawling villas, secret swimming coves and the urban oasis of Parco Virgiliano.

Naples, Pompeii & Around Highlights

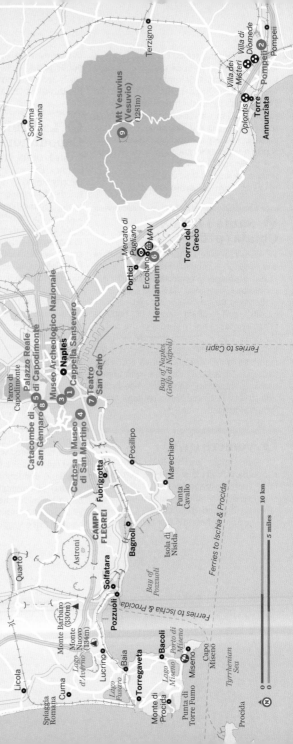

1 Cappella Sansevero (p55) Admiring Giuseppe Sanmartino's *Cristo velato*.

2 Pompeii (p111) Seeing how the ancients lived in a frozen-in-time town.

3 Museo Archeologico Nazionale (p52) Admiring Italy's finest ancient treasures.

4 Certosa e Museo di San Martino (p76) Combining cloisters, carriages and royal barges with panoramic bay and city views.

5 Museo di Capodimonte (p54) Dabbling with Caravaggio, Warhol and regal excess at a hilltop royal palace.

6 Herculaneum (p107) Snooping around millennia-old homes, shops and baths.

7 Teatro San Carlo (p69) Applauding at the country's grandest opera house.

8 Catacombe di San Gennaro (p78) Exploring ancient frescoes and tombs.

9 Mt Vesuvius (p110) Peering into the ashen mouth of a slumbering volcano.

NAPLES

♪ 081 / POP 966.145

Until recently snubbed by many, Naples is quickly evolving into one of Italy's tourist hot spots. Revamped museums, hip new bars and eateries, and swelling visitor numbers are pumping the city with newfound confidence and buzz.

◉ Sights

◉ Centro Storico

Cappella Sansevero　　　　　CHAPEL
See p55.

★**Duomo**　　　　　CATHEDRAL
(Map p58; ♪081 44 90 97; Via Duomo 149; cathedral/baptistry free/€2; ⊙cathedral 8.30am-1.30pm & 2.30-7.30pm Mon-Sat, 8.30am-1.30pm & 4.30-7.30pm Sun, baptistry 8.30am-12.30pm & 3.30-6.30pm Mon-Sat, 8.30am-1pm Sun, Cappella di San Gennaro 8.30am-1pm & 3-6.30pm Mon-Sat, 8.30am-1pm & 4.30-7pm Sun; ☐147, 182, 184 to Via Foria, ⓂPiazza Cavour) Whether you go for Giovanni Lanfranco's fresco in the Cappella di San Gennaro (Chapel of St Janarius), the 4th-century mosaics in the baptistry, or the thrice-annual miracle of San Gennaro, do not miss Naples' cathedral. Kick-started by Charles I of Anjou in 1272 and consecrated in 1315, it was largely destroyed in a 1456 earthquake. It has had copious nips and tucks over the subsequent centuries.

Among these is the gleaming neo-Gothic facade, only completed in 1905. Step inside and you'll immediately notice the central nave's gilded coffered ceiling, studded with late-mannerist art. The high sections of the nave and the transept are the work of baroque overachiever Luca Giordano.

Off the right side of the nave, the **Cappella di San Gennaro** (also known as the Chapel of the Treasury) was designed by Theatine priest and architect Francesco Grimaldi, and completed in 1646. The most sought-after artists of the period worked on the chapel, creating one of Naples' greatest baroque legacies. Highlights here include Jusepe de Ribera's gripping canvas *St Gennaro Escaping the Furnace Unscathed* and Giovanni Lanfranco's dizzying dome fresco. Hidden away in a strongbox behind the altar is a 14th-century silver bust

(Continued on page 56)

NAPLES IN...

One Day
Start with a burst of baroque in the Chiesa del Gesù Nuovo (p57), then clear your mind in the majolica-tiled cloister of the Complesso Monumentale di Santa Chiara (p56). Stop at Palazzo Venezia (p89) for coffee in a secret garden, then get breathless over Giuseppe Sanmartino's *Cristo velato* (Veiled Christ) sculpture in the Cappella Sansevero. Lunch at Tandem (p84) or super-cheap Trattoria Mangia e Bevi (p84) before spending the afternoon exploring the ancient treasures of the Museo Archeologico Nazionale (p52). Revive with aperitivo on Piazza Bellini (p65) before dinner at bistro-style Salumeria (p85) or cult-status pizzerias Concettina Ai Tre Santi (p88) or Pizzeria Gino Sorbillo (p84).

Two Days
Start day two with firebrand espresso at belle-époque Caffè Gambrinus (p90), before catching the Capodimonte shuttle bus to explore the gilded, art-crammed halls of the Palazzo Reale di Capodimonte (p54). Alternatively, catch a funicular to the richly historic Certosa e Museo di San Martino (p76). Either way, head down to the shore in the afternoon, lunching at Officina del Mare (p87) or no-frills Trattoria Castel dell'Ovo (p87) and taking in the views from atop neighbouring Castel dell'Ovo (p73). From here, it's an easy walk to Chiaia, home to chic boutiques, the cinematic staircase of Palazzo Mannajuolo (p75) and buzzing aperitivo bars like Ba-Bar (p91) and Barril (p90).

Three Days
Head into the suburbs and up Mt Vesuvius (p110) for dizzying views and a face-to-face with its deceptively peaceful crater. Back down the slope, walk the ghostly streets of ancient Pompeii (p111) or Herculaneum (p107) before heading back to town in time for a (pre-booked) performance at the revered Teatro San Carlo (p92).

TOP SIGHT
MUSEO ARCHEOLOGICO NAZIONALE

The stuff history dreams are made of, Naples' Museo Archeologico Nazionale houses one of the world's most important collections of ancient treasures. Its assets include many of the finest frescoes, mosaics and epigraphs from ill-fated Pompeii and Herculaneum, not to mention the largest single sculpture from antiquity unearthed to date.

Toro Farnese & Hercules

The undisputed star of the ground-floor Farnese collection of colossal Greek and Roman sculptures is the *Toro Farnese* (Farnese Bull). Mentioned in the *Natural History* of Pliny the Elder, the early-3rd-century masterpiece – most likely a Roman copy of a Greek original – is the largest single sculpture recovered from antiquity. Unearthed in Rome in 1545, the piece was restored by Michelangelo before being escorted to Naples by warship in 1788. Sculpted from a single block of marble, the masterpiece depicts the humiliating demise of Dirce, Queen of Thebes, tied to a raging bull and violently dragged to her death. Directly opposite the work is mighty *Ercole* (Hercules), also discovered at Rome's Baths of Caracalla, albeit without his legs. Michelangelo commissioned Guglielmo della Porta to sculpt replacement pins. The original legs were later uncovered and reinstated by the Bourbons. An inscription on the rock below Hercules' club attributes the work to Athenian sculptor Glykon.

DON'T MISS

➡ Toro Farnese & Hercules statues

➡ Alexander the Great mosaic

➡ Gabinetto Segreto (Secret Chamber)

➡ First-floor frescoes and Villa dei Papiri sculptures

PRACTICALITIES

➡ Map p58

➡ ☎ 848 800288

➡ www.museo archeologiconapoli.it

➡ Piazza Museo Nazionale 19

➡ adult/reduced €18/2

➡ ⊙ 9am-7.30pm Wed-Mon

➡ Ⓜ Museo, Piazza Cavour

Mezzanine Mosaics & Ancient Erotica

The museum's mezzanine level is awash with precious mosaic panels, most of which hail from ancient Pompeii. Room LIX is home to the playful *Scena di commedia: Musici ambulanti,* depicting four roaming musicians, as well as the allegorical *Memento mori,* in which a skull represents death, a butterfly the soul, and the wheel fate. The mosaics in rooms LX and LXI are even more impressive. Once adorning the largest home in Pompeii, the Casa del Fauno, they include an action-packed mural of Alexander the Great in battle against Persian king Darius III. Considered one of the most important works of art from antiquity, it's a precise copy of a famous Hellenistic painting from the second half of the 4th century BC. The mosaics found in the Casa del Fauno were created by lauded craftsmen from Alexandria, Egypt, active in Italy between the end of the 2nd century BC and the beginning of the 1st century BC. The mezzanine is also home to the Gabinetto Segreto (Secret Chamber), a small, once-scandalous collection of erotically themed artworks and objects. Its most famous piece is a marble sculpture of the mythical half-goat, half-man Pan copulating with a nanny goat.

First-Floor Frescoes & Sculptures

The 1st floor is a tour de force of ancient frescoes, pottery, glassware and sculpture. From the Sala del Meridione, the collection commences with frescoes retrieved from Vesuvian villas. Room LXXII is home to the largest known depiction of Perseus and Andromeda, in which the hero rescues his young bride after slaying a sea monster. More beast slaying occurs in Room LXXIII, home to a notable depiction of *Theseus the Liberator*. In Room LXXV, *Bacchus and Vesuvius* is believed to represent Vesuvius as it looked before the eruption of AD 79, with one summit instead of two. A notorious clash between rival spectators at Pompeii's amphitheatre in AD 59 is captured in Room LXXVIII's *Riot between Pompeians and Nucerians*. At the end of the building is a collection of impressive sculptures found at the Villa dei Papiri. Room CXVI houses the five bronzes known collectively as the *Daughters of Danaus*. Dating from the Augustan period (27 BC– AD 14), the figures represents mythical siblings condemned to pouring water for eternity after murdering their cousins (and bridegrooms) to appease their father, who sought revenge on his own sibling, Aegyptus.

BASEMENT TREASURES

The museum's basement claims one of the world's most important collections of ancient Greek, Italic and Latin epigraphs (stone inscriptions), representing both public and private life in ancient times. Adjoining it is a collection of Egyptian treasures, which, in Italy, is outshone only by Turin's Museo Egizio.

***

The Museo Archeologico Nazionale occupies the Palazzo degli Studi, built in the late 16th century as a cavalry barracks. It was extended and modified over the centuries by architects including Giulio Cesare Fontana, the son of the great late-Renaissance architect Domenico Fontana. The building's pièce de résistance is its 1st-floor Salone della Meridiana (Hall of the Sundial), its own origins in the early 17th century. The arresting vault fresco, by Neapolitan artist Pietro Bardellino, pays tribute to King Ferdinand IV and his wife Maria Carolina of Austria.

TOP SIGHT
PALAZZO REALE DI CAPODIMONTE

Former summer residence of the kings of the Two Sicilies, the Palazzo Reale di Capodimonte claims one of Italy's largest and richest art collections. Waiting beyond it is the Parco di Capodimonte, Naples' glorious, green, panoramic lungs.

Museum Masterpieces

The Museo di Capodimonte constitutes a number of historic collections, most notably the Farnese Collection. First-floor highlights include Masaccio's shimmering *Crucifixion,* Botticelli's *Madonna with Child and Angels,* Bellini's *Transfiguration* and Parmigianino's *Antea,* all of which are subject to room changes within the museum. Second-floor highlights include a series of early 16th-century tapestries depicting the 1525 Battle of Pavia, a pivotal moment in the Italian War of 1521–26 and Caravaggio's *Flagellation of Christ* (Room 78). Rooms 88 to 95 offer a feast of Neapolitan baroque paintings.

Parco di Capodimonte

Designed by Ferdinando Sanfelice in 1742 as a royal hunting reserve, the Parco di Capodimonte sprawls across 134 hectares in a series of themed gardens and woods. East of the palace building lies the park's Porta di Mezzo (Middle Gate), from where five paths radiate out into the woods in one of the finest examples of late-baroque garden architecture. The central path leads to the *Statua del Gigante* (Statue of the Giant), named for its colossal dimensions.

DON'T MISS

➡ Museum masterpieces

➡ Royal park

PRACTICALITIES

➡ Map p80

➡ ☎ 081 749 91 11

➡ www.museo capodimonte. beniculturali.it

➡ Via Miano 2

➡ adult/reduced €12/8

➡ ⊙ 8.30am-7.30pm Thu-Tue

➡ 🚌 R4, 178 to Via Capodimonte, 🚌 Shuttle Capodimonte

TOP SIGHT
CAPPELLA SANSEVERO

Former stamping ground – and final resting place – of the city's most infamous alchemist, the Capella Sansevero lays claim to the *Cristo velato* (Veiled Christ; pictured), a sculpture so extraordinary that many have questioned how only a talented artist's hand could achieve such perfection.

Cristo Velato

Dating from 1753, Giuseppe Sanmartino's depiction of a spent, crucified Christ features a marble veil so thin that many have wondered whether the chapel's alchemist patron, Prince Raimondo di Sangro, had found a way to transform cloth into stone.

Ceiling Fresco

The Cappella Sansevero is crowned by Francesco Maria Russo's bombastic *Gloria del Paradiso* (Glory of Heaven). The prince himself formulated the long-lasting colours used by the artist, which have allowed the fresco to remain intense and untouched since its completion in 1749.

Subterranean Chamber

Beneath the chapel lies di Sangro's secret chamber, home to a pair of meticulously preserved human arterial systems, one of a man, the other of a woman. According to one legend, they belonged to di Sangro's hapless servants, murdered for minor disobedience.

DON'T MISS

➡ *Cristo velato* sculpture

➡ *Gloria del Paradiso* ceiling fresco

➡ Subterranean chamber

PRACTICALITIES

➡ Map p58

➡ ☎ 081 551 84 70

➡ www.museosansevero.it

➡ Via Francesco de Sanctis 19

➡ adult/reduced €7/5

➡ ⊘ 9am-7pm Wed-Mon

➡ Ⓜ Dante

Naples

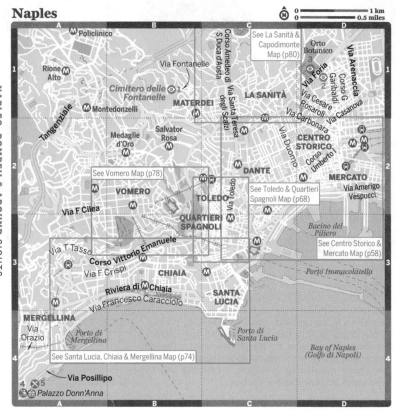

Naples

◎ Top Sights
1 Cimitero delle Fontanelle.....................B1

◎ Sights
2 Mercato Sant'Antonio Abate..............D1
3 Orto Botanico di Napoli.......................D1

✪ Activities, Courses & Tours
4 Kayak Napoli...A4

✪ Eating
5 Palazzo Petrucci...................................A4

(Continued from page 51)

in which sit the skull of San Gennaro and the two phials that hold his miraculously liquefying blood.

The next chapel eastwards contains an urn with the saint's bones and a cupboard full of femurs, tibias and fibulas. Below the high altar is the **Cappella Carafa**, a Renaissance chapel built to house yet more of the saint's remains.

Off the left aisle lies the 4th-century **Basilica di Santa Restituta**, the subject of an almost complete makeover after the earthquake of 1688. From it you can access the **Battistero di San Giovanni in Fonte**. It is Western Europe's oldest baptistry and is encrusted with fragments of glittering 4th-century mosaics.

The Duomo's subterranean **archaeological zone**, which includes fascinating remains of Greek and Roman buildings and roads, remains closed indefinitely.

★ **Complesso Monumentale di Santa Chiara**   BASILICA
(Map p58; ☎081 551 66 73; www.monasterodi santachiara.it; Via Santa Chiara 49c; basilica free, Complesso Monumentale adult/reduced €6/4.50; ⊙basilica 7.30am-1pm & 4.30-8pm, Complesso Monumentale 9.30am-5.30pm Mon-Sat, 10am-2.30pm Sun; Ⓜ Dante) Vast, Gothic and cleverly

deceptive, the mighty **Basilica di Santa Chiara** stands at the heart of this tranquil monastery complex. The church was severely damaged in WWII: what you see today is a 20th-century recreation of Gagliardo Primario's 14th-century original. Adjoining it are the basilica's **cloisters**, adorned with brightly coloured 17th-century majolica tiles and frescoes.

While the Angevin porticoes date back to the 14th century, the cloisters took on their current look in the 18th century thanks to the landscaping work of Domenico Antonio Vaccaro. The walkways that divide the central garden of lavender and citrus trees are lined with 72 ceramic-tiled octagonal columns connected by benches. Painted by Donato and Giuseppe Massa, the tiles depict various rural scenes, from hunting sessions to vignettes of peasant life. The four internal walls are covered with soft, whimsical 17th-century frescoes of Franciscan tales.

Adjacent to the cloisters, a small and elegant **museum** of mostly ecclesiastical props also features the excavated ruins of a 1st-century spa complex, including a remarkably well-preserved *laconicum* (sauna).

Commissioned by Robert of Anjou for his wife Sancia di Maiorca, the monastic complex was built to house 200 monks and the tombs of the Angevin royal family. Dissed as a 'stable' by Robert's ungrateful son Charles of Anjou, the basilica received a luscious baroque makeover by Domenico Antonio Vaccaro, Gaetano Buonocore and Giovanni Del Gaizo in the 18th century. It took a direct hit during an Allied air raid on 4 August 1943 and its reconstruction was completed in 1953. Features that did survive the fire resulting from the bombing include part of a 14th-century fresco to the left of the main door and a chapel containing the tombs of the Bourbon kings from Ferdinand I to Francesco II.

The church forecourt makes a cameo in Pier Paolo Pasolini's film *Il Decameron* (The Decameron), itself based on Giovanni Boccaccio's 14th-century novel.

Chiesa del Gesù Nuovo   CHURCH
(Map p58; ☑ 081 557 81 51; Piazza del Gesù Nuovo; ☺ 7.15am-12.45pm & 4-8pm Mon-Sat, 8am-2pm & 4-9pm Sun; Ⓜ Dante) The extraordinary Chiesa del Gesù Nuovo is an architectural Kinder Surprise. Its shell is the 15th-century, Giuseppe Valeriani–designed facade of Palazzo Sanseverino, converted to create the 16th-century church. Inside, *piperno*-stone

sobriety gives way to a gob-smacking blast of baroque that could make the Vatican blush: a vainglorious showcase for the work of top-tier artists such as Francesco Solimena, Luca Giordano and Cosimo Fanzago.

The church is the final resting place of much-loved local saint Giuseppe Moscati (1880–1927), a doctor who served the city's poor. Adjacent to the right transept, the Sale di San Giuseppe Moscati (Rooms of St Joseph Moscati) include a recreation of the great man's study, complete with the armchair in which he died. Scan the walls for *ex-voti*, gifts offered by the faithful for miracles purportedly received. The church itself received a miracle of sorts on 4 August 1943, when a bomb dropped on the site failed to explode. Its shell is aptly displayed beside the *ex-voti*.

The church flanks the northern side of beautiful **Piazza del Gesù Nuovo**, a favourite late-night hang-out for students and lefties. At its centre soars Giuseppe Genuino's lavish **Guglia dell'Immacolata**, an obelisk built between 1747 and 1750. On 8 December, the Feast of the Immacolata, a firefighter scrambles up to the top to place a wreath on the statue of the Virgin Mary.

★ **Pio Monte della Misericordia**   CHURCH, MUSEUM
(Map p58; ☑ 081 44 69 44; www.piomonte dellamisericordia.it; Via dei Tribunali 253; adult/reduced €7/5; ☺ 9am-6pm Mon-Sat, to 2.30pm Sun; Ⓜ Piazza Cavour) The 1st-floor gallery of this octagonal, 17th-century church delivers a satisfying, digestible collection of Renaissance and baroque art, including works by Francesco de Mura, Jusepe de Ribera, Andrea Vaccaro and Paul van Somer. It's also home to contemporary artworks by Italian and foreign artists, each inspired by Caravaggio's masterpiece *Le sette opere di Misericordia* (The Seven Acts of Mercy). Considered by many to be the most important painting in Naples, you'll find it above the main altar in the ground-floor chapel.

Magnificently demonstrating the artist's chiaroscuro style, which had a revolutionary impact in Naples, *Le sette opere di Misericordia* was considered unique in its ability to illustrate the various acts in one seamlessly choreographed scene. Pio Monte della Misericordia's archives are home to the *Declaratoria del 14 Ottobre 1607,* an original church document acknowledging payment of 400 ducats to Caravaggio for the painting. A photocopy of the document is on display

Centro Storico & Mercato

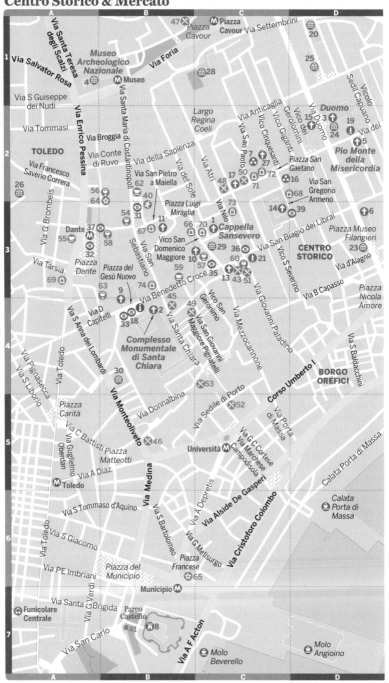

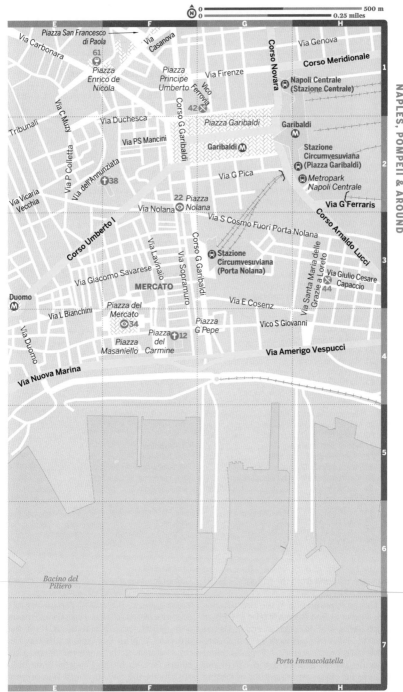

Centro Storico & Mercato

Top Sights
1 Cappella Sansevero C3
2 Complesso Monumentale di Santa Chiara B4
3 Duomo D2
4 Museo Archeologico Nazionale A1
5 Pio Monte della Misericordia D2

Sights
6 Basilica di San Giorgio Maggiore D3
7 Basilica di San Paolo Maggiore C2
8 Castel Nuovo B7
9 Chiesa del Gesù Nuovo B4
10 Chiesa di San Domenico Maggiore C3
11 Chiesa di San Pietro a Maiella B3
12 Chiesa di Santa Maria del Carmine F4
13 Chiesa di Sant'Angelo a Nilo C3
14 Chiesa e Chiostro di San Gregorio Armeno C3
15 Complesso Monumentale dei Girolamini D2
16 Complesso Monumentale di San Lorenzo Maggiore C2
17 Complesso Museale di Santa Maria delle Anime del Purgatorio ad Arco C2
18 Guglia dell'Immacolata B4
19 Guglia di San Gennaro D2
20 MADRE D1
21 Maradona Shrine C3
22 Mercato di Porta Nolana F2
23 Museo Civico Filangieri D3
24 Museo del Tesoro di San Gennaro D2
Museo delle Arti Sanitarie .... (see 28)
25 Museo Diocesano di Napoli D1
26 Museo Nitsch A2
27 Napoli Sotterranea C2
28 Ospedale degli Incurabili C1
29 Palazzo dei Di Sangro C3
30 Palazzo Orsini in Gravina B4
31 Piazza Bellini B3
32 Piazza Dante A3
33 Piazza del Gesù Nuovo B4
34 Piazza del Mercato F4
35 Piazza San Domenico Maggiore C3
36 Piazzetta Nilo C3
37 Port'Alba B3
38 Santissima Annunziata F2
39 Via San Gregorio Armeno D3

Activities, Courses & Tours
40 Centro di Alimentazione Consapevole B3
41 City Sightseeing Napoli B7

Eating
42 Attanasio G1
43 Donna Romita C3
44 La Masardona H3
45 La Taverna a Santa Chiara B4
46 'O Sfizio B5
47 Pasticceria Di Costanzo B1
48 Pizzeria Gino Sorbillo C2
49 Salumeria B4
50 Serafino C2
51 Tandem C3
52 Trattoria Mangia e Bevi C5
53 Vero GastroBar C4

Drinking & Nightlife
54 Caffè dell'Epoca B3
55 Caffè Mexico A3
56 Il Birraiuolo B2
57 Jamón C3
58 Libreria Berisio B3
59 Palazzo Venezia Napoli B3
60 Shanti Art Musik Bar C3
61 Spazio Intolab E1
62 Spazio Nea B2
63 Superfly B3

Entertainment
64 Bourbon Street B2
65 Teatro Mercadante B6

Shopping
66 Bottega 21 .... B3
67 Colonnese B3
68 Ferrigno D2
69 Gay Odin A3
70 Kiphy C3
71 La Scarabattola C2
72 Limonè C2
73 MAC Ceramics C3
74 Scriptura B3

in the 1st-floor gallery, where you can also view the painting from the gallery's Sala del Coretto (Coretto Room).

On the opposite side of the street stands the **Guglia di San Gennaro** (Map p58; Piazza Riario Sforza; R2 to Corso Umberto I). Dating back to 1636, with stonework by Cosimo Fanzago and a bronze statue by Tommaso Montani, the obelisk is a soaring *grazie* (thank you) to the city's patron saint for protecting Naples from the 1631 eruption of Mt Vesuvius.

Chiesa di San Domenico Maggiore CHURCH
(Map p58; 333 8638997; www.museosandomenicomaggiore.it; Piazza San Domenico Maggiore 8a; guided tour adult/reduced from €5/4; 10am-6pm; M Dante) Completed in 1324 on the orders of Charles I of Anjou, this was the royal church of the Angevins. Pietro Cavallini's frescoes in the Cappella Brancaccio are among the few surviving 14th-century remnants. Take the guided tour (in Italian,

with an English information sheet) to view the **sacristy**, crowned by a ceiling fresco by Francesco Solimena and home to the sarcophagi of 45 Aragon princes and other nobles. The tour includes a peek at rare historical garments retrieved from the coffins.

The longer tour (adult/reduced €7/5) also takes in the former monastic cell of St Thomas Aquinas, where you can still see the bell he would ring to call his students. English-language guides are available but need to be requested in advance (by email via the website).

Back in the church, the Cappellone del Crocifisso is home to the miraculous 13th-century *Crocifisso tra La Vergine e San Giovanni*, said to have spoken to St Thomas Aquinas. It asked him: *'Bene scripsisti di me, Thoma; quam recipies a me pro tu labore mercedem?'* (You've written good things about me, Thomas; what will you get in return?) – *'Domine, non aliam nisi te'* (Nothing if not you, O Lord), Thomas replied diplomatically. The first bishop of New York, Richard Luke Concanen (1747–1810) is also buried in the church.

MADRE   GALLERY
(Museo d'Arte Contemporanea Donnaregina; Map p58; ☑ 081 1973 7254; www.madrenapoli.it; Via Settembrini 79; adult/reduced €8/4; ⊙ 10am-7.30pm Mon & Wed-Sat, to 8pm Sun; Ⓜ Piazza Cavour) When *Madonna and Child* overload hits, reboot at Naples' museum of modern and contemporary art. In the lobby, French conceptual artist Daniel Buren sets the mood with his playful, mirror-panelled installation *Work in Situ*, with other specially commissioned installations from heavyweights like Anish Kapoor, Rebecca Horn and Sol LeWitt on level one. Level two houses the bulk of MADRE's permanent collection of painting, sculpture, photography and installations from other prolific 20th- and 21st-century artists, designers and architects.

**Complesso
Monumentale di
San Lorenzo Maggiore**   ARCHAEOLOGICAL SITE
(Map p58; ☑ 081 211 08 60; www.laneapolissotterrata.it; Via dei Tribunali 316; church free, museum & excavations guided tour adult/reduced €10/7.50; ⊙ church 8am-7pm, excavations & museum 9.30am-5.30pm; Ⓜ Dante) The **basilica** at this richly layered religious complex is deemed one of Naples' finest medieval buildings. Aside from Ferdinando Sanfelice's facade, the Cappella al Rosario and the Cappellone

di Sant'Antonio, its baroque makeover was stripped away last century to reveal its austere, Gothic elegance. Beneath the basilica is a sprawl of extraordinary Graeco-Roman **ruins**, accessible on a one-hour guided tour.

**Chiesa e Chiostro
di San Gregorio Armeno**   CHURCH, CLOISTER
(Map p58; ☑ 081 420 63 85; Via San Gregorio Armeno 44; ⊙ 9.30am-noon Mon-Fri, to 1pm Sat & Sun; Ⓜ Dante) Overstatement knows no bounds at this richly ornamented 16th-century monastic complex. The church packs a visual punch with its lavish wood and papier-mâché choir stalls, sumptuous altar by Dionisio Lazzari, and Luca Giordano's masterpiece fresco *The Embarkation, Journey and Arrival of the Armenia Nuns with the Relics of St Gregory*. Excess gives way to soothing tranquillity in the picture-perfect cloisters, accessible through the gate on Vico Giuseppe Maffei.

Giordano's famous fresco recounts the 13th-century exile of nuns fleeing persecution in Constantinople. Once in Naples, the holy escapees set up this monastic complex, naming it after the Bishop of Armenia, San Gregorio, whose earthly remains they were carrying with them. More famously, though, they also kept the relics and dried blood of Santa Patrizia (St Patricia), who, having escaped from Constantinople, died in Naples sometime between the 4th and 8th centuries. Patricia's powdered blood is said to liquefy every Tuesday, unlike that of Naples' patron saint, San Gennaro (p84), which can only manage it three times a year.

The cloisters feature a whimsical baroque fountain embellished with masks, dolphins and sea horses, and two exquisite statues portraying Christ and the Samaritan by Matteo Bottigliero. At the southern end is the convent's old bakery, which is still hung with cooking utensils. Close by is the *Cappella della Madonna dell'Idria*. Adorned with paintings by baroque artist Paolo de' Matteis, the chapel is the only remnant of the original medieval convent.

From the cloisters you can enter the beautifully decorated *coro delle monache* (nuns' choir stall), which looks down on the church nave and altar. If you're lucky, you might catch a glimpse of the choir's 612-year-old wooden nativity scene, usually hidden away in a cabinet on the southern wall. Either way, take note of the discreet windows lining the oval cupola above the choir stall. These belong to a secret second choir stall, hidden so that even ill, bed-ridden nuns could attend Mass.

Via San Gregorio Armeno   STREET

(Map p58; **M**Dante) Dismissed by serious collectors, this narrow street nonetheless remains famous across Italy for its *pastori* (nativity-scene figurines). Connecting Spaccanapoli with Via dei Tribunali, the *decumanus maior* (main road) of ancient Neapolis, its clutter of shops and workshops peddle everything from doting donkeys to kitsch celebrity caricatures. At No 8 you'll find the workshop of Ferrigno (Map p58; ☑ 081 552 31 48; www.arteferrigno.com), whose terracotta figurines are the most famous and esteemed on the strip.

Ospedale degli Incurabili   HISTORIC BUILDING

(Map p58; ☑ 081 44 06 47; www.museoartisan itarie.it; Via Maria Longo 50; museum €4, 90min museum & pharmacy tour adult/reduced €10/6; ☺pharmacy tours & museum 9am-5pm Wed, Fri & Sat, to 1pm Sun, Orto Medico & Chiostro Santa Maria delle Grazie 9am-5pm; **M**Piazza Cavour, Museo) It's at this 16th-century hospital and monastic complex that you'll find the Museo delle Arti Sanitarie (Museum of the History of Medicine & Health), a small museum home to rare, historical surgical instruments, as well as a curious tableau of *pastori* (nativity-scene figurines) inflicted with diseases common in the 18th century. The complex also houses the Farmacia Storica degli Incurabili, a breathtaking 18th-century apothecary that can be visited on a guided tour.

Tours of the *farmacia* run on Wednesday, Friday, Saturday and Sunday and can be booked by emailing or calling the museum. If you're already at the museum, you may be able to join the next tour. The tours are usually in Italian, though English-language tours can be organised if requested a few weeks in advance.

Divided into a glorious reception hall and a laboratory, the apothecary's lavish walnut shelves are lined with decorative majolica vases, while Pietro Bardellino's epic ceiling painting portrays an episode from Homer's *Iliad,* in which Machaon is curing the wounded Menelaus. A more unusual feature of the reception hall is a rococo inlay portraying an allegory of caesarean birth.

Some of Naples' finest baroque architects and artists worked on the apothecary: Domenico Antonio Vaccaro styled the facade, Bartolomeo Vecchione designed the interior, and Gennaro di Fiore engraved the shelves,

the latter also collaborating with Carlo Van-vitelli at the Reggia di Caserta (p70). The majolica vases were painted by Lorenzo Salandra and Donato Massa (whose most famous tilework is found in the cloister of the Basilica di Santa Chiara (p56)). Not surprisingly, the pharmacy is widely considered to be one of the city's finest examples of early-18th-century craftmanship.

Both the museum and *farmacia* face the Cortile degli Incurabili (Courtyard of the Incurables), from which stairs lead up to the main hospital building. Enter it and cross the lobby to access the Orto Medico (Medical Garden), a raffish garden dotted with medicinal plants and herbs. At its centre is a small fountain and a beautiful 400-year-old camphor tree. Walk a little further on and you'll stumble upon the smaller Chiostro Santa Maria delle Grazie, its lush tropical foliage framed by a frescoed, vaulted portico.

Chiesa San Giovanni a Carbonara   CHURCH

(Map p80; ☑ 081 29 58 73; Via Carbonara 5; ☺9am-1pm Mon, Tue, Thu & Sat, to 6pm Wed & Fri; ☐147, 182, 184 to Via Foria, **M**Piazza Cavour) Sumptuous sculpture and Technicolor frescoes makes this Gothic church worth a detour. Andrea de Firenze, Tuscan sculptors and northern-Italian artists collaborated on the Gothic-Renaissance mausoleum of King Ladislas, soaring 18m behind the main altar. Behind it, the circular Cappella Caracciolo del Sole uplifts with its vivid 15th-century frescoes and Leonardo da Besozzo's tomb for Giovanni Caracciolo, the ambitious lover of King Ladislas' sister Queen Joan II of Naples.

Caracciolo's increasing political power led the queen to plot his demise and in 1432 he was stabbed to death in the nearby Castel Capuano.

Other important works include the Cappella Caracciolo di Vico (renowned for showcasing early-16th-century Roman style in southern Italy), the *Monumento Miroballo* by Tommaso Malvito and Jacopo dell Pila; and the colourful 14th-century Cappella Somma, complete with mannerist frescoes and an exquisite 16th-century altar executed by Annibale Caccavello and Giovan Domenico d'Auria. The church is also home to Giorgio Vasari's painting *Crocifissione* (Crucifixion), a brooding 16th-century composition whose style echoes that of Vasari's contemporary, Michelangelo.

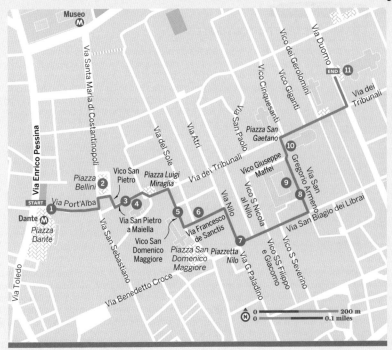

City Walk
Centro Storico: A World Heritage Wander

START PORT'ALBA
END DUOMO
LENGTH 1.8KM; 2.5 HOURS

Start the walk at the old city gate of ① **Port'Alba**, inaugurated in 1625 by the Spanish viceroy of Naples, Antonio Alvárez. The gate leads into Via Port'Alba, flanked by a handful of bookshops and street-art creations. Turn left into Via Santa Maria di Costantinopoli to reach bar-flanked ② **Piazza Bellini** (p65), one of Naples' most popular nocturnal hangouts. The ruins in the middle of the square are from the city's 4th-century-BCE walls. The southern end of Piazza Bellini leads to Via San Pietro a Maiella, where the soft sounds of strings emanate from the Conservatorio di Musica di San Pietro a Majella. Drop into erudite bookshop ③ **Colonnese** (p93) to browse vintage Neapolitan prints, then slip into the ④ **Chiesa di San Pietro a Maiella** (p66) to swoon over Mattia Preti's baroque paintings in the coffered wooden ceiling. The church bookends Via Tribunali, one of

Naples' main Graeco-Roman *decumani* (main streets). Head east along it and turn right into ⑤ **Vico San Domenico Maggiore**, flanked by a number of idiosyncratic boutiques selling local wares. Turn left into Via Francesco de Sanctis to view Giuseppe Sanmartino's *Veiled Christ* sculpture inside the ⑥ **Cappella Sansevero** (p55), then turn right in Via Nilo to reach ⑦ **Piazzetta Nilo** (p66), home to a river-god statue erected by ancient Alexandrian merchants. From here, continue east along Via San Biagio dei Librai – another of the city's original *decumani* – and turn left into ⑧ **Via San Gregorio Armeno** to eye up the street's famous nativity-crib vendors and its show-stopping ⑨ **Chiesa e Chiostro di San Gregorio Armeno** (p61). The latter adjoins a blissful cloister, open in the mornings. Further up the street lies the Gothic simplicity of the ⑩ **Basilica di San Lorenzo Maggiore** (p61), worth a peek before turning right into bustling Via Tribunali. At Via Duomo, turn left to reach Naples' ⑪ **Duomo** (p51), home to spectacular baroque interiors and the oldest baptistry in Western Europe.

LOCAL KNOWLEDGE

BANKSY, STREET ART & NAPLES

The obvious draw on Via dei Tribunali's Piazza dei Girolamini may be its namesake baroque church (p251), but scan the wall of the building to the right and you'll discover an altogether more contemporary attraction: a stencil of the Madonna under a pistol. Typically Neapolitan in its intermingling of the sacred and the profane, the easily missed work is by celebrated street artist Banksy. The British artist's second work in Naples – an interpretation of Bernini's St Teresa with a McDonald's meal and Coca-Cola on her lap – was destroyed by a less talented graffiti writer in 2010.

Banksy's Madonna is one of many engaging, whimsical and downright provocative street-art creations in the city, whose homegrown talent includes the duo cyop & kaf (www.cyopekaf.org), Diego Miedo (www.diegomiedo.org), Felice Pignataro (www.felice pignataro.org) and Jorit Agoch (www.jorit.it). The latter artist is known for his epicly scaled murals. Among these is a soaring depiction of a personal friend as San Gennaro, located beside the **Basilica di San Giorgio Maggiore** (Map p58; ☑ 081 28 79 32; Via Duomo 237; ⊗ 8.30am-noon & 5-7.30pm Mon-Sat, 8.30am-1.30pm Sun; ☑ R2 to Corso Umberto I, Ⓜ Duomo) in the *centro storico*.

If you're itching to explore the local scene, consider booking a two-hour walking tour of the city's curb-side creativity with Napoli Paint Stories (p82).

The 18th-century double-flight staircase leading up to the church itself is the work of baroque great Ferdinando Sanfelice.

The church derives its name from its location, on the former site of an Angevin *carbonarius* (waste-disposal and incineration site).

Museo Civico Filangieri   MUSEUM

(Map p58; ☑ 081 20 31 75; www.salviamoil museofilangieri.org; Via Duomo 288; adult/reduced €7/5; ⊗ 10am-4pm Tue-Sat, to 2pm Sun; ☑ R2 to Corso Umberto I) This kooky museum serves up an eclectic collection of treasures, from historic Asian and European armour and weaponry to sumptuous paintings spanning the 15th to the 19th centuries. Much of the collection belonged to 19th-century prince Gaetano Filangieri, whose private, walnut-panelled *biblioteca* (library) afforded him commanding views of the handsome Sala Agata (Agatha Hall), worth the entry fee itself.

Complesso Museale
di Santa Maria delle
Anime del Purgatorio ad Arco   CHURCH

(Map p58; ☑ 081 21 19 29; www.purgatorio adarco.it; Via dei Tribunali 39; guided tour adult/ reduced €6/5; ⊗ 30min guided tours every 45min 10am-6pm Mon-Sat, to 2pm Sun Apr-early Jan, reduced hours rest of year; Ⓜ Dante) Consecrated in 1638, the engrossing *chiesa delle cape di morte* (the church of the skulls) sits on two levels. While the upper church boasts fine paintings – namely Luca Giordano's

The Death of St Alessio and Massimo Stanzione's *Virgin with the Souls of Purgatory* – the lower church (only accessible by guided tour) is most famous as a hotspot for the cult-like worship of the *anime pezzentelle* (poor souls).

Between the 17th and early 19th centuries, the large, nameless grave at the centre of the lower church received the remains of countless locals who could not afford to be buried in the church. Heaving with anonymous bones, the hypogeum became an epicentre for the cult of the *anime pezzentelle*, in which followers adopted skulls and prayed for souls. It was hoped that once the souls reached heaven, they would offer graces and blessings as gratitude. Up to 60 Masses were held here each day, and on All Souls' Day, queues leading into the underground vault would reach the Duomo, 450m away. Although burials on this site ceased soon after the declaration of the Edict of Saint-Cloud (a Napoleonic order banning burials within the city's borders), the wall shrines remained. The most famous of these belongs to 'Lucia' – a tiara-crowned skull named for a neon sign left at her shrine. According to legend, the skull was that of an 18th-century teenage bride, whose tragic death from tuberculosis saw her become the unofficial protector of young brides. To this day, you will find gifts of jewellery and bridal bouquets at her shrine, left by those who still believe in the cult.

The guided tour also takes in the upper church's sacristy, home to a small but beautiful collection of devotional art and ecclesiastical robes. The church is sometimes used for classical-music concerts – check the website (in Italian) to see what might be in the wings.

Piazza Bellini PIAZZA

(Map p58; Ⓜ Dante) One of the best spots to chill with a *spritz* is this free-spirited, bar-lined square. Featuring excavated ruins from the city's 4th-century Greek city walls, it's the classic go-to for bohemians and best experienced in the evening when it heaves with uni students, left-leaning crowds and a healthy dose of flirtatious glances. Generally speaking, bars at the western end of the square attract the bulk of locals, while those on the eastern side draw the out-of-town crowds.

Museo Diocesano di Napoli MUSEUM

(Map p58; ☑ 081 557 13 65; www.museodiocesano napoli.it; Largo Donnaregina; adult/reduced €6/4; ☺ 9.30am-4.30pm Mon & Wed-Sat, 9.30am-2pm Sun; Ⓜ Piazza Cavour) Once a baroque place of prayer, this is now a repository for religious paintings, triptychs and sculptures, many from defunct churches. Notable works include Luca Giordano's final canvases (either side of the main altar), Paolo de Matteis' *St Sebastian Healed by St Irene*, and a young Francesco Solimena's fresco *The Miracle of the Roses of St Francis*, in the Coro delle Monache (Nuns' Choir). Accessed from the museum, the Gothic **Chiesa di Donnaregina Vecchia** houses Naples' largest cycle of 14th-century frescoes.

Mercato di Porta Nolana MARKET

(Map p58; Porta Nolana; ☺ 8am-2pm; 🚇 R2 to Corso Umberto I, Ⓜ Garibaldi) Naples at its most vociferous and intense, the Mercato di Porta Nolana is a heady, gritty street market where bellowing fishmongers and greengrocers collide with fragrant delis and bakeries, contraband cigarette vendors and Bangladeshi takeaways and grocery stores. Dive in for anything from luscious tomatoes and mozzarella to golden-fried street snacks, cheap luggage and bootleg CDs.

The market's namesake is medieval city gate **Porta Nolana**, which stands at the head of Via Sopramuro. Its two cylindrical towers, optimistically named Faith and Hope, support an arch decorated with a bas-relief of Ferdinand I of Aragon on horseback.

Chiesa di Santa Maria del Carmine CHURCH

(Map p58; ☑ 081 20 11 96; Piazza del Carmine; ☺ 6.30am-12.30pm & 4.30-7.30pm Mon-Sat, 6.30am-12.30pm & 5.30-7.30pm Sun; 🚇 151, 154 to Via Nuova Marina) Its 17th-century *campanile* (bell tower) is Naples' tallest, and this iconic church is home to a famously nimble crucifix. Now hanging in a tabernacle beneath the church's main arch, the cross reputedly dodged a cannonball fired at the church in 1439 during the war between Alfonso of Aragon and Robert of Anjou. Equally miraculous is the 13th-century Byzantine icon of the *Madonna della Bruna,* held behind the main altar, and celebrated with fireworks each 16 July.

Indeed, the much-loved Chiesa di Santa Maria del Carmine is shrouded in legend. According to Neapolitan folklore, when Conrad (Corradino) of Swabia was charged with attempting to depose Charles I of Anjou in 1268, his mother, Elisabetta di Baviera, desperately tried to collect the money required to free her son. Alas, the money arrived too late, Conrad lost his head and his grief-stricken mamma handed the cash to the church (on the condition that the Carmelite brothers prayed for him every day). They agreed, the church went up and a monument to Conrad still remains in the transept.

Just northwest of the church and Piazza del Carmine, the **Piazza del Mercato** has an even more macabre past. The starting point for the deadly plague of 1656, it was here that over 200 supporters of the ill-fated Parthenopean Republic of 1799 were systematically executed.

Museo del Tesoro di San Gennaro MUSEUM

(Map p58; ☑ 081 29 49 80; www.museosangenn aro.it; Via Duomo 149; €6; ☺ 9am-5pm; 🚇 147, 182, 184 to Via Foria) If you're intrigued by Naples' cultish love affair with San Gennaro, eye up his glittering treasury at the Museo del Tesoro di San Gennaro, adjacent to the Duomo. Gifts made to Naples' patron saint include ambitious bronze busts, silver ampullae and even a gilded 18th-century sedan chair used to transport his bust on rainy procession days. The star attraction, however, is Matteo Treglia's extraordinary 18th-century mitre, adorned with 3694 gems: 3328 diamonds, 198 emeralds and 168 rubies.

Upstairs, the **Sacrestia dell'Immacolata** (Sacristy of the Immaculate Conception) shines with 17th-century frescoes by Luca Giordano and Giacomo Farelli. The frescoes in the adjoining **Antesacrestia** are the work of Francesco Maria Russo, their solid hues reminiscent of his more famous work inside Naples' Cappella Sansevero (p55). Luca Giordano makes another appearance in the adjoining **Sacrestia Nuova** (New Sacristy), his signed ceiling fresco one of the few works the artist began *and* completed alone.

Chiesa di San Pietro a Maiella CHURCH

(Map p58; ☑ 081 45 90 08; Piazza Luigi Miraglia 25; ⊗ 8.30am-1pm Mon-Sat, 10-11.30am Sun; Ⓜ Dante) Dedicated to hermit Pietro del Morrone, who was promoted to Pope Celestine V in 1294, this Gothic veteran is most famous for its series of baroque ceiling paintings, executed by Mattia Preti between 1657 and 1673 and depicting episodes from the lives of Celestine V and St Catherine of Alexandria. To the left of the altar, the **Cappella Pipino** holds 14th-century frescoes of Mary Magdalene, attributed to an anonymous artist known simply as the Maestro di Giovanni Barrile.

Basilica di San Paolo Maggiore CHURCH

(Map p58; ☑ 081 45 40 48; Piazza San Gaetano 76; ⊗ 9am-4.30pm Mon-Sat; ☐ R2 to Corso Umberto I, Ⓜ Duomo) Despite dating from the 8th century, this glorious basilica was almost entirely rebuilt at the end of the 16th century. Its huge, gold-stuccoed interior features paintings by Massimo Stanzione and Paolo de Matteis and a striking geometric floor by Nicola Tammaro. Top billing, however, goes to the sumptuous **sacristy**, lavished with luminous frescoes by baroque-meister Francesco Solimena.

Built in 1603, the double staircase adorning the basilica's main facade is the work of Francesco Grimaldi. Much older are the two columns flanking the entrance, taken from the Roman temple to Castor and Pollux that stood on the site.

Napoli Sotterranea ARCHAEOLOGICAL SITE

(Underground Naples; Map p58; ☑ 081 29 69 44; www.napolisotterranea.org; Piazza San Gaetano 68; adult/reduced €10/8; ⊗ English tours 10am, noon, 2pm, 4pm & 6pm; Ⓜ Dante) This evocative guided tour leads you 40m below street level to explore Naples' ancient labyrinth of aqueducts, passages and cisterns.

The passages were originally hewn by the Greeks to extract tufa stone used in construction and to channel water from Mt Vesuvius. Extended by the Romans, the network of conduits and cisterns was more recently used as an air-raid shelter in WWII. Part of the tour takes place by candlelight via extremely narrow passages – not suitable for expanded girths!

Chiesa di Sant'Angelo a Nilo CHURCH

(Map p58; ☑ 081 420 12 22; Vico Donnaromita 15; ⊗ 8.30am-1pm & 4.30-6.30pm Mon-Sat, 8.30am-1pm Sun; Ⓜ Dante) This modest 14th-century church houses one of the first great artworks to grace the Neapolitan Renaissance – the majestic tomb of Cardinal Rinaldo Brancaccio, the church's founder. Although considered a part of Naples' artistic heritage, the sarcophagus was actually sculpted in Pisa by Donatello, Michelozzo and Pagno di Lapo Portigiani. Taking a year to complete, the chiselled marvel was shipped to Naples in 1427.

Piazzetta Nilo PIAZZA

(Map p58; Via Nilo; Ⓜ Dante) You'll stumble across two deities in this dusty little square. First is ancient-Egyptian river god Nilo: the marble **Statua del Nilo** was erected by Alexandrian merchants who lived in the area during Roman times. The sculpture mysteriously disappeared when the Egyptian expats moved out, turning up headless in the 15th century. Its restored bearded bonce was added in the 18th century.

Opposite the statue, **Bar Nilo** is home to a tongue-in-cheek **shrine** (Map p58; Via San Biagio dei Librai 129; ⊗ 7.30am-8pm Mon-Sat, to 4.30pm Sun; Ⓜ Dante) to Argentine footballer and ex-Napoli deity Diego Maradona.

◉ Toledo & Quartieri Spagnoli

Museo Archeologico Nazionale MUSEUM

See p52.

★ Palazzo Reale PALACE

(Royal Palace; Map p74; ☑ 081 40 05 47; www.coopculture.it; Piazza del Plebiscito 1; adult/reduced €6/3; ⊗ 9am-8pm Thu-Tue; ☐ R2 to Via San Carlo, Ⓜ Municipio) Envisaged as a 16th-century monument to Spanish glory (Naples was under Spanish rule at the time), the magnificent Palazzo Reale is home to the **Museo del Palazzo Reale**, a rich and eclectic collection of baroque and neoclassical furnishings, porcelain, tapestries, sculpture and paintings, spread across the palace's royal apartments.

Among the many highlights is the **Teatrino di Corte**, a lavish private theatre created

ART IN TRANSIT

Underground art means just that in Naples, with many of the city's metro stations designed or decorated by top-tier artists, both homegrown and foreign. You'll find Mario Merz' blue neon digits at Vanvitelli; a witty Fiat installation by Perino & Vele at Salvator Rosa; and Technicolor wall drawings by Sol LeWitt at Materdei. And that's before we mention the snapshots by heavyweight Italian photographers at Museo or Jannis Kounellis' eerie shoe installation at Dante.

Most of the city's 'Art Stations' are on the recently extended Line 1. Among the most striking is Università, brainchild of Egyptian-born industrial designer Karim Rashid. True to Rashid's style, the station is a playful, candy-coloured ode to the digital age. White tiles clad the station entrance, each one printed with a word orginating in the last century. In the station itself you'll find lenticular icons that change perspective and colour, a sculpture reflecting the nodes and synapses of the brain, platform steps decorated with abstracted portraits of Dante and Beatrice, and even platform walls adorned with glowing, 'animated' artwork (stare persistently).

Even more breathtaking is Toledo station. Topping a CNN list of Europe's most impressive metro stations in 2014, its lobby features ruins from an Aragonese fortress and a spectacular wall mosaic by conceptual artist William Kentridge. Depicted in the latter is a medley of Neapolitan icons, from San Gennaro and a *pizzaiolo* (pizza maker) to the Museo Archeologico Nazionale's famous *Atlante farnese* sculpture. Another Kentridge mural hovers above the escalators (it's said that the cat represents the artist himself). Toledo station reaches a depth of 50m below sea level, a fact not lost on the station's colour scheme, which goes from ochre (representing Naples' iconic tufa stone) to a dazzling blue as you descend the escalators. It's here, 'below the sea', that you'll find a spectacular mosaic porthole, streaming down light from the sky above. The porthole's light installation is by artist Robert Wilson, whose concourse 'Light Panels' ripple as you hurry past them.

Designed by architects Alvaro Siza and Eduardo Souto De Mura, Municipio station will eventually include its own museum space, home to some of the 3000 artefacts unearthed during the station's construction. Among the astounding finds are remnants of the city's ancient Greek and Roman ports, as well as Roman vessels. The base of a 14th-century Angevin tower – the Torre dell'Incoronata – is showcased in the station's concourse, beside a specially commissioned installation by Israeli artist Michal Rovner. The ancient and the cutting edge also collide at the still-incomplete Duomo station, where a street-level glass-and-steel bubble designed by Italian starchitect Massimiliano Fuksas sheds light on a Roman temple used for the Isolympic Augustan Roman Italic Games, a local version of Greece's ancient Olympics.

For more information on Naples' art stations, download the free PDF information sheets on the ANM website (www.anm.it); click on the Metro Art link. Either way, grab a metro ticket, head underground and get inspired.

by Ferdinando Fuga in 1768 to celebrate the marriage of Ferdinand IV and Marie Caroline of Austria. Incredibly, Angelo Viva's statues of Apollo and the Muses set along the walls are made of papier mâché.

Sala (Room) VIII is home to a pair of vivid, allegorical 18th-century French tapestries representing earth and water respectively. Further along, Sala XII will leave you sniggering at the 16th-century canvas *Gli esattori delle imposte* (The Tax Collectors). Painted by Dutch artist Marinus Claeszoon Van Reymerswaele, it confirms that attitudes to tax collectors have changed little in

500 years. Sala XIII used to be Joachim Murat's study in the 19th century, but was used as a snack bar by Allied troops in WWII. Meanwhile, what looks like a waterwheel in Sala XXIII is actually a nifty rotating reading desk made for Queen Maria Carolina of Austria by Giovanni Uldrich in the 18th century.

The Cappella Reale (Royal Chapel) houses an 18th-century *presepe napoletano* (Neapolitan nativity scene). Fastidiously detailed, its cast of *pastori* (nativity-scene figurines) were crafted by a series of celebrated Neapolitan artists, including Giuseppe Sanmartino,

Toledo & Quartieri Spagnoli

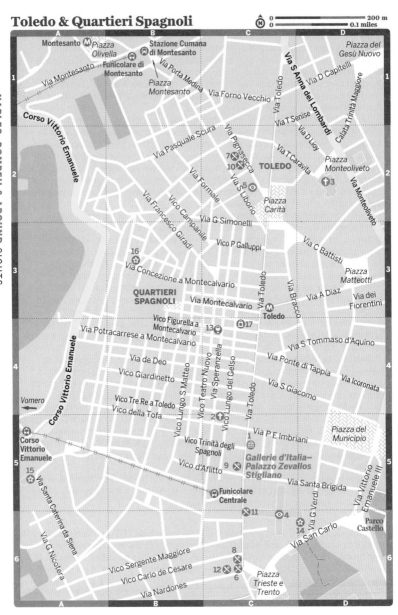

creator of the *Cristo velato* (Veiled Christ) sculpture in the Cappella Sansevero.

The palace is also home to the **Biblioteca Nazionale di Napoli** (National Library; Map p74; 081 781 91 11; www.bnnonline.it; 8.30am-7pm Mon-Fri, to 1.30pm Sat, papyri exhibition by appointment only, Sezione Lucchesi Palli 8.30am-6.45pm Mon-Thu, to 3.30pm Fri) **FREE**, its own priceless treasures including at least 2000 papyri discovered at Herculaneum. You will need to email the library a month ahead to organise a viewing of its ancient papyri, retrieved from Herculaneum. Thankfully, you won't need to book

Toledo & Quartieri Spagnoli

ahead to view the library's exquisite **Biblioteca Lucchesi Palli** (Lucchesi Palli Library; closed Sat). Crafted by some of Naples' most celebrated 19th-century artisans, it's home to numerous fascinating artistic artefacts, including letters by composer Giuseppe Verdi. Bring photo ID to enter the Biblioteca Nazionale.

Theatre and opera fans can buy the combination ticket (€11) for entry to both the Palazzo Reale and adjoining **MeMus theatre museum** (Museum & Historical Archive of the Teatro San Carlo; Map p74; http://memus. squarespace.com; adult/reduced €6/5; ⊗9am-7pm Mon, Tue & Thu-Sat, to 3pm Sun).

Piazza del Plebiscito   PIAZZA
(Map p74; Via San Carlo; ☐R2 to Via San Carlo, ⓂMunicipio) For Continental grandeur, it's hard to beat Piazza del Plebiscito. Whichever way you look, the view is show-stopping. To the northwest, vine-covered slopes lead up to Castel Sant'Elmo (p77) and the Certosa di San Martino (p76); to the east, the pink-hued Palazzo Reale (p66) shows off its oldest facade. And to the west stands Pietro Banchini's neoclassical facsimile of Rome's Pantheon, the **Basilica di San Francesco di Paola** (Map p74; ☑081 1948 4893; ⊗8.30am-noon & 4-7pm).

A later addition to the columned colonnade of Joachim Murat's original 1809 piazza design, the church was commissioned by Ferdinand I in 1817 to celebrate the restoration of his kingdom after the Napoleonic interlude. Standing guard outside are Antonio Canova's statue of a galloping King Charles VII of the Bourbons and Antonio Calì's rendering of Charles' son Ferdinand I.

At its northern end, Piazza Plebiscito spills onto Piazza Trieste e Trento, the city's buzzing heart and home to its most glamorous cafe, Caffè Gambrinus (p90).

★**Teatro San Carlo**   THEATRE
(Map p74; ☑081 797 24 12; www.teatrosancarlo. it; Via San Carlo 98; guided tour adult/reduced €9/7; ⊗guided tours in English 11.30am & 3.30pm, in Italian 10.30am, 12.30pm, 2.30pm & 4.30pm; ☐R2 to Via San Carlo, ⓂMunicipio) An evening at Italy's largest opera house is magical. Although the original 1737 theatre burnt down in 1816, Antonio Niccolini's 19th-century reconstruction is pure Old World opulence. If you can't make it to a performance, consider taking one of the 45-minute guided tours of the venue. Tours usually take in the foyers, elegant main hall and royal box (the best seat in the house) and tour tickets can be purchased at the theatre up to 15 minutes before each tour begins.

Next door, the Palazzo Reale is home to the theatre's museum, MeMus.

★**Gallerie d'Italia –
Palazzo Zevallos Stigliano**   GALLERY
(Map p68; ☑081 42 50 11; www.palazzozevallos. com; Via Toledo 185; adult/reduced €5/3; ⊗10am-7pm Tue-Fri, to 8pm Sat & Sun; ⓂMunicipio) Built for a Spanish merchant in the 17th century and reconfigured in belle-époque style by architect Luigi Platania in the early 20th century, Palazzo Zevallos Stigliano houses a compact yet stunning collection of Neapolitan and Italian art spanning the 17th to early 20th centuries. Star attraction is Caravaggio's mesmerising swansong, *The Martyrdom of St Ursula* (1610). Completed weeks

REGGIA DI CASERTA: THE ITALIAN VERSAILLES

The one compelling reason to stop at the otherwise nondescript town of Caserta, 30km north of Naples, is to gasp at the colossal, World Heritage–listed **Reggia di Caserta** (Palazzo Reale; ☑ 0823 44 80 84; www.reggiadicaserta.beniculturali.it; Viale Douhet 22, Caserta; adult/reduced €12/6; ⊙ palace 8.30am-7.30pm Wed-Mon, park to 7pm Wed-Mon Apr-Sep, reduced hr Oct-Mar, Giardino Inglese to 6pm Wed-Mon Apr-Sep, reduced hr Oct-Mar; ℝ Caserta). With film credits including *Mission: Impossible 3* and the interior shots of Queen Amidala's palace in *Star Wars Episode 1: The Phantom Menace* and *Star Wars Episode 2: Attack of the Clones,* this former royal residence is Italy's monumental swan song to the baroque.

The complex began life in 1752 after Charles VII ordered a palace to rival Versailles. Not one to disappoint, Neapolitan architect Luigi Vanvitelli delivered a palace bigger than its French rival. With its 1200 rooms, 1790 windows, 34 staircases and 250m-long facade, it was reputedly the largest building in 18th-century Europe.

Vanvitelli's immense staircase leads up to the **Royal Apartments**, lavishly decorated with frescoes, art, tapestries, period furniture and crystal.

The back rooms off the **Sala di Astrea** (Room of Astraea) house an extraordinary collection of historic wooden models of the Reggia, along with architectural drawings and early sketches of the building by Luigi Vanvitelli and his son, Carlo. The apartments are also home to the Mostra Terrea Motus, an underrated collection of international modern art commissioned after the region's devastating earthquake in 1980.

To clear your head afterwards, explore the elegant landscaped park, which stretches for some 3km to a waterfall and a fountain of Diana. Within the park is the famous **Giardino Inglese** (English Garden), a romantic oasis of intricate pathways, exotic flora, pools and cascades. Bicycle hire (from €4) is available at the back of the palace building, as are pony-and-trap rides (€50 for 40 minutes, up to five people).

If you're feeling peckish, consider skipping the touristy palace cafeteria for local cafe **Martucci** (☑ 0823 32 08 03; www.facebook.com/martucci.caffe; Via Roma 9, Caserta; pastries from €1.50, sandwiches from €3.50, salads €7.50; ⊙ 5am-10.30pm; 🖥), 250m east of the complex.

Regular trains connect Naples to Caserta (€3.40, 30 to 50 minutes); always plan ahead and check times online before hitting the station. Caserta train station is located opposite the palace grounds. If you're driving from Naples, exit the A1 (E45) at Caserta Sud and follow signs for Caserta and the Reggia.

before the artist's lonely death, the painting depicts a vengeful king of the Huns piercing the heart of his unwilling virgin-bride-to-be, Ursula.

Positioned behind the dying martyr is a haunted Caravaggio, an eerie premonition of his own impending fate. The tumultuous history of both the artist and the painting is documented in the free and highly informative tablet audio guide.

Caravaggio's masterpiece is one of around 120 works on display in the *palazzo*'s sumptuous rooms. Among the numerous standouts are Luca Giordano's robust *The Rape of Helen,* a graphic *Judith Beheads Holofernes* attributed to Louis Finson, Francesco Solimena's *Hagar and Ishmael in the Desert Confronted by the Angel* and a series of bronze and terracotta sculptures by Vincenzo Gemito.

A fine collection of landscape paintings includes Gaspar van Wittel's *View of Naples with the District of Chiaia from Pizzofalcone* and his *View of Naples with Largo di Palazzo,* both of which offer a fascinating depiction of the city in the early 18th century. The latter painting – which depicts what is now Piazza del Plebiscito – includes the triple-arched Fontana dell'Immacolatella. Designed by Michelangelo Naccherini and Pietro Bernini in 1601, the fountain is now located at the corner of Via Partenope and Via Nazario Sauro, beside Borgo Marinaro. Gaspar van Wittel was the father of celebrated Neapolitan architect Luigi Vanvitelli.

Galleria Umberto I   ARCHITECTURE
(Map p68; Via San Carlo; ℝ R2 to Via San Carlo, Ⓜ Municipio) Recalling Milan's Galleria Vittorio Emanuele, Naples' most famous

19th-century arcade is a breathtaking pairing of richly adorned neo-Renaissance fronts and a delicate glass ceiling capped by a lofty 56m dome. Complete with a sumptuous marble floor, the *galleria* is at its most spectacular at night, when it becomes a surreal setting for impromptu soccer games.

La Pignasecca   MARKET

(Map p68; Via Pignasecca; ⊗8am-1pm; Ⓜ Toledo) Naples' oldest street market is a multisensory escapade into a world of wriggling seafood, fragrant delis and clued-up *casalinghe* (homemakers) on the hunt for perfect produce. Fresh produce aside, the market's street-side stalls flog everything from discounted perfume and linen to Neapolitan hip-hop CDs and oh-so-snug *nonna* slippers.

Chiesa di Sant'Anna
dei Lombardi   CHURCH

(Map p68; ☑081 551 33 33; Piazza Monteoliveto; adult/reduced €5/3; ⊗9.30am-6.30pm Mon-Sat; Ⓜ Toledo) This magnificent church is testament to the close links that once existed between the Neapolitan Aragonese and the Florentine Medici dynasty. One particular highlight is Guido Mazzoni's spectacular *Pietà*. Dating from 1492, the terracotta ensemble is made up of eight life-size terracotta figures surrounding the lifeless body of Christ. Originally the figures were painted, but even without colour they still make quite an impression. Also impressive is baroque painter Francesco Solimena's arresting depiction of St Christopher.

The **sacristy** is a work of art in itself. The walls are graced with gloriously inlaid wood panels by Giovanni da Verona, while the ceiling bursts with 16th-century frescoes by Giorgio Vasari depicting the *Allegories and Symbols of Faith*.

Across Via Monteoliveto from the church is the 16th-century **Palazzo Orsini in Gravina** (Map p58; Via Monteoliveto 3), the seat of Naples University's architecture faculty.

Castel Nuovo   CASTLE

(Map p58; ☑081 795 77 22; Piazza Municipio; adult/reduced €6/3; ⊗8.30am-6pm Mon-Sat, 10am-1pm Sun; Ⓜ Municipio) Locals know this 13th-century castle as the Maschio Angioino (Angevin Keep), and its Cappella Palatina is home to fragments of frescoes by Giotto; they're on the splays of the Gothic windows. You'll also find Roman ruins under the glass-floored Sala dell'Armeria (Armoury

Hall). The castle's upper floors (closed on Sunday) house a collection of mostly 17th- to early-20th-century Neapolitan paintings. The top floor houses the more interesting works, including landscape paintings by Luigi Crisconio and a watercolour by architect Carlo Vanvitelli.

The history of the castle stretches back to Charles I of Anjou, who upon taking over Naples and the Swabians' Sicilian kingdom found himself in control not only of his new southern Italian acquisitions but also of possessions in Tuscany, northern Italy and Provence (France). It made sense to base the new dynasty in Naples, rather than Palermo in Sicily, and Charles launched an ambitious construction program to expand the port and city walls. His plans included converting a Franciscan convent into the castle that still stands in Piazza Municipio.

Christened the Castrum Novum (New Castle) to distinguish it from the older Castel dell'Ovo (p73) and **Castel Capuano**, it was completed in 1282, becoming a popular hang-out for the leading intellectuals and artists of the day – Giotto repaid his royal hosts by painting much of the interior. Of the original structure, however, only the Cappella Palatina remains; the rest is the result of Aragonese renovations two centuries later, as well as a meticulous restoration effort prior to WWII.

The two-storey Renaissance triumphal arch at the entrance – the **Torre della Guardia** – commemorates the victorious entry of Alfonso I of Aragon into Naples in 1443, while the stark stone **Sala dei Baroni** (Hall of the Barons) is named after the barons slaughtered here in 1486 for plotting against King Ferdinand I of Aragon. Its striking ribbed vault fuses ancient Roman and Spanish late-Gothic influences.

Casa e Chiesa di
Santa Maria Francesca
delle Cinque Piaghe   CHURCH, HISTORIC SITE

(Map p68; ☑081 42 50 11; Vico Tre Re a Toledo 13; ⊗church 7am-12.15pm, apartment 9.30am-12.15pm, plus 4.30-7.30pm on the 6th of every month; Ⓜ Toledo) The very essence of Naples' cultish brand of Catholicism, this holy sanctuary was once the stamping ground of stigmatic and mystic Santa Maria Francesca delle Cinque Piaghe, the city's only canonised woman. It is also home to her miraculous wooden chair: infertile believers come to be blessed while sitting on it in the hope of falling pregnant.

You'll find the holy furniture piece in the saint's meticulously preserved 18th-century **apartment**. Here, walls heave with modern baby trinkets and vivid 18th- and 19th-century paintings depicting fantastical holy healings – *ex voti* offered by those whose prayers have been answered. Other household objects include the stigmatic's blood-stained clothes, her bed and pillow, her self-flagellation cords and a rare, hand-painted *spinetta* (spinet or harpsichord) from 1682.

The apartment sits above a tiny **chapel** famed for its beautiful 18th-century Neapolitan liturgical art, including glass-eyed holy statues. Particularly rare is the statue of the *Divina pastora* (Divine Shepherdess) on the left side of the nave. The only sculpture of its kind in Naples, it features an unusual depiction of the Virgin Mary reclined and wearing a shepherdess' hat that has its roots in 18th-century Spain. To the left of the nave, a statue of Santa Maria Francesca contains the holy local's bones.

Museo Nitsch   MUSEUM
(Map p58; ☑ 081 564 16 55; www.museonitsch.org; Vico Lungo Pontecorvo 29d; adult/reduced €10/5; ☉ 10am-7pm Mon-Fri, to 2pm Sat; Ⓜ Dante) In 1974, experimental Austrian artist Hermann Nitsch was invited to perform one of his 'actions' (a bloody, ritualistic art performance) in Naples, leading to his immediate arrest and deportation from Italy. Not one for the squeamish or easily offended, this savvy museum and cultural centre documents the now revered artist's intriguing, symbolic, confronting works through photographs, video, painting and props.

Piazza Dante   PIAZZA
(Map p58; Ⓜ Dante) On hot summer evenings, Piazza Dante turns into a communal living room, packed with entire families who

---

SEEKING FERRANTE

Declared one of the 100 most influential people by *Time* magazine in 2016, Elena Ferrante has firmly established herself as the queen of Italy's contemporary literary scene. Writing under a pseudonym, Ferrante's quartet of Neapolitan Novels have sold almost 6 million copies worldwide, and spawned both theatrical and TV adaptations.

The quartet – *My Brilliant Friend, The Story of a New Name, Those Who Stay and Those Who Leave* and *The Story of the Lost Child* – explore the intense bond between childhood friends Elena Greco (Lenù) and Raffaella Cerullo (Lila), born into a mid-century Naples of grit, poverty and tumultuous social change. The third protagonist is Naples itself, with Ferrante's evocative depictions of the city drawing literary pilgrims seeking the streets, squares and *palazzi* inhabited by her protagonists.

The impoverished neighbourhood in which Elena and Lila grow up was inspired by Rione Luzzatti, a pocket of drab 20th-century apartment blocks directly south of the Mercato Caramanico a Poggioreale (p93). Skirting the southern edge of the district is Via Taddeo da Sessa, the street referred to as the *stradone* in the novels. The road leads towards Piazza Garibaldi, from where Corso Umberto I heads southwest with its cache of kitschy bridal boutiques. It's here that young bride-to-be Lila seeks her own wedding gown. To the north is the *centro storico*, where Elena gets political with the radical-left Brigate Rosse (Red Brigades) on Via Tribunali and wanders with her father on bookish Port'Alba.

Elena sips at gilded Caffè Gambrinus (p90) with her daughters and old school friend, Gigliola, and delves into the city's history at the equally sumptuous Biblioteca Nazionale di Napoli (p68). Just north of both is Via Toledo, where siblings Marcello and Michele Solara cruise in their Fiat 1100. From Caffè Gambrinus, Via Chiaia leads to Chiaia, a neighbourhood that enchants Elena and Lila with its elegance and chic *signore*. It's here that Lila window shops on Via dei Mille, that Elena presents her book at La Fetrinelli and that the Solara brothers have their shoe shop in fashionable **Piazza dei Martiri** (Map p74; ☒ E6 to Piazza dei Martiri). The latter's centrepiece is Enrico Alvino's 19th-century monument to Neapolitan martyrs, with four lions representing the anti-Bourbon uprisings of 1799, 1820, 1848 and 1860.

For further insight, **Looking for Lila** (☑ 389 8463510; www.lookingforlila.com; 5hr tour for 2 people €250) runs private, bespoke tours of the city inspired by the novels.

stroll, eat, smoke, play cards, chase balloons and whinge about the in-laws.

Dominating the eastern flank of the square is the enormous facade of the **Convitto Nazionale**, the pièce de résistance of Luigi Vanvitelli's spectacular 18th-century square. Dedicated to the Bourbon king Charles VII, its protagonist is now a sand-blasted marble Dante looking out over Via Toledo.

Below it all, the **Dante metro station** doubles as a contemporary-art space, with installations from some art-world heavyweights. As you head down on the escalator, look up and catch Joseph Kosuth's *Queste cose visibili* (These Visible Things) above you. Eye-squintingly huge and neon, it's an epic quotation from Dante's *Il convivio*. Along the wall at the bottom of the escalator you'll find artist Jannis Kounellis' renegade train tracks running over abandoned shoes. Right behind you, above the second set of escalators, sits *Intermediterraneo,* Michelangelo Pistoletto's giant mirror map of the Mediterranean Sea.

☉ Santa Lucia & Chiaia

★ **Galleria Borbonica** HISTORIC SITE
(Map p74; ☑ 081 764 58 08, 366 2484151; www.galleriaborbonica.com; Vico del Grottone 4; 1hr standard tour adult/reduced €10/5; ☺ standard tour 10am, noon, 3pm & 5pm Fri-Sun; ☒ R2 to Via San Carlo, ☒ Chiaia-Monte di Dio) Traverse five centuries along Naples' Bourbon Tunnel. Conceived by Ferdinand II in 1853 to link the Palazzo Reale (p66) to the barracks and the sea, the never-completed escape route is part of the 17th-century Carmignano Aqueduct system, itself incorporating 16th-century cisterns. The standard tour does not require prebooking, though the Adventure Tour (85 minutes; adult/reduced €15/10) and adults-only Speleo Light Tour (90 minutes; €15) do.

The Via delle Memorie Tour (60 minutes; adult/reduced €10/5) is only available in English for groups; see the website for details. Note that there are two other entrances to the Galleria Borbonica: one at Via Domenico Morelli 61 and the other at Via Monte di Dio 14.

Museo Pignatelli MUSEUM
(Map p74; ☑ 081 761 23 56; www.polomuseale campania.beniculturali.it/index.php/il-museo-pignatelli; Riviera di Chiaia 200; adult/reduced €5/2.50; ☺ 8.30am-5pm Wed-Mon; ☒ 140 to

Riviera di Chiaia) When Ferdinand Acton, a minister at the court of King Ferdinand IV (1759–1825), asked Pietro Valente to design Villa Pignatelli in 1826, Valente whipped up this striking Pompeiian facsimile. Now the Museo Pignatelli, its aristocratic hoard includes sumptuous furniture and decorative arts, as well as a beautiful collection of 19th- and 20th-century carriages in the adjoining **Museo delle Carrozze**.

Bought and extended by the Rothschilds in 1841, Villa Pignatelli became home to the Duke of Monteleone, Diego Aragona Pignatelli Cortés, in 1867, before his granddaughter Rosina Pignatelli donated it (and its treasures) to the state. Permanent-collection highlights include a small yet fine array of local and foreign porcelain in the Salotto Verde (Green Room), and a leather-lined smoking room (known as the Biblioteca). The 1st floor – whose bathroom features a tub made from a single block of Carrara marble – also hosts regular temporary exhibitions, mostly photographic.

Castel dell'Ovo CASTLE
(Map p74; ☑ 081 795 45 92; Borgo Marinaro; ☺ 9am-7.30pm Mon-Sat, to 2pm Sun Apr-Oct, reduced hr Nov-Mar; ☒ E6, 128 to Via Santa Lucia) FREE Built by the Normans in the 12th century, Naples' oldest castle owes its name (Castle of the Egg) to Virgil. The Roman scribe reputedly buried an egg on the site where the castle now stands, warning that when the egg breaks, the castle (and Naples) will fall. Thankfully, both are still standing, and walking up to the castle's ramparts will reward you with a breathtaking panorama.

Santa Lucia, Chiaia & Mergellina

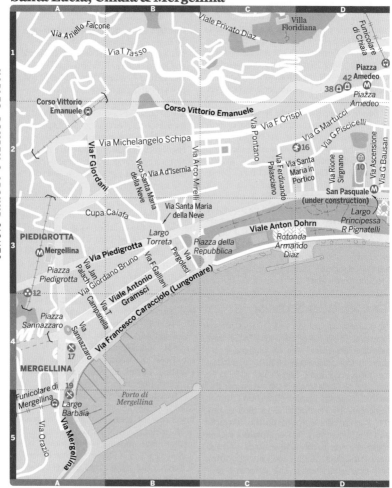

Used by the Swabians, Angevins and Alfonso of Aragon, who modified it to suit his military needs, the castle sits on the rocky, restaurant-lined 'island' of **Borgo Marinaro**. According to legend, the heartbroken siren Partenope washed ashore here after failing to seduce Ulysses with her song. It's also where the Greeks first settled the city in the 7th century BC, calling the island Megaris. Its commanding position wasn't wasted on the Roman general Lucullus either, who had his villa here long before the castle hit the skyline.

Views aside, the castle is also the setting for temporary art exhibitions, special events, and no shortage of posing brides and grooms.

Lungomare STREET, PARK

(Seafront; Map p74; Via Caracciolo & Via Partenope; ☐ C25 to Piazza Vittoria) When you need a break from Naples' hyperactive tendencies, take a deep breath on its pedestrianised seafront strip. Stretching 2.5km along Via Partenope and Via Caracciolo, its views are nothing short of exquisite, taking in the bay, Mt Vesuvius, two castles and Vomero's

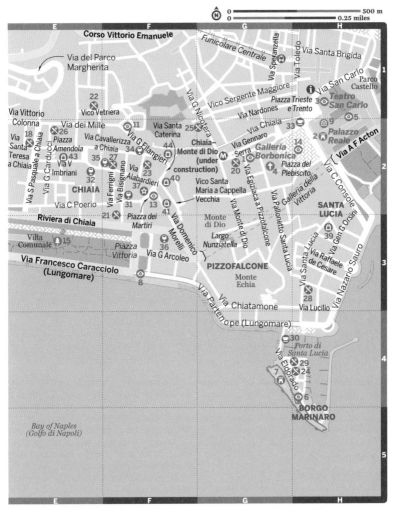

Liberty-style villas. It's particularly romantic at dusk, when Capri and the volcano take on a mellow orange hue.

Palazzo Mannajuolo ARCHITECTURE
(Map p74; Via Filangieri 36; ⏰ 8am-9pm; 🚇 E6 to Piazza dei Martiri, Ⓜ Piazza Amedeo) Commissioned by entrepreneur and engineer Giuseppe Mannajuolo, this distinguished *palazzo* was built between 1910 and 1911. It's one of the city's finest examples of Italian art nouveau architecture, known as *stile Liberty* (Liberty style). The building's western facade is especially impressive, its alternating convex and concave elements crowned by

a faux dome. The star attraction, however, is the building's cinematic indoor staircase, a jaw-dropping elliptical creation adorned with wrought-iron parapets and embossed marble steps.

Villa Comunale PARK
(Map p74; Piazza Vittoria; ⏰ 7am-midnight; 🚇 C25 to Piazza Vittoria, 128, 140 to Riviera di Chiaia) Another Luigi Vanvitelli production, this long, leafy seaside strip was originally built for Bourbon royalty. Called the Passeggio Reale (Royal Walkway), it was off limits to the plebs except on 8 September, the day of the Festa di Piedigrotta. Rumour has it that

Santa Lucia, Chiaia & Mergellina

taking one's wife to the park on that day was a clause in many a marital contract. Husbands across the city must have heaved a sigh of relief when the park finally went public in 1869.

◉ Vomero

★ Certosa e Museo di San Martino
MONASTERY, MUSEUM

(Map p78; ☑ 081 229 45 03; www.polomuseale campania.beniculturali.it/index.php/certosa-e-museo; Largo San Martino 5; adult/reduced €6/3; ⊘ 8.30am-7.30pm Tue & Thu-Sat, to 6.30pm Sun; Ⓜ Vanvitelli, ⓕ Montesanto to Morghen) The high point (quite literally) of the Neapolitan baroque, this charterhouse-turned-museum was built as a Carthusian monastery between 1325 and 1368. Centred on one of the most beautiful cloisters in Italy, it has been decorated, adorned and altered over the centuries by some of Italy's finest talent, most importantly architect Giovanni Antonio Dosio in the 16th century and baroque sculptor Cosimo Fanzago a century later. Nowadays, it's a superb repository of Neapolitan and Italian artistry.

The monastery's **church** and the sacristy, treasury and chapter house that flank it contain a feast of frescoes and paintings by some of Naples' greatest 17th-century artists, among them Battista Caracciolo, Jusepe de Ribera, Guido Reni and Massimo Stanzione. In the nave, Cosimo Fanzago's inlaid marble work is simply extraordinary.

Adjacent to the church, the **Chiostro dei Procuratori** is the smaller of the monastery's two cloisters. A grand corridor on the left leads to the larger **Chiostro Grande** (Great Cloister). Originally designed by Dosio in the late 16th century and added to by Fanzago, it's a sublime composition of Tuscan-Doric porticoes, marble statues and vibrant camellias. The balustrade marks the Certosa's small cemetery, adorned with skulls created by Fanzago.

Just off the Chiostro dei Procuratori, the **Sezione Navale** documents the history of the Bourbon navy from 1734 to 1860, and features a small yet extraordinary collection of royal barges. The **Sezione Presepiale** – which faces the refectory – houses a whimsical collection of rare Neapolitan *presepi* (nativity scenes) from the 18th and 19th centuries, including the colossal 19th-century Cuciniello creation, which covers one wall of what used to be the monastery's kitchen. The **Quarto del Priore** in the southern wing houses the bulk of the monks' historic picture collection, as well as one of the museum's most famous sculptures, the tender *Madonna col Bambino e San Giovannino* (Madonna and Child with the Infant John the Baptist). The piece is the work of Pietro Bernini, father of the more famous Gian Lorenzo Bernini. Also noteworthy is a statue of St Francis of Assisi by 18th-century master sculptor Giuseppe Sanmartino, creator of the *Cristo velato* (Veiled Christ) housed in Naples' Cappella Sansevero.

A pictorial history of Naples is told in **Immagini e Memorie della Città e del Regno** (Images and Memories of the City and Kingdom of Naples). Here you'll find portraits of historic characters; antique maps, including a 35-panel copper map of 18th-century Naples in Room 45; and rooms dedicated to major historical events such as the eruption of Mt Vesuvius and the Revolt of the Masaniello (Room 36) and the plague (Room 37). Room 32 boasts the beautiful *Tavola Strozzi* (Strozzi Table); its fabled depiction of maritime Naples in the second half of the 15th century is one of the city's most celebrated historical records.

It's worth noting that some sections of the museum are only open at various times of the day; see the website for specific times.

Below the Certosa is the imposing **Sotterranei Gotici** (Gothic basement). The austere vaulted space holds around 150 marble sculptures and epigraphs. Note that at the time of writing, tours were suspended indefinitely; contact the museum for updates.

Castel Sant'Elmo   CASTLE
(Map p78; ☑ 081 558 77 08; www.polomuseale campania.beniculturali.it/index.php/il-castello; Via Tito Angelini 22; adult/reduced Wed-Mon €5/2.50, Tue €2.50/1.25; ⊙ castle 8.30am-7.30pm daily, museum 9.30am-5pm Wed-Mon, reduced hours winter; Ⓜ Vanvitelli, Ⓡ Montesanto to Morghen) Star-shaped Castel Sant'Elmo was originally a church dedicated to St Erasmus. Some 400 years later, in 1349, Robert of Anjou turned it into a castle before Spanish viceroy Don Pedro de Toledo had it further fortified in 1538. Used as a military prison until the 1970s, it's now famed for its jaw-dropping panorama, which takes in much of the city, its bay, islands and beyond. It's also known for its **Museo del Novecento**, dedicated to 20th-century Neapolitan art.

NAPLES, POMPEII & AROUND SIGHTS

THE CAPTAIN'S CURSE

Of the many macabre tales about the Cimitero delle Fontanelle (p79), none intrigues quite like that of *il Capitano* (The Captain), the centre skull at the base of the cemetery's three Calvary crosses.

According to legend, a pious young woman from La Sanità adopted the skull, a common practice in Naples until the late 1960s. As incongruous as it seems, the Cimitero delle Fontanelle doubled as a lovers' lane for lovebirds with nowhere else to go. This was not lost on the woman's less-than-pious boyfriend, who tried to convince her to lose her virginity at the site.

Pensive and nervous, the young woman approached the Captain, asking the skull to bless their relationship and grant them a happy marriage. Not one for superstitious beliefs, the boyfriend began mocking her and the Captain, poking the skull's eye socket and daring it to turn up at their wedding. Adding insult to injury, he took his lover's virginity then and there.

Fast forward to the couple's wedding banquet, where a stranger entered wearing an eye patch and an old-fashioned officer's uniform. No less cocky than at the cemetery that fateful day, the young groom cornered the guest as he was leaving, demanding to know who had invited him. The officer turned around, smiled, and replied, 'You did...at the Fontanelle', before opening his coat to reveal a full skeleton that immediately crumbled to the floor.

Not surprisingly, the shock killed both the groom and his bride, whose final resting place suitably remains a mystery. While some say that the couple's remains lie in the Cimitero delle Fontanelle, others believe that a funerary fresco of a couple in the Catacombe di San Gaudioso (p79) indicates their place of eternal regret.

Vomero

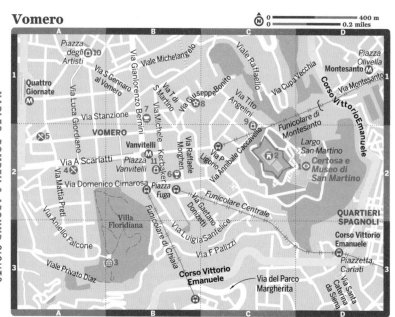

Vomero

Museo Duca di Martina
& Villa Floridiana   MUSEUM, GARDENS
(Map p78; ☏081 578 84 18; www.polomuseale
campania.beniculturali.it/index.php/il-museo; Via
Cimarosa 77; adult/reduced €4/2; ⊙museum

8.30am-5pm Wed-Mon, gardens 8.30am-7pm; Ⓜ Vanvitelli, ⛟ Chiaia to Cimarosa, Centrale to Piazza Fuga) The Museo Duca di Martina houses a beautiful collection of ceramics, with priceless Chinese Ming (1368–1644) ceramics and Japanese Edo (1615–1867) vases on the lower floor, lively Renaissance majolica on the midde floor, and more European ceramics (including some sumptuous Meissen pieces) on the top floor. You'll also find a smattering of paintings from greats such as Francesco Solimena, Francesco De Mura and Vincenzo Camuccini.

The museum's home is the stately Villa Floridiana, a not-so-modest gift from King Ferdinand I to his second wife, the Duchess of Floridia. Its lush, manicured gardens are worth the trip alone, with dreamy bay and city views, and a pretty little fountain sprinkled with tortoises.

◉ La Sanità & Capodimonte

Museo di Capodimonte   MUSEUM
See p54.

★ Catacombe di San Gennaro   CATACOMB
(Map p80; ☏081 744 37 14; www.catacombedi
napoli.it; Via Capodimonte 13; adult/reduced €9/6; ⊙1hr tours hourly 10am-5pm Mon-Sat, to 2pm Sun; ⛟R4, 178 to Via Capodimonte) Naples' oldest

and most sacred catacombs became a Christian pilgrimage site when San Gennaro's body was interred here in the 5th century. The carefully restored site allows visitors to experience an evocative other world of tombs, corridors and broad vestibules, its treasures including 2nd-century Christian frescoes, 5th-century mosaics and the oldest known portrait of San Gennaro, dating from the second half of the 5th century.

The catacombs are home to three types of tomb, each corresponding to a specific social class. The wealthy opted for the open-room *cubiculum*, originally guarded by gates and adorned with colourful wall frescoes. One *cubiculum* to the left of the entrance features an especially beautiful funerary fresco of a mother, father and child: it's made up of three layers of fresco, one commissioned for each death. The smaller, rectangular wall niches, known as *loculum*, were the domain of the middle classes, while the *forme* (floor tombs) were reserved for the poor.

Further ahead you'll stumble upon the *basilica minore* (minor basilica), home to the tombs of San Gennaro and 5th-century archbishop of Naples Giovanni I. Sometime between 413 and 431, Giovanni I accompanied the martyr's remains from Pozzuoli to Naples, burying them here before Lombard prince Sico I of Benevento snatched them in the 9th century. The *basilica minore* also harbours fragments of a fresco depicting Naples' first bishop, Sant'Aspreno. The city's bishops were buried here until the 11th century.

Close to the *basilica minore* is a 3rd-century tomb whose Pompeiian-hued artwork employs both Christian and pagan elements. In the image of three women building a castle, the figures represent the three virtues, while the castle symbolises the Church.

The lower level is even older, dating back to the 2nd century and speckled with typically pagan motifs like fruit and animals. The painting on the side of San Gennaro's tomb – depicting the saint with Mt Vesuvius and Mt Somma in the background – is the first known image of San Gennaro as the protector of Naples. Also on the lower level is the Basilica di Agrippino, named in honour of Sant'Agrippino. The sixth bishop of Naples, Agrippino was also the first Christian to be buried in the catacombs, back in the 3rd century.

Tours of the catacombs are run by the Co-operativa Sociale Onlus 'La Paranza' (p82),

whose ticket office is to the left of the **Chiesa di Madre di Buon Consiglio** (Map p80; ☑ 081 741 00 06; Via Capodimonte 13; ☺ 8am-noon & 5-7pm Mon-Sat, 9am-1pm & 5-7pm Sun; ☐ R4, 178 to Via Capodimonte), a snack-sized replica of St Peter's in Rome completed in 1960. Tickets can also be purchased in advance online.

The cooperative also runs a fascinating Sunday morning walking tour called **Il Miglio Sacro** (The Holy Mile; adult/reduced €15/13), which explores the neighbouring Sanità district. The Holy Mile tour must be prebooked and is offered in Italian unless requested in English, French or Spanish in advance; see the website for details.

The catacombs themselves also host occasional special events, including theatrical and live-music performances; see the website.

★ **Cimitero delle Fontanelle** CEMETERY
(☑ 081 1925 6964; www.cimiterofontanelle.com; Via Fontanelle 80; ☺ 10am-5pm; ☐ C51 to Via Fontanelle, Ⓜ Materdei) 𝐅𝐑𝐄𝐄 Holding about eight million human bones, the ghoulish Fontanelle Cemetery was first used during the 1656 plague, before becoming Naples' main burial site during the 1837 cholera epidemic. At the end of the 19th century it became a hot spot for the *anime pezzentelle* (poor souls) cult, in which locals adopted skulls and prayed for their souls. Lack of information at the site makes joining a tour much more rewarding; reputable outfits include Cooperativa Sociale Onlus 'La Paranza' (p82).

**Basilica Santa Maria
della Sanità & Catacombe
di San Gaudioso** CHURCH, CATACOMB
(Map p80; ☑ 081 744 37 14; www.catacombe dinapoli.it; Piazza Sanità 14; basilica free, catacomb adult/reduced €9/6; ☺ basilica 9am-1pm daily, 1hr catacomb tours 10am, 11am, noon, 1pm daily; ☐ C51 to Piazza Sanità, Ⓜ Piazza Cavour, Museo) While we love the baroque paintings by Andrea Vaccaro and Luca Giordano – not to mention the two contemporary sculptures by Riccardo Dalisi – it's the eerie, one-of-a-kind catacombs beneath this 17th-century basilica that makes the place so utterly unforgettable. Entered through the 5th-century **cripta** (crypt) below the high altar, its damp walls reveal a rather macabre method of medieval burial.

First, bodies would be stored in the arched wall niches, where the *schiattamorti* (literally 'corpse squashers') would poke

La Sanità & Capodimonte

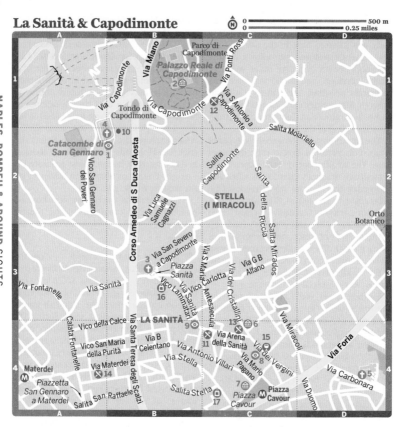

La Sanità & Capodimonte

them to release all blood and bodily fluids. Once dried out, the body would be buried, while the skull would be cemented to the wall and set over a fresco of the dearly de-parted. These frescoes are clearer than ever thanks to recent restoration work. The skull positioned above a frescoed body depicted with paintbrushes and a ruler belonged to

16th-century mannerist painter Giovanni Balducci. The Florentine artist had struck a deal with the Dominicans – in return for decorating their catacomb free of charge, they would allow him to be buried here (considered a privilege at the time).

Another fascinating feature is the so-called *Trionfo della croce* (Triumph of the Cross) mosaic. Created in the 5th or 6th century, its earthy tones and unusually large lambs suggest that the artist hailed from Africa. The African connection continues with the catacomb's namesake, San Gaudioso, a North African bishop who died in Naples in AD 452 and was buried on the site.

In the crypt itself, scan the walls for an intensely colourful 9th-century fresco of the Madonna and Child flanked by figures believed to be St Gregory and St Marciano. The image was discovered in the 1990s beneath a 19th-century fresco.

Catacomb guided-tour tickets can be purchased online or at the basilica.

Palazzo Sanfelice ARCHITECTURE
(Map p80; Via Arena della Sanità 6; 🚌C51, C52 to Via Arena della Sanità, 🇲Piazza Cavour) Ferdinando Sanfelice's debut staircase is this double-ramped diva inside the Palazzo Sanfelice. Upon its completion in 1726 it became the talk of the town, and from then on there was no stopping Sanfelice, who perfected his dramatic design in various *palazzi* across the city, culminating in his masterpiece at the Palazzo dello Spagnuolo.

Palazzo dello Spagnuolo ARCHITECTURE
(Map p80; Via dei Vergini 19; 🚌C51, C52 to Via dei Vergini, 🇲Piazza Cavour) In baroque-rich Naples, even staircases can be an event and the masterpiece gracing the courtyard of this *palazzo* is one of its most showstopping. Designed by Ferdinando Sanfelice and dating from 1738, its double-ramped, five-arched flights were put to good use in film classics such as Luigi Zampa's *Processo alla città* (The City Stands Trial) and Vittorio de Sica's *Giudizio universale* (The Last Judgment).

Laboratorio Oste MUSEUM
(Map p80; 📱349 4433422; www.annibale oste.com/esperienza-oste/; Via dei Cristallini 138; ⊙usually 9am-6pm Mon-Fri; 🚌C51, C52 to Via dei Vergini, 🇲Piazza Cavour, Museo) The late Annibale Oste was one of Naples' most celebrated sculptors and designers; his workshop is now a small gallery-archive showcasing some of his works, including whimsical light

sculptures, vases, and fantastical furniture pieces spanning 2001 to 2010. The venue, charming in itself, is now lovingly run by his artist children, Mariasole and Vincenzo. Vincenzo's striking contemporary jewellery (p95) is also on display (and for sale).

Deemed a visionary by his peers, Annibale Oste breathed a sense of energy and playfulness into materials as diverse as bronze, steel, wood, alabaster and glass. His use of fibreglass in the 1970s was lauded as pioneering, and his creations – which include a storage unit that evokes a deliciously giant chocolate block – are an extraordinary symphony of textures, shapes and colours. Interestingly, the building's courtyard was once used for staging plays, with the workshop's office used as a changing room by local actors. Among them was a young Totò, who would go on to become one of Italy's greatest comic film stars.

If you plan on visiting, it's always a good idea to email (vincenzooste@gmail.com) or call ahead to ensure that someone is there to let you in.

⊙ Mergellina & Posillipo

**Parco Sommerso
di Gaiola** MARINE RESERVE
(Map p104; 📱081 240 32 35; www.areamarina protettagaiola.it; Discesa Gaiola; ⊙10am-4pm Apr-Sep, to 2pm Oct-Mar; 🚌140 to Discesa Coroglio) Steep steps lead down to this marine reserve, rich in biodiversity and submerged Roman ruins. Due to its size, only 100 bathers are allowed through its gates at any one time (bring photo ID). Admittedly, the association managing the fragile reserve tolerates rather than encourages bathers. Instead, visitors should consider one of the educational activities offered, including year-round tours of the marine reserve and the clifftop **Parco Archeologico del Pausilypon**, littered with the ruins of the 1st-century BC Villa di Pollione.

The once-luxurious villa belonged to Publius Vedius Pollio, a wealthy friend of Emperor Augustus and, according to accounts by Pliny the Elder, a cruel, murderous figure who bred *murene* (large eels) in the coastal grottoes below, which are also visited on the guided tours.

Bequeathed to Augustus after Pollio's death in 15 BC, the grounds include a Roman theatre, the venue for weekly sunset concerts and theatre performances in the summer. Known as the **Pausilypon:**

Suggestioni all'Imbrunire (www.suggestioni allimbrunire.org), the season usually runs from mid-June to late July.

The marine reserve offers daily kayaking, snorkelling and diving tours all year round. Guided archaeological tours (adult/reduced €6/3.50) run at from noon Tuesday to Friday, 10am and noon on Saturday, and 10am, 11am and noon on Sunday between April and September (no 11am Sunday tour the rest of the year). Glass-bottom boat tours (adult/reduced €12/10) run at 10.30am, 12.30pm and 3pm on Saturday and Sunday from around April to the end of October. Check the reserve's website for more information.

Parco Virgiliano   PARK

(Map p104; Viale Virgilio; ⊗ 7am-1am late Jun-Sep, to midnight May–mid-Jun, to 9pm rest of year; 🚌 140 to Via Posillipo) Perched high above the shimmering sea on the westernmost tip of posh Posillipo hill, this much-loved, somewhat neglected park is the place to kick back on a terrace and soak up the spectacular coastal views: Capri to the south; Nisida, Procida and Ischia to the southwest; and the Bay of Pozzuoli and Bagnoli to the west. Posillipo market takes place outside the main gates on Thursday between 7am and 2pm.

History buffs may know that the tiny island of Nisida is where Brutus reputedly conspired against his over-achieving nemesis Julius Caesar.

Parco Vergiliano   ARCHAEOLOGICAL SITE

(Map p74; ☎ 081 66 93 90; Salita della Grotta 20; ⊗ 9am-2pm Wed-Mon; Ⓜ Mergellina) Head up the steep steps at this off-the-radar park and you'll find yourself peering into the world's longest Roman tunnel. Designed by the architect Lucius Cocceius Auctus, the 700m-long engineering feat once linked Naples to Pozzuoli. At the top of the steps lies the tomb of Virgil, who died in Brindisi in 19 BC. Legend has it that the Roman poet's remains were carted to Naples and buried in this Augustan-era vault.

🏃 Activities

★ Kayak Napoli   KAYAKING

(☎ 338 2109978, 331 9874271; www.kayaknapoli. com; Bagno Sirena, Via Posillipo 357; tours €25-30; 🚌 140 to Via Posillipo) 🛶 Popular kayak tours head along the Neapolitan coastline, gliding past often-inaccessible ruins, neoclassical villas and luscious gardens, and into secret sea grottoes. Tours cater to rookie and experienced paddlers, with day and night options. While the 'Naples and its Villas' Tour departs from Via Posillipo 357, the 'Wild Posillipo' and 'Sunset' Tours leave from Via Posillipo 68, also in the Posillipo neighbourhood.

Tours are subject to weather conditions and should be booked ahead. The outfit also offers stand-up paddleboarding rental (from €15) and tours (three-hour tour €30).

Culinary Backstreets   FOOD

(https://culinarybackstreets.com/culinary-walks/ naples; 5½hr tour adult/7-12yr US$135/67.50) This reputable international outfit runs food-themed walking tours of Naples' World Heritage–listed *centro storico*. Tours explore everything from market stalls and regionally grown produce to classic street-food vendors and speciality food shops. Book tours directly on the website.

Toffini Academy   COOKING

(Map p74; ☎ 081 66 53 36; www.toffini.it/Corsi; Via Martucci 35; 3hr cooking course from €60; 🚌 627 to Via Crispi, Ⓜ Piazza Amedeo) Toffini Academy runs relaxed, enjoyable Neapolitan cooking courses suitable for both novices and domestic kitchen gods and goddesses. English-language options include home-made pizza making, pasta and seafood, as well as local Sunday-lunch favourite, *ragù napoletano*. Italian speakers can also choose from other options, among them risotto and gelato making. The kitchen is sleek, contemporary and smartly designed to feel communal.

👉 Tours

★ Cooperativa Sociale
Onlus 'La Paranza'   TOURS

(Map p80; ☎ 081 744 37 14; www.catacombedi napoli.it; Via Capodimonte 13; ⊗ information point 10am-5pm Mon-Sat, to 2pm Sun; 🚌 R4, 178 to Via Capodimonte) Runs tours of the Catacombe di San Gennaro (p78) as well as a fascinating Sunday-morning walking tour called Il Miglio Sacro (The Holy Mile; adult/reduced €15/13), which explores the earthy Sanità district. The Holy Mile tour is in Italian only and must be pre-booked; see the website for details. The ticket office is to the left of the Chiesa di Madre di Buon Consiglio (p79).

Napoli Paint Stories   WALKING

(☎ 333 6290673; www.napolipaintstories.it; tour adult/reduced €15/12; ⊗ varies, usually Sat & Sun)

WORTH A TRIP

CUMA

Dating back to the 8th century BC, the **Parco Archeologico di Cuma** (Scavi Archeologici di Cuma; Map p104; ☑ 081 854 30 60; Via Montecuma; adult/reduced €4/2; ☉ 9am-1hr before sunset; ◪ Cumana to Fusaro, then EAV bus to Cuma) is the site of the first Greek settlement on the Italian mainland. Its ruins are shrouded in ancient mythology: in Virgil's *The Aeneid*, the **Antro della Sibilla Cumana** (Cave of the Cumaean Sibyl) is where the oracle reputedly passed on messages from Apollo. The ancient Roman poet, probably inspired by a visit to the cave himself, writes of Aeneas coming here to seek the sibyl, who directs him to Hades (the underworld), entered from nearby Lago d'Averno. More prosaic are recent studies that maintain that the 130m-long trapezoidal tunnel was actually built as part of Cuma's defence system.

Even more fantastical is the **Tempio di Apollo** (Temple of Apollo), built on the site where Daedalus is said to have flown in Italy. According to Greek mythology, Daedalus and his son Icarus took to the skies to escape King Minos in Crete. En route Icarus flew too close to the sun and plunged to his death as his wax-and-feather wings melted from the heat. At the top of the ancient acropolis stand the ruins of the **Tempio di Giove** (Temple of Jupiter). Dating back to the 5th century BC, it was later converted into a Christian basilica, of which the remains of the altar and the circular baptismal font are visible.

To reach the site, take the Cumana train from Naples or Pozzuoli to Fusaro station, then walk 150m north to Via Fusaro. From here, Cuma-bound EAV buses run roughly every 30 minutes from Monday to Saturday and every hour on Sunday.

Napoli Paint Stories runs two-hour walking tours focused on the city's booming street-art scene. Expect to see works by Italian talent like Jorit Agoch, Blu, cyop & kaf, Ericailcane and Diego Miedo, as well as the work of British great Banksy. Tours – offered in Italian and English – should be booked at least one week in advance.

City Sightseeing Napoli   BUS
(Map p58; ☑ 081 551 72 79; www.city-sightseeing.it/en/naples; adult/reduced €23/11.50) City Sightseeing Napoli operates a hop-on, hop-off bus service with three routes across the city. All depart from Largo Castello, beside the Castel Nuovo. Tickets are available on board and children under five travel free. Tour commentaries are provided in a number of languages, including English.

The bus company also runs two museum shuttle services; one to the Museo di Capodimonte and another to the Reggia di Caserta.

🎆 Festivals & Events

Festival MANN   CULTURAL
(www.festivalmann.it; ☉ Mar/Apr) Naples' Museo Archeologico Nazionale (p52) serves up eight days of dynamic theatre, dance, concerts, art exhibitions, film screenings and panel discussions, both Italian and international.

Maggio dei Monumenti   CULTURAL
(www.comune.napoli.it; ☉ May) A month-long cultural feast, with a bounty of concerts, performances, exhibitions, guided tours and other events across Naples. The festival program is usually released on the Comune di Napoli (Naples City Council) website.

Wine & The City   WINE
(www.wineandthecity.it; ☉ May) A 10-day celebration of regional vino, with free wine tastings and cultural events in palaces, museums, boutiques and eateries across the city.

★ Napoli Teatro Festival Italia   THEATRE
(www.napoliteatrofestival.it; ☉ Jun/Jul) One month of local and international theatre, dance and performance art, staged in conventional and unconventional venues.

Festa della Madonna del Carmine   RELIGIOUS
(☉ 16 Jul) Pilgrims and fireworks on Piazza del Carmine, in honour of the Chiesa di Santa Maria del Carmine's miraculous Madonna.

Napoli Film Festival   FILM
(www.napolifilmfestival.com; ☉ Sep-Oct) The one-week Napoli Film Festival is well known for showcasing lesser-known independent

talent, including filmmakers based in Campania. The program also includes web series and video blogs made in southern Italy.

Festa di San Gennaro RELIGIOUS
(Duomo; ⊙ Sat before 1st Sun in May, 19 Sep, 16 Dec) The faithful flock to the Duomo to witness the miraculous liquefaction of San Gennaro's blood three times a year.

Eating

Centro Storico

Tandem NEAPOLITAN €
(Map p58; ☑ 081 1900 2468; Via G Paladino 51; meals €19; ⊙ 12.30-3.30pm & 7-11.30pm; ☜; Ⓜ Dante) *Ragù* might be a Sunday-lunch staple in Naples, but laid-back Tandem serves it up all week long. Whether you're tucking into *rigatoni al ragù* or a *ragù* fondue, expect rich, fragrant, warming goodness that could make your nonna weep. Complete with vegetarian options, it's a small, simple spot with a cult following, so head in early or (on weekends) book.

'O Sfizio NEAPOLITAN €
(Map p58; ☑ 081 1895 8824; Via Santa Maria la Nova 50; panini €3.50-5, dishes €4-5; ⊙ 7am-7pm Mon-Sat; ⓠ R4 to Via Monteoliveto, Ⓜ Università, Toledo) It's not atmosphere that draws fans to humble 'O Sfizio, a bargain-priced takeaway by a traffic-ridden thoroughfare. It's the *parmigiana di melanzana* that's so good that many locals vote it above their own mothers' versions. 'O Sfizio's iteration is simply gorgeous, never oily or heavy yet generously laden with Parmigiano, mozzarella and slightly crisp aubergine.

Pizzeria Gino Sorbillo PIZZA €
(Map p58; ☑ 081 44 66 43; www.sorbillo.it; Via dei Tribunali 32; pizzas from €4; ⊙ noon-3.30pm & 7-11.30pm Mon-Sat; ☜; Ⓜ Dante) Day in, day out, this cult-status pizzeria is besieged by hungry hordes. While debate may rage over whether Gino Sorbillo's pizzas are the best in town, there's no doubt that his giant, wood-fired discs – made using organic flour and tomatoes – will have you licking fingertips and whiskers. Head in superearly or prepare to wait.

La Masardona NEAPOLITAN €
(Map p58; Via Capaccio Giulio Cesare 27; pizza fritta €3.30-7; ⊙ 7am-4pm Mon-Fri, 7am-4pm & 7pm-midnight Sat; ☜; Ⓜ Garibaldi) Naples' remarkably light *pizza fritta* – deep-fried

pizza dough traditionally stuffed with pork *cicoli* (dried lard cubes), salami, *provola*, ricotta and tomato – is best savoured at this legendary joint. Most regulars order it *senza ricotta* (without ricotta) and wash it down with sweet marsala wine. Other versions include numerous vegetarian combos. The snack-sized version (known as *battilocchio*) is actually quite generous.

Serafino SICILIAN €
(Map p58; ☑ 081 557 14 33; Via dei Tribunali 44; arancini, cannoli €2.50; ⊙ 10.30am-10.30pm Mon-Thu, to midnight Fri-Sun) A veritable porthole to Sicily, this takeaway stand peddles authentic island street food. Savoury bites include various types of *arancini* (deep-fried rice balls), among them *al ragù* (with meat sauce) and *alla Norma* (with fried aubergine and ricotta). The real reason to head here, however, is for the crisp, flawless cannoli, filled fresh with silky Sicilian ricotta and sprinkled with pistachio crumbs. Bliss.

Donna Romita NEAPOLITAN €
(Map p58; ☑ 081 1851 5074; www.donnarom ita.it; Vico Donnaromita 14; cheese & charcuterie platter for two €20, meals €20-25; ⊙ 7pm-1.30am Tue-Thu, to 2am Fri, 12.30-3.30pm & 7pm-2am Sat, 12.30-3.30pm & 7pm-12.30am Sun; ☜; Ⓜ Dante) With a street-level bar and basement dining room, hip, minimalist Donna Romita serves gorgeous, locavore fare with competent modern tweaks. The emphasis is on regional ingredients from smaller producers, whether it's sweet, fragrant Montoro onions or organic olive oil from the Vallo di Diano. Even the wine list is an all-Campanian affair, from the *bollicine* (sparkling wines) to the post-dinner *grappe*.

Da Michele PIZZA €
(☑ 081 553 92 04; www.micheleintheworld.com; Via Cesare Sersale 1; pizzas from €4; ⊙ 10.30am-11.30pm Mon-Sat; ⓠ R2 to Corso Umberto I) Veteran pizzeria Da Michele continues to keep things plain and simple: unadorned marble tabletops, brisk service and two types of pizza – margherita or marinara. Both are delicious. Expect lengthy queues.

Trattoria Mangia e Bevi NEAPOLITAN €
(Map p58; ☑ 081 552 95 46; Via Sedile di Porto 92; meals €7; ⊙ 12.30-3.30pm Mon-Fri; ☜; Ⓜ Università) Gigi Grasso's loud and lively Eat & Drink sees everyone from pierced students to bespectacled *professori* squeeze around the communal tables for delicious home cooking at rock-bottom prices. Scan

the daily-changing menu, jot down your choices and prepare yourself for classic hits like grilled *provola*, earthy *salsiccia* (pork sausage) and *peperoncino*-spiked *friarielli* (local broccoli).

La Taverna a Santa Chiara NEAPOLITAN €

(Map p58; ☑ 393 9557558; www.tavernaasantachiara.it; Via Santa Chiara 6; meals €22; ☺ 1-2.30pm Mon, Wed & Thu, to 3pm Fri-Sun, 8-11pm Mon-Sat; 🖤; Ⓜ Dante) Gragnano pasta, Agerola pork, *salsiccia rossa di Castelpoto* (cured pork sausage with toasted peppers) and *conciato romano* (regional cheese made with cow's, sheep's and goat's milk and aged in terracotta amphorae): this modest, two-level eatery is healthily obsessed with small, local producers and Slow Food ingredients. The result is a beautiful, seasonal journey across Campania.

★ Salumeria NEAPOLITAN €€

(Map p58; ☑ 081 1936 4649; www.salumeriaupnea.it; Via San Giovanni Maggiore Pignatelli 34/35; sandwiches from €5.50, charcuterie platters from €8.50, meals around €30; ☺ 12.30-5pm & 7.15pm-midnight Thu-Tue; 🖤; Ⓜ Dante) Small producers, local ingredients and contemporary takes on provincial Campanian recipes drive bistro-inspired Salumeria. Nibble on quality charcuterie and cheeses or fill up on artisanal *panini*, hamburgers or Salumeria's sublime *ragù napoletano* (pasta served in a rich tomato-and-meat sauce slow-cooked over two days). Even the ketchup here is made in-house, using DOP Piennolo tomatoes from Vesuvius.

Vero GastroBar VEGETARIAN €€

(Map p58; ☑ 081 341 0049; www.facebook.com/verogastrobar; Piazzetta Teodoro Monticelli 4; meals €25; ☺ 12.30-3.30pm & 7-11pm Tue-Sun; 🖋; Ⓜ Università) Modern, casual Vero serves flavour-packed, flesh-free food at piazza-side tables and in an intimate, barrel-vaulted basement. The menu celebrates fusion fare, from a Neapolitan empanada stuffed with olives, capers, escarole and raisins to a baobun burger with seitan, avocado cream, rucola, Tropea onions and tomatoes. Libations include bottled and draught craft beers, as well as wines from smaller producers.

✖ Toledo & Quartieri Spagnoli

★ Il Gelato Mennella GELATO €

(Map p68; ☑ 081 40 44 58; www.pasticceriamennella.it; Via Toledo 110; gelato from €2.50; ☺ 10am-11.30pm Mon-Fri, to 1am Sat & Sun; 🚌 R2

to Via San Carlo, Ⓜ Municipio) Could it be ingredients like prized Campanian *noccioIe* (hazelnuts) from Giffoni and Sicilian pistachios from Bronte? Perhaps it's the absence of artificial nasties? Whatever the secret, Mennella scoops out smashing gelato, bursting with real, vivid flavours and velvety texture. The waffles cones are made fresh on-site and a number system means no queue jumping!

There are other branches around town, including in Chiaia and Vomero; see the website.

Osteria della Mattonella NEAPOLITAN €

(Map p74; ☑ 081 41 65 41; Via Giovanni Nicotera 13; meals €15-25; ☺ 12.30am-4pm & 7.30-11.30pm Mon-Sat, 12.30-4pm Sun; 🖤; 🚌 E6 to Via Giovanni Nicotera) In Italian, *mattonella* means tile, an apt name for this classic Neapolitan *osteria*, its walls clad in 18th-century majolica tiles. Matriarch Antonietta has been running the place since 1978, her faithful regulars here for comforting, home-cooked classics. The *primi* (first courses) are particularly notable, from the *ragù* and *pasta e provola* to a nourishing lentil and broccoli *zuppa* (soup).

Antica Pizzeria e Trattoria al '22 NEAPOLITAN €

(Map p68; ☑ 081 552 27 26; www.al22pizzeria.it; Via Pignasecca 22; pizzas from €4, meals €16-25; ☺ 11am-4pm & 6.30-11.30pm Mon-Thu, to 11.45pm Fri & Sat; Ⓜ Toledo) Despite its pizza-centric menu, loud, familial Al '22 is famous for its *parmigiana di melanzane* (aubergine parmigiana), baked in terracotta ramekins and fired in the wood-fired oven. The result is a crisp, charred top that seals the cheesy, gooey bliss beneath. The pizza selection is amble, with spin-offs including golden, fried *calzoni* stuffed with satisfying combos like *provola* and sautéed escarole.

Antica Pizza Fritta da Zia Esterina Sorbillo PIZZA €

(Map p68; ☑ 081 442 13 64; www.sorbillo.it; Piazza Trieste e Trento 53; pizza fritta from €3.50; ☺ 11am-10pm Mon-Thu, to 11pm Fri & Sun, to midnight Sat; 🚌 R2 to Via San Carlo, Ⓜ Municipio) This takeaway hotspot serves up huge, superlative *pizza fritta*, deep-fried pizza dough traditionally filled with pork *cicoli* (dried lard cubes), *provola*, ricotta and tomato. A handful of variations are available, all made fresh to order using organic flour and high-quality ingredients. And while it is filling, it's also surprisingly light: the key to a perfect rendition of this Neapolitan classic.

Pizzeria da Attilio　　　　　　　PIZZA €

(Map p68; ☑081 552 04 79; www.pizzeriada
attilio.com; Via Pignasecca 17; pizzas from €4.50;
☺noon-4pm & 7pm-midnight Mon-Sat; Ⓜ Toledo)
Its more-famous rivals might get much of
the international press, but this come-as-
you-are veteran fires some of the best pie
in town. Lording over the front-room pizza
oven is *pizzaiolo* Attilio Bachetti, whose
grandfather (also Achille Bachetti) opened
the place in 1938. Must-try pizzas include
the sun-shaped Carnevale, the eight points
of its crust filled with ricotta.

Trattoria San Ferdinando　　NEAPOLITAN €€

(Map p68; ☑081 42 19 64; Via Nardones 117;
meals €25-35; ☺12.30-3.30pm Mon-Sat, 7.30-
11pm Tue-Fri; ☐R2 to Via San Carlo, Ⓜ Municipio)
Hung with theatre posters, cosy, family-run
San Ferdinando pulls in theatre crowds
and the odd intellectual. For a Neapolitan

taste trip, ask for a rundown of the day's
antipasti and choose your favourites for an
antipasto misto (mixed antipasto). Seafood
standouts include a delicate *seppia ripieno*
(stuffed squid), while nonna Lina's homemade desserts make for a scandalously good
dénouement.

✖ Santa Lucia & Chiaia

Antica Osteria Da Tonino　　　ITALIAN €

(Map p74; ☑081 42 15 33; Via Santa Teresa a
Chiaia 47; meals around €16; ☺12.30-3.30pm
daily, plus 7.30-11.30pm Fri & Sat; Ⓜ Piazza Amedeo) Wood-panelled, family-run Da Tonino
has been feeding locals since 1880. Now
run by the fifth and sixth generations, its
gingham-print tables lure everyone from
Rubinacci suits to old-timers and the odd
Nobel Prize winner (Dario Fo ate here). The
day's menu – hand-written and photocopied

SWEET TREATS

Naples is no place for counting calories. Neapolitans adore their sweets and no Sunday
lunch is complete without a tray of fresh, runny, succulent *paste* (pastries) from the local
pasticceria (pastry shop). Locals have a particular soft spot for the iconic *sfogliatella*;
filled with cinnamon-spiced, sweetened ricotta, the pastry comes in two forms: denser
frolla (made with shortbread pastry) and flakier *riccia* (made using filo pastry).

Sfogliatella Mary (Map p68; sfogliatelle €1.80; ☺8am-8.30pm Tue-Sun; ☐R2 to Via San
Carlo, Ⓜ Municipio) At the Via Toledo entrance to Galleria Umberto I, this tiny takeaway
vendor is widely considered the queen of the *sfogliatella*.

Pintauro (Map p68; ☑081 41 73 39; Via Toledo 275; sfogliatelle €2; ☺9am-8pm Mon-Sat,
9.20am-2pm Sun, closed mid-Jul–early Sep; ☐R2 to Via San Carlo, Ⓜ Municipio) This local
institution has been selling superlative *sfogliatelle* since the early 1800s, when its
founder supposedly brought them to Naples from their culinary birthplace on the Amalfi
Coast.

Attanasio (Map p58; ☑081 28 56 75; Vico Ferrovia 1-4; sfogliatelle €1.30; ☺6.30am-7.30pm
Tue-Sun; Ⓜ Garibaldi) So you thought a *sfogliatella* from Pintauro was crispy perfection?
Bite into the piping-hot ricotta filling at this retro pastry peddler and prepare to reassess.

Pasticceria Mennella (Map p74; ☑081 42 60 26; www.pasticceriamennella.it; Via Carducci
50-52; pastries from €1.50; ☺6.30am-9.30pm Mon-Fri, to 10.30pm Sat, 7am-9.30pm Sun;
Ⓜ Piazza Amedeo) If you eat only one sweet treat in Naples (good luck with that!), make
it Mennella's spectacular *frolla al limone*, a shortbread pastry filled with heavenly lemon
cream.

Pasticceria Poppella (Map p80; ☑081 45 53 09; www.facebook.com/pasticceriapop
pella; Via Arena della Sanità 29; ☺6am-10pm; Ⓜ Piazza Cavour, Museo) Neapolitans from
across the city revere this upbeat pastry shop for its *fiocco di neve* (snowflake), a soft,
small brioche, dusted in icing sugar and packed with a light, vanilla-scented filling of
ricotta and Italian pastry cream.

Pasticceria Di Costanzo (Map p58; ☑081 45 01 80; www.dicostanzopasticceria.it; Piazza
Cavour 133-135; pastries from €1; ☺7.15am-8.15pm Thu-Tue; Ⓜ Piazza Cavour, Museo) Colourful, technically impressive and ridiculously cute, Mario Di Costanzo's sweet treats are
what Instagram dreams are made of.

– offers simple, beautiful home cooking. If it's on offer, order the heavenly *polpette al ragù* (meatballs in tomato sauce).

Muu Muuzzarella Lounge NEAPOLITAN €

(Map p74; ☑ 081 40 53 70; www.muumuuz zarellalounge.it; Vico II Alabardieri 7; dishes €6-16; ☺ noon-midnight Tue-Sun; ☎ 🖉; 🚇 E6 to Piazza dei Martiri) Pimped with milking-bucket lights and cow-hide patterned cushions, playful, contemporary Muu is all about super-fresh Campanian mozzarella, from cheese and charcuterie platters to creative dishes like buffalo bocconcini with creamy pesto and crunchy apple. Leave room for the chef's secret-recipe white-chocolate cheesecake, best paired with a glass of Guappa (buffalo-milk liqueur). Numerous non-meat options too.

★ L'Ebbrezza di Noè ITALIAN €€

(Map p74; ☑ 081 40 01 04; www.lebbrezzadi noe.com; Vico Vetriera 9; meals €35-40, cheese & charcuterie platters €10; ☺ 6-11pm Tue-Thu, to midnight Fri & Sat, 1-3pm Sun; ☎; Ⓜ Piazza Amedeo) A wine shop by day, 'Noah's Drunkenness' transforms into an intimate culinary hot spot by night. Slip inside for *vino* and conversation with sommelier Luca at the bar, or settle into one of the bottle-lined dining rooms for seductive, market-driven dishes such as house special *paccheri fritti* (fried pasta stuffed with aubergine and served with fresh basil and a rich tomato sauce).

Topping it off are about 2800 wines, including nearly 500 champagnes from smaller producers. Book ahead.

★ Da Ettore NEAPOLITAN €€

(Map p74; ☑ 081 764 35 78; Via Gennaro Serra 39; meals €25; ☺ 1-3pm & 8-10pm Tue-Sat, 1-3pm Sun; ☎; 🚇 R2 to Via San Carlo, Ⓜ Chiaia-Monte di Dio) This homey, eight-table trattoria has an epic reputation. Scan the walls for famous fans like comedy great Totò, and a framed passage from crime writer Massimo Siviero, who mentions Ettore in one of his tales. The draw is solid regional cooking, which includes one of the best *spaghetti alle vongole* (spaghetti with clams) in town. Book two days ahead for Sunday lunch.

Pescheria Mattiucci SEAFOOD €€

(Map p74; ☑ 081 251 2215; www.pescheriamat tiucci.com; Vico Belledonne a Chiaia 27; crudo €25, cooked dishes €12-15; ☺ 12.30-3pm & 7-10.30pm Tue-Sat; 🚇 E6 to Piazza dei Martiri, Ⓜ Piazza Amedeo) Run by brothers Francesco, Gennaro and

Luigi, this local Chiaia fishmonger transforms daily into a wonderfully intimate, sociable seafood eatery. Perch yourself on a bar stool, order a vino, and watch the team prepare your superfresh, tapas-style *crudo* (raw seafood) to order. You'll also find a number of simple, beautifully cooked surf dishes.

Dialetti ITALIAN €€

(Map p74; ☑ 081 248 1158; www.facebook.com/ DialettiNapoli; Vico Satriano 10; meals around €32; ☺ noon-3.30pm & 6pm-midnight Mon-Sat; ☎; 🚇 128, 140, 151 to Riviera di Chiaia) On-point Dialetti takes its cues from cities like New York, London and Sydney. You'll find a snug, vintage-pimped lounge corner at the front, a communal dining table with views of the glassed-in kitchen, and a softly lit dining room beyond it. Service is attentive and the daily changing menu champions gorgeous ingredients, cooked beautifully and with subtle contemporary tweaks.

Officina del Mare SEAFOOD €€

(Map p74; ☑ 081 1935 3543; Piazzetta Marinari 20-21; meals around €40; ☺ 11.30am-11.30pm; 🚇 128, E6 to Via Santa Lucia) While this place lacks the waterfront views of its neighbours, it also lacks the dated kitsch. Furthermore, both the chef and sommelier hail from Naples' illustrious Grand Hotel Parker's, translating into gracious service and beautifully prepared dishes made with top-notch seafood. Top choices include the *crudo*, pasta (most notably the *scialatiello* with seafood) and the grilled fish mains.

Trattoria Castel dell'Ovo SEAFOOD €€

(Map p74; ☑ 081 764 63 52; Via Luculliana 28; meals €25; ☺ 8-11pm Fri-Wed Jul-Sep, 1-3.15pm & 8-11pm Mon-Wed, Fri & Sat, 1-3.15pm Sun Oct-Jun; 🚇 128 to Via Santa Lucia) Many locals ditch the bigger, more touristy restaurants on Borgo Marinaro for this cheaper, friendlier bolthole. Sit beside bobbing boats and tuck into surf staples like *zuppa di pesce* (fish soup) and *insalata di polipo* (octopus salad with fresh tomato). Even if it's not on the menu, it's worth requesting the spaghetti with prawns, mussels, zucchini and Parmigiano. Cash only.

Ristorantino dell'Avvocato NEAPOLITAN €€

(Map p74; ☑ 081 032 00 47; www.ilristorantino dellavvocato.it; Via Santa Lucia 115-117; meals €40-45; ☺ noon-3pm & 7.30-11pm Tue-Sat, noon-3pm Sun; ☎; 🚇 128, E6 to Via Santa Lucia) This elegant yet welcoming restaurant is a favourite

Side margin: NAPLES, POMPEII & AROUND EATING

of Neapolitan gastronomes. Apple of their eye is affable lawyer turned head chef Raffaele Cardillo, whose passion for Campania's culinary heritage merges with a knack for subtle, refreshing twists – think coffee papardelle served with mullet *ragù*.

The degustation menus (€50 to €60) are good value. Book ahead.

✗ Vomero

Antica Pizza Fritta da Zia Esterina Sorbillo
STREET FOOD €

(Map p78; ☑ 081 1932 3779; www.sorbillo.it; Via Luca Giordano 33-35; pizza fritta from €3.50; ⊙ 11am-10pm Mon-Thu, to 11pm Fri, to midnight Sat; Ⓜ Vanvitelli) A neon-framed image of San Gennaro greets visitors at Zia Esterina, famed for its *pizza fritta*. Surprisingly light, its choice of fillings ranges from the classic (dried lard, *provola*, ricotta and tomato) to the more novel. Simply order at the counter, wait for your number to be called, then gobble at one of the bar tables or benches (standing room only).

La Frescheria
SEAFOOD €€

(Map p78; ☑ 081 578 2149; www.facebook.com/lafrescheriabottegadelgusto; Via Francesco Fracanzano 8c; lunch dishes €10, dinner around €40; ⊙ 12.30-3pm & 7.30-11.30pm Tue-Sat, 12.30-3pm Sun; 🐾; Ⓜ Quattro Giornate) Contemporary, attentive La Frescheria serves smashing seafood at its street-level *crudo* bar and softly lit, basement dining room. The day's catch – much of it from Pozzuoli's famous fish market – determines the simple, compact lunch menu. Dinner is more extensive (and expensive), with highlights including *crudo mediterraneo* (raw fish) and panko-crusted, paprika-dusted octopus served with housemade herb mayo.

✗ La Sanità & Capodimonte

★ Concettina Ai Tre Santi
PIZZA €

(Map p80; ☑ 081 29 00 37; www.pizzeria oliva.it; Via Arena della Sanità 7; pizzas from €5; ⊙ noon-midnight Mon-Sat, to 5pm Sun; 🐾; Ⓜ Piazza Cavour, Museo) Head in by noon (or 7.30pm at dinner) to avoid a long wait at this hot-spot pizzeria, made famous thanks to its young, driven *pizzaiolo* Ciro Oliva. The menu is an index of fastidiously sourced artisanal ingredients, used to top Ciro's flawless, wood-fired bases. Traditional Neapolitan pizza aside, you'll also find a string of creative seasonal options.

★ Pizzeria Starita
PIZZA €

(Map p80; ☑ 081 557 36 82; www.pizzeriastarita.it; Via Materdei 28; pizzas from €4; ⊙ noon-3.30pm & 7pm-midnight Tue-Sun; Ⓜ Materdei) The giant fork and ladle hanging on the wall at this historic pizzeria were used by Sophia Loren in *L'oro di Napoli,* and the kitchen made the *pizze fritte* sold by the actress in the film. While the 60-plus pizza varieties include a tasty *fiorilli e zucchine* (zucchini, zucchini flowers and *provola*), our allegiance remains to its classic *marinara*.

Da Luisa
NEAPOLITAN €

(Map p80; ☑ 081 44 97 66; Via Capodimonte 19; pizzas from €4, meals €18; ⊙ noon-3.30pm & 7-11pm Tue-Sun) Opposite the Museo di Capodimonte, neighbourly Da Luisa offers a short menu of uncomplicated, classic dishes. Pique the appetite with prosciutto and mozzarella before moving onto comforting pasta dishes such as fusilli with porcini mushrooms and pork sausage or *orechiette* with broccoli and pancetta. Simple *secondi* (main courses) span both surf and turf, and it also dishes out bubbling pizzas.

✗ Mergellina & Posillipo

★ 50 Kalò
PIZZA €

(Map p74; ☑ 081 1920 4667; www.50kalò.it; Piazza Sannazzaro 201b; pizza from €5; ⊙ 12.30-4pm & 7.30pm-12.30am; 🐾; Ⓜ Mergellina) That this trendy pizzeria's name roughly translates as 'good dough' in Neapolitan is no coincidence. At the helm is third-generation *pizzaiolo* Ciro Salvo, whose obsessive research into Naples' most famous edible translates into wonderfully light, perfectly charred wood-fired pizzas. Quality is the key here: from the olive oil to the rustic pork salami, ingredients are sourced directly from local and artisanal producers.

Chalet Ciro Mergellina
GELATO €

(Map p74; ☑ 081 66 99 28; www.chaletciro.it; Via Caracciolo; gelato from €2.50, cono graffa €5; ⊙ 6.45am-2.30am Mon, Tue, Thu & Sun, to 3am Fri, to 4am Sat; Ⓜ Mergellina) This retro seafront chalet sells everything from coffee and pastries to crêpes, but you head here for the *graffe* (doughnuts) and the gelato. Indeed, find both in Ciro's obscenely decadent *cono graffa,* gelato served in a doughnut cone. Locals justifiably call it a *bomba* (bomb). Pay inside, choose your flavours at the street-side counter, then kill the cals with a bayside saunter.

Palazzo Petrucci   MODERN ITALIAN €€€

(⌧081 575 75 38; www.palazzopetrucci.it; Via Posillipo 16C; meals €75, degustation menus €90-150; ⊙12.30-2.30pm & 7.30-10.30pm Tue-Sat, dinner only Mon, lunch only Sun; ⌐140 to Via Posillipo) Fine-dining, beachside Petrucci excites palates with unexpected takes on Italian traditions. Here, 'lasagna' might mean mozzarella with raw prawn and broccoli cream, while a dish of *tubettone* pasta could include a clever, unorthodox pairing of oysters, white-truffle pearls and cauliflower cream. Polished service and views over Capri and the legend-riddled Palazzo Donn'Anna make it a spot to celebrate something special. Book ahead.

Drinking & Nightlife

Although Neapolitans aren't big drinkers, Naples offers an increasingly varied selection of venues in which to imbibe. You'll find well-worn wine bars and a new wave of options focused on craft beer, cocktails and even speciality coffee. The main hubs are the *centro storico* and Chiaia. The former is generally cheaper and more alternative, the latter more fashionable and scene-y.

Centro Storico

★**Spazio Intolab**   CLUB

(Map p58; ⌧333 9126318; www.facebook.com/intolab; Piazza Enrico De Nicola 46; cover €5-15; ⊙9.30pm-4am Fri & Sat; ⛾; ⓂGaribaldi) Housed on the 1st floor of the Lanificio – a Bourbon-era wool factory and 15th-century cloister turned culture hub – Spazio Intolab draws an easy, arty, cosmopolitan crowd with its all-night parties. Regular DJ sets include in-the-know names from Italy and abroad, playing anything from deep house and techno to live electronica. Check the venue's Facebook page for upcoming events.

Jamón   WINE BAR

(Map p58; ⌧081 420 24 58; Piazza San Domenico Maggiore 9; sandwiches €5, cheese & charcuterie tasting plates €5; ⊙10am-midnight; ⓂDante) Great for a piazza-side graze, this savvy little deli–wine bar sits at the top of sweeping Piazza San Domenico Maggiore. Offerings include niche and harder-to-find charcuterie and cheese; think cinnamon-seasoned Tuscan mortadella and *prosciutto di suino nero dei Nebroli* (Sicily's answer to Spanish *pata negra*). Savour them in a tasting plate, or sliced and freshly stuffed into a crusty *panino*.

Palazzo Venezia Napoli   CAFE

(Map p58; ⌧081 552 87 39; www.palazzovenezianapoli.com; Via Benedetto Croce 19; ⊙10am-1.30pm & 3.30-7pm Mon-Sat; ⓂDante) This richly historic *palazzo* was gifted to the Venetian Republic in the 15th century as a base for its envoys. The building's 1st floor now houses a small cafe, with a scattering of tables and chairs in a tranquil secret garden. Wind down with a herbal tea or an *aperitivo spritz* surrounded by irises, citrus trees, palms and ferns.

You'll also find works by local artists and artisans for sale.

Shanti Art Musik Bar   BAR

(Map p58; ⌧081 551 49 79; www.facebook.com/ShantiSPACCANapoli; Via Giovanni Paladino 56; ⊙10.30am-2.30am Mon-Wed, 11am-3am Thu-Sat; ⛾; ⓂDante) Under Tibetan prayer flags, shabby Shanti draws a cosmopolitan crowd of arty and indie types, both local and foreign. While the place serves lunchtime grub, head here in the evenings, when party people congregate at upcycled, candlelit tables to chat, flirt and party well into the night. Drinks are well priced.

Superfly   BAR

(Map p58; ⌧081 551 03 88; www.facebook.com/soulbar.superfly; Via Cisterna dell'Olio 12; ⊙7pm-1.30am Mon, Wed, Thu & Sun, to 3am Fri & Sat; ⓂDante) They may be a little older, but the '90s kids are still partying at this tiny veteran bar, tucked away on a *centro-storico* side street. Here, well-mixed drinks, old-school tunes and fun, easy vibe make it a hit with artists, radicals and middle-class peeps, who spill out onto the skinny street, chatting, toasting and making the odd new friend.

Spazio Nea   CAFE

(Map p58; ⌧081 45 13 58; www.spazionea.it; Via Costantinopoli 53; ⊙9am-2am, to 3am Fri & Sat; ⛾; ⓂDante) Aptly skirting bohemian Piazza Bellini, this whitewashed gallery features its own cafe-bar speckled with books, flowers, cultured crowds and al fresco seating at the bottom of a baroque staircase. Eye up exhibitions of contemporary Italian and foreign art, then kick back with a *caffè* or a *spritz*. Check Nea's Facebook page for upcoming readings, live-music gigs or DJ sets.

Caffè dell'Epoca   BAR

(Map p58; Via Santa Maria di Costantinopoli; ⊙7am-2am Mon-Sat, to 2pm Sun; ⛾; ⓂDante) You're not here for the drab decor and

CAFFÈ GAMBRINUS

Gambrinus is Naples' oldest and most venerable **cafe** (Map p74; ☑ 081 41 75 82; www.grancaffegambrinus.com; Via Chiaia 1-2; ☺ 7am-1am Sun-Fri, to 2am Sat; ☐ R2 to Via San Carlo, Ⓜ Municipio), serving superlative Neapolitan coffee under flouncy chandeliers. Oscar Wilde knocked back a few here and Mussolini had some rooms shut to keep out left-wing intellectuals. Sit-down prices are steep, but the *aperitivo* nibbles are decent and sipping a *spritz* or a luscious *cioccolata calda* (hot chocolate) in its belle-époque rooms is something worth savouring.

sallow lighting but for Piazza Bellini's hottest bargains: €1.50 bottles of Peroni and €2 *spritz*. These cut-price libations draw no shortage of art- and music-school students and staffers, who spill out onto the street for fun, boisterous evening sessions. Bantering owner Peppe will even let you bring in a takeaway pizza.

Libreria Berisio   BAR
(Map p58; ☑ 081 549 90 90; www.facebook.com/Berisio; Via Port'Alba 28-29; ☺ 9.30am-1.30am Mon-Thu, to 3am Fri, 9.30am-1.30pm & 7pm-3.30am Sat, 6.30pm-1.30am Sun; ☎; Ⓜ Dante) This midcentury bookshop doubles as buzzing cocktail bar, its wine-red interiors drawing a predominantly young, international crowd. Sip a well-crafted negroni while browsing floor-to-ceiling bookshelves...or the cute peeps in the crowd.

🍸 Toledo & Quartieri Spagnoli

Il Birraiuolo   BAR
(Map p58; ☑ 081 549 27 03; www.facebook.com/ilbirraiuolo; Via Bellini 48; ☺ 6.30pm-midnight Wed, Thu & Sun, to 2am Fri & Sat; Ⓜ Dante) Should you swill a barrel-aged saison from the Veneto's Crak, a Tasmanian IPA from Lombardy's Hop Skin, or jump the border and down a Pannepot Grand Reserva from Belgium's De Struise Brouwers? It's the kind of conundrum you'll face at this intimate, affable temple to craft brews. Staff are clued up about what they pour and you'll also find a solid selection of whiskies.

Caffè Mexico   CAFE
(Map p58; Piazza Dante 86; ☺ 5.30am-8.30pm Mon-Sat, 6.30am-2.30pm Sun; Ⓜ Dante) One of Naples' best (and best-loved) coffee bars – even the local cops stop by for a quick pick-me-up – is a retro-tastic combo of old-school baristas, an orange espresso machine and velvety, full-flavoured *caffè*. The espresso is served *zuccherato* (sweetened), so request it *amaro* if you fancy a bitter hit.

Cammarota Spritz   BAR
(Map p68; ☑ 320 2775687; www.facebook.com/cammarotaspritz; Vico Lungo Teatro Nuovo 31; ☺ 4pm-midnight Mon & Wed, noon-midnight Tue & Thu-Sat; Ⓜ Toledo) This threadbare bar has developed a cult following for its €1 Aperol *spritz*, drawing hordes of students and travellers wanting to get happy on the cheap. Seating is minimal, with most punters happily chatting, texting and flirting while standing on the skinny street. There's also €1 beer and wine, though the vino would be better off dressing a salad. Stick to the *spritz*.

🍸 Santa Lucia & Chiaia

★ L'Antiquario   COCKTAIL BAR
(Map p74; ☑ 081 764 53 90; www.facebook.com/AntiquarioNapoli; Via Gaetani 2; ☺ 7.30pm-2.30am; ☐ 151, 154 to Piazza Vittoria) If you take your cocktails seriously, slip into this sultry, speakeasy-inspired den. Wrapped in art nouveau wallpaper, it's the domain of Neapolitan barkeep Alex Frezza, a finalist at the 2014 Bombay Sapphire World's Most Imaginative Bartender Awards. Straddling classic and contemporary, the drinks are impeccable, made with passion and meticulous attention to detail. Live jazz-centric tunes add to the magic on Wednesdays.

★ Barril   BAR
(Map p74; ☑ 393 9814362; www.barril.it; Via G Fiorelli 11; ☺ 7pm-2am Tue-Thu & Sun, to 3am Fri & Sat; ☎; Ⓜ Piazza Amedeo) From street level, stairs lead down to this softly lit, buzzing garden bar, where grown-up, fashionable types mingle among birdcage seats and vintage Cinzano posters. Fresh, competent cocktails include giant, creamy piña coladas, and you'll also find over 40 gins with numerous tonic waters for a customised G&T. Bites include cheese and charcuterie platters, plus a decent selection of complimentary *aperitivo*-time snacks.

★ Ba-Bar
BAR

(Map p74; ✆ 081 764 35 25; www.ba-bar.it; Via Bisignano 20; ⊗5pm-2am Mon & Sun, 11am-3.30pm & 5pm-2am Tue & Wed, 11am-3.30pm & 5pm-3am Thu-Sat; ☎; ▣ E6 to Piazza dei Martiri) Swinging, candlelit Ba-Bar is a solid all-rounder, punctuated with quirky vintage objects and pulling a friendly, mixed crowd. It's a top spot for a pre-dinner *aperitivo*, a lingering catch-up in the cosy back room, or a foosball game in the basement. Cocktails are well mixed, with a rotating list of interesting Italian wines, as well as local and foreign beers.

On the food front, bites range from graze-friendly platters of quality regional cheeses and charcuterie, to *panini*, pasta dishes, salads and a handful of mains.

Cantine Sociali
BAR

(Map p74; ✆ 338 3511375; www.facebook.com/CantineSocialiNapoli; Piazza Giulio Rodinò 28; ⊗6pm-2am Mon-Wed, to 3am Thu-Sun; ▣ E6 to Piazza dei Martiri) Cantine Sociali is hugely popular, drawing a stylish, mixed-age crowd to its timber deck each night. The wine list is extensive and competent (if not especially cheap), the cocktails well mixed, and the free *aperitivo* buffet a satisfying spread that usually includes couscous, vegetables and *pizzette* (small pizzas).

Enoteca Belledonne
BAR

(Map p74; ✆ 081 40 31 62; www.enotecabelledonne.com; Vico Belledonne a Chiaia 18; ⊗5pm-1am Mon, 10am-1.30pm & 4.30pm-2am Tue-Thu, 10am-1.30pm & 4.30pm-3am Fri & Sat, 7pm-2am Sun; ☎; ▣ E6 to Piazza dei Martiri) Bottle-lined timber shelves set a cosy scene at this classic Chiaia wine shop and bar. Swill, sniff and eavesdrop over a list of well-chosen, mostly Italian wines, including over 30 by the glass. The decent grazing menu includes Italian and Spanish charcuterie and cheese (from €8), as well as just-caught *crudo* platters (€25) from nearby Pescheria Mattiucci (p87).

Al Barcadero
CAFE

(Map p74; ✆ 334 1790987; Banchina Santa Lucia 2; ⊗8am-2am Tue-Sun May-Oct, to 8pm Tue-Sun Nov-Apr; ▣ 128, E6 to Via Santa Lucia) Turn left down the steps as you walk towards Borgo Marinaro and you'll find this unpretentious waterfront bar. Plonk yourself by the water and gaze out at boat-rowing fishermen and a menacing Mt Vesuvius while sipping a notoriously strong negroni.

⚲ Vomero

★ Ventimetriquadri
CAFE

(Map p78; ✆ 345 5328421; www.facebook.com/ventimetriquadri.specialtycoffee; Via Bernini 64A; ⊗3-11pm Mon, 9am-11pm Tue-Fri, 10am-midnight Sat, 10am-2pm & 6-11pm Sun; ☎; Ⓜ Vanvitelli) What was once an old printing shop (note the vintage printer-drawer tabletops and bookish wallpaper) is now the city's first speciality-coffee cafe. The chances are you'll find owner Vincenzo Fioretto behind the counter, carefully preparing your brew from seven single origins or the house blend. Brewing methods include espresso, V60 and Aeropress brewing, with quality teas available for those who prefer leaves to beans.

Options also include thoughtfully chosen wines and regional craft beers, as well as cakes and boards of artisinal cheeses and cured meats.

Fonoteca
BAR

(Map p78; ✆ 081 556 03 38; www.fonoteca.net; Via Raffaele Morghen 31 C/F; ⊗noon-1am Mon-Thu, to 2am Fri & Sat, 6.30pm-1.30am Sun; ☎; Ⓜ Vanvitelli, ▣ Centrale to Piazza Fuga) Groove away at this Vomero favourite, a hybrid music shop/cafe/bar. Hunt for new and used vinyl and CDs spanning electronica and classic rock to jazz, blues and world, flick through art and music-themed tomes, or head straight to the back bar for a *caffè*, cocktail or Neapolitan craft beer. There's also an ample selection of teas, including herbal options.

⚲ La Sanità & Capodimonte

Antica Cantina Sepe
BAR

(Map p80; ✆ 081 45 46 09; Via dei Vergini 55; ⊗9am-8.30pm, to midnight Thu; Ⓜ Piazza Cavour, Museo) This pocket-sized cantina and grocery store has become an unlikely hotspot thanks to next-gen owner, Francesco Sepe, and his on-tap local vino, sold at €1.50 a glass. Fancier wines cost no more than €3.50 a pop, while Thursday nights see mamma Giovanna make a small feast for the weekly *aperitivo* session, which features DJ sets, live music or other cultural events.

★ Entertainment

Although Naples is no London or Milan on the entertainment front, it does offer world-class opera, ballet, classical music and jazz, thought-provoking theatre and in-the-know DJs. To see what's on, scan Italian-language

Corriere del Mezzogiorno (https://corriere delmezzogiorno.corriere.it/napoli) or *La Repubblica* (http://napoli.repubblica.it), or ask at the tourist office.

★ Teatro San Carlo
OPERA, BALLET

(Map p74; ☑box office 081 797 23 31; www.teatro sancarlo.it; Via San Carlo 98f; ☺box office 10am-9pm Mon-Sat, to 6pm Sun; ☐R2 to Via San Carlo, Ⓜ Municipio) San Carlo's opera season runs from November or December to June, with occasional summer performances. Sample prices: a place in the 6th tier (from €35), the stalls (€75 to €130) or the side box (from €40). Ballet season runs from late October to April or early May; tickets range from €30 to €110.

Be aware that not all shows take place on the main stage, with other venues including the smaller Teatrino di Corte in neighbouring Palazzo Reale (p66).

Centro di Musica Antica Pietà de' Turchini
CLASSICAL MUSIC

(Map p68; ☑081 40 23 95; www.turchini.it; Via Santa Caterina da Siena 38; adult/reduced €10/7; ☐Centrale to Corso Vittorio Emanuele) Classical-music buffs are in for a treat at this beautiful deconsecrated church, an evocative setting for concerts of mostly 17th- to 19th-century Neapolitan works. Upcoming concerts are listed on the venue's website. Note that some concerts are held at other venues, including the Palazzo Zevallos Stigliano (p69).

Associazione Scarlatti
CLASSICAL MUSIC

(Map p74; ☑081 40 60 11; www.associazione scarlatti.it; Piazza dei Martiri 58; ☐E6 to Piazza dei Martiri) Naples' premier classical-music association organises chamber-music concerts in venues that include the Museo Diocesano di Napoli. Local talent mixes it with foreign guests, which have included the Amsterdam Baroque Orchestra, St Petersburg's Mariinsky Theatre Orchestra and Belgian composer Philippe Herreweghe.

Tickets are normally available at the venue an hour before show time; expect to pay between €13 and €18, depending on the seat.

Teatro Mercadante
THEATRE

(Map p58; www.teatrostabilenapoli.it; Piazza Municipio; Ⓜ Municipio) Dating from 1779, the Teatro Mercadante is home to the city's leading theatre company, the Teatro Stabile Napoli. The company performs a mix of mainly 19th- and 20th-century classics from playwrights as diverse as Luigi Pirandello, Henrik Ibsen, David Mamet and the Roberto Alajmo. Productions are generally in Italian.

Bourbon Street
JAZZ

(Map p58; ☑338 8253756; www.bourbon streetjazzclub.com; Via Bellini 52; ☺8.30pm-2am Tue-Thu & Sun, to 3am Fri & Sat; closed Jul-early Sep; Ⓜ Dante) Bourbon Street is one of the top spots for live jazz and blues, drawing a mixed crowd of seasoned jazz nerds and rookies. Acts are mostly local, with Wednesday, Thursday and Sunday nights featuring 'JamJazz' sessions, when musicians hit the stage for impromptu collaborations. Check the venue's Facebook page (Bourbon Street Napoli Jazz Club) to see who's up next.

Galleria Toledo
THEATRE

(Map p68; ☑081 42 50 37; https://galleria toledo.info; Via Concezione a Montecalvario 34; Ⓜ Toledo) If it's cutting edge, independent or experimental, the chances are it's playing at this cult-status theatre in the Quartieri Spagnoli. Offerings span local and global plays and live music, with the odd offbeat arthouse flick thrown in for good measure. Online and phone bookings are taken, with collection at the theatre 30 minutes prior to the performance.

Blue Around Midnight
JAZZ

(Map p78; ☑081 1837 0171; www.facebook.com/ Bluearoundmidnightmidnightjazzclub; Via Bonito 32a; ☺6pm-2am Thu-Sat May-Sep, 6pm-2am Tue-Sun Oct-Apr; ☎; Ⓜ Vanvitelli, ☐Montesanto to Morghen) One of Naples' oldest and most famous jazz clubs, this tiny swinging bolt-hole features mostly home-grown live gigs, with the occasional blues band putting in a performance. Best of all, you can nosh while you tap those toes (meals around €20 to €25). Booking recommended.

🔒 Shopping

🔒 Centro Storico

★ Bottega 21
FASHION & ACCESSORIES

(Map p58; ☑081 033 55 42; www.bottegaventu no.it; Vico San Domenico Maggiore 21; ☺9.30am-8pm Mon-Sat) Top-notch Tuscan leather and traditional, handcrafted methods translate into coveted, contemporary leather goods at Bottega 21. Block colours and clean, simple designs underline the range, which

TO MARKET, TO MARKET

Porta Nolana and La Pignasecca are only two of Naples' loud and legendary markets. Stock up on cheap shoes, cut-price kitchenware and the odd vintage gem at the following favourites.

Mercato Caramanico a Poggioreale (☎327 5973834; www.facebook.com/Mercato Caramanico; Via Marino di Caramanico; ⊙6.30am-2pm Fri-Mon, closed Aug; ☐130, 190, 601 to Via Nuova Poggioreale) Also known as the *Mercatino delle Scarpe* (Shoe Market), Naples' largest open-air market is famous for its kicks, from designer overstock to no-frills everyday brands. Located 2.5km northeast of Napoli Centrale (catch bus 601 from Piazza Garibaldi), the place has over 550 stalls, with other good buys including handbags, casual wear, suits, colourful rolls of fabric, and kitchenware.

Mercatino dell'Umberto (Map p74; Via Imbriani; ⊙8.30am-2pm Mon-Sat; ☐128, 140, 151 to Riviera di Chiaia) Hit the stalls on Via Imbriani for well-priced fashionable frocks, jumpers and cardigans, tasteful bijou jewellery, shoes, high-end fakes and the odd treasure (think vintage *foulard* scarves). There's a high turnover of stock to boot. Don't haggle. This is Chiaia, darling.

Mercatino di Antignano (Map p78; Piazza degli Artisti; ⊙7am-1.30pm Mon-Sat; Ⓜ Quattro Giornate) Up high in mild-mannered Vomero, this atmospheric place is popular for bags, jewellery, linen, kitchenware and shoes, as well as fresh produce and deli items ranging from silky olives to pungent cheese and rustic *salsiccie* (pork sausage). There's even an outdoor kiosk pouring well-priced *spritz* when (not if) you need a break.

Mercato Sant'Antonio Abate (O' Buvero; Via Sant'Antonio Abate; ⊙9am-7.30pm Mon-Sat; ☐147, 182, 184, 185 to Via Forio, 201, 202, 254 to Corso Garibaldi) Running along ramshackle Via Sant'Antonio Abate, O' Buvero is a hyperactive, rough-and-ready neighbourhood market peddling everything from fresh fruit and vegetables to seafood, local cheeses and *salumi* (charcuterie). It's also an evocative spot to experience Napoli at its most intense.

Mercatino di Posillipo (Map p104; Parco Virgiliano; ⊙7am-2pm Thu; ☐140 to Via Posillipo) Located outside the main gates of Parco Virgiliano, this isn't the cheapest market, but it's generally the best for quality goods. Top buys include women's swimwear, underwear, boots, linen, and cut-price jewellery and cosmetics. You'll also find racks of 'designer' clothing, predominantly for women.

---

includes stylish totes, handbags, backpacks and duffel bags, as well as wallets and coin purses, unisex belts, gloves, sandals, tobacco pouches and, occasionally, notebook covers.

There's a second branch further down the street at No 11.

★ La Scarabattola ARTS & CRAFTS
(Map p58; ☎081 29 17 35; www.lascarabattola.it; Via dei Tribunali 50; ⊙10.30am-2pm & 3.30-7.30pm Mon-Fri, 10am-8pm Sat; Ⓜ Dante) La Scarabattola's handmade sculptures of *magi* (wise men), devils and Neapolitan folk figures constitute Jerusalem's official Christmas crèche, and the artisanal studio's fans also include fashion designer Stefano Gabbana and Spanish royalty. Figurines aside, sleek ceramic creations (like Pulcinella-inspired place-card holders) inject Neapolitan folklore with refreshing contemporary style.

Scriptura FASHION & ACCESSORIES
(Map p58; ☎081 552 66 69; Via San Sebastiano 45; ⊙10am-8pm Mon-Sat; Ⓜ Dante) Family-run Scriptura is a must for artisanal leather goods made using high-quality Campanian leather. Its range includes handbags, satchels, duffel bags and backpacks, as well as belts, men's and women's gloves, jackets, wallets, tobacco pouches, eyeglass cases and leather-bound notebooks. Styles and colours cover both the classic and the contemporary and, best of all, prices are reasonable given the quality.

Colonnese ARTS, BOOKS
(Map p58; ☎081 45 98 58; https://colonnese.it; Via San Pietro a Maiella 32-33; ⊙10am-7.30pm; Ⓜ Dante) Neighbour to one of Italy's most esteemed music conservatories, this erudite bookshop fills with the sound of practising musicians. Most new and vintage-edition

titles are in Italian, though English-language titles include Colonnese's editions of Nea-politan-themed classics. You'll find quality original and reproduction Neapolitan prints from the 18th and 19th centuries, as well collectible postcards from the late 19th and early 20th centuries.

Kiphy
COSMETICS

(Map p58; ☑340 2849691; www.kiphy.it; Vico San Domenico Maggiore 3; ☺10.30am-2pm & 4-7.30pm Mon-Sat; ⓂDante) ✐ In her heavenly scented workshop, Pina Malinconico crafts handmade slabs of soap that look as beautiful as they smell. Lined up under low-slung lights, varieties include a refreshing orange-and-cinnamon blend. The freshly made shampoos, creams and oils use organic, fair-trade ingredients and can be personally tailored. Best of all, products are gorgeously packaged, reasonably priced and made with love.

MAC Ceramics
CERAMICS

(Map p58; ☑333 6031376; www.facebook.com/bottegadiceramica; Via Nilo 12; ☺10am-7pm Mon-Sat; ⓂDante) MAC sells playful, contemporary ceramics created by talented local couple Antimo De Santis and Marina Pascali. Everything is handmade from scratch, from the cube-shaped, pastel-hued necklaces to the polka-dot espresso cups and textile-imprinted dishes. Prices are reasonable, ranging from around €10 for an espresso cup and saucer to around €35 for a teapot.

Limonè
FOOD & DRINKS

(Map p58; ☑081 29 94 29; www.limoncellodinapoli.it; Piazza San Gaetano 72; ☺11am-8.30pm; ⓂDante) For a take-home taste of Napoli, stock up on a few bottles of Limonè's homemade *limoncello* (lemon liqueur), made with organic lemons from the Campi Flegrei. For something a little sweeter, opt for the *crema di limone*, a gorgeous lemon liqueur made with milk. Other take-home treats include lemon pasta and risotto, lemon-infused chocolate, jars of rum-soaked *babà*, even lemon-infused grappa.

🏠 Toledo & Quartieri Spagnoli

Gay Odin
CHOCOLATE

(Map p58; ☑081 551 34 91; www.gay-odin.it; Via Toledo 427; ☺9.30am-8pm Mon-Sat, 10am-2pm Sun; ⓂDante) One of several branches around town, Gay Odin is famous for its delectable artisanal chocolates.

Talarico
FASHION & ACCESSORIES

(Map p68; ☑081 40 77 23; www.mariotalarico.it; Vico Due Porte a Toledo 4b; ☺8am-8pm Mon-Sat; ⓂToledo) Mario Talarico and his nephew have turned the humble umbrella into a work of art. Sought after by heads of state, each piece is a one-off, with mother-of-pearl buttons, a horn tip and a handle made from a single tree branch. While top-of-the-range pieces can fetch €500, there are more affordable options that will keep the budget-conscious singing in the rain.

🏠 Santa Lucia & Chiaia

Asad Ventrella:
Contemporastudio
JEWELLERY

(Map p74; ☑081 247 99 37; www.asadventrella.it; Via Crispi 50; ☺10am-1.30pm & 4-7.30pm Mon-Fri, 10am-1.30pm Sat; ⓂPiazza Amedeo) Asad Ventrella is one of Naples' most talented, respected names in jewellery design, producing statement-making wearables that are equally playful, experimental and stylish. The labyrinth is a recurring motif, as is Mediterranean mythology, underscoring objects that include rings, necklaces, bracelets and money clips. Quirkier pieces include a pasta-shaped necklace made of solid silver. These are whimsical, confident creations with a strong sense of place.

Mattana Design
JEWELLERY

(Map p74; ☑081 66 88 31; www.mattanadesign.com; Via Crispi 24; ☺10am-2pm & 4.30-7.30pm Mon-Sat; ⓂPiazza Amedeo) Pimp your fingers, wrists or neckline with Mattana's meticulously detailed creations for men and women. The studio's DNapoli line is especially intriguing, taking its inspiration ancient Neapolitan history, mythology and culture, whether it be sirens and saints, or traditional playing cards.

Livio De Simone
FASHION & ACCESSORIES

(Map p74; ☑081 764 38 27; www.liviodesimone.com; Via Domenico Morelli 17; ☺10am-1.30pm & 4.30-8pm Mon-Sat; ☒E6 to Piazza dei Martiri) The late Livio De Simone put Capri on the catwalk, dressing Audrey Hepburn and Jackie O in his bold, colourful creations. Inspired by the island, summer and the sea, his daughter, Benedetta, keeps the vision alive with the label's distinctive hand- and block-printed *robe chemesiers* (shirt dresses), frocks, suits, coats, and matching bags, purses, luggage tags, cushion covers and bowls.

Tramontano FASHION & ACCESSORIES
(Map p74; ☑ 081 41 48 37; www.tramontano.it; Via Chiaia 143-144; ☺ 10am-1.30pm & 4-8pm Mon-Sat, 10am-1.30pm & 4.30-8pm Sun; ⬚ E6 to Piazza dei Martiri) Tramontano has a solid rep for its exquisitely crafted, handmade Neapolitan leather goods. Fawn over elegant women's handbags, clutches and totes, as well as preppy-chic satchels and duffels for men. Tramontano also stocks handsome rolling luggage.

Bowinkel ANTIQUES
(Map p74; ☑ 081 764 07 39; www.bowinkel.it; Via Santa Lucia 25; ☺ 10am-1.30pm & 4-7.30pm Mon-Fri, to 1.30pm Sat; ⬚ 128, E6 to Via Santa Lucia) The city's finest vintage prints, photographs, paintings and frames. If you can't find what you're looking for here, check out its sister branch (☑ 081 764 82 30) at Via Calabritto 1, where you're just as likely to stumble across a Liberty-era fan or a model of a long-gone tram. Perfect if shopping for someone who has it all.

🏠 Vomero

Riot Laundry Bar FASHION & ACCESSORIES
(Map p78; ☑ 081 1957 8491; www.facebook.com/riotlaundrybarandclothes; Via Kerbaker 19; ☺ shop 10am-2pm & 4-8pm Mon-Thu, to midnight Fri, 10am-midnight Sat, cafe/bar 8am-2am Mon-Thu & Sun, to 4am Fri & Sat; Ⓜ Vanvitelli, ⬚ Centrale to Piazza Fuga) Revamp your wardrobe or record collection *and* kick back with a coffee or beer at this split-level shop-and-bar. Street-smart threads include indie names like Wood Wood, Libertine and local denim label Derriere Heritage. The latter offers custom-ised jeans, with your choice of cut, wash and detailing. The process takes about a week (shipping available), with a pair costing be-tween €90 and €150.

De Paola Cameos JEWELLERY
(Map p78; ☑ 081 1916 8284; www.cameofactorydepaola.it; Via Annibale Caccavello 69; ☺ 9.30am-8pm Mon-Sat, to 1.30pm Sun; Ⓜ Vanvitelli, ⬚ Montesanto to Morghen) Head to this corner workshop for a beautiful range of finely carved cameos, including pieces made on-site. Small pendants start from around €50. Other options include classic coral necklaces, earrings, pendants and bracelets. Wearables aside, you'll also find a small se-lection of whimsical porcelain from Naples' renowned Capodimonte.

🏠 La Sanità & Capodimonte

★ Omega FASHION & ACCESSORIES
(Map p80; ☑ 081 29 90 41; www.omegasrl.com; Via Stella 12; ☺ 8.30am-6pm Mon-Fri; Ⓜ Piazza Cavour, Museo) Despite hiding away on the 3rd floor of a nondescript building, Paris, New York and Tokyo know all about this family-run glove factory, whose clients in-clude Dior and Hermes. Omega's men's and women's leather gloves are meticulously handcrafted using a traditional 25-step pro-cess, and best of all, they retail for a fraction of the price charged by the luxury fashion houses.

You can expect to pay between €30 and €110 for a pair of gloves, depending on the style. The workshop is now run by the fourth and fifth generations of the family: affable Mauro Squillace and his son Alberto. Mauro offers free 45-minute tours of the workshop and glove-making process if he's not busy, and no reservations are necessary to drop by the place, whether to shop or simply take a peek.

Vincenzo Oste Gioielli JEWELLERY
(Map p80; ☑ 349 4433422; www.vincenzooste.it; Via dei Cristallini 138; ☺ 8am-7.30pm Mon-Fri; Ⓜ Piazza Cavour, Museo) While the late Anni-bale Oste made a name from himself as a visionary sculptor and designer, son Vincen-zo wows aesthetes with his extraordinary jewellery design. Working predominantly in sterling silver, his pieces exude intense drama and energy, with sinuous, highly cre-ative forms that render rings, bracelets and earrings as wearable sculptures worthy of a gallery plinth.

Prices start at around €180 for a ring and €240 for a pair of earrings.

Cioccolato Mario Gallucci CHOCOLATE
(Map p80; ☑ 081 45 64 42; www.cioccolato napoli.com; Vico Lammatari 38; ☺ 8.30am-1pm & 2-7pm Mon-Fri, to 1pm Sat; ⬚ C51 to Piazza Sanità, Ⓜ Piazza Cavour, Museo) Hidden away down a Sanità side street, this vintage chocolatier has been ruining waistlines since 1890. Its selection of dark, milk and white chocolate pralines and truffles come in a few local shapes, including *tazzine di caffè* (coffee cups) and *cozze* (mussels). You might even find giant chocolate lemons or a chocolate *caffettiera* (coffee percolator), complete with edible *tazze* (cups).

❶ Information

EMERGENCY

Italy's country code	☎ 39
International access code	☎ 00
Ambulance	☎ 118
Police	☎ 112/113
Fire	☎ 115

TOURIST INFORMATION

Tourist Information Office (Map p58; ☎ 081 551 27 01; www.inaples.it; Piazza del Gesù Nuovo 7; ☻9am-5pm Mon-Sat, to 1pm Sun; Ⓜ Dante) In the *centro storico*.

Tourist Information Office (Map p74; ☎ 081 40 23 94; www.inaples.it; Via San Carlo 9; ☻9am-5pm Mon-Sat, to 1pm Sun; 🚇 R2 to Via San Carlo, Ⓜ Municipio) At Galleria Umberto I, directly opposite Teatro San Carlo.

❶ Getting There & Away

AIR

Naples International Airport (Capodichino) (☎ 081 789 62 59; www.aeroportodinapoli. it; Viale F Ruffo di Calabria), 7km northeast of the city centre, is southern Italy's main airport. It's served by a number of major airlines and low-cost carriers, including easyJet, which operates flights to Naples from London, Paris, Amsterdam, Vienna, Berlin and several other European cities.

BOAT

Fast ferries and hydrofoils for Capri, Ischia, Procida and Sorrento depart from Molo Beverello in front of Castel Nuovo; hydrofoils for Capri, Ischia and Procida also sail from Mergellina.

Ferries for Sicily, the Aeolian Islands and Sardinia sail from Molo Angioino (right beside Molo Beverello) and neighbouring Calata Porta di Massa.

BUS

Most national and international buses leave from **Metropark Napoli Centrale** (Map p58; ☎ 800 650006; Corso Arnaldo Lucci; Ⓜ Garibaldi), on the southern side of Napoli Centrale train station. The bus station is home to **Biglietteria Vecchione** (☎ 331 88969217; ☻6.30am-9.15pm Mon-Fri, to 7pm Sat, 7am-7pm Sun), a ticket agency selling national and international bus tickets.

Metropark Napoli Centrale serves numerous bus companies offering regional and interregional services, among them FlixBus (https://global.flixbus.com), CLP (www.clpbus.it), Marino (www.marinobus.it), Miccolis (www.miccolis-spa. it) and SAIS (www.saistrasporti.it). It also serves **Fiumicino Express** (☎ 391 3998081; www.fiumi cinoexpress.com), which runs to/from Rome's Fiumicino and Ciampino airports via Caserta.

The bus stop for SITA Sud (www.sitasud trasporti.it) services to the Amalfi Coast is just around the corner on Via Galileo Ferraris (in front of the hulking Istituto Nazionale della Previdenza Sociale office building).

CAR & MOTORCYCLE

Naples is on the north–south Autostrada del Sole, the A1 (north to Rome and Milan) and the A3 (south to Salerno and Reggio di Calabria).

Among other locations, the following carrental agencies have branches at Naples International Airport:

Avis (☎ 081 28 40 41; www.avisautonoleggio. it; Piazza Garibaldi 92, Starhotels Terminus; ☻8am-7.30pm Mon-Fri, 8.30am-4.30pm Sat, 9am-1pm Sun)

Europcar (☎ 081 780 56 43; www.europcar.it; ☻7.30am-11.30pm)

Hertz (☎ 081 20 28 60; www.hertz.it; Corso Arnaldo Lucci 171; ☻8.30am-1pm & 2.30-7pm Mon-Fri, 8.30am-1pm Sat)

Maggiore (☎ 081 28 78 58; www.maggiore.it; Napoli Centrale; ☻8.30am-7.30pm Mon-Fri, to 6pm Sat, to 12.30pm Sun)

For scooter rental, contact **Vespa Sprint** (☎ 081 764 34 52; http://vespasprint.it/noleggio-vespa-scooter-napoli; Via Santa Lucia 36, Naples; scooter hire per day from €60; ☻8am-8pm Mon-Sat, 10am-6pm Sun), in the city's Santa Lucia district.

TRAIN

Naples is southern Italy's rail hub and on the main Milan–Palermo line, with good connections to other Italian cities and towns.

The city's main train station is **Napoli Centrale** (Stazione Centrale; ☎ 081 554 31 88; Piazza Garibaldi), just east of the *centro storico*. From here, the national rail company Trenitalia (www.trenitalia.com) runs regular direct services to Rome (2nd class €13 to €48, 70 minutes to three hours, around 66 daily). High-speed private rail company **Italo** (☎ 892020; www.italotreno.it) also runs daily direct services to Rome (2nd class €15 to €40, 70 minutes, around 20 daily). Most Italo services stop at Roma Termini and Roma Tiburtina stations.

❶ Getting Around

Naples' city centre is relatively compact and best explored on foot. The city is also serviced by an affordable network of buses, funiculars and both metro and suburban trains.

BUS

ANM (☎ 800 639525; www.anm.it) operates city buses in Naples. There's no central bus station, but most buses pass through Piazza Garibaldi. Buses generally run from around 5.30am to about 11pm, depending on the route and day. Some routes do not run on Sunday. A small number of routes run through the night, marked with an 'N' before their route number.

Useful city routes include the following:

140 Santa Lucia to Posillipo (via Mergellina)

154 Port area to Chiaia (along Via Volta, Via Vespucci, Via Marina, Via Depretis, Via Acton, Via Morelli and Piazza Vittoria)

C51 Piazza Cavour to La Sanità (along Via Foria, Via Vergini, Via Sanità and Via Fontanelle)

E6 Piazza Trieste e Trento to Chiaia (along Via Monte di Dio, Via Santa Lucia, Via Morelli, Piazza dei Martiri and Via Filangieri)

R2 Napoli Centrale to Piazza Trento e Trieste (along Corso Umberto I and Piazza Municipio)

R4 Via Toledo to Capodimonte (via Piazza Dante and Via Santa Maria di Costantinopoli)

CAR & MOTORCYCLE

Nonresident vehicles are banned in much of central Naples, though there is no need for a car as a visitor.

FUNICULAR

Three services connect central Naples to Vomero, while a fourth connects Mergellina to Posillipo. All operate from 7am to 10pm daily. ANM transport tickets are valid on funicular services.

Funicolare Centrale (www.anm.it; ◷7am-10pm) Travels from Piazzetta Augusteo to Piazza Fuga.

Funicolare di Chiaia (www.anm.it; ◷7am-10pm) Travels from Via del Parco Margherita to Via Domenico Cimarosa.

Funicolare di Montesanto (www.anm.it; ◷7am-10pm) Travels from Piazza Montesanto to Via Raffaele Morghen.

Funicolare di Mergellina (www.anm.it; ◷7am-10pm) Connects the waterfront at Via Mergellina with Via Manzoni.

TAXI

Official taxis are white and metered. Always ensure the meter is running.

The minimum starting fare is €3.50 (€6.50 on Sunday), with a baffling range of additional charges, all of which are listed at www.taxinapoli.it/tariffe. These extras include the following:

➡ €1.50 for a radio taxi call

➡ €4 for an airport run

➡ €5 for trips starting at the airport and €0.50 per piece of luggage in the boot (trunk). Guide dogs, wheelchairs and strollers are carried free of charge.

There are taxi stands at most of the city's main piazzas.

Book a taxi by calling any of the following companies:

Consortaxi (☎ 081 22 22; www.consortaxi.com)

Radio Taxi Partenope (☎ 081 01 01; www.radiotaxilapartenope.it)

Taxi Napoli (☎ 081 88 88; www.taxinapoli.it)

TRAIN
Metro Line 1

Like city buses, **Metro Line 1** (Linea 1; www.anm.it) is operated by ANM.

➡ Trains run from Garibaldi (Napoli Centrale) to Vomero and the northern suburbs via the city centre.

➡ Useful stops include Duomo and Università (southern edge of the *centro storico*), Municipio (hydrofoil and ferry terminals), Toledo (Via Toledo and Quartieri Spagnoli), Dante (western edge of the *centro storico*) and Museo (National Archaeological Museum).

➡ Trains run from about 6am to around 11.30pm.

Metro Line 2

Metro Line 2 (Linea 2; www.trenitalia.com/tcom/Treni-Regionali/Campania) is operated by Italy's state-owned Ferrovie dello Stato (FS).

➡ Trains runs from Gianturco to Garibaldi (Napoli Centrale) and on to Pozzuoli.

➡ Useful stops include Piazza Cavour (La Sanità and northern edge of *centro storico*), Piazza Amedeo (Chiaia) and Mergellina (Mergellina ferry and hydrofoil terminal). Change for Line 1 at Garibaldi or Piazza Cavour (known as Museo on Line 1).

➡ Trains run from about 5.30am to around 11.30pm.

Circumvesuviana

Circumvesuviana (☎ 800 211388; www.eavsrl.it) trains (follow signs from Napoli Centrale station) run to Sorrento (€3.90, 68 minutes) via Ercolano (Herculaneum; €2.20, 17 minutes), Pompeii (€2.80, 36 minutes) and other towns along the coast. Trains run from about 6am to around 10pm.

Ferrovia Cumana

Ferrovia Cumana (☎ 800 21 13 88; www.eavsrl.it) trains run to Pozzuoli (€2.20, 22 minutes) and the Campi Flegrei. In Naples, Cumana trains depart from Stazione Cumana di Montesanto on Piazza Montesanto, 500m southwest of Piazza Dante. Trains run from around 5.30am to about 10pm.

The Baroque

Innately extravagant, effusive and loud, Naples found its soulmate in the baroque. As a booming metropolis, Naples was hungry for big, bold and bombastic – the baroque ensured it got it.

Reggia di Caserta (p70) **2.** Certosa e Museo di San Martino (p76)
Cappella di San Gennaro (p51)

Cappella Sansevero

Incredibly, Francesco Maria Russo's vivid vault fresco has remained untouched since its debut in 1749. Then again, the di Sangro family chapel (p55) is not short of jaw-dropping revelations, among them Giuseppe Sanmartino's *Cristo velato* sculpture.

Reggia di Caserta

Four courtyards, 1000-plus rooms, two dozen state apartments, a library, theatre and one of Europe's most ambitious landscaped gardens: Caserta's Unesco-listed royal palace (p70) made sure the baroque went out with a very loud bang.

Cappella di San Gennaro

Every patron saint deserves a little attention, and Naples' San Gennaro gets plenty in the chapel (p51) that houses his liquefying blood. From Cosimo Fanzago's sculptures to Giovanni Lanfranco's 'Paradise' fresco, it's a spiritual tour de force.

Certosa e Museo di San Martino

The Carthusian monks at this charterhouse (p76) commissioned the baroque's finest to pimp their church. Their prayers were answered with luscious sculptures, canvases, and inlaid stone and wood.

Farmacia Storica degli Incurabili

Diva of Italian drugstores, the Farmacia Storica degli Incurabili (p62) is the country's most faithfully preserved 18th-century pharmacy, not to mention a high-inducing feast of walnut cabinets, majolica ceramics and brooding oil brushstrokes.

DIEGO FIORE/SHUTTERSTOCK ©

1. Tempio di Cerere, Paestum (p203) 2. Casa di Nettuno e Anfitrite, Herculaneum (p109) 3. Pompeii ruins (p111) 4. Parco Archeologico di Baia, Campi Flegrei (p103)

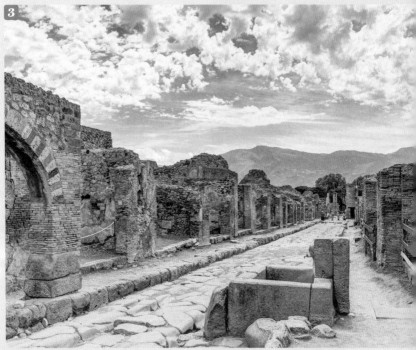

GREG ELMS/LONELY PLANET ©

Historical Riches

Few Italian regions can match Campania's historical legacy. Colonised by the ancient Greeks and loved by the Romans, it's a sun-drenched repository of A-list antiquities, from World Heritage wonders to lesser-known archaeological gems.

Paestum

Great Greek temples never go out of vogue and those at Paestum (p203) are among the greatest outside Greece itself. With the oldest structures stretching back to the 6th century BC, this place makes Rome's Colosseum feel positively modern.

Herculaneum

A bite-sized Pompeii, Herculaneum (p109) is even better preserved than its nearby rival. This is the place to delve into the details, from once-upon-a-time shop advertisements and furniture, to quirky mosaics and even an ancient security device.

Pompeii

Short of stepping into the Tardis, Pompeii (p111) is your best bet for a little time travel. Snap-locked in ash for centuries, its excavated streetscapes offer a tangible, 3D encounter with the ancients and their daily lives.

Subterranean Naples

Eerie aqueducts, mysterious burial crypts and ancient streetscapes: beneath Naples' hyperactive streets lies a wonderland of Graeco-Roman ruins. For a taste, head below the Complesso Monumentale di San Lorenzo Maggiore (p61) or follow the leader on a Napoli Sotterranea (p66) tour.

Campi Flegrei

The Phlegraean Fields simmer with ancient clues. Roam where emperors bathed at the Parco Archeologico di Baia (p103), sneak into a Roman engineering marvel at the Piscina Mirabilis, or spare a thought for doomed martyrs at the Anfiteatro Flavio (p102).

CAMPI FLEGREI

Stretching west of Posillipo Hill to the Tyrrhenian Sea, the oft-overlooked Campi Flegrei (Phlegrean Fields) counterbalances its ugly urban sprawl with steamy active craters, lush volcanic hillsides and priceless ancient ruins. While its Greek settlements are Italy's oldest, its Monte Nuovo is Europe's youngest mountain. Gateway to the region is the port town of Pozzuoli, home to archaeological must-sees and handy for ferries to Ischia and Procida.

ⓘ Getting There & Away

Metro Line 2 runs frequently from Naples to Bagnoli (€1.30) and Pozzuoli (€2.20) in the Campi Flegrei. Ferrovia Cumana (p97) commuter trains also run frequently between Naples, Bagnoli and Pozzuoli. In Naples, Cumana trains depart Stazione Cumana di Montesanto on Piazza Montesanto, 500m southwest of Piazza Dante. The Cumana line is also handy for Lucrino (€2.20, 29 minutes) and Fusaro (€2.80, 33 minutes).

EAV (☑ 800 211388; www.eavsrl.it) runs bus services throughout the Campi Flegrei, connecting Cumana trains to Bacoli and Cuma. That said, connections are often inconvenient and services unreliable. Beyond Pozzuoli, the easiest way to explore the Campi Flegrei is with a reputable local tour outfit such as Yellowsudmarine Food Art & Tours (p113).

Pozzuoli & Around

Pozzuoli is Naples' older, slightly calmer sibling. Founded around 530 BC by political exiles from the Aegean island of Samos, it's here that St Paul is said to have landed in AD 61, that San Gennaro was beheaded and that screen goddess Sophia Loren spent her childhood. The city is littered with ancient relics, from one of Italy's largest Roman arenas to subterranean taverns and graffiti-scrawled slave cells. Lively bars and restaurants dot the seafront and surrounding streets, the latter perfect spots to sample some of Campania's freshest local seafood.

◉ Sights

Rione Terra   HISTORIC SITE, RUIN
(Map p104; ☑ 081 1993 6286; www.cattedrale pozzuoli.it; Largo Sedile di Porto; archaeological area adult/reduced €5/2.50; ⊙ Duomo 10am-noon & 5.30-7.30pm Sat, 10.30am-1pm & 5.30-7.30pm Sun, archaeological area 9am-4.30pm Sat & Sun; Ⓜ Pozzuoli, Ⓡ Cumana to Pozzuoli) Rione Terra is Pozzuoli's oldest quarter and its ancient acropolis. The original 2nd-century-BC temple to Jupiter, Juno and Minerva was replaced by a temple to Augustus in the 1st century. The latter's marble columns now form part of the 17th-century Duomo, home to 13 paintings by 17th-century greats including Artemisia Gentileschi, Giovanni Lanfranco and Jusepe De Ribera. Below the current cluster of buildings is a trove of an ancient ruins.

Dating back to when Pozzuoli was the ancient port of Puteoli, the ruins include the *decumanus maximus* (main street), flanked by ancient taverns, millers' shops (complete with intact grindstones) and graffiti written by the poet Catallus in a slaves' cell. Archaeologists made the startling find after volcanic activity in the 1970s forced a mass evacuation of the quarter.

Anfiteatro Flavio   RUINS
(Map p104; ☑ 848 80 02 88; Corso Nicola Terra cciano 75; adult/reduced €4/2; ⊙ 9am-1hr before sunset Wed-Mon; Ⓜ Pozzuoli, Ⓡ Cumana to Pozzuoli) Back in its ancient heyday, Italy's third-largest amphitheatre – desired by Nero, and completed by Vespasian from AD 69 to 79 – could hold over 20,000 spectators and was occasionally flooded for mock naval battles. Its best-preserved remains lie under the main arena. Wander among the fallen columns and get your head around the complex mechanics involved in hoisting caged wild beasts up to their waiting victims through the overhead 'skylights'.

Tempio di Serapide   RUINS
(Map p104; Via Serapide; ⊙ 24hr; Ⓜ Pozzuoli, Ⓡ Cumana to Pozzuoli) Just east of the port, sunken in a leafy piazza, sits the Tempio di Serapide, which can be viewed from the street but not visited. Despite its name, it wasn't a temple at all but an ancient *macellum* (town market) – the site is named after a statue of the Egyptian god Serapis found here in 1750. Its toilets (at either side of the eastern apse) are considered works of ancient ingenuity.

Monte Nuovo   PARK
(New Mountain; Map p104; ☑ 081 804 14 62; Via Virgilio; ⊙ 9am-1hr before sunset Mon-Sun, to 1pm Sun; Ⓡ Cumana to Arco Felice) At 8pm on 29 September 1538, a crack appeared in the earth near the ancient Roman settlement of Tripergole, violently spewing out a concoction of pumice, fire and smoke over six days. By the end of the week, Pozzuoli had a new 134m-tall neighbour. Today, Europe's newest

mountain is a lush and peaceful nature reserve, its shady sea-view slopes the perfect spot for a picnic.

Eating

Exytus Caffè
CAFE €

(Map p104; ☑081 526 70 90; Corso della Repubblica 126; cornetti €0.80; ⊙7.30am-2am; Ⓜ Pozzuoli, Ⓡ Cumana to Pozzuoli) It might just be a tiny hole-in-the-wall (OK, technically, there are two holes in the wall), but Exytus is a street cafe with a big reputation. Join the curbside crowd for espresso with perfect *schiuma zuccherata* (sugared froth), best enjoyed with a scrumptious *cornetto* (croissant); we have a crush on the *crema e amarena* (custard-and-cherry) combo.

Pizzaló
PIZZA, NEAPOLITAN €€

(Map p104; ☑081 658 75 66; Corso Umberto I 17/19; meals €30; ⊙noon-3.30pm & 7pm-midnight; ☎; Ⓜ Pozzuoli, Ⓡ Cumana to Pozzuoli) Facing Pozzuoli's popular esplanade, upbeat restaurant-pizzeria Pizzaló serves decent pizzas, as well as Neapolitan dishes with unexpected twists; *parmigiana di melanzane* (aubergine parmigiana) made with squid, or *paccheri alla genovese* (tube-shaped pasta with slow-cooked onion) laced with seafood. From extended families to local Kardashian wannabes, the outdoor tables are highly coveted on sunny days.

Lucrino, Baia & Bacoli

This string of towns spreads west from Pozzuoli along a built-up and inspiring coastal road. First up is Lucrino, where you'll find peaceful Lago d'Averno (the mythical entrance to hell) and a famous thermal spa centre. A further 3km southwest, Baia takes its name from Baios, a shipmate of Ulysses' who died and was buried here. A glamorous Roman holiday resort with a sordid reputation, the ancient town is now mostly under water, though evocative ruins and a recently expanded archaeological museum help kickstart the imagination. A further 4km south is the sleepy fishing town of Bacoli, home to the magical Piscina Mirabilis.

◉ Sights & Activities

Parco Archeologico di Baia
RUINS

(Map p104; ☑081 868 75 92; www.coopculture. it; Via Sella di Baia, Baia; adult/reduced €4/2;

⊙9am-8pm Tue-Sun May-Aug, reduced hours rest of year; Ⓡ EAV to Baia, Ⓡ Cumana to Fusaro) In Roman times, these 1st-century-BC ruins were part of a sprawling palace and spa complex. Emperors would entertain themselves and their guests in a series of lavishly decorated thermal baths that descended to the sea. Among the surviving snippets are exquisite floor mosaics, a beautifully stuccoed *balneum* (bathroom), an outdoor theatre and the impressive **Tempio di Mercurio**, its oculus-punctured dome predating Rome's Pantheon. The dome once covered a *frigidarium* (cold bath), located approximately 7m below the current water level.

To get here on public transport, catch the Cumana train to Fusaro station and walk 150m north to Via Fusaro. From here, the site is a 900m walk east along Via Fusaro. Alternatively, from Via Fusaro, you can catch a Monte di Procida–bound EAV bus to the site (services run roughly every 20 minutes Monday to Saturday, with reduced services on Sunday). This bus can also be caught in central Naples, at Piazza Municipio or Piazza Vittoria.

Museo Archeologico dei Campi Flegrei
MUSEUM, CASTLE

(Archaeological Museum of the Campi Flegrei; Map p104; ☑081 523 37 97; www.coopculture.it; Via Castello 39, Bacoli; adult/reduced €4/2; ⊙9am-2.30pm Tue-Sun, last entry 1pm; Ⓡ EAV to Baia) This usually crowd-free museum occupies the commanding Castello di Baia, built in the late 15th century by the Aragonese as a defence against possible French invasion. Later enlarged by Spanish viceroy Don Pedro de Toledo, it served as a military orphanage for most of the 20th century. Today, it's

---

ⓘ BEFORE YOU EXPLORE

⋯⋯⋯⋯⋯⋯⋯⋯⋯⋯⋯⋯⋯⋯⋯

The Campi Flegrei offers a good-value **combined ticket**. Valid for two days, it includes entry to the Anfiteatro Flavio, Parco Archeologico di Baia, Museo Archeologico dei Campi Flegrei and Parco Archeologico di Cuma (p83). The ticket costs €8 (€4 for EU citizens aged 18 to 24) and can be purchased at any of the four sights. Keep in mind that the Parco Archeologico di Baia and Museo Archeologico dei Campi Flegrei are closed on Monday, while the Anfiteatro Flavio is closed on Tuesday.

Campi Flegrei

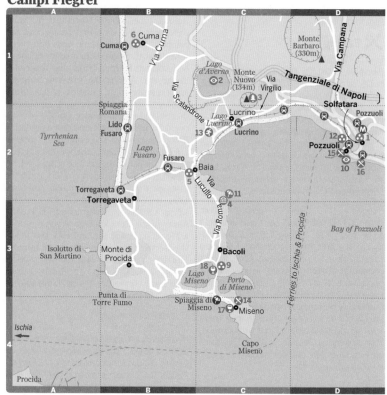

Campi Flegrei

home to an interesting collection of local archaeological treasures.

These include items from the area's original Greek settlement, as well as arte-facts from Pozzuoli's Rione Terra. Due to funding and management issues, access to various parts of the collection are notoriously changeable; on our last visit, both the

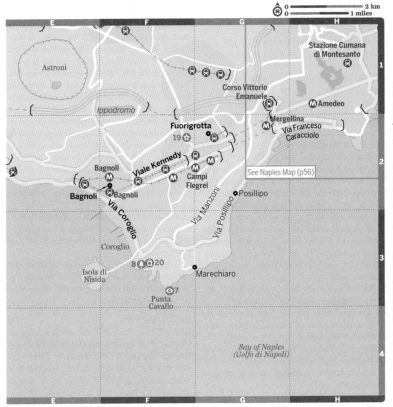

museum's *nymphaeum* (shrine to the water nymph, dredged up from underwater Baiae) and a bronze equestrian statue of the Emperor Domitian were off limits.

Spiaggia del Castello
BEACH

(Castle Beach; Map p104; ☑ 333 2629253; www. spiaggiacastellodibaia.it; ☑ EAV to Baia) Right below the Castello di Baia sits the wonderful Castle Beach. A sandy double-sided affair, it's only accessible by boat (adult/child return from €3/1.50) from a nearby jetty. To reach the jetty, catch the EAV bus to Baia and get off outside the FIART factory just south of town. Walk a further 250m south and turn left into the driveway beside the green gate at the curve.

At the end sits the car park and jetty, where you can hire a deckchair (€5/6 weekdays/weekends) or umbrella (€5/6) for convenient waterside sunning. Avoid the weekend summer crowds by coming earlier in the week.

Lago d'Averno
LAKE, RUIN

(Lake Averno; Map p104; Via Lucrino Averno, Lucrino; ☑ Cumana to Lucrino) In Virgil's *Aeneid,* it is from Lago d'Averno that Aeneas descends into the underworld. It's hard to imagine hell in such a bucolic setting, where old vineyards and citrus groves fringe the ancient crater. A popular walking track now circles the perimeter of the lake, located an easy 1km walk north of Lucrino train station.

The lake's name stems from the Greek word άορνος, meaning 'without birds': according to legend, birds who flew over the lake would fall out of the sky. A likely explanation for this phenomenon was the release of poisonous volcanic gases from the lake's fumaroles. While it may have been unlucky for feathered critters, Lago d'Averno proved useful to Roman general Marcus Vipsanius Agrippa, who in 37 BC linked it to nearby Lago Lucrino and the sea, turning hell's portal into a strategic naval dockyard. The battleships may have gone, but the lakeside ruins of the **Tempio di Apollo** (Temple of Apollo) remain. Built during the reign of Hadrian in the 2nd century AD, this thermal complex once sported a domed roof almost the size of the Pantheon's in Rome. Alas, only four great arched windows survive.

Terme Stufe di Nerone   SPA

(Map p104; ☑ 081 868 80 06; www.termestufedi nerone.it; Via Stufe di Nerone 37, Bacoli; day entry €30, 50min massage from €40; ⊙ 8am-8pm daily Jun-Aug, 8am-8pm Mon, Wed & Sat, to 11pm Tue, Thu & Fri, to 6pm Sun rest of year; ☒ Cumana to Lucrino) Your body will thank you after a trip to this verdant thermal-spa complex. Built on the site of an ancient Roman prototype (spot the remnants in the bar), its steamy grottoes, mineral baths and pools are a soothing antidote to Naples' muscle-tensing energy. Day passes must be booked via the website, where you can also book beauty treatments and massages.

Book treatments at least two days in advance. Swimming caps are obligatory for use of the pools and can be purchased (along with a towel) for €8. From Lucrino train station, walk 500m southwest along Via Miliscola before turning right into Via Stufe di Nerone. The entrance is 200m ahead. If you have your own wheels, on-site parking costs €2.50.

STADIO SAN PAOLO

Naples' football team, Napoli, is the fourth most supported in Italy after Juventus, AC Milan and Inter Milan, and watching it play at **Stadio San Paolo** (Map p104; Piazzale Vincenzo Tecchio; Ⓜ Napoli Campi Flegrei), the country's third-largest stadium, is a rush. The season runs from late August to late May; seats cost from around €20 to €100. Tickets are available from selected tobacconists, the agency inside Naples' **Feltrinelli** (Map p74; ☑ 199 15 11 73; www.lafeltrinelli.it; Via Santa Caterina 23; ⊙ 9am-9pm; ☒ E6 to Piazza dei Martiri), or **Box Office** (Map p68; ☑ 081 551 91 88; www.boxofficenapoli.it; Galleria Umberto I 17; ⊙ 9.30am-8pm Mon-Fri, 10am-1.30pm & 4.30-8pm Sat; ☒ R2 to Piazza Trieste e Trento, Ⓜ Municipio); bring photo ID.

✕ Eating & Drinking

★ Capo Blu   ITALIAN €€

(Map p104; ☑ 081 523 61 22; Via Sacello di Miseno 122, Miseno; meals €25-35; ⊙ 8pm-midnight Tue-Sun Jun-Aug, 8pm-midnight Tue-Sat & 1-4pm Sun rest of the year; ☎; ☒ Cumana to Torregavata, then EAV bus to Miseno) Decked out in model boats and local artwork, casual, affable Capo Blu serves up antipasti worthy of a fine-dining menu. The multicourse *assaggio di antipasti* (antipasto tastings) is a veritable meal, its ever-changing repertoire including anything from white polenta paired with sea snails and *papacelle* (Neapolitan peppers) salsa, to *sfogliatina* made with buffalo ricotta, orange-marinated anchovies, artichoke and mint.

Try to leave room for dessert, whose seasonal options might include cheesecake with mandarin sauce made with fruit from the garden.

Book ahead and request a table in the mosaic-graced *sala intima* (intimate dining room) or, in the summer, on the *terrazzino* (small outdoor terrace).

Beach Brothers   BAR

(Map p104; ☑ 081 523 31 83; Via Dragonara 22, Miseno; ⊙ 7.30am-3am daily May-Sep, 9am-7.30pm Thu-Tue Oct-Apr; ☎; ☒ Cumana to Torregavata, then EAV bus to Miseno) Right on Miseno's sandy beach, Beach Brothers is a blissful spot to kick back with a beer or *spritz* and watch the sun set lazily over Procida and Ischia. The young owners are passionate about good music, hosting contemporary Neapolitan singer-songwriters throughout the year. Sun loungers (€5 in peak season) are available for hire, with simple fish and seafood dishes for the peckish.

Beach Brothers is best experienced from September to May, when the place is free from peak-season crowds and traffic.

Roof & Sky   BAR

(Map p104; ☑ 333 2761608; www.astecoecielo.it; Via Miseno, Bacoli; ⊙ 7.30am-1am Tue-Thu & Sun, to 4am Fri & Sat; ☎; ☒ Cumana to Fusaro, then EAV bus to Bacoli) From May to September, the floating pontoon bar sets sail to the centre of Lago di Miseno (Miseno Lake) at around 9.30pm each night, with a shuttle-boat service providing access to and from the Bacoli lakeshore. At any time of the year, the place is a good bet for well-mixed cocktails, *taglieri* (platters) and decent *aperitivi* snacks.

PISCINA MIRABILIS

You'll need to book (by phone) at least two hours ahead to visit the world's largest Roman cistern, the Piscina Mirabilis (Marvellous Pool; Map p104; ☑ 333 6853278; Via Piscina Mirabile 27, Bacoli; donation appreciated; ⊗ 8am-4.30pm Tue-Sun Apr-Oct, to 3pm Tue-Sun Nov-Mar; ℝ Cumana to Fusaro, then EAV bus to Bacoli). It's well worth the effort to stand in this underrated ancient wonder. Bathed in an eerie light and featuring 48 soaring pillars and a barrel-vaulted ceiling, the Marvellous Pool is more 'subterranean cathedral' than 'giant water tank'. While there is no entrance fee, a small tip (around €3 per person) is appropriate.

The cistern was an Augustan-era creation, its 12,600-cu-metre water supply serving the military fleet at nearby Miseno. Fresh water flowed into the cistern from the Serino river aqueduct, which was then raised up to the terrace with hydraulic engines, exiting through doors in the central nave. Engineers still marvel at its technical sophistication.

The cistern is a short walk from Via Miseno in the centre of Bacoli; follow the signpost-ed steps to the left of Osteria Il Garum at Via Miseno 19.

GULF OF NAPLES

Buried for centuries beneath metres of volcanic debris, the archaeological sites scattered between Naples and Castellammare to the south are among the most spectacular Roman relics in existence. These include the ruins of Pompeii and the smaller yet better-preserved ruins of Herculaneum. Beyond them are lesser-known yet worthy archaeological wonders, including the lavishly frescoed villa of Oplontis. Their common nemesis, Mt Vesuvius, offers jaw-dropping summit views and bucolic hiking trails. To the west of Naples lie the sulphuric Campi Flegrei, speckled with Graeco-Roman legends, evocative yet little-visited ruins, and an impressive archaeological museum.

Herculaneum (Ercolano)

Ercolano is an uninspiring Neapolitan suburb that's home to one of Italy's best-preserved ancient sites: Herculaneum. A superbly conserved fishing town, the site is smaller and less daunting than Pompeii, allowing you to visit without the nagging feeling that you're bound to miss something.

◉ Sights

★ Ruins of
Herculaneum   ARCHAEOLOGICAL SITE
(☑ 081 777 70 08; http://ercolano.beniculturali
.it; Corso Resina 187, Ercolano; adult/reduced
€13/2; ⊗ 8.30am-7.30pm, last entry 6pm Apr-
Oct, 8.30am-5pm, last entry 3.30pm Nov-Mar; ℙ;
ℝ Circumvesuviana to Ercolano–Scavi) Herculaneum harbours a wealth of archaeologi-
cal finds, from ancient advertisements and stylish mosaics to carbonised furniture and terror-struck skeletons. Indeed, this superbly conserved Roman fishing town of 4000 inhabitants is easier to navigate than Pompeii, and can be explored with a map and highly recommended audio guide (€8).

To reach the ruins from Ercolano–Scavi train station, walk downhill to the very end of Via IV Novembre and through the archway across the street. The path leads down to the ticket office, which lies on your left. Ticket purchased, follow the walkway around to the actual entrance to the ruins, where you can also hire audio guides.

Herculaneum's fate runs parallel to that of Pompeii. Destroyed by an earthquake in AD 62, the AD 79 eruption of Mt Vesuvius saw it submerged in a 16m-thick sea of mud that essentially fossilised the city. This meant that even delicate items, such as furniture and clothing, were discovered remarkably well preserved. Tragically, the inhabitants didn't fare so well; thousands of people tried to escape by boat but were suffocated by the volcano's poisonous gases. Indeed, what appears to be a moat around the town is in fact the ancient shoreline. It was here in 1980 that archaeologists discovered some 300 skeletons, the remains of a crowd that had fled to the beach only to be overcome by the terrible heat of clouds surging down from Vesuvius.

The town itself was rediscovered in 1709 and amateur excavations were carried out intermittently until 1874, with many finds carted off to Naples to decorate the houses of the well-to-do or ending up in museums. Serious archaeological work began again in

Ruins of Herculaneum

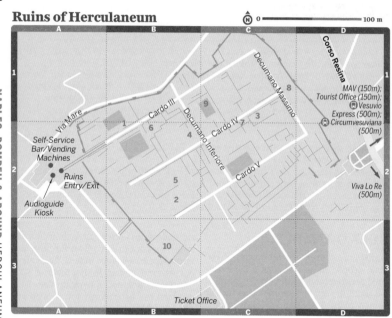

1927 and continues to this day; with much of the ancient site buried beneath modern Ercolano, it's slow going.

Note that at any given time some houses will invariably be shut for restoration.

➡ **Casa d'Argo**

(Argus House) This noble house would originally have opened onto Cardo II (as yet unearthed). Its porticoed garden opens onto a *triclinium* (dining room) and other residential rooms.

➡ **Casa dello Scheletro**

(House of the Skeleton) The modest Casa dello Scheletro features five styles of mosaic flooring, including a design of white arrows at the entrance to guide the most disoriented of guests. In the internal courtyard,

don't miss the skylight, complete with the remnants of an ancient security grill. Of the house's mythically themed wall mosaics, only the faded ones are originals; the others now reside in Naples' Museo Archeologico Nazionale (p52).

➡ **Terme Maschili**

(Men's Baths) The Terme Maschili were the men's section of the **Terme del Foro** (Forum Baths). Note the ancient latrine to the left of the entrance before you step into the *apodyterium* (changing room), complete with bench for waiting patrons and a nifty wall shelf for sandal and toga storage.

While those after a bracing soak would pop into the *frigidarium* (cold bath) to the left, the less stoic headed straight into the *tepadarium* (tepid bath) to the right. The sunken mosaic floor here is testament to the seismic activity preceding Mt Vesuvius' catastrophic eruption. Beyond this room lies the *caldarium* (hot bath), as well as an exercise area.

➡ **Decumano Massimo**

Herculaneum's ancient high street is lined with shops, and fragments of advertisements; look for the wall fresco advertising wines by colour code and price per weight. Note the one to the right of the Casa del Salone Nero. Further east along the street, a crucifix found in an upstairs room of the **Casa del Bicentenario** (Bicentenary House) provides possible evidence of a Christian presence in pre-Vesuvian Herculaneum.

➡ Casa del Bel Cortile

(House of the Beautiful Courtyard) The Casa del Bel Cortile is home to three of the 300 skeletons discovered on the ancient shore by archaeologists in 1980. Almost two millennia after the volcanic eruption, it's still poignant to see the forms of what are understood to be a mother, father and young child huddled together in the last, terrifying moments of their lives.

➡ Casa di Nettuno e Anfitrite

(House of Neptune & Amphitrite) This aristocratic pad takes its name from the extraordinary mosaic in the *triclinium* (dining room), which also features a mosaic-encrusted *nymphaeum* (fountain and bath as a shrine to the water nymph). The warm colours in which the sea god and his nymph bride are depicted hint at how lavish the original interior must have been.

➡ Casa del Tramezzo di Legno

(House of the Wooden Partition) Unusually, this house features two atria, which likely belonged to two separate dwellings that were merged in the 1st century AD. The most famous relic here is a wonderfully well-preserved wooden screen, separating the atrium from the *tablinum,* where the owner talked business with his clients. The second room off the left side of the atrium features the remains of an ancient bed.

➡ Casa dell'Atrio a Mosaico

(House of the Mosaic Atrium; ⊘ closed for restoration) An ancient mansion, the House of the Mosaic Atrium harbours extensive floor tilework, although time and nature have left the floor buckled and uneven. Particularly noteworthy is the black-and-white chessboard mosaic in the atrium.

➡ Casa dei Cervi

(House of the Stags) The Casa dei Cervi is an imposing example of a Roman noble family's house that, before the volcanic mud slide, boasted a seafront address. Constructed around a central courtyard, the two-storey villa contains murals and some beautiful still-life paintings. Waiting for you in the courtyard is a diminutive pair of marble deer assailed by dogs, and an engaging statue of a drunken, peeing Hercules.

➡ Terme Suburbane

(Suburban Baths) Marking Herculaneum's southernmost tip is the 1st-century-AD Terme Suburbane, one of the best-preserved Roman bath complexes in existence, with deep pools, stucco friezes and bas-reliefs looking down upon marble seats and floors. This is also one of the best places to observe the soaring volcanic deposits that smothered the ancient coastline.

MAV MUSEUM

(Museo Archeologico Virtuale; ☑ 081 777 68 43; www.museomav.com; Via IV Novembre 44; adult/reduced €10/8; ⊘ 9am-5.30pm daily Mar-May, 10am-6.30pm daily Jun-Sep, to 4pm Tue-Sun Oct-Feb; ⚹; ☒ Circumvesuviana to Ercolano–Scavi) Using computer-generated recreations, this 'virtual archaeological museum' brings ruins such as Pompeii's forum and Capri's Villa Jovis back to virtual life. Some of the displays are in Italian only. The short documentary gives an overview of the history of Mt Vesuvius and its infamous eruption in AD 79...in rather lacklustre 3D. The museum is on the main street linking Ercolano–Scavi train station to the ruins of Herculaneum.

Eating

Viva Lo Re NEAPOLITAN €€

(☑ 081 739 02 07; www.vivalore.it; Corso Resina 261, Ercolano; meals €32; ⊘ noon-3.30pm & 7.30-11.30pm Tue-Sat, noon-3.30pm Sun; ⛭) Whether you're after an inspired meal or a simple glass of vino, this refined yet relaxed *osteria* (casual tavern) is a solid choice. The wine list is extensive and impressive, while the menu offers competent, produce-driven regional cooking with subtle modern twists. For an appetite-piquing overview, start with the multitaste *antipasto Viva Lo Re.*

The *osteria* lies 500m southeast of the Herculaneum ruins on Corso Resina; dubbed the *Miglio d'Oro* (Golden Mile) for its once glorious stretch of 18th-century villas.

ⓘ Information

Tourist Office (☑ 081 788 13 75; Via IV Novembre 44; ⊘ 9am-2pm Mon-Fri & 2.30-5pm Tue & Thu; ☒ Circumvesuviana to Ercolano–Scavi) Ercolano's tourist office is in the same building as MAV, between the Circumvesuviana Ercolano–Scavi train station and the Herculaneum *scavi* (ruins).

❶ Getting There & Away

CAR & MOTORYCLE

If driving from Naples, the A3 runs southeast along the Bay of Naples. To reach the ruins of Herculaneum, exit at Ercolano Portico and follow the signs to car parks near the site. From Sorrento, head north along the SS145, which spills onto the A3.

TRAIN

If travelling by Circumvesuviana (p97) train (€2.20 from Naples or €2.90 from Sorrento), get off at Ercolano–Scavi station and walk 500m downhill to the ruins – follow the signs for the scavi down the main street, Via IV Novembre.

From mid-March to mid-October, tourist train Campania Express runs four times daily between Naples (Porta Nolana and Piazza Garibaldi Circumvesuviana stations) and Sorrento, stopping at Ercolano–Scavi and Pompei Scavi–Villa dei Misteri en route. One-day return tickets from Naples to Ercolano (€7) or from Sorrento to Ercolano (€11) can be purchased at the stations or online at EAV (p102).

Mt Vesuvius

Rising formidably beside the Bay of Naples, Mt Vesuvius forms part of the Campanian volcanic arch, a string of active, dormant and extinct volcanoes that include the Campi Flegrei's Solfatara and Monte Nuovo, and Ischia's Monte Epomeo. Infamous for its explosive Plinian eruptions and surrounding urban sprawl, it's also one of the world's most carefully monitored volcanoes. Another full-scale eruption would be catastrophic. More than half a million people live in the so-called 'red zone', the area most vulnerable to pyroclastic flows and crushing pyroclastic deposits in a major eruption. Yet, despite

---

OFF THE BEATEN TRACK

VESUVIUS ON HORSEBACK

For a different take on Mt Vesuvius, **Horse Riding Tour Naples** (☑345 8560306; www.horseridingnaples.com; guided tour €60) runs daily morning and afternoon horse-riding tours of the Parco Nazionale del Vesuvio (weather permitting). The tour, of around two to two-and-a-half hours on horseback, includes transfers to/from your hotel in Naples or to either Pompeii or Ercolano (Herculaneum). Helmet, saddle and guide are included.

---

government incentives to relocate, few residents are willing to leave.

◉ Sights

Mt Vesuvius   VOLCANO
(☑081 239 56 53; www.parconazionaledelvesuvio. it; crater adult/reduced €10/8; ⊙crater 9am-6pm Jul & Aug, to 5pm Apr-Jun & Sep, to 4pm Mar & Oct, to 3pm Nov-Feb, ticket office closes 1hr before crater) Since exploding into history in AD 79, Vesuvius has blown its top more than 30 times. What redeems this slumbering menace is the spectacular panorama from its crater, which takes in Naples, its world-famous bay, and part of the Apennine Mountains. Vesuvius is the focal point of the **Parco Nazionale del Vesuvio** (Vesuvius National Park), with nine nature walks around the volcano – download a simple map from the park's website. Horse Riding Tour Naples also runs daily horse-riding tours.

The mountain is widely believed to have been higher than it currently stands, claiming a single summit rising to about 3000m rather than the 1281m of today. Its violent outburst in AD 79 not only drowned Pompeii in pumice and pushed the coastline back several kilometres but also destroyed much of the mountain top, creating a huge caldera and two new peaks. The most destructive explosion after that of AD 79 was in 1631, while the most recent was in 1944.

❶ Getting There & Away

BUS

Vesuvius can be reached by bus from Pompeii and Ercolano.

The cheapest option is to catch the public EAV bus (p102) service, which departs from Piazza Anfiteatro and stops outside Pompei Scavi–Villa dei Misteri train station en route. Buses depart every 50 minutes from 8am to 3.30pm and take around 50 minutes to reach the summit car park. Once here, purchase your entry ticket to the summit area (adult/reduced €10/8) and follow the 860m gravel path up to the crater (roughly a 25-minute climb). In Pompeii, ignore any touts telling you that the public bus only runs in summer; they are merely trying to push private tours. Bus tickets cost €3.10 one way and can be purchased on board.

In Ercolano, private company **Vesuvio Express** (☑081 739 36 66; www.vesuvioexpress. it; Piazzale Stazione Circumvesuviana, Ercolano; return incl admission to summit €20; ⊙every 40min, 9.30am-5pm Jul & Aug, to 4pm Apr-Jun & Sep, to 2.10pm Oct-Mar) runs buses to the summit car park from Piazzale Stazione Circumvesuviana, outside Ercolano–Scavi train station. A word of warning: this company has received very mixed reviews, with numerous claims of unreliability from travellers.

When the weather is bad the summit path is shut and bus departures are suspended.

CAR & MOTORCYCLE
If travelling by car, exit the A3 at Ercolano Portico and follow signs for the Parco Nazionale del Vesuvio. From the summit car park (€5), a shuttle bus (return €2) reaches the ticket office and entry point further up the volcano.

Pompeii

Modern-day Pompeii (Pompei in Italian) may feel like a nondescript satellite of Naples, but it's here that you'll find Europe's most compelling archaeological site: the ruins of Pompeii. Sprawling and haunting, the site is a stark reminder of the destructive forces that lie deep inside Vesuvius.

⊙ Sights

★ **Ruins of Pompeii** ARCHAEOLOGICAL SITE
(☎ 081 857 53 47; www.pompeiisites.org; entrances at Porta Marina & Piazza Anfiteatro; adult/reduced €16/2; ⊙ 9am-7.30pm Mon-Fri, from 8.30am Sat & Sun, last entry 6pm Apr-Oct, 9am-5.30pm Mon-Fri, from 8.30am Sat & Sun, last entry 3.30pm Nov-Mar; ⊞ Circumvesuviana to Pompei Scavi–Villa dei Misteri) The ghostly ruins of ancient Pompeii make for one of the world's most engrossing archaeological experiences. Much of the site's value lies in the fact that the town wasn't simply blown away by Vesuvius in AD 79 but buried under a layer of *lapilli* (burning fragments of pumice stone). The result is a remarkably well-preserved slice of ancient life, where visitors can walk down Roman streets and snoop around millennia-old houses, temples, shops, cafes, amphitheatres and even a brothel.

The origins of Pompeii are uncertain, but it seems likely that it was founded in the 7th century BC by the Campanian Oscans. Over the next seven centuries, the city fell to the Greeks and the Samnites before becoming a Roman colony in 80 BC.

In AD 62, a mere 17 years before Vesuvius erupted, the city was struck by a major earthquake. Damage was widespread and much of the city's 20,000-strong population was evacuated. Fortunately, many had

not returned by the time Vesuvius blew, but 2000 men, women and children perished nevertheless.

After its catastrophic demise, Pompeii receded from the public eye until 1594, when the architect Domenico Fontana stumbled across the ruins while digging a canal. Exploration proper, however, didn't begin until 1748. Audio guides are a sensible investment (€8) and a good guidebook will also help – try *Pompeii,* published by Electa Napoli.

Maintenance work is ongoing, with new discoveries unearthed regularly.

➡ **Terme Suburbane**
Just outside ancient Pompeii's city walls, this 1st-century-BC bathhouse is famous for several erotic frescoes that scandalised the Vatican when they were revealed in 2001. The panels decorate what was once the *apodyterium* (changing room). The room leading to the colourfully frescoed *frigidarium* (cold bath) features fragments of stuccowork, as well as one of the few original roofs to survive at Pompeii. Beyond the *tepadarium* (tepid bath) and *caldarium* (hot bath) rooms are the remains of a heated outdoor swimming pool.

➡ **Tempio di Apollo**
(Temple of Apollo) The oldest and most important of Pompeii's religious buildings, the Tempio di Apollo largely dates from the 2nd century BC, including the striking columned portico. Fragments remain of an earlier version dating from the 6th century BC. The statues of Apollo and Diana (depicted as archers) on either side of the portico are copies; the originals are housed in Naples' Museo Archeologico Nazionale (p52).

➡ **Basilica**
The basilica was the 2nd-century-BC seat of Pompeii's law courts and exchange. The semicircular apses would later influence the design of early Christian churches.

➡ **Foro**
(Forum) A huge rectangle flanked by limestone columns, the *foro* was ancient Pompeii's main piazza, as well as the site of gladiatorial games before the Anfiteatro (p116) was constructed. The buildings surrounding the forum are testament to its role as the city's hub of civic, commercial, political and religious activity. At its northern end are the remains of the Tempio di Giove (Capitolium; p112), the heart of religious life in Pompeii.

Pompeii

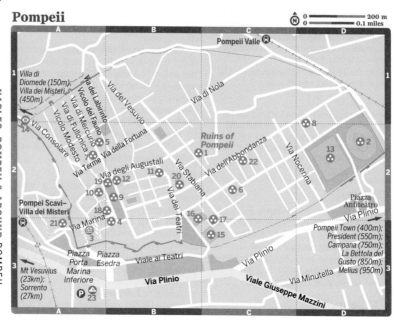

Pompeii

◎ Top Sights
1 Ruins of Pompeii	B2

◎ Sights
2 Anfiteatro	D2
3 Antiquarium	A3
4 Basilica	B3
5 Casa del Fauno	A2
6 Casa del Menandro	C2
7 Casa del Poeta Tragico	A2
8 Casa della Venere in Conchiglia	D1
9 Foro	B2
10 Granai del Foro	A2
11 Lupanare	B2
12 Macellum	B2
13 Palestra Grande	D2
14 Porta Ercolano	A1
15 Quadriportico dei Teatri	C3
16 Teatro Grande	B2
17 Teatro Piccolo	C3
18 Tempio di Apollo	B2
19 Tempio di Giove	B2
20 Terme Stabiane	B2
21 Terme Suburbane	A3
22 Via dell'Abbondanza	C2

⛺ Sleeping
23 Camping Spartacus	A3

➡ **Tempio di Giove**

(Temple of Jupiter) Built in the 2nd-century BC in honour of Jupiter, Juno and Minerva, the Tempio di Giove was a nexus of religious activity. Its surviving elements include fluted columns and the two triumphal arches that flanked the temple. A large-scale sculpture of Jupiter's head found here can be viewed at the Museo Archeologico Nazionale (p52).

➡ **Granai del Foro**

(Forum Granary) The Granai del Foro is now used to store hundreds of amphorae and a number of body casts that were made in the late 19th century by pouring plaster into the hollows left by disintegrated bodies. Among these casts is a pregnant slave; the belt around her waist would have displayed the name of her owner.

➡ **Macellum**

Dating from the 2nd century BC, the *macellum* was the city's main produce market. Note the 12 bases at the centre of the market, which were once stands for the timber poles that supported the market's conical roof. Surviving frescoes reveal some of the goods for sale, including prawns.

Casa del Poeta Tragico

(House of the Tragic Poet) The 1st-century AD Casa del Poeta Tragico features the world's first-known 'beware of the dog' – *cave canem* – warnings. Visible through a protective glass panel, the floor mosaic is one of the best preserved at the ruins. The house itself is featured in Edward Bulwer-Lytton's 1834 novel *The Last Days of Pompeii*.

Casa del Fauno

Covering an entire *insula* (city block) and claiming two atria at its front end (humbler homes had one), Pompeii's largest private house is named after the delicate bronze statue in the *impluvium* (shallow pool). It was here that early excavators found Pompeii's greatest mosaics, most of which are now in Naples' Museo Archeologico Nazionale (p52). Valuable on-site originals include a beautifully patterned marble floor.

Villa dei Misteri

This restored, 90-room villa is one of the most complete structures left standing in Pompeii. The **Dionysiac frieze**, the most important fresco still on-site, spans the walls of the large dining room. One of the biggest and most arresting paintings from the ancient world, it depicts the initiation of a bride-to-be into the cult of Dionysus, the Greek god of wine.

A farm for much of its life, the villa's vino-making area is still visible at the northern end.

Follow Via Consolare northwest out of the town through **Porta Ercolano**. Continue past **Villa di Diomede** and you'll come to Villa dei Misteri.

Lupanare

The explicit frescoes at this ancient brothel provided visual 'inspiration' for clients. Once ready, visitors would indulge in one of the five rooms on the ground floor, each complete with a stone bed and latrine. Scan the walls for declarations of love and hope, written in various languages by the brothel's workers.

Terme Stabiane

At this typical 2nd-century-BC bathing complex, bathers would enter from the vestibule, stop off in the vaulted *apodyterium* (changing room), and then pass through to the *tepidarium* (tepid bath) and *caldarium* (hot bath). Particularly impressive is the stuccoed vault in the men's changing room, complete with whimsical images of *putti* (winged babies) and nymphs.

ⓘ POMPEII TOURS

You'll almost certainly be approached by a guide outside the ticket office. Authorised guides wear identification tags.

Reputable tour operators include the following:

Yellowsudmarine Food Art & Tours (☑ 329 1010328; www.yellowsudmarine. com; 2hr Pompeii guided tour €150, plus entrance fee)

Walks of Italy (www.walksofitaly.com; 3hr Pompeii guided tour per person €59)

Via dell'Abbondanza

(Street of Abundance) The Via dell'Abbondanza was one of ancient Pompeii's main streets. The elevated stepping stones allowed people to cross the street without stepping into the waste that washed down the thoroughfare.

Teatro Grande

The 2nd-century-BC Teatro Grande was a huge 5000-seat theatre carved into the lava mass on which Pompeii was originally built. The site hosts the annual Pompeii Theatrum Mundi (p116), a summer season of classical theatre.

Quadriportico dei Teatri

Behind the Teatro Grande's stage, the porticoed Quadriportico dei Teatri was initially used as a place for the audience to stroll between acts and later as a barracks for gladiators.

Teatro Piccolo

(Odeon) The Teatro Piccolo was once an indoor theatre renowned for its acoustics.

Casa del Menandro

Better preserved than the larger Casa del Fauno), luxurious Casa del Menandro has an elegant peristyle (a colonnade-framed courtyard) beyond its beautifully frescoed atrium. On the peristyle's far right side a doorway leads to a private bathhouse, lavished with exquisite frescoes and mosaics. The central room off the far end of the peristyle features a striking fresco of the ancient Greek dramatist Menander, after whom the rediscovered villa was named.

Palestra Grande

Lithe ancients kept fit at the Palestra Grande, an athletics field with an impressive portico dating from the Augustan period. Used both as a training ground for gladiators and as a meeting centre for youth associations, its

Tragedy in Pompeii

24 AUGUST AD 79

8am Buildings including the ❶ **Terme Suburbane** and the ❷ **Foro** are still undergoing repair after an earthquake in AD 63 caused significant damage to the city. Despite violent earth tremors overnight, residents have little idea of the catastrophe that lies ahead.

Midday Peckish locals pour into the ❸ **Thermopolium di Vetutius Placidus**. The lustful slip into the ❹ **Lupanare**, and gladiators practise for the evening's planned games at the ❺ **Anfiteatro**. A massive boom heralds the eruption. Shocked onlookers witness a dark cloud of volcanic matter shoot some 14km above the crater.

3pm–5pm Lapilli (burning pumice stone) rains down on Pompeii. Terrified locals begin to flee; others take shelter. Within two hours, the plume is 25km high and the sky has darkened. Roofs collapse under the weight of the debris, burying those inside.

25 AUGUST AD 79

Midnight Mudflows bury the town of Herculaneum. Lapilli and ash continue to rain down on Pompeii, bursting through buildings and suffocating those taking refuge within.

4am–8am Ash and gas avalanches hit Herculaneum. Subsequent surges smother Pompeii, killing all remaining residents, including those in the ❻ **Orto dei Fuggiaschi**. The volcanic 'blanket' will safeguard frescoed treasures like the ❼ **Casa del Menandro** and ❽ **Villa dei Misteri** for almost two millennia.

TOP TIPS

➡ Visit in the afternoon.
➡ Allow three hours.
➡ Wear comfortable shoes and a hat.
➡ Bring drinking water.
➡ Don't use flash photography.

Terme Suburbane
The *laconicum* (sauna), *caldarium* (hot bath) and large, heated swimming pool weren't the only sources of heat here; scan the walls of this suburban bathhouse for some of the city's raunchiest frescoes.

Villa di Diomede

Casa del Poeta Tragico

Porta Ercolano

Casa del Fauno

Basilica

Tempio di Apollo

Porta Marina

Terme del Foro

Macellum

Teatro Grande

Quadriportico dei Teatri

Porta di Stabia

Teatro Piccolo

Foro
An ancient Times Square of sorts, the forum sits at the intersection of Pompeii's main streets and was closed to traffic in the 1st century AD. The plinths on the southern edge featured statues of the imperial family.

Villa dei Misteri
Home to the world-famous *Dionysiac Frieze* fresco. Other highlights at this villa include *trompe l'oeil* wall decorations in the *cubiculum* (bedroom) and Egyptian-themed artwork in the *tablinum* (reception).

Lupanare
The prostitutes at this brothel were often slaves of Greek or Asian origin. Mattresses once covered the stone beds and the names engraved in the walls are possibly those of the workers and their clients.

Thermopolium di Vetutius Placidus
The counter at this ancient snack bar once held urns filled with hot food. The *lararium* (household shrine) on the back wall depicts Dionysus (the god of wine) and Mercury (the god of profit and commerce).

Casa dei Vettii

Porta del Vesuvio

EYEWITNESS ACCOUNT

Pliny the Younger (AD 61–c 112) gives a gripping, first-hand account of the catastrophe in his letters to Tacitus (AD 56–117).

Porta di Nola

Casa della Venere in Conchiglia

Porta di Sarno

Tempio di Iside

3

7

6

Grande Palestra

5

Orto dei Fuggiaschi
The Garden of the Fugitives showcases the plaster moulds of 13 locals seeking refuge during Vesuvius' eruption – the largest number of victims found in any one area. The huddled bodies make for a moving scene.

Anfiteatro
Magistrates, local senators and the games' sponsors and organisers enjoyed front-row seating at this veteran amphitheatre, home to gladiatorial battles and the odd riot. The parapet circling the stadium featured paintings of combat, victory celebrations and hunting scenes.

Casa del Menandro
This dwelling most likely belonged to the family of Poppaea Sabina, Nero's second wife. A room to the left of the atrium features Trojan War paintings and a polychrome mosaic of pygmies rowing down the Nile.

huge, portico-flanked courtyard includes the remains of a swimming pool.

➡ **Anfiteatro**

(Amphitheatre) Gladiatorial battles thrilled up to 20,000 spectators at the grassy *anfiteatro*. Built in 70 BC, it's the oldest known Roman amphitheatre in existence. In 59 AD, the venue witnessed violent clashes between spectators from Pompeii and Nucera, documented in a fresco now found in Naples' Museo Archeologico Nazionale (p52).

➡ **Casa della Venere in Conchiglia**

(House of the Venus Marina, House of Venus in a Shell) Casa della Venere in Conchiglia harbours a lovely peristyle looking onto a small, manicured garden. It's here in the garden that you'll find the large, striking Venus fresco, after which the house is named. Venus – whose hairstyle in this depiction reflects the style popular during Emperor Nero's reign – was the city's patron goddess.

Antiquarium   MUSEUM

Pompeii's small museum hosts rotating exhibitions showcasing the site's archaeological finds and exploring various aspects of ancient Roman culture. The space also includes an impressive multimedia presentation that digitally reconstructs a number of ancient Pompeii's buildings, making it a helpful stop before roaming the ruins themselves. The building also houses the site's bookshop.

🎭 Festivals & Events

Pompeii Theatrum Mundi   THEATRE

(www.teatrostabilenapoli.it/pompeii-theatrum-mundi; ☉ Jun-Jul) Pompeii's ancient Teatro Grande is the venue for this acclaimed summertime season of classical theatre, performed by Naples' Teatro Stabile.

🍴 Eating & Drinking

Melius   NEAPOLITAN €

(☑ 081 850 25 98; www.salumeriamelius.com; Via Lepanto 156-160; cheese/cured-meat platter €12, meals around €25; ☉ 9am-11pm Tue-Sat, to 3pm Sun; 🚊 FS to Pompei, Circumvesuviana to Pompei Scavi–Villa dei Misteri) Stop by this luscious gourmet deli to revel in the taste of Campania. There's a vibrant in-house restaurant where you can sit down to local delicacies such as fresh *mozzarella di bufala* (buffalo mozzarella), Graniano pasta, smoked Cilento salamis, and anchovies from Cetara, or you can buy to take away.

La Bettola del Gusto   ITALIAN €€

(☑ 081 863 78 11; www.labettoladelgusto.it; Via Sacra 48; meals €25-30, degustation menu €35; ☉ 12.30-3.30pm & 7.30-11pm Tue-Sun; 🕿; 🚊 FS to Pompei, Circumvesuviana to Pompei Scavi–Villa dei Misteri) Inspired by their mother Rosa's cooking, twins Alberto and Vincenzo Fortunato are the force behind this warm, good-value restaurant. The kitchen revels in all things artisanal, whether it be the *provolone del Monaco* or vegetables from the family's own patch. Savour thoughtful dishes like seared prawns wrapped in crunchy Irpinia *guanciale* (cured pork jowl).

★President   CAMPANIAN €€€

(☑ 081 850 72 45; www.ristorantepresident.it; Piazza Schettini 12; meals €80, tasting menus €80-120; ☉ noon-3.30pm & 7pm-late Tue-Sun; 🚊 FS to Pompei, Circumvesuviana to Pompei Scavi–Villa dei Misteri) At the helm of this Michelin-starred standout is charming owner-chef Paolo Gramaglia, whose passion for local produce, history and culinary whimsy translates into bread made to ancient Roman recipes, yellowtail carpaccio with bitter orange and citrus zest, lemon emulsion and buffalo mozzarella, or impeccably glazed duck breast lifted by vinegar cherries, orange sauce and nasturtium.

The menu's creative and visual brilliance is matched by sommelier Laila Buondonno's swoon-inducing wine list, which features around 600 drops from esteemed and lesser-known Italian winemakers; best of all, the staff are happy to serve any bottle to the value of €100 by the glass.

A word of warning: if you plan on catching a *treno regionale* (regional train) back to Naples from nearby Pompei station (a closer, more convenient option than the Pompei Scavi–Villa dei Misteri station on the Circumvesuviana train line), check train times first as the last service from Pompei can depart as early as 9.53pm.

Campana   COFFEE

(☑ 081 1966 4530; www.facebook.com/campana bottega; Via Sacra 44; ☉ 7.30am-10.30pm Tue-Fri, to 11.30pm Sat & Sun; 🚊 FS to Pompei, Circumvesuviana to Pompei Scavi–Villa dei Misteri) Friendly, laid-back Campana is Campania's first speciality-coffee roastery, the passion project of young maverick roaster Paola Campana. Sip and slurp from a rotating cast of single origins, or try the intriguing house blend, made with no fewer than six single origins. Brewing options include V60, Aeropress,

OFF THE BEATEN TRACK

VINTAGE VILLAS

Buried beneath the unappealing streets of Torre Annunziata, Oplontis (☎081 857 53 47; www.pompeiisites.org; Via dei Sepolcri, Torre Annunziata; adult/reduced incl Boscoreale €7/2; ☉8.30am-7.30pm, last entry 6pm Apr-Oct, 8.30am-5pm, last entry 3.30pm Nov-Mar; ⊠Circumvesuviana to Torre Annunziata) was once a blue-ribbon seafront suburb under the administrative control of Pompeii. First discovered in the 18th century, only two of its houses have been unearthed, and only one, Villa Poppaea, is open to the public. This villa is a magnificent example of an *otium* villa (a residential building used for rest and recreation), thought to have belonged to Sabina Poppaea, Nero's second wife. Particularly outstanding are the richly coloured 1st-century wall paintings in the *triclinium* (dining room) and *calidarium* (hot bath) in the west wing. Marking the villa's eastern border is a garden with an envy-inducing swimming pool (17m by 61m). The villa is a straightforward 300m walk south from Torre Annunziata Circumvesuviana train station along Via Sepolcri.

South of Oplontis, Stabiae (☎081 857 53 47; www.pompeiisites.org; Via Passeggiata Archeologica, Castellammare di Stabia; ☉8.30am-7.30pm, last entry 6pm Apr-Oct, 8.30am-5pm, last entry 3.30pm Nov-Mar; ⊠Circumvesuviana to Via Nocera) FREE stood on the slopes of the Varano hill overlooking what was then the sea and is now modern Castellammare di Stabia. Here at Stabiae you can visit two villas: the 1st-century-BC Villa Arianna and the larger Villa San Marco, said to measure more than 11,000 sq metres. Neither is in mint condition, but the frescoes in Villa Arianna suggest that it must once have been quite something. Stabiae is a 1.1km walk south of Via Nocera Circumvesuviana station.

Some 3km north of Pompeii, the archaeological site of Boscoreale (☎081 857 53 47; www.pompeiisites.org; Via Settetermini, Boscoreale; adult/reduced incl Oplontis €7/2; ☉8.30am-7.30pm, last entry 6pm Apr-Oct, 8.30am-6.30pm, last entry 5pm Nov-Mar; ⊠Circumvesuviana to Villa Regina–Antiquarium) consists of a rustic country villa dating back to the 1st century BC, and a fascinating antiquarium showcasing artefacts from Pompeii, Herculaneum and the surrounding region. Among the more unusual items on display are shreds of Roman fabric, eggshells from Pompeii and a carbonised loaf of bread. To reach the site on public transport, take the Circumvesuviana train to Villa Regina–Antiquarium station. From the station, it's an easy 700m walk to the ruins – head north along Via Settetermini, then turn left into Viale Villa Regina. The route is signposted.

Oplontis and Boscoreale are covered by a single ticket (adult/reduced €7/4). The sites are also covered by a three-sites combination ticket (adult/reduced €18/10), which also includes Pompeii. Admission to Stabiae is currently free.

Chemex, syphon and cold brew, with just good ol' espresso for the old-schoolers.

❶ Getting There & Away

CAR & MOTORCYCLE

If driving from Naples, head southeast on the A3, using the Pompei exit and following the signs to Pompei Scavi. Car parks are clearly marked and vigorously touted. Close to the ruins, **Camping Spartacus** (☎081 862 40 78; www.camping spartacus.it; Via Plinio 127; adult/child per night €7.50/4, car/camper/caravan €5/10/12; 🛜💺) offers good-value, all-day parking (€5). This is a much cheaper option than the main car park located directly north of the Circumvesuviana train station.

From Sorrento, head north along the SS145, which connects to the A3 and Pompeii.

TRAIN

To reach the *scavi* (ruins) by Circumvesuviana (p97) train (€2.80 from Naples, 36 minutes; €2.40 from Sorrento, 30 minutes), alight at Pompei Scavi–Villa dei Misteri station, beside the main entrance at Porta Marina. Regional trains (www.trenitalia.com) stop at Pompei station in the centre of the modern town.

From mid-March to mid-October, tourist train Campania Express runs four times daily between Naples (Porta Nolana and Piazza Garibaldi Circumvesuviana stations) and Sorrento, stopping at Ercolano–Scavi, Torre Annunziata (Oplontis), Pompei Scavi–Villa dei Misteri, Castellammare and Vico Equense en route. One-day return tickets from Naples to Pompeii (€11, 29 minutes) or from Sorrento to Pompeii (€7, 24 minutes) can be purchased at the stations or online at EAV (p102).

AT A GLANCE

POPULATION
88,695

HIGHEST POINT
Monte Epomeo
(788m; p145)

**BEST
ISCHIAN CUISINE**
Il Focolare (p141)

BEST BEACH
Spiaggia di Faro
(p131)

**BEST
ROMAN RUINS**
Villa Jovis (p128)

WHEN TO GO
Apr, May, Sep & Oct
Best months to visit,
with generally clear
skies and mild to
warm temperatures.
Easter can be
crowded.

Jun-Aug Try to avoid
August, which is
when most Italians
take their annual
holiday.

Nov-Mar Most
tourist facilities shut
down in winter.

Procida (p151)
IACOMINO FRIMAGES/SHUTTERSTOCK ©

The Islands

Tossed like colourful dice into the beautiful blue Bay of Naples, the islands of the Amalfi Coast are justifiably famous and sought out. They are surprisingly diverse as well. Procida, Ischia and Capri vary not just in ambience and landscape but also in their sights, activities and size. Pretty Procida is the smallest of the trio; tiny, tranquil and unspoiled, and possible to explore in just a few hours. The fashionable flipside is Capri, with its celebrity circuit of experiences, sights and shops. Ischia is the largest island, with natural spas, botanical gardens, hidden coves and exceptional dining. If that all sounds too challenging, make a beeline for the beaches – they are the Bay of Naples' best.

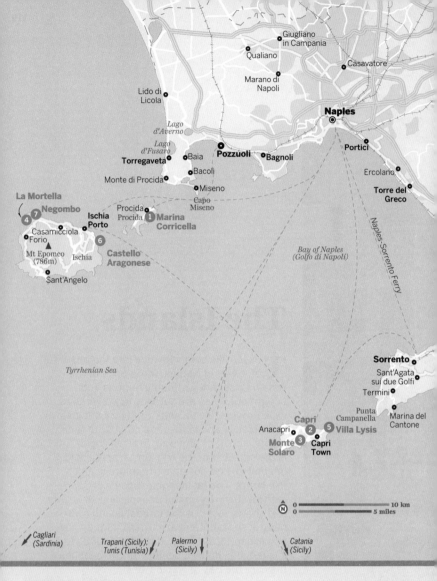

The Islands Highlights

1 Marina Corricella (p151) Enjoying a lazy lunch at a seafood restaurant in Procida's pretty fishing port.

2 Capri Whales (p135) Cruising the turquoise waters around Capri.

3 Monte Solaro (p129) Taking the chairlift to the top of Capri's highest mountain.

4 La Mortella (p148) Exploring the lush garden paradise of late British composer William Walton.

5 Villa Lysis (p128) Admiring the architectural majesty of this clifftop villa, which mixes classical architecture with elements of art nouveau.

6 Castello Aragonese (p143) Losing yourself in this labyrinth of a fortress off the east coast of Ischia.

7 Negombo (p145) Relaxing amid thermal pools, exotic plants and modern sculpture in Ischia's finest spa.

CAPRI

081 / POP 14,120

Capri is beautiful – seriously beautiful. There's barely a grubby building or untended garden to blemish the splendour. Steep cliffs rise majestically from an impossibly blue sea; elegant villas drip with wisteria and bougainvillea; even the trees seem to be carefully manicured.

Long a preserve of celebrities and the super-rich, this small, precipitous island off the west end of the Sorrento Peninsula has a tangible deluxe feel. Your credit card can get a lot of exercise in its expensive restaurants and museum-quality jewellery shops – a cappuccino alone can cost €7. But, regardless of this, Capri is worth visiting, whatever your budget. Glide silently up craggy Monte Solaro on a chairlift. Relive erstwhile poetic glories in Villa Lysis. Find a quiet space in the sinuous lanes of Anacapri. In the process, you'll enjoy some sublime moments.

ⓘ Getting There & Away

Unless you're prepared to pay €1850 for a **helicopter transfer** (0828 35 41 55, 348 586 28 30; www.capri-helicopters.com) from Naples International Airport (20 minutes), you'll arrive in Capri by boat.

BOAT

The two major ferry routes to Capri are from Naples and Sorrento, although there are also seasonal connections with Ischia and the Amalfi Coast (Amalfi, Positano and Salerno).

Caremar (081 837 07 00; www.caremar.it; Marina Grande) Operates hydrofoils and ferries to/from Naples (€12.50 to €18, 40 minutes to 1¼ hours, up to seven daily) and hydrofoils to/from Sorrento (€14.40, 25 minutes, four daily).

Navigazione Libera del Golfo (NLG; 081 552 07 63; www.navlib.it; Marina Grande)

Operates hydrofoils to/from Naples (from €19, 45 minutes, up to nine daily).

SNAV (081 428 55 55; www.snav.it; Marina Grande) Operates hydrofoils to/from Naples (from €22.50, 45 minutes, up to nine daily).

ⓘ Getting Around

Capri is a small island and easily walkable if you're moderately fit and have time to spare. The walk from Marina Grande to Capri Town takes about 20 minutes. From Marina Grande to Anacapri via the Scala Fenicia takes about an hour. Both walks are uphill (with steps).

BOAT

Motoscafisti di Capri (p135) Runs trips to the Blue Grotto from Marina Grande. The rowing boat into the cave is not included – you'll have to pay for this at the entry to the cave. Boat tickets purchased online are €1 cheaper. The company also runs a two-hour trip around the island (at kiosk/online €18/17), which includes a visit to the Blue Grotto.

BUS

Autobus ATC (081 837 04 20; tickets €2, day pass €6) Runs buses between Marina Grande, Capri Town, Marina Piccola and Anacapri.

Staiano Autotrasporti (081 837 24 22; www.staianotourcapri.com; Bus Station, Viale de Tommaso, Anacapri; tickets €2) Runs regular buses to the Grotta Azzurra and Punta Carena *faro* (lighthouse) from Anacapri.

FUNICULAR

Funicular (Via Colombo 18; tickets €2; 6.30am-9.30pm) The first challenge facing visitors is how to get from Marina Grande to Capri Town. The most enjoyable option is the funicular, if only for the evocative en-route views over the lemon groves and surrounding countryside. The ticket booth in Marina Grande is not at the funicular station itself; it's behind the tourist office (turn right onto Via Marina

---

ⓘ GETTING YOUR BEARINGS

All hydrofoils and ferries arrive at Marina Grande, the island's transport hub. From here, the quickest way up to Capri Town is by funicular, but there are also buses and more costly taxis. On foot, it's a 2.3km uphill climb along Via Marina Grande. At the top, turn left (east) at the junction with Via Roma for the centre of town or right (west) for Via Provinciale Anacapri, which eventually becomes Via Orlandi as it leads up to Anacapri.

Pint-sized Piazza Umberto I is the focal point of Capri Town. A short hop to the east, Via Vittorio Emanuele leads down to the main shopping street, Via Camerelle.

Up the hill in Anacapri, buses and taxis drop you off in Piazza Vittoria, from where Via Giuseppe Orlandi, the main strip, runs southwest and Via Capodimonte heads northeast up to Villa San Michele di Axel Munthe.

It is possible to walk to Anacapri from Marina Grande in about an hour along the Scala Fenicia (Map p122), an uphill path with 921 steps.

Capri

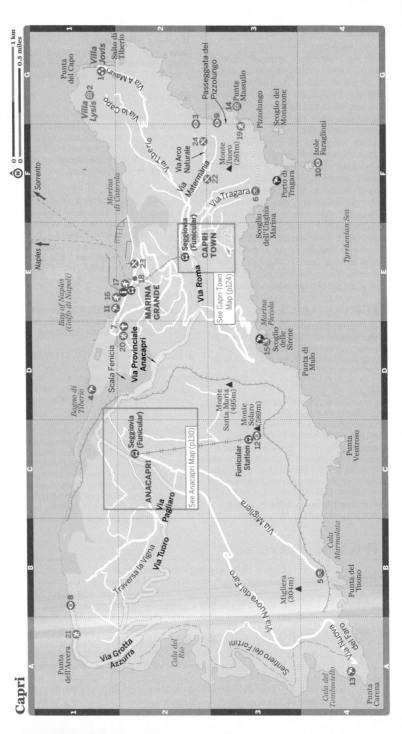

Capri

Grande from the ferry port). Note that the funicular usually closes from January through March for maintenance; a substitute bus service is in place during this period.

SCOOTER

Capri Scooter (☑338 3606918, 081 362 00 83; www.capriscooter.com; Via Marina Grande 280, Marina Grande; per 2/24hr €30/65) If you're looking to hire a scooter at Marina Grande, stop here. There's another outlet in **Anacapri** (☑081 837 38 88; www.capriscooter. com; Piazza Barile 20, Anacapri; per 2/24 hr €30/65).

TAXI

From Marina Grande, a **taxi** (☑in Anacapri 081 837 11 75, in Capri Town 081 837 66 57) costs from €17 to Capri Town and from €23 to Anacapri; from Capri Town to Anacapri costs around €18. These rates include one bag per vehicle. Each additional bag (with dimensions exceeding 40cm by 20cm by 50cm) costs an extra €2.

Capri Town

☑ 081 / POP 7210

With its whitewashed stone buildings and tiny, car-free streets, Capri Town exudes a cinematic air. A diminutive model of upmarket Mediterranean chic, it's a well-tended playground of luxury hotels, expensive bars, smart restaurants and high-end boutiques. In summer the centre swells with crowds of camera-wielding day trippers and yacht-owning playboys (and girls), but don't be put off from exploring the atmospheric and ancient side streets, where the crowds quickly thin. The walk east out of town to Villa Jovis is especially wonderful.

⊙ Sights

Giardini di Augusto   GARDENS
(Gardens of Augustus; Map p124; €1; ⊙9am-7.30pm summer, reduced hr rest of yr) As their name suggests, these gardens near the Certosa di San Giacomo were founded by Emperor Augustus. Rising in a series of flowered terraces, they lead to a lookout point offering breathtaking views over to the Isole Faraglioni, a group of three limestone stacks rising out of the sea.

From the gardens, pretty, hairpin Via Krupp winds down to Marina Piccola and past a bust of Vladimir Lenin overlooking the road from a nearby platform. The Russian revolutionary visited Capri in 1908, during which time he was famously snapped engaged in a game of chess with fellow revolutionary Alexander Bogdanov. Looking on in the photograph is Russian writer Maxim Gorky, who called the island home between 1906 and 1909.

Certosa di San Giacomo   MONASTERY
(Map p124; ☑081 837 62 18; Viale Certosa 40; adult/reduced €6/2; ⊙10am-6pm Tue-Sun Apr-Sep, to 3pm Oct-Mar) Founded in 1363, this substantial monastery is generally considered to be the finest remaining example of Caprese architecture and today houses a school, a library, a temporary exhibition space and a museum with some evocative 17th-century paintings. Be sure to look at the cloisters, which have a real sense of faded glory (the smaller is 14th-century, the larger 16th-century).

To get here take Via Vittorio Emanuele III, east of Piazza Umberto I, which meanders down to the monastery.

Capri Town

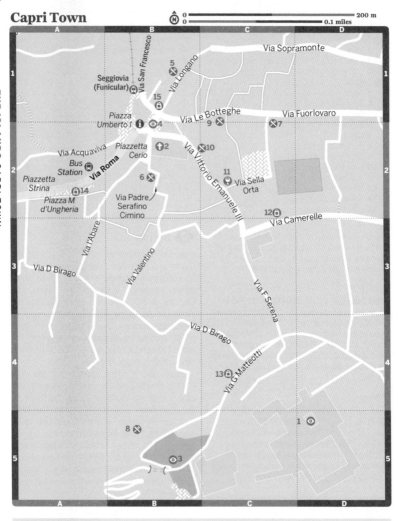

Capri Town

THE ISLANDS IN....

One Day
Escape the clamour and crowds of Naples and enjoy a day of tranquillity a short ferry hop away on the charmingly unspoilt island of Procida. After a gentle stroll in the *centro storico* (historic centre), pull up a chair at lovely Marina Corricella (p151) for a simple meal of fresh seafood overlooking the fishing boats. Take an afternoon boat trip (p153) around the island's evocative hidden coves.

Two Days
Plan on an early arrival in Ischia, then head for the botanical gardens of La Mortella (p148) for a wander along the shady, cool pathways surrounded by exotic plants. Spend lunch near the beach at languid Sant'Angelo (p150). In the afternoon, catch a water taxi to Terme Cavascura (p151), the island's oldest natural spa, for an afternoon of restorative relaxation. Round off the day poking around the eclectic mix of shops (p141) on Via Roma, within walking distance of the ferry pier.

Three Days
Turn up before the Capri day trippers descend and join the local who's-who brigade at the emblematic square La Piazzetta (p127). Leave the surrounding sophisticated strut of shops behind as you head towards the nearby Giardini di Augusto (p123), with flower-filled terraces and some of the best views on the island. Pick a restaurant overlooking the water, then enjoy the beauty of the island's trails (p127), with either a country amble or a more demanding hike.

The monastery's history is a harrowing one: it became the stronghold of the island's powerful Carthusian fraternity and was viciously attacked during Saracen pirate raids in the 16th century. A century later, monks retreated here to avoid the plague and were rewarded by an irate public (whom they should have been tending), who tossed corpses over the walls. There are some soothing 17th-century frescoes in the church, which will hopefully serve as an antidote as you contemplate the monastery's dark past.

Piazza Umberto I   PIAZZA
(Map p124) Located beneath the 17th-century clock tower and framed by see-and-be-seen cafes, this showy, open-air salon is central to your Capri experience, especially in the evening when the main activity in these parts is dressing up and hanging out. Be prepared for the cost of the front-row seats – the moment you sit down for a drink, you're going to pay handsomely for the grandstand views (around €7 for a coffee and €18 for a couple of glasses of wine).

Chiesa di Santo Stefano   CHURCH
(Map p124; ☑ 081 837 23 96; Piazza Umberto I; ⊙ 9am-7pm summer, 10am-2pm winter) Though not remarkable in itself, Capri's main church, named after its patron saint, is a

tempting haven from the bottlenecks of tourists on the streets outside. The wooden doors embellished with imitation marble date from the mid-18th century and were inspired by Villa Jovis on Capri. Note the pair of languidly reclining patricians in the chapel to the south of the main altar, who seem to mirror some of the mildly debauched folk in the cafes outside.

✖ Eating

There's no shortage of restaurants and trattorias in Capri Town, most of which focus on traditional regional cuisine. To be expected, prices are on the higher side. Those wanting a cheap bite on the go should head to Gelateria Buonacore, which peddles fresh, flavourful Italian street food. Call ahead to reserve restaurant tables in the peak summer season.

Gelateria Buonacore   FAST FOOD €
(Map p124; ☑ 081 837 78 26; Via Vittorio Emanuele III 35, Capri Town; snacks €2-10, gelato from €2.50; ⊙ 8am-midnight Jul-Sep, reduced hours rest of year, closed Tue Oct-Jun; ⚑) Ideal for quick takeaways, this popular, down-to-earth snack bar does a roaring trade in savoury and sweet treats. Hit the spot with *panini* (sandwiches), stuffed peppers, waffles and the legendary ice cream. Hard to beat, though, are the delicate but filling

sfogliatelle (cinnamon-infused ricotta in a puff-pastry shell; €2.50) and the feather-light speciality *caprilu al limone* (lemon and almond cakes).

★ È Divino ITALIAN €€

(Map p124; ☑ 081 837 83 64; www.edivinocapri. com/divino; Via Sella Orta 10a, Capri Town; meals €33-48; ⊙ 8pm-1am daily Jun-Aug, 12.30-2.30pm & 7.30pm-midnight Tue-Sun rest of year; 🐊) Proudly eccentric (what other restaurant has a bed in its dining room?), this diligent purveyor of Slow Food is a precious secret to those who know it. Whether dining among lemon trees in the garden or among antiques, chandeliers and contemporary art (and that bed!) inside, expect a thoughtful, regularly changing menu dictated by what's fresh from the garden and market.

Favourites include a sultry pasta dish of *paccheri* (short, fat pasta tubes) with tuna, olives, capers and datterini tomatoes.

★ La Palette ITALIAN €€

(Map p122; ☑ 081 837 72 83; www.lapalette.it; Via Matermània 36; meals from €35; ⊙ 11am-midnight Apr-early Nov) Local Caprese ingredients are combined into the most flavour-filled, creative dishes possible here. Expect the delights of zucchini flowers stuffed with ricotta, fresh and tangy octopus salad, and an aubergine *parmigiana* that seems to taste so much better than everyone else's. An easy 10-minute walk from Capri Town, it has swooningly romantic bay views.

Backed up with a fabulous wine cellar and knowledgeable, passionate staff, La Palette has quickly risen to the top of Capri's gilded restaurant list.

WORTH A TRIP

LE GROTTELLE

This **restaurant** (Map p122; ☑ 081 837 57 19; Via Arco Naturale 13; meals €30-40; ⊙ noon-2.30pm & 7-11pm Fri-Wed summer, noon-3pm Fri-Wed Apr, May & Oct, closed Nov-Mar; 🐊) is a great place to impress someone – not so much for the food, which is decent enough, but for the dramatic setting: its two dining areas are set in a cave and on a hillside terrace with sea views. Dishes are rustic, from homemade fusilli pasta with shrimps and courgettes to rabbit with onions, garlic and rosemary. The restaurant is an easy 1km walk east of Capri Town.

Al Grottino NEAPOLITAN €€

(Map p124; ☑ 081 837 05 84; www.ristoranteal grottino.net; Via Longano 27; meals from €30; ⊙ 11.45am-3.30pm & 6.30pm-midnight Apr-Oct) Expect a queue here. Dating from 1937, Al Grottino was a VIP spot in the '50s and '60s (check out the photos in the window), and it continues to lure locals and visitors with traditional Neapolitan dishes like *ravioli alle Caprese* (ravioli with Parmesan and marjoram) and specials like *cocotte* (hand-made pasta with mixed seafood served in a paella-like pan).

The small dining space is reassuringly traditional, right down to the decorative chianti bottles.

Donna Rachele TRATTORIA €€

(Map p124; ☑ 081 837 53 87; www.donnarachele. com; Via Padre Serafino Cimmino 2; pizza from €7, meals €30-35; ⊙ noon-3.30pm & 7pm-midnight; 🐊) Tucked away in a corner, this place has a traditional trattoria atmosphere, with small rooms, decorative tiles and walls lined with bottles. Vegetarians will do well, with such antipasti choices as grilled artichokes, sautéed spinach and white beans, while seafood lovers will enjoy specialities on the main menu like *alici del menaica* (anchovies caught using an ancient Campanese fishing method).

★ Il Geranio SEAFOOD €€€

(Map p124; ☑ 081 837 06 16; www.geraniocapri. com; Via Matteotti 8, Capri Town; meals €45-50; ⊙ noon-3pm & 7-11pm mid-Apr–mid-Oct) Time to pop the question or quell those predeparture blues? The terrace at this sophisticated spot offers heart-stealing views over the pine trees to Isole Faraglioni. Seafood is the speciality, particularly the salt-baked fish. Other fine choices include octopus salad and linguine with saffron and mussels. Book at least three days ahead for a terrace table in high season.

La Capannina TRATTORIA €€€

(Map p124; ☑ 081 837 07 32; www.capannina capri.com; Via le Botteghe 12; meals €40-50; ⊙ noon-3pm & 7-11.30pm mid-Mar–Oct) Dating back to 1931, this is the island's most famous traditional trattoria and a long-time favourite on the celebrity circuit. Set up to look like a Hollywood version of a rustic resturant – pink tablecloths, pink roses, hanging copper pots and carved wooden chairs – it serves a classic island menu of comfort food. Reservations are recommended.

> ## OFF THE BEATEN TRACK
>
> ### PASSEGGIATA DEL PIZZOLUNGO
>
> Surprisingly for such a small place, Capri offers some memorable hiking. A network of well-maintained paths weaves its way across the island, leading through areas that even in the height of summer are all but deserted; the tourist offices can provide reasonable maps. One especially fine option is the Passeggiata del Pizzolungo, which can be done as a circuit from the centre of Capri Town. It's spectacular even by Capri standards, taking in a necklace of west-coast sights including the Arco Naturale, Faraglioni and several grottoes and *belvederi* (lookouts). Most of the path is paved and there are quite a few steps, though it is not inordinately difficult. The walk should take about an hour and is roughly marked on most local maps available at the tourist office.
>
> From Capri Town, head east to the **Arco Naturale** (Map p122), a curious eroded-limestone arch dating back to the Paleolithic era and formed by millennia of natural wear and tear. At the end of Via Matermània, backtrack to Le Grottelle restaurant and take the set of stairs beside it (Passeggiata del Pizzolungo). About halfway down you'll pass the **Grotta di Matermània** (Map p122), a giant natural cave used by the Romans as a *nymphaeum* (shrine to the water nymph). You can still see traces of the mosaic wall decorated with shells. At the bottom, continue down the path as it follows the rocky coastline south. The striking flat-roofed red villa you eventually see on your left, on the Punta Massullo promontory, is **Villa Malaparte** (Map p122), the former holiday home of Tuscan writer Curzio Malaparte (1898–1957). Carrying on, the sea views become increasingly impressive as the path continues westward around the lower wooded slopes of Monte Tuoro. A few hundred metres further along and you will arrive at a staircase on your right, which leads up to the **Belvedere di Tragara** (Map p122), a prime viewing point for the pointed, limestone **Isole Faraglioni** (Map p122). From here, follow Via Tragara back to the town centre.

Popular dishes include high-quality seafood pasta, *ravioli caprese* (ravioli stuffed with ricotta and herbs), grilled meat and fresh fish, as well as the speciality, *linguine al sugo di scorfano* (flat ribbons of pasta with scorpion fish).

Drinking & Nightlife

Capri's nightlife is a showy business. The main activity is styling up and hanging out, ideally at one of the cafes on **La Piazzetta** (Piazza Umberto I). Aside from the cafes, the nightlife here is fairly staid, with only a handful of clubs.

Taverna Anema e Core   CLUB
(Map p124; ☏ 329 4742508; www.anemaecore. com; Via Sella Orta 39e, Capri Town; ⊗ 11pm-late Jun-Aug, closed Wed Apr, May, Sep & Oct, closed rest of the yr) Behind a humble exterior is one of the island's most famous nightspots, run by the charismatic Guido Lembo. This smooth and sophisticated bar-club attracts an appealing mix of superchic and casually dressed punters, here for the relaxed atmosphere and regular live music, including unwaveringly authentic Neapolitan guitar strumming and singing.

Shopping

★ La Parisienne   FASHION & ACCESSORIES
(Map p124; ☏ 081 837 02 83; www.laparisienne capri.it; Piazza Umberto I 7, Capri Town; ⊗ 9am-10pm) First opened in 1906 (yes, that is not a misprint!) and best known for introducing Capri pants in the 1960s – famously worn by Audrey Hepburn, who bought them here – La Parisienne can run you up a made-to-measure pair within a day. It also sells off-the-hook Capri pants (from €250).

Jackie O was a customer, and Clark Gable apparently favoured the fashions here, particularly the Bermuda shorts, which (believe it or not) were considered quite raffish in their day.

Carthusia I Profumi di Capri   COSMETICS
(Map p124; ☏ 081 837 53 93; www.carthusia.it; Via Matteotti 2d, Capri Town; ⊗ 9am-8pm Apr-Sep, to 5pm rest of yr) Allegedly, Capri's famous floral perfume was established in 1380 by the prior of the Certosa di San Giacomo. Caught unawares by a royal visit, he displayed the island's most beautiful flowers for the queen. Changing the water in the vase, he discovered a floral scent. This became the

LUXE VILLAS OF THE PAST

Capri's northeastern corner is home to two of the island's most evocative former abodes.

A 40-minute walk from Piazza Umberto I in Capri Town, the beautifully melancholic art nouveau **Villa Lysis** (Map p122; www.villalysiscapri.com; Via Lo Capo 12; €2; ⊙10am-7pm Thu-Tue Jun-Aug, to 6pm Apr, May, Sep & Oct, to 4pm Nov & Dec) was the one-time retreat of French poet Jacques d'Adelsward-Fersen, who came to Capri in 1904 to escape a gay sex scandal in Paris. Unlike other stately homes, the interior has been left almost entirely empty; this is a place to let your imagination flesh out the details.

One notable curiosity is the 'Chinese room' in the basement, which includes a semi-circular opium den with a swastika emblazoned on the floor. Fersen became addicted to opium following a visit to Ceylon in the early 1900s; the swastika is the Sanskrit symbol for well-being. Equally transfixing is the sun-dappled garden, a triumph of classical grandiosity half given over to nature.

Afterwards, it is possible to take a steep, winding path, the Sentiero delle Calanche, to **Villa Jovis** (Jupiter's Villa; Map p122; Via A Maiuri; adult/reduced €6/4; ⊙10am-7pm Jun-Sep, to 6pm Apr, May & Oct, to 4pm Mar, Nov & Dec, closed Jan & Feb), a 20-minute walk away. Villa Jovis was the largest and most sumptuous of 12 Roman villas commissioned by Roman Emperor Tiberius (r AD 14–37) on Capri, and his main island residence. A vast complex, now reduced to ruins, it famously pandered to the emperor's supposedly debauched tastes, and included imperial quarters and extensive bathing areas set in dense gardens and woodland.

The villa's spectacular location posed major headaches for Tiberius' architects. The main problem was how to collect and store enough water to supply the villa's baths and 3000-sq-metre gardens. The solution they eventually hit upon was to build a complex canal system to transport rainwater to four giant storage tanks, whose remains you can still see today.

Beside the ticket office is the 330m-high **Salto di Tiberio** (Tiberius' Leap), a spectacular sheer cliff from where, as the story goes, Tiberius had out-of-favour subjects hurled into the sea.

From Capri Town, Villa Jovis is a 45-minute walk east along Via Tiberio.

---

base of the classic perfume now sold at this smart laboratory outlet.

Women's and men's fragrances aside, the shop also sells heavenly scented skincare, candles and room fragrances.

Capri Watch FASHION & ACCESSORIES
(Map p124; ☑ 081 837 71 48; www.capricapri.com; Via Camerelle 21, Capri Town; ⊙9am-5pm Mon-Sat) The flashy selection of watches here is made by local watchmaker Silvio Staiano. The prices start surprisingly low, around €70 for a relatively straightforward timepiece, spiralling up to several zeros worth of precious and semi-precious jewel-encrusted numbers.

There are several other branches on the island.

Da Costanzo SHOES
(Map p124; ☑ 081 837 80 77; Via Roma 49, Capri Town; ⊙9am-8.30pm Mar-Nov) In 1959 Clark Gable stopped off at this tiny, unpretentious shoe shop to get a pair of handmade leather sandals, and the shop still sells a range of colourful styles to passers-by and shoe aficionados. Prices start at around €90 – a small investment for a piece of Hollywood history.

🛈 Information

Tourist Office (Map p124; ☑ 081 837 06 86; www.capritourism.com; Piazza Umberto I, Capri Town; ⊙8.30am-8.45pm summer, 9am-1pm & 3.30-6.45pm Mon-Sat winter) On the main square. Can provide a map of the island, plus accommodation listings, ferry timetables and other useful information.

🛈 Getting There & Away

Autobus ATC (☑ 081 837 04 20; tickets €2, day pass €6) runs regular buses to/from Anacapri. The **bus station** (Map p124) is on Via Roma, an easy 150m walk southwest of Piazza Umberto I.

Anacapri & Around

Traditionally Capri Town's more subdued neighbour, Anacapri is no stranger to tourism. The focus is largely limited to Villa San Michele di Axel Munthe and the souvenir shops on the main streets. Delve further, though, and you'll discover that Anacapri is still, at heart, the laid-back, rural village that it's always been.

⊙ Sights

★ **Villa San Michele
di Axel Munthe**   MUSEUM, GARDENS
(Map p130; ✆ 081 837 14 01; www.villasan michele.eu; Via Axel Munthe 34; €8; ⊙ 9am-6pm May-Sep, reduced hr rest of yr) The former home of Swedish doctor, psychiatrist and animal-rights advocate Axel Munthe, San Michele di Axel Munthe should be included on every visitor's itinerary. Built on the site of the ruins of a Roman villa, the gardens make a beautiful setting for a tranquil stroll, with pathways flanked by immaculate flowerbeds. There are also superb views from here, plus some fine photo props in the form of Roman sculptures.

If you are here between June and August, you may be able to catch one of the classical concerts that take place in the gardens. Check the website for the current program and reservation information.

Chiesa di San Michele   CHURCH
(Map p130; Piazza San Nicola; €3; ⊙ 9.30am-7pm) Anacapri's chief building is famous for its handsome floor, a veritable work of art depicting the Adam and Eve story in multicoloured tiles. So masterful is the detail that the floor of the hexagonal church has been left uncovered to allow closer inspection. For the best vista, head up a coiled spiral staircase to a tiny viewing gallery.

Belvedere di Migliera   VIEWPOINT
(Map p122) This panoramic platform, reached via a 30-minute walk along a paved path from Anacapri, has spectacular sea views. From Piazza Vittoria, take Via Caposcuro and carry on straight along its continuation, Via Migliera. Along the way you'll pass orchards, vineyards and small patches of woodland.

Once at the belvedere you can return to Anacapri via the Torre di Materita or, if you've still got the legs, continue up Monte Solaro – but note that this tough walk is graded medium–difficult.

Casa Rossa   MUSEUM
(Map p130; ✆ 081 838 21 93; Via Orlandi 78; €3.50; ⊙ 10am-1.30pm & 5.30-8pm) The striking Moroccan-style 'Red House' was built by American colonel John Clay MacKown in 1876. Constructed around a 16th-century defensive tower, the building houses an

THE ISLANDS ANACAPRI & AROUND

DON'T MISS

MONTE SOLARO

Rising 589m above Anacapri, Monte Solaro (Map p122) is Capri's highest point. The easiest way to reach the top is on the Seggiovia del Monte Solaro (Map p130; ✆ 081 837 14 38; www.capriseggiovia.it; Via Caposcuro; single/return €8/11; ⊙ 9.30am-5pm May-Oct, 9am-4pm Mar & Apr, to 3.30pm Nov-Feb) from Piazza Vittoria. Sitting in an old-fashioned chairlift above the white houses, terraced gardens and hazy hillsides of Anacapri as you rise to the top of Capri's highest mountain has to be one of the island's most sublime experiences. The ride takes an all-too-short 13 minutes, but when you get there, the views, framed by dismembered classical statues, are outstanding.

If you have energy to burn, you can also reach the summit on foot; a 45-minute to one-hour walk one way. To do the latter, take Via Axel Munthe and turn right up Via Salita per il Solaro. The hike climbs steadily uphill but is not difficult if you're relatively fit. Follow the steep stony trail until you come to the pass known as La Crocetta, marked by a distinctive iron crucifix. Here the path divides: turn right for the summit and its spectacular views over the Bay of Naples and the Amalfi Coast, or take a left for the valley of Cetrella and the small hermitage of Santa Maria a Cetrella.

The hermitage dates from the 16th century, its bell tower and two barrel-vaulted naves forming the oldest part of the structure. The sacristy and a number of service rooms were added in the early 17th century. The hermitage is not always open to the public, so check with the tourist office beforehand if you fancy snooping around it.

Anacapri

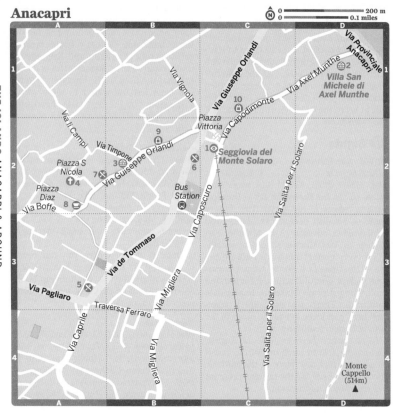

Anacapri

eclectic collection of 19th-century paintings, including some evocative scenes of Capri by Gonsalvo Carelli (1818–1900), and by French painter Eduard Alexandre Sain, who ably captures the island's spirit in works such as *Wedding in Capri*. Also here is a colossal 1st-century Roman statue discovered during 19th-century excavations of the Blue Grotto.

✕ Eating & Drinking

Anacapri is home to a number of trattorias and restaurants, serving mainly traditional regional fare and pizza.

Trattoria Il Solitario TRATTORIA €
(Map p130; ☎ 081 837 13 82; Via Orlandi 96; meals €20-30; ⊙ noon-3.30pm & 7-11.30pm Apr-Oct; 🍴) Eating here is a bit like being invited to

someone's home: tables are set in a small backyard with lemon trees and children's toys in the corner, and the ambience is one of unhurried holiday time. The menu lists the usual island fare – pasta, seafood, grilled meat, pizzas – but the helpings are large and the quality high.

The pizzas include a vast pizza *bianche* selection, which is handy if you're tiring of tomatoes.

La Rondinella
ITALIAN €€

(Map p130; ☑081 837 12 23; www.ristorante larondinella.com; Via Orlandi 295; meals €30-40, pizzas from €7; ☺noon-2.30pm & 7-11.30pm, closed Nov-Mar) Graham Greene's favourite hang-out when he lived in these parts, La Rondinella sits in the heart of white-washed Anacapri. Who knows what literary nuggets the author dreamt up as he sat at his preferred corner table, or whether, like contemporary visitors, he found inspiration in the *linguine alla ciammura,* a pasta dish with a creamy anchovy, garlic and parsley sauce.

The *torta di mandorle* (chocolate and almond tart) sits like an epilogue at the end of the menu crying out to be tasted.

Le Arcate
CAMPANIAN, PIZZA €€

(Map p130; ☑081 837 35 88; Via de Tommaso 24; pizzas €7-11, meals €30; ☺noon-3pm & 7pm-midnight) This is the restaurant that the locals recommend – and frequent. An unpretentious place with hanging baskets of ivy, sunny yellow tablecloths and well-aged terracotta tiles, it specialises in subtly simple *primi* (first courses) and pizzas. Stop by for the island classic: *ravioli alla caprese* (pasta stuffed with ricotta, Parmesan and marjoram, with a tomato or sage and butter sauce).

Caffè Michelangelo
CAFE

(Map p130; ☑333 7784331; Via Orlandi 138, Anacapri; ☺8am-2am Jul & Aug, to 1am Sep-Jun, closed Thu Nov & Dec; ☎) On a street flanked by tasteful shops and near two lovely piazzas, this is the best place in Anacapri to park your gluteus maximus for a bit of tourist-watching. Rate the passing parade over a *spritz con Cynar,* a less-sweet take on the classic Aperol *spritz,* made using a herbacious Italian bitter liqueur. It also does wine by the glass.

SPIAGGIA DI FARO

The most 'local' beach on Capri, Spiaggia di Faro (Map p122) is by the lighthouse and away from the action, and known for its wonderful sunsets. There are a couple of private beach clubs, plus a public area with a cafe. The beach, as with most in Capri, is mainly made up of rocks – not that this dampens its popularity. Catch a Faro-bound bus from Anacapri to get there.

Shopping

Limoncello Capri Canale Massimo
DRINKS

(Map p130; ☑081 837 29 27; www.limoncello.com; Via Capodimonte 27, Anacapri; ☺9am-7.30pm, closed mid-Jan–mid-Feb) Don't be put off by the gaudy yellow display: this historic shop stocks some of the island's best *limoncello.* In fact, it was here that the drink was first concocted (or at least that is the claim). Apparently, the grandmother of current owner Massimo made the tot as an after-dinner treat for the guests in her small guesthouse.

Nowadays, the shop produces some 70,000 bottles each year, as well as lemon and orange chocolates, lemon honey, and a tasty lemon sorbet (€2.50; 2% alcohol).

Elegantia
FASHION & ACCESSORIES

(Map p130; Via Orlandi 75, Anacapri; ☺9am-8pm Mon-Sat) Always fancied yourself flouncing around in one of those sherbet-yellow, baby-pink or powder-blue floppy hats? Then this is the place to pick one up (€15). The owner can also run up copies of clothing and do alterations and repairs.

Information

Tourist Office (Map p130; ☑081 837 15 24; www.capritourism.com; Via Orlandi 59, Anacapri; ☺8.30am-4.15pm daily Jun–mid-Sep, to 2.30pm Mon-Sat rest of year) Can provide a map of the island, along with hotel listings and other useful information.

Getting There & Away

Autobus ATC (p128) Runs regular buses to/from Marina Grande and Capri Town. Change at Anacapri's **bus station** (Map p130; Piazzetta Cimitero) for minibuses to Grotta Azzurra and the *faro* (lighthouse).

FRANK CHMURA/GETTY IMAGES ©

1. Picturesque Procida (p151)
Pastel-painted houses on the beautiful island of
Procida.

2. Marina Corricella (p151), Procida
The multihued waterfront village of Marina
Corricella is a riot of colours overlooking a boat-
filled habour.

3. La Mortella (p148), Ischia
Maypop flower in La Mortella, one of Italy's finest
botanical gardens with more than 1000 rare and
exotic plants.

4. Monte Solaro (p129), Capri
View from atop Monte Solaro, Capri's highest
peak. It's easily reached via a chairlift.

KAREL GALLAS/SHUTTERSTOCK ©

Marina Grande

📄 081

Capri's main port is a shabbily attractive place and very Italian, with little evidence of the cosmopolitan flair that awaits up the hill. For those desperate for a swim, there's an attractive 200m-long pebble beach (Capri's largest) to the west of the port.

⊙ Sights & Activities

Bagni di Tiberio   BEACH
(Map p122; ⊙9am-sunset Apr-Sep) This pebble beach is home to the island's most popular beach club (entry €20), where you can swim amid the ruins of a Roman villa. It's a 10-minute walk or a short boat ride from Marina Grande.

Chiesa di San Costanzo   CHURCH
(Map p122; Via Marina Grande) This is the island's oldest church and the only real sight around the marina. Dating from the 5th century, the whitewashed *chiesa* is dedicated to the island's patron saint, who settled on Capri after escaping a vicious storm en route from Constantinople to Rome. Its original incarnation was built over an earlier Roman construction, although the Byzantine version you see today is the result of a 10th-century makeover. Inside, the sign of the building's great antiquity is its characterfully patched and mismatched columns

Banana Sport   BOATING
(Map p122; 📄 348 5949665; Marina Grande; 2hr/day rental 5-person boat €80/220; ⊙May–mid-Oct) Located on the eastern edge of the waterfront, Banana Sport hires out five-person motorised dinghies, allowing you to explore secluded coves and grottoes. You can also visit the popular swimming spot **Bagno di Tiberio** (€10), a small inlet west of Marina Grande; it's said that Tiberius once swam here.

Tours

Capri's two classic water tours are to the Grotta Azzurra and a circumnavigation of the island. Both cost around €18 and take between one and two hours. Be warned – they're incredibly popular. Various companies offer these excursions, including Laser Capri and Motoscafisti di Capri.

GROTTA AZZURRA

Capri's most famous attraction is the **Grotta Azzurra** (Blue Grotto; Map p122; €14; ⊙9am-5pm), an unusual sea cave illuminated by an other-worldly blue light. The easiest way to visit is to take a boat tour from Marina Grande; tickets include the return boat trip but the rowing boat into the cave and admission are paid separately. Beautiful though it is, the Grotta is extremely popular in the summer and the crowds coupled with long waiting times and tip-hungry guides can make the experience underwhelming for some.

The grotto had long been known to local fishermen when it was rediscovered by two Germans – writer Augustus Kopisch and painter Ernst Fries – in 1826. Subsequent research, however, revealed that Emperor Tiberius had built a quay in the cave around AD 30, complete with a nymphaeum (shrine to the water nymph). Remarkably, you can still see the carved Roman landing stage towards the rear of the cave.

Measuring 54m by 30m and rising to a height of 15m, the grotto is said to have sunk by up to 20m in prehistoric times, blocking every opening except the 1.3m-high entrance. And this is the key to the magical blue light. Sunlight enters through a small underwater aperture and is refracted through the water; this, combined with the reflection of the light off the white sandy seafloor, produces the vivid blue effect to which the cave owes its name.

The Grotta can also be accessed from land. Take a bus from Marina Grande to Anacapri and then another bus to the road's end at Grotta Azzurra. From here, a staircase leads down to a small dock where rowing boats await to take passengers into the adjacent cave.

Bear in mind that the time actually spent in the Grotta during a tour amounts to 10 minutes maximum. The singing row-boat 'captains' are included in the price, so don't feel any obligation if they push for a tip.

The grotto is closed if the sea is too choppy and swimming in it is forbidden, although you can swim outside the entrance.

LOCAL KNOWLEDGE

CELEBRITY ISLAND

A byword for Mediterranean chic, Capri has long enjoyed a reputation as a haunt for the famous and infamous. Dive into a local restaurant and, more often than not, you'll find a photo wall of spaghetti-eating and negroni-drinking celebrities.

The first big name to decamp here was Emperor Tiberius in AD 27. A man of sadistic sexual perversions, at least if the Roman author Suetonius is to be believed, he had 12 villas built on the island, including the vast Villa Jovis. He also left deep scars and, until modern times, his name was equated with evil by the islanders. When the Swedish doctor Axel Munthe first began picking about the Roman ruins on the island in the early 20th century and built his villa on the site of a Tiberian palace, locals would observe that it was all *'roba di Tiberio'* – Tiberius' stuff.

But more than Tiberius' rumoured capers, it was the discovery of the Grotta Azzurra in 1826 that paved the way for Capri's celebrity invasion. As news of the spectacular cave spread so artists such as John Singer Sargent, musicians including Debussy, intellectuals, industrialists and writers began to visit, attracted by the island's isolated beauty and, in some cases, the availability of the local lads. An early habitué, Alfred Krupp, the German industrialist and arms manufacturer, was involved in a gay scandal, while author Norman Douglas and French count Jacques Fersen set all manner of tongues wagging.

The island also proved an escape for Russian revolutionaries. In 1905 the author Maxim Gorky moved to Capri after failing to topple the Russian tsar, and Vladimir Lenin visited the island in 1908 and 1910. In the course of the early 20th century Chilean poet Pablo Neruda and German author Thomas Mann visited regularly, British writers Compton Mackenzie and Graham Greene lived here for extended periods, and Britain's wartime singer Gracie Fields retired here.

More recently, singer Mariah Carey was spotted shopping with (now ex) billionaire beau James Packer, while Beyoncé and Jay-Z were snapped eating dinner in Capri Town. Such celebrities help keep Capri's reputation for star-spangled *dolce vita* alive – and its overworked paparazzi in business.

For more peace and quiet (and money), you can organise your own private boat with or without a skipper. You don't need a boat licence to do this, although some nautical experience is handy. For private rentals, try Banana Sport or Capri Whales.

★ **Capri Whales**   BOATING
(Map p122; ☑ 081 837 58 33; www.capriwhales.it; Marina Grande 17; 2hr private boat tours from per boat €150, day trip to Positano from €650, boat hire 2hr/full day €100/250, kids under 6yr free; ☺ year round; 🖳) A congenial business based on the main quay offering guided boat tours of the island as well as longer full-day trips to Positano. Alternatively, you can hire your own boat for three hours or a full day. Trips are family-friendly, with a child life vest and water toys provided.

Laser Capri   BOATING
(Map p122; ☑ 081 837 52 08; www.lasercapri. com; Via Colombo 69; Blue Grotto/island tour €18) With a ticket office right on the port (it's usually the one with the longest queue), Laser Capri offer the two island classics: boat

trips to the Grotta Azzurra (not including entry fee) and a one-hour boat tour of the whole island.

If you're limited for time, go for the island tour – granted, it's popular, but you'll still get spectacular views of Villa Jovis, the Arco Naturale, I Faraglioni and the Grotta Verde from a comfortable pew.

Motoscafisti di Capri   BOATING
(Map p122; ☑ 081 837 56 46; www.motoscafisti capri.com; Private Pier 0; Grotta Azzurra/island trip €15/€18) This outfit runs trips to the Grotta Azzurra from Marina Grande. The rowing boat into the cave is not included – you'll have to pay for this at the entry to the cave. Boat tickets purchased online are €1 cheaper. The company also runs a two-hour trip around the island, which also includes a visit to the Grotta Azzurra.

Sercomar   BOATING
(Map p122; ☑ 081 837 87 81; www.caprisea service.com; Via Colombo 64, Marina Grande; tours around €18; ☺ Apr-Oct; 🖳) Offers boat tours of Capri – two-hour trips at competitive rates.

SENTIERO DEI FORTINI

Snaking its way along Capri's oft-overlooked western coast, the 5.2km **Sentiero dei Fortini** (Path of the Small Forts; Map p122) is a wonderful if somewhat arduous walk that takes you from Punta dell'Arcera near the Grotta Azzurra in the north to Punta Carena at the island's southwestern tip, where it is possible to go for a refreshing swim.

Named after the three coastal forts (Pino, Mèsola and Orrico) along the way, it passes through some of Capri's most unspoilt countryside. Give yourself three hours to complete the walk and carry plenty of water.

✖ Eating

You'll find a string of generally average, overpriced tourist traps facing the port on Via Marina Grande. You'll find better options in both Capri Town and Anacapri.

L'Approdo   ITALIAN €€
(Map p122; ☑ 081 837 89 90; www.approdocapri.com; Piazzetta Ferraro 8; pizzas from €4.50, meals €25-40; ◷ 11.30am-4pm & 6.30pm-midnight) If you've arrived on the ferry with an appetite, head here, a two-minute walk to the left from where you disembark. You can easily fill up on the superb antipasti spread, and the pizzas are agreeably blistered and varied – try the *sfilatino* with ricotta, ham and mozzarella. Seafood is pricier but as fresh as the day's catch.

There are good views of the colourful fishing boats and nets from the sprawling outdoor terrace, with little to remind you of Capri's fabled glitz up the hill.

ⓘ Information

Tourist Office (Map p122; ☑ 081 837 06 34; www.capritourism.com; Banchina del Porto; ◷ 8.30am-4.15pm, closed Sat & Sun Jan-Mar & Nov) Can provide a map of the island, plus accommodation listings, ferry timetables and other useful information.

ⓘ Getting There & Around

Marina Grande is Capri's main port of entry with numerous daily ferries and hydrofoils to Naples and Sorrento (and the Amalfi coast in the summer).

On foot, it's a 20-minute uphill climb to Capri Town, or you can take the funicular (p121),

which connects directly to Piazza Umberto I. In addition, Autobus ATC (p128) runs minibuses to Capri Town, Marina Piccola and Anacapri.

ISCHIA

☑ 081 / POP 64,110

The volcanic outcrop of Ischia is the most developed and largest of the islands in the Bay of Naples. An early colony of Magna Graecia, first settled in the 8th century BC, Ischia today is famed for its thermal spas, manicured gardens, striking Aragonese castle and unshowy, straightforward Italian airs – a feature also reflected in its food. Ischia is a refreshing antidote to glitzy Capri.

Most visitors head straight for the north-coast towns of Ischia Porto, Ischia Ponte, Forio and Lacco Ameno. Of these, Ischia Porto boasts the best bars, while Forio and Lacco Ameno have the prettiest spas and gardens. On the calmer south coast, the car-free perfection of Sant'Angelo offers a languid blend of a cosy harbour and lazy beaches. In between the coasts lies a less-trodden landscape of chestnut forests, vineyards and volcanic rock, loomed over by Monte Epomeo, Ischia's highest peak.

History

Ischia was an important stop on the trade route from Greece to northern Italy in the 8th century but has since seen its fair share of disaster. The 1301 eruption of the now extinct (and unfortunately named) Monte Arso forced the locals to flee to the mainland, where they remained for four years. Five centuries later, in 1883, an earthquake killed more than 1700 people and razed the burgeoning spa town of Casamicciola. To this day, the town's name signifies 'total destruction' in the Italian vernacular.

ⓘ Information

Tourist Office (Map p142; ☑ 081 507 42 31; www.infoischiaprocida.it; Via Iasolino 7, Ischia Porto; ◷ 9am-2pm & 3-8pm Mon-Sat Apr-Sep, 9am-2pm Mon-Fri Oct-Mar) Has a slim selection of maps and brochures; next to the ferry port.

ⓘ Getting There & Away

Ischia's main ferry terminal is in Ischia Porto. However, there are also other smaller terminals in Casamicciola and Forio.

Alilauro (☑ 081 497 22 42; www.alilauro.it) Operates hydrofoils from Naples to Ischia Porto

(€20.10, 50 minutes, up to 12 daily) and up to six hydrofoils daily between Forio and Naples (€21.50). There are also two daily ferries to Sorrento (€22.90, one hour) from Ischia Porto.

Caremar (☑ 081 98 48 18; www.caremar.it; Via Iasolino) Operates up to six daily hydrofoils from Naples to Ischia Porto (€17.90, 45 minutes) and Procida (€8.70, 20 minutes), as well as ferries.

SNAV (Map p138; ☑ 081 428 55 55; www.snav.it) Operates hydrofoils from Naples to the Ischian town of Casamicciola (€20.20 to €21.20, one hour, five daily).

ℹ Getting Around

Ischia's main circular highway can get clogged with traffic in the height of summer. This, combined with the penchant the local youth have for overtaking on blind corners and the environmental impact of just too many cars, means that you may want to consider riding the excellent network of buses (cheap!) or hopping in a taxi (not cheap!) to get around. The distance between attractions and the lack of pavements on the busy roads makes walking unappealing.

The island's main **bus station** (Map p142; cnr Via Iasolino & Via della Foce) is a one-minute walk west of the **ferry and hydrofoil terminal** (Map p142; Via Iasolino), at Ischia Porto, with buses servicing all other parts of the island.

BUS

There are two principal lines: the CS (Circolo Sinistro, or Left Circle), which circles the island anticlockwise, and the CD line (Circolo Destro, or Right Circle), which travels in a clockwise direction, passing through each town and departing every 15 to 30 minutes. Buses pass near all hotels and campgrounds. A single-trip ticket (corsa singola) costs €1.50 (€2 if bought on board). An all-day, multi-use ticket (biglietto giornaliero) costs €4.50 and should be bought from tobacconists.

CAR & SCOOTER

You can do this small island a favour by not bringing your car. If you want to hire a car or a scooter for a day, there are plenty of hire companies. **Balestrieri** (☑ 081 98 56 91; www.autonoleggiobalestrieri.it; Via Iasolino 35, Ischia Porto; car per day/week from €30/140) hires out cars and scooters, and it also has mountain bikes (€15 per day). Note that you can't take a hired vehicle off the island.

If you're hiring a car in high season, parking is going to be a headache. Go for a smart car if you can, which takes up minimal space. There's a small car park at the entrance to Sant'Angelo (two hours €3) and Ischia Porto and Ischia Ponte both have signposted central car parks (€1.50 per hour).

Ischia Porto & Ischia Ponte

Although technically two separate towns, Ischia Porto and Ischia Ponte are bookends to one long, sinuous sprawl of pastel-coloured buildings, terrace bars and restaurants, and palm-fringed shops and hotels, all of which makes for a relaxed saunter.

The ferry port itself was a crater lake, opened up to sea at the request of Spanish king Ferdinand II in 1854. While the story goes that he couldn't stand the stench of the lake, his request was more likely inspired by the prospect of increasing shipping-tax revenue.

Whatever the reason, it was a great idea, and now the harbour is fringed by a string of restaurants serving fresh seafood. Head further east and you'll hit the **Spiaggia dei Pescatori**, where the compelling scene of brightly painted fishing boats and lurid beach umbrellas is backed by the pyramid silhouette of the imposing Castello Aragonese.

◎ Sights & Activities

Santa Maria Assunta   CATHEDRAL
(Map p142; Via Mazzella, Ischia Ponte; ⊙ 8am-12.30pm & 4.30-8pm) A striking 15th-century watchtower, Torre del Mare, now serves as the bell tower to this church that is also Ischia's cathedral. The current church, designed by Antonio Massinetti and completed in 1751, stands on the site of two older churches, one 13th century and the other 17th century. Step inside its fanciful baroque interior and you'll find an ancient baptismal font salvaged from the nearby castle and propped up by marble statues of the virtues, and a sombre Romanesque wooden crucifix.

Museo del Mare   MUSEUM
(Map p142; ☑ 081 98 11 24; Via San Giovanni da Procida 2, Ischia Ponte; adult/reduced €2.50/free; ⊙ 10.30am-12.30pm Wed, Fri & Sun; 4-8pm Tue, Thu & Sat; ⊞) If you are an old salt at heart (or have a penchant for model ships), don't miss Ischia's maritime museum with its lovingly documented exhibits. Objects include cult ex-votos (offerings to the saints) from sailors to saints, ancient urns, beautifully crafted model ships and revealing photographs of island life in the 20th century, including the arrival of Ischia's very first American car in 1958 – you can just imagine what a celebratory occasion that must have been.

THE ISLANDS ISCHIA PORTO & ISCHIA PONTE

Ischia

THE ISLANDS ISCHIA PORTO & ISCHIA PONTE

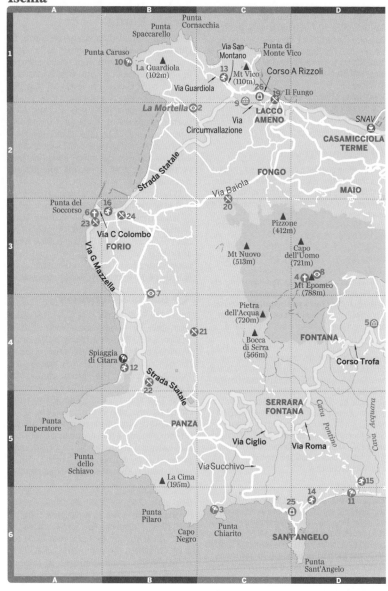

Ischia Diving DIVING
(Map p142; ☑081 98 18 52; www.ischiadiving.net;
Via Iasolino 106, Ischia Porto; single dive €40) This
well-established diving outfit offers some
attractively priced dive packages, such as
five dives including equipment for €180.

Eating

Both Ischia Porto and Ischia Ponte offer a
good number of decent restaurants. Fresh
fish and seafood are the speciality. For waterside dining, consider the restaurants
along Via Porto, which flanks the eastern

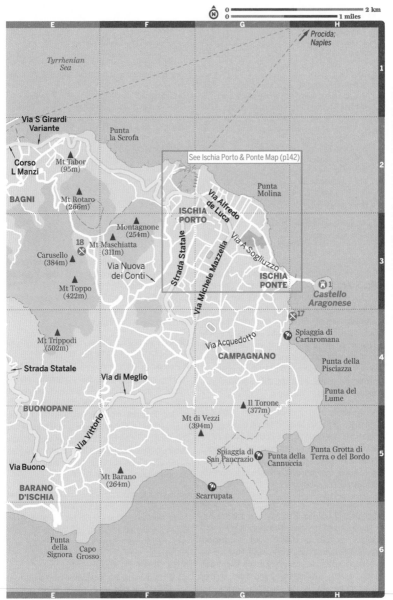

side of Ischia Porto's harbour. Always ask if the seafood is *surgelato* (frozen) or *fresco* (fresh); it's the latter you want to be eating.

Ristorante Aglio, Olio & Pomodoro ITALIAN €
(Map p142; ☑ 081 1914 3460; Via Mazzella 84, Ischia Ponte; meals €20; ☉ 12.30-3pm & 7-11pm)

Garlic, olive oil and tomatoes are the base for a lot of simply executed dishes at this warmly welcoming trattoria serving local dishes such as rabbit, plus excellent pizzas and – of course – seafood. It's not the most elegant option in town, but it's reasonably priced and great fun.

Ischia

Al Pontile
ITALIAN €

(Map p142; ☑ 081 98 34 92; Via Mazzella 15, Ischia Ponte; meals from €20; ⊗ noon-3pm & 7pm-midnight Mar-Oct) Sit outside, front or back, with the castle as an evocative backdrop to the shopping street or sea. The reassuringly brief menu includes pasta mainstays like *puttanesca* with capers, tomatoes and olives, and reliable meat and fish mains. Smile sweetly and the owner will bring a bottle of *limoncello* along with the bill, allowing you your fill of lemony top-ups.

Bar de Maio
GELATO €

(Map p142; ☑ 081 99 18 70; Piazza Antica Reggia 9, Ischia Porto; ice cream from €1.50; ⊗ 24hr) Technically a bar close to the port; in reality, it's better known as a prime gelato spot. According to some residents, it's the best ice-cream parlour on the island.

Da Ciccio
CAFE €

(Map p142; ☑ 081 199 13 14; Via Porto 1, Ischia Porto; snacks from €1; ⊗ 8am-midnight; 🛜) Old and popular enough to qualify as an 'institution' (1947 and counting), Da Ciccio (not to be confused with the restaurant of the same name) is an always-busy bar and casual eating place plying ice cream, pastries and coffee to people catching up on their email (thanks to the free wi-fi). It's slap-bang in the middle of the port area.

Gran Caffè Vittoria
CAFE €

(Map p142; ☑ 081 199 16 49; Corso Colonna 110, Ischia Porto; pastries from €2.50; ⊗ 8am-11pm) At the smarter end of the port, this posh cafe employs old-school bow-tied waiters to serve an artistic-looking selection of cakes, pastries, coffees and other such delights. The bulk of the clientele prefers to lounge al fresco on the outdoor terrace on the other side of the pedestrian street.

★ Ristorante La Pantera Rosa
ITALIAN €€

(Map p142; ☑ 081 99 24 83; Via Porto 53, Ischia Porto; meals €30; ⊗ noon-2.30pm & 7-11.30pm) In the long line of Ischia's portside eating establishments, the 'pink panther' might be the best. First, there's the owner, Amedeo, a skilled linguist who manages to be charismatic in five different languages. Then there's the food: all the traditional pasta and pizza choices, plus specialities like *risotto alla pescatora* (seafood risotto), which comes highly recommended.

Gardenia Mare
MEDITERRANEAN €€

(Map p138; ☑ 081 99 11 07; www.gardeniamare.it; Via Nuova Cartaromana 66, Ischia Ponte; meals €35-40; ⊗ 9am-6pm & 8.30-11.30pm) With bamboo furniture, surrounding greenery and wonderful views of the Castello Aragonese, this makes for a fantastically romantic sunset dinner spot. It's a beach-club restaurant (no fee if you just want to eat here), so you can work up your appetite for the seafood dishes with a swim first.

Da Raffaele
ITALIAN €€

(Map p142; ☑ 081 99 12 03; www.daraffaele.it; Via Roma 29, Ischia Porto; meals €28; ⊗ noon-3pm & 6.30-11.30pm Mar-Nov; 🖈) Handily situated in the middle of Via Roma, this brightly lit,

WORTH A TRIP

IL FOCOLARE

A good choice for those seeking a little turf instead of surf, **Il Focolare** (Map p138; ☑ 081 90 29 44; www.trattoriailfocolare.it; Via Creajo al Crocefisso 3, Barano d'Ischia; meals €30-35; ⊙12.30-2.45pm Thu-Sun & 7.30-11.30pm daily Jun-Oct, closed Wed Nov-May, closed Feb) is one of the island's best-loved restaurants. Family-run, homey and rustic, it has a solidly traditional meat-based menu with steaks, lamb cutlets and specialities including *coniglio all'Ischitana* (a typical local rabbit dish with tomatoes, garlic and herbs). On the sweet front, the desserts are homemade and exquisite.

Owner Riccardo D'Ambra (who runs the restaurant together with his son, Agostino) is a leading local advocate of the Slow Food movement. If you want seafood, coffee or soft drinks, you'll have to go elsewhere; they're not on the menu here.

welcoming place has few surprises on the menu but prepares everything well. Try the *frittura di pesce all'ischitana* (mixed fried fish) or *melanzane a funghetti* (fried aubergine with tomatoes, mushrooms, garlic and basil). It might be the best place in Ischia for street-side beer and pizza.

Ristorante da Ciccio ITALIAN €€
(Map p142; ☑ 081 99 16 86; Via Mazzella 32, Ischia Ponte; meals €25-30; ⊙noon-3.30pm & 7.30-11.30pm, closed Tue Dec-Feb) In the seafood game since 1963 and currently overseen by charming host Carlo, Ristorante da Ciccio (Italian street-slang for 'dude' or 'chubby') is an atmospheric trattoria where the uncomplicated menu pushes you unapologetically towards the fish. The pasta with prawns, clams and courgettes sings out loudly.

Tables spill out onto the pavement in summer, from where there are fabulous castle views.

 Drinking & Nightlife

Ischia is not Ibiza. That said, the area around Ischia Porto has the best buzz, with a handful of bars and clubs that stay open way past cocoa time.

Bar Calise BAR
(Map p142; ☑ 081 99 12 70; www.barcalise.com; Piazza degli Eroi 69, Ischia Porto; ⊙11am-4pm & 6pm-2am Thu-Sun) One of the oldest bars on the island, founded in 1925 and located near the harbour. The atmosphere here is one of languid gentility: waistcoated waiters serve cocktails and coffees to a background of live Latin, swing and folk music.

Attached to the bar, the *pasticceria* (pastry shop) is a great place to pick up *sfogliatelle* (cream-filled pastry with thin leaf-like outer shell) and other treats.

Valentino Ischia CLUB
(Map p142; ☑ 081 98 25 69; www.valentinoischia. eu; Corso Colonna 97, Ischia Porto; ⊙10pm-5am Wed-Sun) A surprisingly lively club playing international house music, and with the aesthetic bonus of some pretty, traditional majolica tilework.

 Shopping

Ischia's shopping is centred on Via Roma and the web of narrow streets leading to Ischia Ponte. From floss-thin bikinis to decadent jars of *babà* (sponge soaked in rum), there's enough shopping on these cobbled streets to shift your credit card into overdrive. For a more low-key experience, explore the tiny boutiques and art galleries in Sant'Angelo and Forio.

Antica Macelleria di Francesco Esposito FOOD
(Map p142; ☑ 081 98 10 11; Via delle Terme 2, Ischia Porto; ⊙8am-1.30pm & 4.30-10pm) This century-old deli is gourmet foodie heaven. Drop in from 8am for fresh mozzarella and wood-fired *casareccio* bread, plus a lip-smacking choice of cheese, prosciutto, homemade *peperoncino* salami and marinated peppers. In fact, it's got everything you need for a picnic on the beach, including the obligatory bottle of Falanghina (dry white wine).

Atelier delle Dolcezze FOOD
(Cioccolateria e Gelateria d'Arte; Map p142; Via Cortese; ⊙9am-1.30pm & 4.30-8.30pm Tue-Sun) A fabulous modern chocolatier, combining ranks of sweet chocolate treats with sumptuous artisanal ice cream. The prettily wrapped boxes make good gifts.

Libreria Imagaenaria BOOKS
(Map p142; ☑ 081 98 56 32; Via Mazzella 46-50, Ischia Ponte; ⊙9am-9.30pm) A beautiful old-school bookshop in Ischia Ponte with

Ischia Porto & Ponte

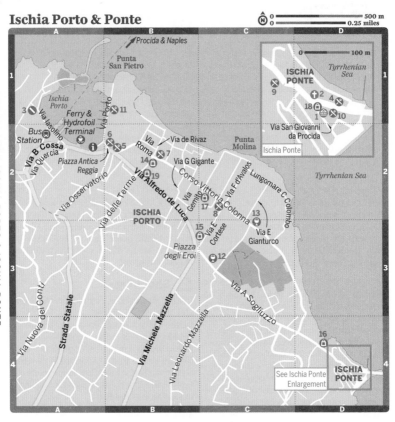

Ischia Porto & Ponte

armchairs, plies of multilingual tomes and some fine local prints on sale too.

Judith Major   FASHION & ACCESSORIES
(Map p142; ☎081 98 32 95; Corso Colonna 174, Ischia Porte; ◷9.30am-1.30pm & 4-8pm) Despite the headmistressy name, this boutique is the exclusive stockist of Italian label Brunello Cucinelli. The look is Polo Ralph Lauren with a sexy Italian twist: cashmere sweaters, suave shirts, blazers and chic womenswear. Shoes include Prada, Barrett and Alberto

Guardiani for men and Stuart Weitzman and Pedro Garcia for women.

Filippo Cianciarelli CERAMICS
(Artigianato Ischitano; Map p142; www.ceramiche cianciarelli.it; Via Mazzella 113, Ischia Ponte; ☺9am-1pm & 4-8pm Mon-Sat) Filippo is a highly original artist who creates vividly patterned pieces, including tall, pyramid-shaped vases, tiled pictures with abstract themes and smaller, easy-to-pack plates, mugs and the like. Displays of his work are combined with more traditional ceramic pieces. The shop sign displays 'Artigianato Ischitano'.

Scaglione Renato JEWELLERY
(Map p142; ☑081 98 45 03; Via Alfredo de Luca 109, Ischia Porto; ☺9am-1pm & 4-8pm Mon-Sat) This little shop has a small but sparkling range of exquisite jewellery, incorporating turquoise, amethyst, amber and coral. Prices are slightly lower than the glitzier options on nearby Via Roma.

❶ Getting There & Away

Ischia Porto is the island's main port with regular daily hydrofoils to Naples with Caremar (p136) and Alilauro (p136).

❶ Getting Around

The island's main bus station (p137) is a one-minute walk west of the ferry terminal in Ischia Porto, with buses servicing all other parts of the island.

CASTELLO ARAGONESE

There are castles and then there's Ischia's **Castello Aragonese** (Aragon Castle; Map p138; ☑342 9618566, 081 99 28 34; www.castelloaragoneseischia.com; Rocca del Castello, Ischia Ponte; adult/reduced €10/6; ☺9am-sunset), a veritable fort-city set on its own craggy islet, looking like a cross between Harry Potter's Hogwarts and Mont Saint Michel. While Syracusan tyrant Gerone I built the first fortress here in 474 BC, the bulk of the current structure dates from the 1400s, when King Alfonso of Aragon gave the older Angevin fortress a thorough makeover, building the fortified bastions, current causeway and access ramp cut into the rock.

At the base of the complex you pay the entrance fee and then ascend via a lift or a series of paths that take you on a looping route through the buildings and lush gardens. The signposted route starts with the relatively modern and plain **Chiesa dell'Immacolata**, built in 1737 over an old church. Commissioned by the adjoining **Convento delle Clarisse** (Convent for Clarisse nuns), it was left in its minimalist state after building funds ran out. Next door, the nuns contributed to the castle's most bizarre and macabre sight. When the erstwhile sisters died, their corpses were taken into the windowless, airless **Cimitero delle Monache Clarisse** where they were propped up on toilet-like chairs. The living nuns were expected to pray daily to the decomposing corpses as a grim reminder of their own mortality. Not surprisingly, many of them caught diseases in the process, some fatal. The empty chairs remain on view in the cellars as a chilling reminder.

Far brighter are the sunbaked, stuccoed ruins of the 14th-century **Cattedrale dell'Assunta**, which collapsed under cannon fire in 1809 as the British tried to shell Napoleon's occupying army into submission. The 11th-century crypt below features snippets of 14th-century frescoes inspired by Giotto.

Carry on until you reach the elegant, hexagonal **Chiesa di San Pietro a Pantaniello** and sombre **Carcere Borbonico**, the one-time prison for leading figures of the Risorgimento (the 19th-century Italian unification movement), such as Poerio, Pironti, Nusco and Settembrini. There's a small and grisly **Museo delle Torture**, with a collection of medieval torture instruments and impressive armour and weaponry.

Elsewhere, you can stroll the castle's terraced grounds dipping into various other small chapels and drinking in the views from the Terrazzo degli Ulivi (Olive tree terrace).

The complex includes a couple of attractive terrace cafes (the highest one offers lovely views across to Capri), as well as an atmospheric **hotel** (☑081 99 24 35; www.albergoilmonastero.it; Castello Aragonese, Rocca del Castello, Ischia Ponte; s €65-90, d €105-145; ☺mid-April–mid-Oct; ⊞ ☎).

LOCAL KNOWLEDGE

ISCHIA ON A FORK

If you wanted to stick the best parts of Ischian cuisine on a fork, you'd need to make it a big one. The island's insularity and rich volcanic soil have thrown up a rich melange of recipes over the years, many of them subtly different from dishes found elsewhere in Campania.

A popular Ischian starter is *caponata*. Unlike Sicilian *caponata* (made with aubergines), the Ischian dish resembles tomato bruschetta with added tuna and olives. It was originally a poor person's food, made for farmers out in the fields from the leftovers of the previous day's stale bread.

For the main course, there's an enticing choice between land and sea. Classic seafood dishes adhere to a cooking method known as *acqua pazza* (crazy water): white fish poached in a herb-heavy broth with locally grown *pomodorini* (cherry tomatoes), garlic and parsley. Typical local fish include *pesce bandiera* (sailfish), the flat castagna, lampuga and *palamide* (a small tuna). Smaller seafood, such as squid, prawns and anchovies, are best enjoyed fried in a *frittura di parzana* (meaning 'from the trawler') and served simply with lemon.

Plump local *pomodorini* reappear in the most classic of all Ischian dishes, *coniglio all'ischitana,* a rabbit stew cooked on the hob in a large terracotta pot with a sauce of olive oil, unpeeled garlic, tomato, chilli, basil, thyme and white wine. Traditionally, rabbits were caught wild, but by the late 20th century cage-bred rabbits had become standard fare on Ischia. In recent years, in a nod to the Slow Food movement, farmers have started to return to rearing rabbits *di fossa* (semiwild in burrows).

Despite its high population density and limited agricultural terrain, Ischia still supports an estimated 800 hectares of vineyards, most of them terraced on the lower slopes of Monte Epomeo. Wine production in Ischia goes back to the ancient Greeks and the island harbours some of Italy's oldest DOCs. With fish or pasta, try a Forastera or a Biancolella (both whites). With the rich *coniglio all'ischitana* go for a ruby red Piedirosso.

If you've room for dessert, opt for chocolate and almond cake (an import from nearby Capri), helped down with an obligatory ice-cold limoncello.

Lacco Ameno

📞 081 / POP 4800

The site of what was possibly the first Greek colony in Italy, Lacco Ameno (the smallest of Ischia's six communes) hides a rich history under its modern cluster of posh spas. The Greeks were the first to settle in the area in around 750 BC. They called Ischia Pithecusae and built an acropolis on Monte Vico, close to where Lacco Ameno now lies. Numerous necropolises have been uncovered nearby.

Lacco's modern renaissance came in the 1950s and 1960s, when Italian film producer Angelo Rizzoli bought the 18th-century Villa Arbusto and rekindled the Roman penchant for thermal spas. French starlets and European royalty came to play at the legendary Terme Regina Isabella spa resort. The stars may have gone, but one local icon remains, sprouting out of the sea: the iconic **Il Fungo** (The Mushroom) is a 10m volcanic rock formation spat out by Monte Epomeo thousands of years ago.

◉ Sights & Activities

**Museo Archeologico
di Pithecusae** MUSEUM

(Map p138; 📞 081 99 61 83; www.pithecusae. it; Corso Rizzoli 210; incl Museo Angelo Rizzoli €5; ⊙ 9.30am-1pm & 3-6.30pm Tue-Sun) Housed in the elegant Villa Arbusto, former home of local celeb Angelo Rizzoli, the Museo Archeologico di Pithecusae enjoys a heady historical location overlooking Monte Vico, site of the ancient settlement and acropolis of Pithecusae. The museum has a fascinating collection of important finds from the island's Hellenic settlement, ranging from imported earthenware to parts of the acropolis itself.

A highlight is the legendary 7th-century-BC Nestor's Cup in Sala (Room) II, bearing one of the oldest-known Greek inscriptions – which, appropriately, celebrates the wine of Ischia. The space also encompasses the Museo Angelo Rizzoli.

Museo Angelo Rizzoli MUSEUM

(Map p138; ☑ 081 99 61 83; www.museoangelo rizzoli.it/; Corso Rizzoli 210; incl Museo Archeolog-ico di Pithecusae €5; ⊙ 9.30am-1pm & 3-6.30pm Tue-Sun; ☝) This pint-sized museum encased in the larger Museo Archeologico di Pithec-usae pays homage to the man who turned humble little Lacco into a celebrity hotspot in the 1950s. Cool paparazzi shots and clip-pings of a Hitchcock-esque Rizzoli and his famous friends decorate rooms that once played host to the likes of Gina Lollabrigida, Grace Kelly and Federico Fellini.

Equally striking are the villa's gardens, complete with lemon trees, fountain, a chil-dren's playground and star-worthy views to-wards the Campi Flegrei.

★ Negombo SPA

(Map p138; ☑ 081 98 61 52; www.negombo.it; Baia di San Montano; all day adult/reduced €35/23, from 3.30pm €23/19; ⊙ 8.30am-7pm mid-Apr-early Oct) This is arguably the best thermal spa on an island full of them, courtesy of its multifaceted attractions. Sure, there are the Zen-like thermal pools, a hammam and private beach, but Negombo is also part of the Grandi Giardini Italiani network, home to more than 500 exotic plant species. Fur-thermore, it ranks as an 'art park' with avant-garde sculptures incorporated into the greenery.

Attractive pools (13 of them) are arranged amid floral foliage, plus there's a Japanese labyrinth pool for weary feet, a decent *tavola calda* (snack bar), and a full range of mas-sage and beauty treatments. A private beach on the Baia di San Montano lies out front, meaning Negombo tends to draw a younger crowd than many other Ischian spa spots.

Those arriving by car or scooter can park all day on-site (car/scooter €5/€3).

Eating

Lacco Ameno offers the usual mix of pizzeri-as and seafood-centric trattorias and restau-rants. Many of the places to eat in town are on, or just off, the main coastal thoroughfare of Corso Angelo Rizzoli.

La Cantina del Mare ITALIAN €

(Map p138; ☑ 081 333 03 22; Corso Rizzoli 20; meals €25; ⊙ noon-2.30pm & 7pm-midnight) This friendly place is just across the road from the beach and serves excellent dishes to locals and wised-up tourists; seafood is the speciality. Sit on the pretty terrace or in the moodily lit interior lined with shelves of wine. The bread is pretty special too: it's made in the island's oldest bread oven and delivered daily.

🛍 Shopping

Stella di Mare CLOTHING

(Map p138; ☑ 081 199 43 96; Corso Rizzoli 150; ⊙ 9.30-1pm & 5-10pm) Pricey and gorgeous womenswear: silk and linen skirts and kaf-tans to keep you cool in every sense, plus sandals, brogues, and fancy tassled and beaded bags.

OFF THE BEATEN TRACK

MONTE EPOMEO & THE HINTERLAND

To anyone of average fitness, an ascent of Ischia's slumbering volcanic peak is practically obligatory. Indeed, the views from the rocky summit of Monte Epomeo are simply superb.

The quickest way to climb Epomeo is from the village of **Fontana** located on the island's southern flank. The 2.5km route (signposted from a bend in the road where the bus stops) weaves up a paved road, diverts onto a track and finishes on a steep-ish path.

The little church near the top of Monte Epomeo is the 15th-century **Cappella di San Nicola di Bari** (Map p138), which features a pretty majolica floor. The adjoining her-mitage was built in the 18th century by an island governor who, after narrowly escaping death, swapped politics for poverty and spent the rest of his days here in saintly solitude.

If the hike leaves you wanting to further explore Ischia's rugged hinterland, **Geo-Ausfluge** (☑ 081 90 30 58; www.eurogeopark.com; walks €17-26) offers a selection of walks throughout the island, led by Italian geologist Aniello Di Lorio. The walks range from three to five hours, with various collection points in Ischia; pick-up in Casamicciola and Panza costs a further €9 return. Although the walks are conducted in German and Italian, they allow participants of all languages to experience some beautiful parts of the island that would be difficult to access solo. For further information and bookings, con-tact Geo-Ausfluge by email or phone.

LAZY BEACH DAYS

While Campania's bewitching landscapes can get your adrenaline pumping, they can also soothe. The region's coastline claims some of Italy's most inviting waters. So bronze, bathe and recharge at the following standout spiagge (beaches).

ISLAND BEACHES

Capri's best beach is at **Marina Grande**, where you'll find some sand among the pebbles. Splash amid ruins at pebbly **Bagni di Tiberio** (p134) or soak up sunsets at in-the-know **Spiaggia di Faro** (p131). On Ischia, **Baia di Sorgeto** (p150) features a bubbling thermal spring, while rocky **Punta Caruso** offers clear, deep water for adult bathers. Across on Procida, bathe on beautiful, sandy **Spiaggia di Chiaia** (p153).

AMALFI COAST BEACHES

The Amalfi Coast's best sandy beach is oft-crowded **Vietri sul Mare** (p193), while steep **Fiordo di Furore** (p183) is perfect for a sheltered dip. One of the Coast's less tourist-centric towns, **Maiori**, claims the region's longest beach, while **Marina di Praia** offers a pebbly cove with good swimming, dive operators (p182) and excellent fish restaurants. Tiny, west-facing **Spiaggia della Gavitelli** (p181) comes with a private beach club and grand sunsets.

CILENTO BEACHES

Sandy, spacious beaches await at squeaky-clean **Spiaggia Grande di Acciaroli** (p208) and **Castellabate** (p206), both in sharp contrast to the Amalfi Coast's rockier, more crowded bathing spots. Also appealing is **Spiaggia Palinuro** (p208) and its slightly quieter sibling, **Spiaggia Marinella** (p208).

1. Marina Grande (p134), Capri
2. Fiordo di Furore (p183), Amalfi Coast

2

❶ Getting There & Away

Both of Ischia's two principal bus lines – the CS and CD – pass through Lacco Ameno on their way around the island. Buses depart every 15 to 30 minutes from the waterfront at the junction of Corso Angelo Rizzoli and SS270.

Forio & the West Coast

The largest town on the island, and apparently the favoured destination of Tennessee Williams and Truman Capote in the 1950s, Forio is home to some of the best restaurants on Ischia, as well as good beaches and a couple of beautifully laid-out botanical gardens.

◎ Sights

★ La Mortella   GARDENS
(Place of the Myrtles; Map p138; ☑ 081 98 62 20; www.lamortella.it; Via F Calese 39; adult/reduced €12/10; ☉ 9am-7pm Tue, Thu, Sat & Sun Apr-early Nov) A symphony of plants, La Mortella (the myrtles) is the former home and gardens of the late British composer William Walton (1902–83) and his Argentine wife, Susana. Designed by Russell Page and inspired by the Moorish gardens of Spain's Alhambra, it is recognised as one of Italy's finest botanical gardens. Stroll among pools, terraces, palms, fountains and more than 1000 rare and exotic plants from all over the world.

The lower section of the garden is humid and tropical, while the upper level features Mediterranean plants and beautiful views over Forio and the coast.

The Waltons first came here in 1949 to establish a new home where they subsequently entertained such venerable house guests as Sir Laurence Olivier, Maria Callas and Charlie Chaplin. Walton's life is commemorated in a small on-site museum, while his ashes are buried beneath a monument in the garden's upper reaches. The gardens host chamber-music recitals and concerts and there's also a rather elegant cafe where you can enjoy a cup of tea amid the greenery.

Giardini Ravino   GARDENS
(Map p138; ☑ 081 99 77 83; www.ravino.it; SS 270; adult/reduced €9/4; ☉ 9am-sunset Wed & Fri-Mon Mar–mid-Nov) The vision of local botanist Giuseppe D'Ambra, who has collected plants since the 1960s, this 6000-sq-metre garden pays homage to the not-so-humble cactus. There is a diverse collection here, as well as other succulent plants, many of which are said to have homeopathic qualities. You can join a guided walk every Sunday at 11am; at other times, reserve in advance.

The gardens are also the site of concerts and art and craft exhibitions, and there are self-catering apartments to rent.

Chiesa di Santa Maria del Soccorso   CHURCH
(Map p138; Via Soccorso 1; ☉ 10am-sunset) This diminutive white church perched above the water in the town centre was originally part of a 14th-century Augustinian monastery; its side chapel and dome were added in 1791 and 1854 respectively, the latter rebuilt after the 1883 earthquake. The 18th-century mismatched majolica tiles adorning the sea-scarred staircase out the front are truly beautiful – as is the view beyond.

🏃 Activities

Giardini Poseidon   SPA
(Poseidon Gardens; Map p138; ☑ 081 908 71 11; www.giardiniposeidonterme.com; Via Mazzella, Spiaggia di Citara; passes per day/half-day/evening €33/€28/€6; ☉ 9am-7pm Apr-Oct) South of Forio lies Ischia's largest day spa, the sprawling Giardini Poseidon, with 20 pools ranging from 28°C (82.4°F) to 40°C (104°F) spread over 6 hectares. The wide choice of treatments and facilities include massages, jacuzzis, saunas, various health treatments, and terraced pools spilling down the volcanic cliffside. Alternatively, settle for the dazzling private beach below.

Westcoast   BOATING
(Map p138; ☑ 081 90 86 04; www.westcoast ischia.it; Porto di Forio; boat hire from €100; ☉ 9am-6.30pm Apr-Nov) Westcoast provides full-day hire of motorised boats and dinghies (with or without a skipper). This is a particularly good idea in August, when the more popular beaches are crowded and you are desperate to find a quiet sandy cove.

🍴 Eating

Forio doesn't lack decent places to eat. Plenty line the portside strip, but some of the best – including a winery – are scattered around the outskirts.

Zi Carmela   ITALIAN €
(Map p138; ☑ 081 99 84 23; Via Schioppa 27; meals €25; ☉ noon-3pm & 7pm-midnight Apr-Oct; 🖭)

WILLIAM & SUSANA WALTON & THE PLACE OF THE MYRTLES

The first meeting between William Walton, renowned 46-year-old British composer, and Susana Gil, a 22-year-old Argentine secretary working for the British Council, has become legend. Spotting Susana at a cocktail party in Buenos Aires, Walton told Benjamin Britten that he intended to marry her. He proposed to Susana, repeating the question every day for two weeks until, to the dismay of her parents, she capitulated – they were married in 1948. It was not to be a fairy tale: Walton had umpteen affairs and made Susana have a dangerous backstreet abortion when she was carrying their child. But from then until the end of her life, her husband, and his music, came first for Susana.

Walton was at the height of his fame at the time of their marriage: he had been knighted in 1951, the same year that the full score of *Façade* was published. This, his most famous work, came about as a collaboration with his patron Edith Sitwell; a setting to music of her surrealistic poems written in 1922, it was greeted as a major contribution to modernism. An innovative viola concerto (1929) was followed by the dazzling and ambitious *First Symphony* in 1935. And, in 1944, Walton wrote the music – by turns masterfully nuanced and clarion-like – for Olivier's film of *Henry V*.

Despite the composer's acclaim, money was tight, and the couple moved from London to the wilds of volcanic Ischia. Their new home, bought despite concerns voiced by their friend Laurence Olivier, was a barren quarry with myrtles *(mortelle)* growing from the rocks. In 1956 Susana and designer Russell Page began to work on La Mortella, transforming the rocky landscape into a layered and theatrical tropical paradise full of rare and exotic plants, such as the huge water lily *Victoria amazonica*, with flowers that turn from white to crimson. As the fame and beauty of the garden increased so Walton's star faded, eclipsed by the progress of Britten: his work came to be seen as old-fashioned, an exercise in orchestral nostalgia.

But the garden was a cherished refuge for the couple, where they were visited by stars such as Laurence Olivier and Vivien Leigh, Maria Callas, Charlie Chaplin and the British dramatist Terence Rattigan.

When Walton died in 1983, Susana encased his ashes in a pyramidal rock at La Mortella, and created the William Walton Trust and Foundation in his memory. She built a recital hall in the garden, featuring busts of the Sitwells, a bronze of Walton himself, and John Piper's design for the ballet version of *Façade*.

Susana's spirited presence in jewel-coloured clothes lit up the garden for visitors into her old age. She died in 2010 aged 83, and the garden is now run by the trust. Visitors to this wonderful place have a double pleasure in store: as well as losing themselves among the lush plants, they will also hear Walton's irresistibly bright and sensual music. And they will see Susana's own memorial, which touchingly recalls a woman who 'loved tenderly, worked with passion and believed in immortality'.

Dating back decades, this restaurant has a lovely terrace decorated with copper pans, ceramic mugs and strings of garlic and chillies. Locals come for seafood dishes such as the *fritturina e pezzogne* (white fish baked in the pizza oven) or *tartare di palamito al profumo d'arancia* (tartare of fish with citrus).

It's perched above an American-style bar (entry is via a side street).

★ **La Casereccia**　　　　CAMPANIAN €€
(Map p138; ☏ 081 98 77 56; www.lacasereccia.com; Via Baiola 269; meals €28-40; ⊙1-3pm & 7.30pm-1am, closed Mon-Wed Feb) Safe in the hands of Mamma Tina, Casereccia delivers plenty of full-flavoured *casereccia* (homemade food). The very Ischian menu pushes seafood, doughy pizzas, island-produced wine and that much vaunted local speciality – *coniglio* (rabbit). Try it either roasted or packaged in delicate ravioli. It's a little out of town on the flanks of Monte Epomeo, but worth the detour.

Montecorvo　　　　ITALIAN €€
(Map p138; ☏ 081 99 80 29; www.montecorvo.it; Via Montecorvo 33; meals €30; ⊙7.30pm-midnight daily yr round, 12.30-3pm Sun mid-Sep–mid-Jun, closed Wed Nov-Mar; ☏) Part of the dining room at hillside Montecorvo is tunnelled into a cave, while the verdant terrace offers

RISTORANTE PIETRATORCIA

Enjoying a bucolic setting among tumbling vines, wild fig trees and rosemary bushes, A-list winery and eatery **Ristorante Pietratorcia** (Map p138; ☑ 081 90 72 32; www.ristorantepietratorcia. it; Via Provinciale Panza 401; menus €35, wine degustations from €20; ☺ 11am-2pm & 5.30pm-midnight Tue-Sun Easter-Oct; ☜) is a showcase for Ischian cooking. Tour the old stone cellars, sip a local drop and eye up a competent, seasonal turf-and-surf menu that is led by rabbit, served with pasta or slow-cooked island style with wine and potatoes. Book ahead in high season. The CD and CS buses stop within metres of the winery's entrance; ask the driver to advise you when to alight.

spectacular sunset views. Owner Giovanni prides himself on the special dishes he makes daily. There's an emphasis on grilled meat and fish, and an especially popular dish of local rabbit, cooked in a woodfired oven.

Despite its sneaky location, hidden amid lush foliage outside Forio, Montecorvo is well signposted along the side street that leads to it.

Umberto a Mare ITALIAN €€€
(Map p138; ☑ 081 99 71 71; www.umbertoamare. it; Via Soccorso 2; meals €45-50; ☺ noon-3pm & 7-11pm Mar-Dec) For 80 years lucky diners have been watching the sun set at this terraced restaurant by the Spanish mission-style Soccorso church in Forio. Pick between a low-key cafe-bar for light snacks or the more formal seasonal restaurant. Restaurant highlights include penne with lobster and asparagus, and a delicate *al profumo di mare* (lightly grilled freshly caught fish).

The orange-sorbet dessert here is highly recommended.

❶ Getting There & Away

It's possible to catch a hydrofoil from Forio's port to Naples with Alilauro (p136).

Both of Ischia's two principal bus lines – the CS and CD – service Forio on their way around the island. Buses depart every 15 to 30 minutes from a bus stop next to the port, at the junction of Via Colombo and Via Panza.

Sant'Angelo & the South Coast

Tiny Sant'Angelo attracts a voguish crowd with its tucked-away boutiques, seafront restaurants and great beaches. Quiet lanes spill down the hill to fashionable Piazzetta Ottorino Troia, where sun-kissed locals sip Campari and soda and take in late-night summer music concerts. Keeping an eye on it all is the great hulking *scoglio* (rock), joined to the village by a sandbar sprinkled with fishing boats, beach umbrellas and *bagnini* (lifeguards).

Catch a brightly painted water taxi from the pier to the sandy **Spiaggia dei Maronti** (Map p138) or the intimate cove of Baia di Sorgeto.

◎ Sights

Casa Museo MUSEUM
(House Museum; Map p138; ☑ 349 7198879; SS 270, Serrara Fontana; ☺ 10am-7pm) **FREE** The good news is that this museum is well signposted and has a car park. The bad news is that it's on a perilous corner on Ischia's mountain road between Buonopane and Fontana. Double back if you can because beguiling Casa Museo is far more interesting than its name suggests. Tunnelled into the rock face, every room contains extraordinary sculptures and carvings made out of stone, wood and pebbles, the latter including such quirky exhibits as a life-size pig.

Other wonderful pieces include a stone head of Neptune, fanciful pebble reptiles, wooden furniture carved out of gnarled tree trunks and intricately patterned pebble mosaics covering the walls, even in the bathroom... Check out the *Alice in Wonderland*-style tunnels that lead here, there – and absolutely nowhere! The museum is free, although a donation is appreciated.

Baia di Sorgeto BEACH
(Map p138; Via Sorgeto) Among all those posh, dreamy (sometimes expensive) spas, it's nice to have access to something that's thermal and free. Located at the bottom of 300 steps, 2km south of the village of Panza, hot thermal water spills into rock pools on the edge of a secluded bay, where it is tempered by the chill of the sea. Choose a spot with an optimum temperature (careful – the water can be scalding), lie back on a rock and luxuriate.

There's a scruffy kiosk at the cove that's only open in the summer.

The cove can also be reached by water taxi from Sant'Angelo (€5 one way).

Activities

Terme Cavascura SPA
(Map p138; ☑ 081 90 55 64, 081 99 92 42; www.cavascura.it; Via Cavascura 1, Spiaggia dei Maronti, Sant'Angelo; basic thermal bath €12, mud & thermal bath €27; ☺ 8.30am-6pm mid-Apr–mid-Oct) Wedged between soaring cliffs, this historic no-frills outdoor spa is Ischia's oldest. Soak in Roman baths hewn into the cliff or sweat it out in a grotto. To get here, catch a water taxi to Cavascura (one way €3.50) and follow signs to Terme Cavascura 300m down a gorge.

For an extra fee, have a mud mask and face massage (€24), manicure (€15) or anti-stress massage (€30). The sulphurous waters are beneficial for rheumatic, bronchial and skin conditions.

Parco Termale Aphrodite Apollon SPA
(Map p138; ☑ 081 99 92 19; www.aphrodite apollon.it; Via Petrelle, Sant'Angelo; per day/half-day €40/30; ☺ 8am-6pm mid-Apr–Oct) A spectacular, partly strenuous 2km walk above the coast from Sant'Angelo (or you can drive) brings you to this luxurious spa, now part of the Miramare Sea Resort. Beyond its ivy-draped entrance is a marble-clad complex of gyms, saunas, lush terraced gardens and 12 differently heated pools, including one for hydro-cycling. The spa offers an extensive range of beauty treatments and therapies.

It is a tad overpriced compared to its more famous (and prettier) competitors.

Shopping

L'Isoletto FOOD
(Map p138; ☑ 081 99 93 74; Via Chiaia delle Rose 36, Sant'Angelo; ☺ 9am-9pm Mon-Sat) Stock up on a mouth-watering selection of local produce, from eye-wateringly spicy *peperoncino* (chilli peppers), rum-soaked *babà* and lemon-cream *cannoncelli* (pastry filled with lemon cream) to Ischian wine and the ubiquitous *limoncello*. Less tasteful – but deliciously kitsch – is the collection of tourist souvenirs, from seashell place mats to 3D souvenir wall plates.

❶ Getting There & Away

Both of Ischia's two principal bus lines – the CS and CD – stop just outside Sant'Angelo, from where the centre of town is about a 10-minute walk further down the road. Buses depart every 15 to 30 minutes.

PROCIDA

☑ 081 / POP 10,465

The Bay of Naples' smallest island is also its best-kept secret. Off the mass-tourist radar, Procida is like the Portofino prototype and is refreshingly real. August aside – when beach-bound mainlanders flock to its shores – its narrow, sun-bleached streets are the domain of the locals: kids clutch fishing rods, parents push prams and old seafolk swap yarns. Here, the hotels are smaller, fewer waiters speak broken German and the island's welcome hasn't been changed by a tidal wave of visitors.

If you have the time, Procida is an ideal place to explore on foot. The most compelling areas (and where you will also find most of the hotels, bars and restaurants) are **Marina Grande**, **Marina Corricella** and **Marina di Chiaiolella**. Beaches are not plentiful here, apart from the Lido di Procida, where, aside from August, you shouldn't have any trouble finding some towel space.

◉ Sights

Abbazia di San Michele Arcangelo CHURCH, MUSEUM
(☑ 334 8514252, 334 8514028; www.abbaziasan micheleprocida.it; Via Terra Murata 89, Terra Murata; ☺ 10am-12.45pm Mon-Sat, from 10.30am Sun) FREE Soak up the dizzying bay views at the belvedere before exploring the adjoining Abbazia di San Michele Arcangelo. Built in the 11th century and remodelled between the 17th and 19th centuries, this one-time Benedictine abbey houses a small museum with some arresting pictures created in gratitude by shipwrecked sailors, plus a church with a spectacular coffered ceiling and an ancient Greek alabaster basin converted into a font.

The church apse features four paintings by Neapolitan artist Nicola Russo. Dating back to 1690, these works include a depiction of St Michael the Archangel protecting Procida from Saracen attack on 8 May 1535.

THE ISLANDS PROCIDA

Procida

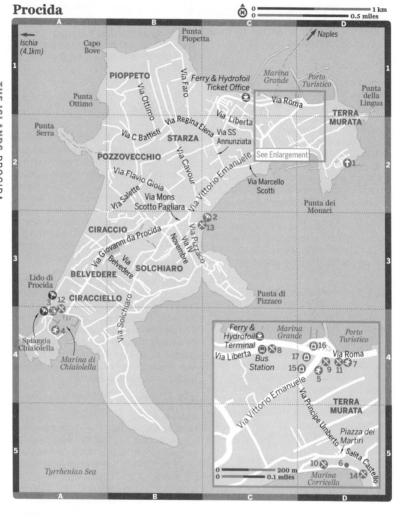

Procida

The painting is especially fascinating for its depiction of Marina Grande in the 16th century.

Free guided tours can be arranged between April and October.

Spiaggia di Chiaia BEACH
Procida has limited beach appeal, but this long, narrow ribbon of brownish sand with views of Marina Corricella in the distance has a loyal local following. Entry is via a stairway off Via Pizzaco, or you can sail in from Marina Corricella or kayak from Marina Chiaiolella. You'll find seafood restaurant La Conchiglia (p154) here.

Isola di Vivara ISLAND
(☑347 7858256; www.comune.procida.na.it; adult/reduced €10/5; ⊙guided tours 10am & 3pm Fri-Sun) Linked to Procida by pedestrian bridge, pocket-sized Vivara is what remains of a volcanic crater dating back some 55,000 years. The island is home to unique flora and abundant birdlife, while archaeological digs have uncovered traces of a Bronze-Age Mycenaean settlement as well as pottery fragments dating back to early Greek colonisation. The island was closed to the public in 2002 and only reopened for guided tours in 2017. Book online 15 days in advance.

Activities

ASD Kayak Procida KAYAKING
(☑348 3487880; www.procidainkayak.it; Via Marina Chiaiolella 30; 4hr circumnavigation €35) Procida is, arguably, the best place in Campania to kayak and this operator excels in fun, friendly and safe paddling trips. The four-hour circumnavigation of the island is an all-time favourite.

Blue Dream Yacht Charter Boating BOATING
(☑081 896 05 79, 339 5720874; www.bluedream charter.com; Via Emanuele 14, Marina Grande; 6/8-person yacht per week from €1600/2800) If you have 'champagne on the deck' aspirations, you can always charter your very own yacht or catamaran from here.

Barcheggiando BOATING
(☑081 810 19 34; Marina Chiaiolella; per day from €100; ⊙8am-8pm Apr-Oct) This outfit hires out motor boats and *gommoni* (wooden boats) at the Marina Chiaiolella.

Sprint CYCLING
(☑339 8659600; www.sprintprocida.com; Via Roma 28, Marina Grande; standard/electric bike per day €10/20; 🚲) One of several bike-hire places on the port at Marina Grande. Bikes are an excellent way of exploring this small, relatively flat island.

Tours

Cesare Boat Trips BOATING
(☑333 4603877; 2½hr tour per person €25; ⊙Mar-Oct) On the harbour at Marina Corricella, ask for friendly Cesare in your best Italian. Check at one of the beach bars or by La Gorgonia restaurant – he won't be far away. Cesare runs some great boat trips.

Eating

Prime waterfront dining here needn't equal an overpriced disappointment, with portside trattorias serving fresh, classic food. Several inland trattorias use home-grown produce and game in their cooking. Try the zesty *insalata al limone,* a lemon salad infused with chilli oil. Marina Grande is the place to mix with the fisherfolk at one of the earthy local bars.

⭐**Da Mariano** ITALIAN €
(☑081 896 73 50; Marina di Chiaiolella; meals €20-25; ⊙noon-3pm & 7pm-midnight Easter-Nov; 🐕) Hugely popular with locals, thanks to simple yet perfectly executed dishes like stuffed calamari and *spaghetti alle vongole* (spaghetti with clams). The fish, including swordfish, is jumping fresh, and you eat looking out at the bay. Round off a meal with the signature *la Procidana*, a *caprese*-style cake made with white chocolate and the juice and rind of local lemons.

Bar Capriccio CAFE, BAR €
(☑081 896 80 16; Via Roma 99; snacks €2-8; ⊙6am-2am Fri-Wed) If you want your cappucino served in a mug by a cool Procida local then head to this internationally flavoured portside bar/cafe. Carb-heavy snacks gravitate from morning pastries to pizza slices and chips by the evening. John Lennon quotes, Route 66 insignias and Cuban flags compete for wall space. The beer's good too.

Bar dal Cavaliere PASTRIES €
(☑081 810 10 74; Via Roma 42, Marina Grande; pastries from €1; ⊙7am-midnight) Procida's prime pastry shop has a sugar-spiked range

THE ISLANDS PROCIDA

of cakes and pastries and is a good place to get acquainted with the local indulgence, *lingua di bue* (ox tongue), a flaky pastry shaped like a tongue and filled with *crema pasticcera* (custard). The place doubles as a cocktail bar and gets insanely busy on weekend afternoons.

Fammivento　　　　SEAFOOD **€**

(⚹ 081 896 90 20; Via Roma 39, Marina Grande; meals €20-30; ⊙ noon-3.30pm & 8-11pm Tue-Sat, noon-3.30pm Sun, closed Dec-Feb) A portside fish restaurant that'll get you started with some stuffed anchovies, before heading on to *linguine pesce spada e melanzane* (linguine with swordfish and aubergine) and finishing off with a *zuppa di crostaci e moluschi* (crustacean and mollusc soup).

Da Giorgio　　　　TRATTORIA **€**

(⚹ 081 896 79 10; Via Roma 36, Marina Grande; meals €24; ⊙ noon-3pm & 7-11.30pm Mar-Oct, closed Tue Nov-Feb) A retro, no-frills neighbourhood trattoria close to the port. The menu holds few surprises, but the ingredients are fresh; try the *spaghetti con frutti di mare* (seafood spaghetti) with some spongy *casareccio* (home-style) bread.

La Lampara　　　　SEAFOOD **€€**

(⚹ 081 896 75 75; Marina Corricella; meals €25-28; ⊙ noon-2.30pm & 7-11pm May-Oct) Enjoying a quaint harbour view that has adorned many a guidebook, La Lampara looks down on Procida's agreeably lived-in marina from its seagull's-eye terrace. Down on your plate, you're looking at seafood, based on the freshest catch of the day. Get your feet wet with the marinated seafood antipasti before taking the plunge with the seafood ravioli.

Caracalè　　　　SEAFOOD **€€**

(⚹ 081 896 91 92; Via Marina Corricella 6, Marina Corricella; meals €28; ⊙ 12.30-3.30pm & 7-11pm, closed Tue Mar-Jun & Sep–mid-Nov) Along this unpretentious marina with its old fishing boats, piled fishing nets and haughty cats, half-a-dozen fine restaurants call out like mythological Sirens. You can't go wrong if you follow the day's catch into Caracalè, tucked away to the left as you face the sea, where the mussels and grilled swordfish slip down nicely with a chilled white wine.

La Conchiglia　　　　SEAFOOD **€€**

(⚹ 081 896 76 02; www.laconchigliaristorante.com; Via Pizzaco 10, Solchiaro; meals €25; ⊙ 1-3.30pm & 8-9.30pm summer) The 'seashell' is secluded on a narrow dark-sand beach with a warped jetty and the pastel jumble of Marina Corricella in the distance (take the steep staircase down from Via Pizzaco). This is a fish speciality restaurant with some interesting vegetable combos. Consider the *stracci* (thick, irregular pasta) with mussels and broccoli, perfect with the house white wine. The sea-facing dining room is pretty casual, and in summer with the windows open the waves provide pleasant background music.

 Shopping

Enoteca Borgo Antico　　　　DRINKS

(⚹ 081 896 96 38; Via Emanuele 13, Marina Grande; ⊙ 9am-9pm) This slick little bottle shop stocks the best of Campanian *vino* and a smattering of other Italian drops. The friendly owner will advise you (in Italian) of the best local wines and the best deals. *Limoncello* and a wide choice of traditional and modern grappas is also available.

ISLAND FESTIVALS

Procession of the Misteri On Good Friday, a wooden statue of Christ and the Madonna Addolorata, along with life-size plaster and papier-mâché tableaux illustrating events leading to Christ's crucifixion, are carted across Procida. Men dress in blue tunics with white hoods, while many of the young girls dress as the Madonna.

Ischia Film Festival (www.ischiafilmfestival.it; ⊙ Jun/Jul) Serves up free flicks and exhibitions in star locations around the island with its HQ in the Castello Aragonese.

Festa di Sant'Anna (www.infoischiaprocida.it; Ischia; ⊙ 26 Jul) The allegorical 'burning of the Castello Aragonese' takes place on the feast day of St Anne; it includes a hypnotic procession of boats and fireworks.

Settembrata Anacaprese (www.capritourism.com; Capri; ⊙ late Aug-early Sep) Annual celebration of the grape harvest with gastronomic events and markets.

Ischia Piano & Jazz (⊙ early Sep) Ischia's annual jazz festival pumps out five days of ivory tinkling with a dash of foreign acts. It's held at various venues across the island.

Maricella   FASHION & ACCESSORIES

(☑081 896 05 61; Via Roma 161, Marina Grande; ☺9am-8.30pm) A sweet little boutique selling brightly coloured accessories, including jewellery that looks good enough to eat: necklaces strung with what resemble M&Ms, brilliant sherbet-yellow earrings and gobstopper-sized rings, as well as pretty sandals, raffia bags and totes for the beach.

Mediterraneo   FASHION & ACCESSORIES

(☑081 196 69 09; Via Roma 32, Marina Grande; ☺9.30am-9pm) The fashions here are made from wispy fine cotton, perfect for those sizzling summer days. Floaty dresses patterned with wild flowers, long light-as-a-feather skirts, snowdrift-white transparent shirts, shopping bags in bold prints and some dressier wear with beautiful colourful designs.

ⓘ Information

Pro Loco (☑081 010 07 24; www.prolocodi procida.it; Via Roma, Stazione Marittima, Marina Grande; ☺10am-1pm daily, 3-5pm Sat & Sun Apr-Oct) Located at the Ferry & Hydrofoil Ticket Office, this modest office has sparse printed information but should be able to advise on activities and the like.

ⓘ Getting There & Away

BOAT

The **Ferry & Hydrofoil Terminal** (Via Roma, Stazione Marittima, Marina Grande) is in Marina Grande.

Caremar (☑081 896 72 80; www.caremar.it) Operates hydrofoils to/from Naples (€14.50,

ⓘ FERRY FACTS

Hydrofoils and ferries are the most likely way of getting to the islands. Note that services departing to/from Positano and Amalfi operate solely from around May to September or October. At other times of the year, you will have to catch services from Naples or Sorrento. In Naples, hydrofoils leave from Molo Beverello, with slower ferries leaving from the adjacent Calata Porta Massa. Generally, there is no need to book: just turn up around 35 minutes before departure in case there's a queue.

40 minutes, up to eight daily) and Ischia (from €13, 20 minutes, up to six daily). It also runs slower ferries to/from both destinations.

SNAV (☑081 428 55 55; www.snav.it) Operates up to four hydrofoils daily to/from Naples (from €17.50, 25 minutes).

ⓘ Getting Around

The island measures a mere 3.8 sq km and can be walked. Apparently, it has been deduced (by an extremely bored person) that no matter where you want to get to on the island, it will take you a maximum of 6000 steps.

BUS

There is a limited bus service (€1.20 from newsagents, or €1.40 on board), with four lines radiating from the **bus station** (cnr Via Roma & Via Libertà) in Marina Grande. Bus L1 connects the port and Via Marina di Chiaiolella (15 minutes).

AT A GLANCE

⭐

LARGEST TOWN
Sorrento 16,400

HIGHEST POINT
Monte Molare
(1444m)

**BEST SEAFOOD
TRATTORIA**
Da Emilia (p167)

**BEST
CHEAP PIZZA**
C'era Una Volta
(p178)

**BEST
DESSERTS**
Sal de Riso (p192)

📅

WHEN TO GO
Apr-Jun & Sep Less
crowded periods.
Best time for hiking,
with colourful
wildflowers and
pleasantly temperate
weather.

Jul & Aug Crowded
and hot, especially in
August.

Oct-Apr The majority
of hotels, bars and
restaurants pull
down their shutters.
Limited water
transportation.

Atrani (p187)
INU/SHUTTERSTOCK ©

The Amalfi Coast

The Amalfi Coast is one of Italy's most memorable destinations. Here, mountains plunge into the sea in a nail-biting scene of precipitous crags, cliff-clinging abodes and verdant woodland. Its string of fabled towns read like a Hollywood cast list. There's jet-set-favourite Positano, with its chic boutiques and sun-kissed sunbathers. Further east, ancient Amalfi lures with its Arabic-Norman cathedral, while mountaintop Ravello stirs hearts with its cultured villas and Wagnerian connection. To the west lies Amalfi Coast gateway Sorrento, a handsome clifftop resort that has miraculously survived the onslaught of package tourism. The region also boasts well-marked hiking trails providing the chance to escape the star-struck coastal crowds.

HIKING ON THE AMALFI COAST

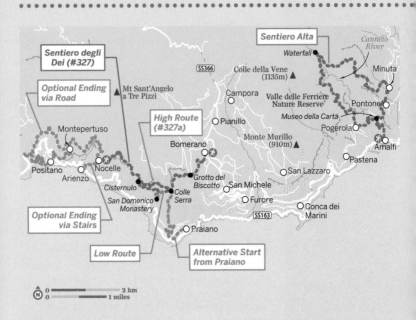

THE SENTIERO DEGLI DEI

START BOMERANO
FINISH NOCELLE
DISTANCE/DURATION 6KM; THREE HOURS

Not only is it spectacular, the Sentiero degli Dei (Path of the Gods) is one of the few Amalfi Coast treks that doesn't involve inordinate amounts of stair-climbing.

The walk starts in the village of Bomerano (a subdivision of Agerola), easily accessible from Amalfi town by SITA bus.

Beginning in the main square, where several cafes, including **Top-VIP Cetarell** (Piazza Paolo Capasso 5; panini from €4; ⊘8am-4pm), despatch portable snacks, follow the red-and-white signs along Via Pennino. The start of the walk proper is marked by a **monument** inscribed with quotes by Italo Calvino and DH Lawrence. Views of terraced fields quickly open out as the path contours around a cliff-face and passes beneath the overhanging **Grotta del Biscotto**

(Biscuit Cave). From here, the trail continues its traverse of the mountainside with some minor undulations. Periodically it dips into thickets of trees and sometimes you'll be required to negotiate rockier sections, but, in the main, the going is relatively easy.

The first main landmark after the Grotta is a path junction at **Colle Serra**. Here you get a choice between a low route or a high route. The low route is more exposed and threads its way through vineyards and rockier sections with magnificent views of Praiano below. Roughly 800m along its course, it is possible to make a short diversion south to the **San Domenico Monastery**. The more popular high route (#327a) sticks to the rocky heights with broad, sweeping vistas. Both paths converge at a point called **Cisternulo**, 1.5km further on. Just below Colle Serra, a path from the Sentiero degli Dei's alternative start in Praiano joins the main trail. Bear in mind that starting in Praiano involves a thigh-challenging climb up 1000 steps before you reach the trail proper.

The Amalfi Coast is laced with ancient footpaths, many of them dating back to the 10th and 11th centuries. Today they offer hikers a more intimate experience of this ethereal region.

After Cisternulo, the path kinks around some half-obscured grotte (caves) and descends into the Valle Grarelle before climbing back up to the finish point in the tiny village of **Nocelle**. A small kiosk selling cold drinks and coffee, served on a charming terrace with fresh flowers, greets you as you enter the village. Alternatively, head a little further through the village to Piazza Santa Croce, where a stall dispenses fantastic freshly squeezed orange and lemon juice.

From here you have three options: 1) take stairs (around 1500 of them!) down through the village to be deposited, via a succession of olive groves, on the coast road 2km east of Positano; 2) catch a bus from the end of Nocelle's one interconnecting road to Positano – small minibuses run by Mobility Amalfi Coast (p181) depart 10 times a day; 3) a much nicer if longer option – especially if you're weary of steps at

this point – is to continue along the path that leads west out of Nocelle towards **Montepertuso**. Don't miss the huge hole in the centre of the cliff at Montepertuso where it looks as though an irate giant has punched through the slab of limestone. In Montepertuso cut down past the church via a series of staircases to hit the northern fringes of Positano.

The CAI (Club Alpino Italiano; Italian Alpine Club) has a website dedicated to the Monti Lattari area (www.caimontilattari.it), with useful information on various trails. Alternatively, the best printed map is from the cart&guide series (map #3) and available in most local bookshops/newsagents (€5). If you prefer a guided hike, there are a number of reliable local guides, including American **Frank Carpegna** (www.positanofrankcarpegna.com), a longtime resident here, and **Zia Lucy** (www.zialucy.it).

The Sentiero degli Dei is not advised for acute vertigo sufferers – if in doubt, take the less exposed upper path (#327a). The trail itself (Bomerano to Nocelle) measures just under 6km one-way, but you'll add on another 3-4km if you continue by foot to Positano at the end. Although sunny days are the norm in spring and summer, it can be cloudy in the dizzy heights but somehow that adds to the drama. Bring a rucksack and plenty of water, and wear proper walking shoes as the going can be rough. You may want to pack swimming gear too and end the walk with a refreshing plunge into the sea.

Inclement weather and/or landslides can sometimes lead to trail closures. Local tourist offices in **Praiano** (p182) and **Bomerano** (☎081 879 10 64; Piazza Paolo Capasso; ⊗8am-1pm & 3-8pm Easter-Sep, 8am-1pm & 2-7pm rest of year☎) can provide more guidance and details.

THE VALLE DELLE FERRIERE VIA SENTIERO ALTO

START/FINISH AMALFI TOWN
DISTANCE/DURATION 11KM; FIVE HOURS

Crossed by the Canneto river and punctuated by waterfalls, the Valle delle Ferriere is a subtropical wooded wonderland tucked away behind Amalfi town. Hit its tracks for a refreshing escape.

In times of old, the Valle delle Ferriere hosted an ironworks (*ferriera*) and various paper factories (*cartiere*). Today the factories are atmospheric mossy ruins and the whole area has been turned into a nature reserve known for its orchids and other endemic flora.

The valley is serviced by two major trails. The longest, the so-called *sentiero alto* (high path), proceeds in an 11km loop through chestnut forests and craggy hills north of Amalfi town. A shorter route, the *sentiero basso* (low path) heads directly up-valley from Amalfi's Museo della Carta.

Whichever route you choose, it's well worth visiting the **Museo della Carta** (p185) first. The Valle delle Ferriere was a hub of paper-making between the 12th and 19th centuries and the museum still harbours a working paper machine.

The *sentiero alta* starts in Amalfi Town just south of the Museo della Carta. Take the Via Casamare uphill continuing as it turns into a gravely path studded with multiple steps – thus begins the long climb to the village of **Pogerola** perched on a crag 252m above. The stairs lead directly into Pogerola's main square overlooked by the **church of Madonna delle Grazie**. From here take the road on the right (standing with your back to the church). After 150m divert right again onto a path (Via Riulo) passing houses and terraced fields before entering a more forested domain. This is the Valle delle Ferriere proper, a **nature reserve** replete with emerald-green ferns and a refreshing array of waterfalls (some up to 20m high). The trail sets out on the wooded west side of the valley, crosses over the **Canneto River** at the largest falls and returns on the more open, craggy east side of the valley. After passing through a tunnel high above Amalfi town, the last few kilometres of the walk traverse more domesticated terrain. Lemon groves and terraced garden plots lead down through the villages of **Minuta** and **Pontone** from where you can drop back into the crowded medieval streets of Amalfi.

HANNAH DENSKI/SHUTTERSTOCK ©

1. Montepertuso (p159) **2.** View from the Sentiero degli Dei **3.** Waterfall, Valle delle Ferriere

TRABANTOS/SHUTTERSTOCK ©

PROSLGN/SHUTTERSTOCK ©

The Amalfi Coast Highlights

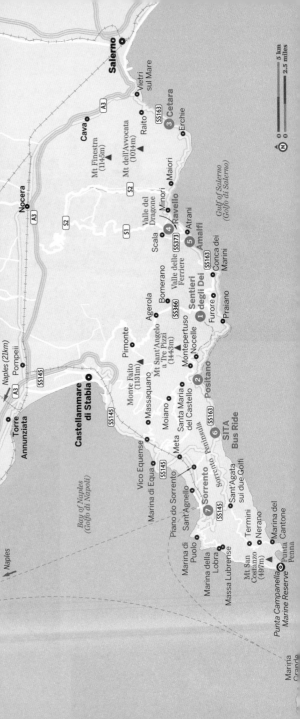

1 Sentiero degli Dei (p158) Thinking you've died and gone to heaven on the spectacular Path of the Gods.

2 Positano (p175) Feeling like you've walked onto the set of a James Bond movie on the vertiginous streets of Campania's poshest town.

3 Cetara (p192) Enjoying a seafood lunch in the Amalfi Coast's bustling fishing town.

4 Villa Cimbrone (p188) Lining up Roman busts and coastal views for a classic Ravello photo from the Belvedere of Infinity.

5 Amalfi (p185) Hiring a boat and floating down the coast in search of the perfect swimming spot.

6 SITA bus ride (p183) Getting a thrill out of the curves and switchbacks of the Amalfi's serpentine coast road.

7 Sorrento (p169) Hunting down traditional marquetry artworks in the narrow streets of the *centro storico*.

ℹ Getting There & Away

AIR

The closest airport to the Amalfi Coast is Naples International Airport (p267). Commonly known as Capodichino, it's served by a number of major airlines and low-cost carriers, with frequent connections to numerous European cities, as well as to New York. Curreri (p172) runs 10 daily buses between the airport and Sorrento (€10, 1¼ hours).

BOAT

Year-round hydrofoils run between Naples and Sorrento (€13, 20 minutes, up to six daily), as well as between Sorrento and Capri (€20.50, 20 minutes, up to 13 daily). From around April/May to October, ferry services connect Sorrento to Positano (€20, 30 minutes, two daily) and Amalfi (€21, 50 minutes, two daily), from where ferries continue to Salerno.

TRAIN

The Circumvesuviana (www.eavsrl.it) runs every 30 minutes between Naples' Garibaldi station (beside Napoli Centrale station) and Sorrento (€3.90, 70 minutes). Trains stop in Ercolano (Herculaneum) and Pompeii en route. Trenitalia (www.trenitalia.com) runs frequent services between Napoli Centrale station and Salerno (€4.70, 40 minutes).

ℹ Getting Around

There are no trains along the coast itself. Instead, there is a regular and efficient SITA Sud (www.sitasudtrasporti.it) bus service running between Sorrento, Positano, Amalfi, Salerno and all the villages in between.

Bicycles and scooters are useful for exploring inland (note: it's hilly away from the coast road), as are your own two legs: the area has an inexhaustible patchwork of walking trails.

SORRENTO

🕾 081 / POP 16,400

A small resort with a big reputation, Sorrento is a town of lemons, high-pedigree hotels and plunging cliffs that cut through the heart of the historical core.

The town's longstanding popularity stems from its location at the western gateway to the Amalfi. It's also on the train line to Pompeii and has regular fast-ferry connections to Naples and Capri.

Tourism has a long history here. It was a compulsory stop on the 19th-century 'Grand Tour' and interest in the town was first sparked by the poet Byron, who inspired a long line of holidaying literary geniuses – including Goethe, Dickens and Tolstoy – to sample the Sorrentine air. The romance persists. Wander through Piazza Tasso on any given Sunday and you'll be exposed to one of Italy's finer *passeggiatas* (strolls), snaking past palatial hotels, magnificent marquetry shops and simple Campanian restaurants serving *gnocchi alla sorrentina* finished off with a shot of ice-cold *limoncello*.

◎ Sights

The centre is compact: all the main sights are within walking distance of Piazza Tasso. Sorrento is a glorious town for an evening stroll: its lively streets are punctuated with jaw-dropping clifftop spots to take in the sunset and views of Mt Vesuvius and Naples.

Centro Storico AREA
(Historic Centre) A major hub for shops, bars and restaurants, recently pedestrianised Corso Italia is the main thoroughfare shooting east-west through the bustling *centro storico*. Duck into the side streets to the north and you'll find narrow lanes flanked by traditional green-shuttered buildings, interspersed with the occasional *palazzo* (mansion), piazza or church. Souvenir and antiques shops, fashion boutiques, trattorias and some fine old buildings also jostle for space in this grid of cobbled backstreets.

Marina Grande HARBOUR
Noticeably detached from the main city and bereft of the hydrofoils and ferries that crowd Marina Piccola, this secluded former fishing village has a timeless maritime air not dissimilar to Marina Corricella on Procida. Bobbing fishing boats and pastel-coloured houses add character to a quarter that's known for its family-run seafood restaurants. The marina also protects the closest thing in Sorrento to a *spiaggia* (beach). If you want to just loll in the sun, nearby jetties sport umbrellas and deckchairs that you can rent for around €12.

Basilica di Sant'Antonino CHURCH
(🕾 081 878 14 37; Piazza Sant'Antonino; ◷ 9am-noon & 5-7pm) Named after Sorrento's patron saint, the town's oldest church barely looks like a church at all from the outside. The interior paints a more ecclesial picture with its Roman artefacts, dark medieval paintings, gilded ceiling, and the oddity of two whale ribs in the lobby by the front door. Apparently, the much-loved saint performed

THE AMALFI COAST SORRENTO

Sorrento

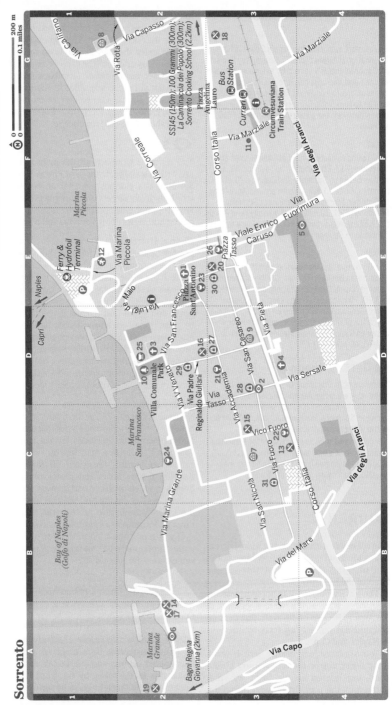

Sorrento

◎ **Sights**

1	Basilica di Sant'Antonino	E2
2	Centro Storico	D3
3	Chiesa & Chiostro di San Francesco	D2
4	Duomo	D3
	Gallery Celentano	(see 3)
5	Il Vallone dei Mulino	E4
6	Marina Grande	A2
7	Museo Bottega della Tarsia Lignea	C3
8	Museo Correale di Terranova	G1
9	Sedile Dominova	D3
10	Villa Comunale Park	D2

🏄 **Activities, Courses & Tours**

11	Gelateria David	F3
12	Sic Sic	E1

🍴 **Eating**

13	AZZ!	C3
14	Da Emilia	A2
15	Inn Bufalito	C3
16	L'Antica Trattoria	D2
17	O'Puledrone	A2
18	Pizzeria Da Franco	G3
19	Soul & Fish	A2
20	Zi'Ntonio	E3

◎ **Drinking & Nightlife**

21	Bollicine	D3
22	Cafè Latino	C3
23	D'Anton	E2
24	La Pergola	C2
25	Risto-Bar La Villa	D2
26	Syrenuse Bar	E3

🛍 **Shopping**

27	Autori Capresi	D3
28	Bottega 21	D3
29	La Feluca	D2
30	Stinga	E3
31	Terrerosse	C3

numerous miracles, including one in which he rescued a child from a whale's stomach. The saint's bones lie beneath the baroque interior in an 18th-century crypt.

Museo Correale di Terranova   MUSEUM
(☑ 081 878 18 46; www.museocorreale.it; Via Correale 50; adult/reduced €8/5; ☺ 9.30am-6.30pm Mon-Sat, to 1.30pm Sat) East of the city centre, this wide-ranging museum is well worth a visit whether you're a clock collector, an archaeological egghead or into delicate ceramics. In addition to the rich assortment of 16th- to 19th-century Neapolitan arts and crafts (including extraordinary examples of marquetry), you'll discover Japanese, Chinese and European ceramics, clocks, fans and, on the ground floor, ancient and medieval artefacts. Among these is a fragment of an ancient Egyptian carving uncovered in the vicinity of Sorrento's Sedile Dominova.

**Chiesa & Chiostro
di San Francesco**   CHURCH
(☑ 081 878 12 69; Via San Francesco; ☺ 7am-7pm) Located next to the Villa Comunale Park, this church is best known for the peaceful 14th-century cloister abutting it, which is accessible via a small door from the church. The courtyard features an Arabic portico and interlaced arches supported by octagonal pillars. Replete with bougainvillea and birdsong, they're built on the ruins of a 7th-century monastery. Upstairs in the Sorrento International Photo School, the

Gallery Celentano (☑ 344 0838503; www.raffaelecelentano.com; adult/reduced €3.50/free; ☺ 10am-9pm Mar-Dec) exhibits black-and-white photographs of Italian life and landscapes by contemporary local photographer Raffaele Celentano.

**Museo Bottega
della Tarsia Lignea**   MUSEUM
(☑ 081 877 19 42; Via San Nicola 28; adult/reduced €8/5; ☺ 10am-6.30pm Apr-Oct, to 5pm Nov-Mar) Since the 18th century, Sorrento has been famous for its *intarsio* (marquetry) furniture, made with elaborately designed inlaid wood. Some wonderful historical examples can be found in this museum, many of them etched in the once fashionable picaresque style. The museum, housed in an 18th-century palace complete with beautiful frescoes, also has an interesting collection of paintings, prints and photographs depicting the town and the surrounding area in the 19th century.

Il Vallone dei Mulino   HISTORIC SITE
(Valley of the Mills; Via Fuorimura) 🌿 Just behind Piazza Tasso, a vertiginous natural phenomenon is on view from Via Fuorimura. Il Vallone dei Mulino is a deep mountain cleft that dates from a volcanic eruption 35,000 years ago. Sorrento was once bounded by three gorges, but today this is the only one that remains. The valley is named after the ancient wheat mills that were once located here. The weed-covered ruins of one are still clearly visible.

Duomo
CATHEDRAL

(📞 081 878 22 48; Corso Italia; ⏰ 8am-12.30pm & 4.30-9pm) Sorrento's cathedral features a striking exterior fresco, a triple-tiered bell tower, four classical columns and an elegant majolica clock. Inside, take note of the marble bishop's throne (1573), as well as both the wooden choir stalls and stations of the cross, decorated in the local *intarsio* style. Although the cathedral's original structure dates from the 15th century, the building has been altered several times, most recently in the early 20th century when the current facade was added.

Villa Comunale Park
PARK

(⏰ 8am-1am Jun-Aug, to midnight May & Sep, reduced hours rest of year) This lofty park is more about vistas than greenery, perched atop Sorrento's famous cliffs with commanding views across the bay to Mt Vesuvius. With its operatic buskers and small bar (📞 081 807 40 90; www.lavillasorrento.it/en; ⏰ 8.30am-11pm; 📶), it's particularly popular at sunset. A lift (€1) at its western edge leads down to the port.

🏃 Activities

Hiring a boat is an excellent way to explore this rugged, seemingly inaccessible coastline. Then there are the hiking paths that cover most of the Sorrento Peninsula, many of them accessible directly from town, if you don't mind an initial uphill slog.

★ Nautica Sic Sic
BOATING

(📞 081 807 22 83; www.nauticasicsic.com; Via Marina Piccola 43, Marina Piccola; ⏰ Apr-Oct) Seek out the best beaches by rented boat, with or without a skipper. This outfit rents a variety of motor boats, starting at around €50 per hour or from €150 per day plus fuel. It also organises boat excursions and wedding shoots.

Bagni Regina Giovanna
SWIMMING

Sorrento lacks a decent beach, so consider heading to Bagni Regina Giovanna, a rocky beach with clear, clean water about 2km west of town, amid the ruins of the Roman Villa Pollio Felix. It's possible to walk here (follow Via Capo), but wear good shoes as it's a bit of a scramble.

Alternatively, you can take the SITA Sud bus headed for Massa Lubrense to save your strength.

Courses

Sorrento Cooking School
COOKING

(📞 081 878 35 55; www.sorrentocookingschool.com; Viale dei Pini 52, Sant'Agnello; ⏰ 10am-2pm Apr-Oct) You can opt for a serious culinary vacation here or one of the popular four-hour classes (€75), learning to make such Italian staples as pizza, ravioli and tiramisu in a beautiful spot surrounded by lemon trees. The class ends with a meal of the dishes prepared, accompanied by local wine.

Classes are held at the Esperidi Resort in Sant'Agnello. Pick-ups can be arranged from Sorrento.

Gelateria David
COOKING

(📞 081 807 36 49; www.gelateriadavidsorrento.it; Via Marziale 19; ⏰ 8am-1am) Impress your dinner-party mates with homemade Italian gelato by taking a course here; classes (€12) last around an hour and culminate in your very own certificate. Times vary according to demand, so call or drop by to organise; they speak excellent English. Specialities include the delicious 'Sorrento moon', with almond and lemons, and *veneziana*, a lemon, orange and mandarin sorbet.

🎊 Festivals & Events

World-class classical concerts are held in the cloisters of the Chiesa di San Francesco (p165) between July and September. Ask at the tourist office for further details.

Sant'Antonino
RELIGIOUS

(⏰ 14 Feb) The city's patron saint, Sant'Antonino, is remembered annually with processions and huge markets. The saint is credited with having saved Sorrento during WWII when Salerno and Naples were heavily bombed.

Settimana Santa
RELIGIOUS

(Holy Week) Famed throughout Italy; the first procession takes place at midnight on the Thursday preceding Good Friday, with robed and hooded penitents in white; the second occurs on Good Friday, when participants wear black robes and hoods to commemorate the death of Christ.

Sagra della Salsiccia e Ceppone
FOOD & DRINK

(⏰ 13 Dec) Sausage lovers can salivate at this annual festival, when hundreds of kilos of sausages are barbecued over a giant bonfire, accompanied by hearty local wine.

THE AMALFI COAST IN...

One Day

Wake up in romantic Ravello (p187) and greet the day in the gardens of Villa Rufolo (p187) and Villa Cimbrone (p188), gazing out over the sea like Wagner once did. Lunch lazily in town before catching a bus down to Amalfi (p183) to explore its extraordinary cathedral (p183) and Paper Museum (p185). Refuel with espresso and *paste* (pastries), then catch a ferry to Positano (p175) in time for dinner and drinks beside Spiaggia Grande.

Two Days

Peruse Positano's chic boutiques, duck into the church and stroll around the cliff to low-key Fornillo (p177). Energetic souls can stride out on the poetically named Sentiero degli Dei (p158), high up in the hills. It takes three hours, but with lunch and numerous admiring-the-view stops you can stretch it out to six. Delightful shorter walks are also available.

Three Days

Catch a morning ferry to Sorrento (p163), hop on a bus and explore the Sorrento Peninsula's spectacular southern tip. From Sorrento, head west on the minor coastal road, admiring the view of Capri from the lookout in **Massa Lubrense** (Largo Vescovado; ☺7am-noon & 4.30-8pm) and continuing south to dramatic Punta Campanella. You can walk to Nerano and on down to Baia di Ieranto (p172) beach, and, for the energetic, carry on to tranquil Sant'Agata sui due Golfi (p174) before bussing it back to Sorrento.

✖ Eating

The centre of town heaves with bars, cafes, trattorias, restaurants and even the odd kebab takeaway shop. Many places, particularly those with waistcoated waiters stationed outside (or eateries displaying sun-bleached photos of the dishes), are tourist traps serving bland food at inflated prices. Don't leave without a dose of *gnocchi alla sorrentina* (gnocchi with tomato sauce and mozzarella).

AZZ!　　　　　　　　　　　　　　　　TAVERNA €
(☎081 877 46 01; Corso Italia 14; mains & snacks €8-10; ☺9.30am-midnight) Like an Italian 'caff' without the greasy spoons, AZZ! delights in its simplicity. Pungent garlic bread, intense lasagna and an appetite-quenching *spaghetti puttanesca* are served at a speed best described as 'allegro' amid multilingual banter between customers and staff. Ideal if you're on your own, in a hurry, and don't want to be surrounded by romantic diners.

La Cantinaccia del Popolo　　　NEAPOLITAN €
(☎366 1015497; Vico Terzo Rota 3; meals €21; ☺11am-3pm & 7-11pm Tue-Sun) Festooned with garlic and with cured hams hanging from the ceiling, this down-to-earth favourite proves that top-notch produce and simplicity are the keys to culinary success. A case in point is the *spaghetti al pomodoro*, a basic dish of pasta and tomato that bursts with flavour, vibrancy and balance. For extra authenticity, it's served directly to you in the pan.

Pizzeria Da Franco　　　　　　　　　PIZZA €
(☎081 877 20 66; Corso Italia 265; pizzas from €6; ☺9am-2am; ☺) Casual Da Franco's long wooden tables are rarely short of customers, many of them here for the superlative pizza. Served in tin trays, it's made the Sorrento way, which means a crisper base than its Neapolitan counterpart. Those hulking Parma *prosciutti* suspended above you also appear on the list of *antipasti*, which include traditional local salami, cheeses and grilled veggies.

100 Grammi　　　　　　　　　　　ITALIAN €
(☎081 533 92 89; Viale Nizza 49; meals €18-25; ☺11.30am-midnight) The Slow Food movement might have originated in Italy, but there isn't always time to wait 45 minutes for your hand-pinched ravioli. In which case, decamp to 100 Grammi, a new quick-fire restaurant where wholesome homemade food arrives promptly. This is a great place to come for simple standards such as *gnocchi alla sorrentino* preceded by a surprise free *antipasto*.

★ Da Emilia　　　　　　　　　　TRATTORIA €€
(☎081 807 27 20; www.daemilia.it; Via Marina Grande 62; meals €22-30; ☺noon-3pm &

DON'T MISS

O'PULEDRONE

The best fish you eat in Sorrento might be one you caught. It's a viable proposition at congenial **O'Puledrone** (☑081 012 41 34; www.opuledrone.com; Via Marina Grande 150; meals €30-35; ☉noon-3pm & 6.30pm-late Apr-Oct). On the harbour at Marina Grande, the joint is run by a cooperative of local fishermen, who can take you out on a three-hour fishing trip (€70). Fish caught, the chef will cook your catch and serve it to you with a carafe of wine. *Perfezione!*

6-10.30pm Mar-Nov; 🖬) Founded in 1947 and still run by the same family, this is a friendly, fast-moving joint overlooking the fishing boats in Marina Grande. There's a large informal dining room, complete with youthful photos of former patron Sophia Loren, a romantic terrace by lapping waves, and a menu of straightforward dishes such as mussels with lemon, clam spaghetti and grilled calamari.

Soul & Fish   SEAFOOD €€
(☑081 878 21 70; www.soulandfish.com; Via Marina Grande 202; meals €38-46; ☉noon-2.30pm & 7-10.30pm, closed Nov-Easter; 🕾) Soul & Fish has a hipper vibe than Marina Grande's no-nonsense seafood restaurants. Your bread comes in a bag, your dessert might come in a Kilner jar and your freshly grilled fish with a waiter ready to slice it up before your eyes. The decor is more chic beach shack than sea-shanty dive bar, with wooden decks, director chairs and puffy cushions.

Inn Bufalito   ITALIAN €€
(☑081 365 69 75; www.innbufalito.it; Vico Fuoro 21; meals €25-30; ☉noon-midnight; 🕾🍴) 🏷 Owner Franco Coppola (no relation to the movie man) exudes a genuine passion for showcasing local produce in his rustic-chic mozzarella bar and restaurant. Buffalo mozzarella can be ordered as part of a tasting platter, while the buffalo itself makes an appearance in numerous dishes, from homemade *paccheri* (short, fat pasta tubes) with buffalo meat *ragù* to grilled buffalo steak.

Zi'Ntonio   ITALIAN €€€
(☑081 878 16 23; www.ristorantezintonio.it; Via Luigi De Maio 9-11; meals around €40; ☉noon-3.30pm & 6pm-midnight) Warm, buzzing and elegantly rustic, multilevel Zi'Ntonio draws everyone from local families and couples to clued-up out-of-towners. While earthy standouts include fried courgette flowers stuffed with buffalo mozzarella and basil, as well as a soul-coaxing lentil and escarole *zuppa* (soup), keep your belly empty if opting for the cult-status *risotto con crostacei*, a huge, flavour-packed paella-style dish laden with seafood.

L'Antica Trattoria   ITALIAN €€€
(☑081 807 10 82; www.lanticatrattoria.com; Via Padre Reginaldo Giuliani 33; meals €49-90; fixed-price menus €49-90; ☉noon-11.30pm; 🍴) Head to the upstairs terrace with its traditional tiles and trailing grape vines and you seem miles away from the alleyways outside. With a deserved reputation as the finest restaurant in town, this posh trattoria has a menu of many delicacies – courgette flowers, quail, and cod *au gratin* included – along with a resident mandolin player.

🍷 Drinking & Nightlife

Despite its popularity, Sorrento is not a major party town. That said, there is no shortage of places to drink. You'll find everything from British-inspired sports bars with pints and Premier League football, to piazza-side *aperitivo* (pre-dinner drink) bars where chatting and people watching is accompanied by occasional live music. The main evening hub is Piazza Tasso.

★D'Anton   LOUNGE
(☑333 1543706; Piazza Sant'Antonio 3/4; ☉10am-11pm mid-Mar–early Jan, to 1.30am summer; 🕾) Welcome to a new and very Italian concept: a cocktail bar doubling up as an interior-design store. That elegant sofa you're sipping a negroni on is for sale. So is that glistening chandelier and that enchanting mirror. Add them to your drinks bill if you're feeling flush, or just admire the candelabras and lampshades over savoury *antipasti* and wicked chocolate-and-almond cake.

Bollicine   WINE BAR
(☑081 878 46 16; Via Accademia 9; ☉6pm-late Mar-Nov; 🕾) The wine list at this unpretentious bar with a dark, woody interior includes all the big Italian names and a selection of interesting local labels. If you can't decide what to go for, the amiable bar staff will advise you. There's also a small menu of *panini* (sandwiches), bruschettas and one or two pasta dishes.

La Pergola
BAR

(☑081 878 10 24; www.bellevue.it; Hotel Bellevue Syrene, Piazza della Vittoria 5; ⊙10.30am-11pm) When love is in the air, put on your best Italian shoes and head for a predinner libation at the Hotel Bellevue Syrene's swoon-inducing terrace bar–restaurant. With its commanding clifftop view across the Bay of Naples towards Mt Vesuvius, it never fails to glam up an otherwise ordinary evening.

Syreneuse Bar
BAR

(☑081 807 55 82; www.barsyrenusesorrento. it; Piazza Tasso; ⊙7.30am-late; 🐾) Hogging Piazza Tasso's busiest spot, the Syrenuse is where locals pile in before, during or after the evening *passeggiata* for an piazza-side *aperitivo*. Drinks are reasonably priced (for Sorrento) and the complimentary bites – such as *pizzette* and *zeppole* (savoury doughnuts) – are a step up from the stock-standard nuts and chips. There's regular live music on Saturday night.

Cafè Latino
BAR

(☑081 877 37 18; www.cafelatinosorrento.it; Vico Fuoro 4a; ⊙10am-1am Easter-Oct; 🐾) Think locked-eyes-over-cocktails time. This is the place to impress your date with cocktails (€8) on the candlelit terrace, surrounded by orange, lemon and banana trees. Sip a spicy Hulk (vodka, grapefruit, sugar cane and jalapeño) or a glass of chilled white wine. If you can't drag yourselves away, you can also eat here (pizzas from €7, meals around €40).

🛍 Shopping

The main Sorrentine craft speciality is marquetry. If you're looking for a quintessential, high-quality souvenir, you can't go wrong an inlaid-wood item – you'll see everything from jewellery boxes to card tables. The best shops, some more than a century old, line the narrow streets of the *centro storico*.

Bottega 21
FASHION & ACCESSORIES

(☑081 807 35 85; www.bottegaventuno.it; Via Torquato Tasso 19; ⊙10am-2pm & 4-10pm Tue & Wed, 10am-2pm & 2.30-10pm Thu-Mon summer, reduced hours rest of year, closed Jan–mid-Mar) This is the Sorrento branch of Neapolitan leather workshop Bottega 21, known for its stylish, handcrafted leather goods. Shop for fetching totes, handbags, duffel bags and backpacks, nifty tobacco pouches, wallets, coin purses and unisex belts. The workshop only uses high-quality Tuscan leather, offered in natural, earthy hues and bolder block colours.

Stinga
ARTS & CRAFTS

(☑081 878 11 65; www.stingatarsia.com; Via Luigi de Maio 16; ⊙9.30am-9.30pm) Well worth seeking out, this place sells distinctive inlaid-wood items made in Sorrento by the same family of craftsmen (and women) for three generations. The pieces are highly original, especially in their use of colour and design, which is often mosaic or geometric. Fine jewellery made by family member Amulè, including coral pieces, is also on display.

Autori Capresi
FASHION & ACCESSORIES

(☑081 877 17 17; www.autoricapresi.it; Via Padre Reginaldo Giuliani 21; ⊙9.30am-10.30pm) If money isn't an issue, pop into unisex Autori Capresi for a serious *costiera* (coastal) makeover. Handmade by Campanian tailors, its casually chic linen creations include trousers, shirts and kaftans, not to mention ridiculously adorable outfits for little fashionistas. You'll also find sweaters, polo necks, belts and accessories. Footwear includes chi-chi sandals and suede loafers worthy of a yacht deck.

La Feluca
ANTIQUES

(☑081 807 24 78; Via Padre Reginaldo Giuliani 60; ⊙10am-9.30pm Mon-Sat, 3-9.30pm Sun) If you're after an obscure memento, make a pit stop at this little treasure trove. You'll find everything from historic photographs of Sorrento and Campania, to old Italian advertising posters, plus the odd sculpture and inlaid-wood *objet*. The green albums on the counter often harbour curious finds; on our last visit we uncovered Fascist-era postcards and a vintage cruise-ship menu.

Terrerosse
CERAMICS

(☑349 7542872, 081 807 32 77; Via Fuoro 73; ⊙10am-10pm Apr-Oct, 10am-1.30pm & 3.30-7pm Nov-Mar) Inspired by local marine life, history and mythology, Alessandro Ottone and his partner Enrica Cerchia create some of Sorrento's most idiosyncratic, textural ceramics. Fish pop out of plates, and surfaces are often etched with whimsical patterns. You'll find everything from platters, coffee cups and table lamps, to jewellery and Christmas-tree decorations. Crockery products are non-toxic and dishwasher safe.

ℹ Information

Main Tourist Office (☑081 807 40 33; www. sorrentotourism.com; Via Luigi de Maio 35; ⊙9am-7pm Mon-Sat, to 1pm Sun Jun-Oct, 9am-4pm Mon-Fri, to 1pm Sat Nov-May; 🐾)

CANADASTOCK/SHUTTERSTOCK ©

LEONS/SHUTTERSTOCK ©

Sorrento (p163)

e vibrant resort town of Sorrento serves
the western gateway to the Amalfi.

2. Villa Rufolo (p187), Ravello

Villa Rufolo is famed for its beautiful,
cascading gardens, which were created
in 1853.

3. Positano (p175)

The Amalfi Coast's most picturesque town,
Positano also boasts smart restaurants and
fashionable retailers.

The town's official tourism office is located in the Circolo dei Forestieri (Foreigners' Club). Ask for the useful publication *Surrentum*.

Station Tourist Information Point (☑ 081 878 21 03; www.tempiotravel.com; Circumvesuviana station; ⊙ 8.30am-7pm Mar-Oct) Run by travel agency Tempio Travel.

❶ Getting There & Away

BOAT

Sorrento is the main jumping-off point for Capri and also has ferry connections to Naples and Amalfi coastal resorts during the summer months from its **ferry and hydrofoil terminal** (Via Luigi de Maio).

Caremar (☑ 081 807 30 77; www.caremar.it) Runs fast ferries to Capri (€14.40, 25 minutes, four daily).

Alilauro (☑ 081 807 18 12; www.alilauro.it) Runs year-round hydrofoils to Naples (€13, 20 minutes, up to six daily) and Capri (€20.50, 20 minutes, up to 13 daily), as well as seasonal services to Ischia (€23, one hour, two to three daily), Positano (€20, 30 minutes, two daily) and Amalfi (€21, 50 minutes, two daily).

BUS

SITA Sud (www.sitasudtrasporti.it) buses serve Naples, the Amalfi Coast and Sant'Agata, leaving from the **bus station** (Piazza Giovanna Battista de Curtis) across from the entrance to the Circumvesuviana train station. Buy tickets at the station or from shops bearing the blue SITA sign.

CAR & MOTORCYCLE

Coming from Naples and the north, take the A3 autostrada until Castellammare di Stabia; exit there and follow the SS145 south.

TRAIN

Sorrento is the last stop on the Circumvesuviana (p272) line from Naples. Trains run every 30 minutes for Naples (€3.90, 70 minutes), via Pompeii (€2.40, 30 minutes) and Ercolano (€2.90, 50 minutes).

❶ Getting Around

TO/FROM THE AIRPORT

Naples International Airport (p267), also known as Capodichino, is the closest airport to Sorrento and the Amalfi Coast.

Curreri (☑ 081 801 54 20; www.curreriviaggi.it) runs 10 daily services to Sorrento from Naples International Airport. Buses leave from outside the departures hall and terminate opposite Sorrento train station. Buy tickets (€10) for the 1¼-hour journey on board.

A taxi from the airport to Sorrento costs around €85.

CAR & MOTORCYLE

The big international car-hire operators, as well as some local outfits, are based in Sorrento.

Autoservizi De Martino (☑ 081 878 28 01; www.admitaly.com/en; Via Parsano 8) has cars from €54 a day, and €280 per week, plus 50cc scooters from €23 for four hours.

Avis (☑ 081 878 24 59; www.avisautonoleggio.it; Corso Italia 322, Sant'Agnello; ⊙ 8.30am-1.30pm & 3.30-7pm Mon-Fri, 9am-1pm Sat) Small cars from €35 per day.

Hertz (☑ 081 807 16 46; www.hertz.it; Corso Italia 261b; ⊙ 8.30am-1pm & 2-8pm Mon-Thu, 8.30am-1pm & 2-8pm Fri) Small cars from €33 per day.

In midsummer, finding a parking spot can be a frustrating business, particularly as much of the parking on the side streets is for residents only and the city centre is closed to traffic for most of the day. There are well-signposted car parks near the ferry terminal, on the corner of Via degli Aranci and Via Renato, and heading west out of town near Via Capo (€2 per hour).

SORRENTO PENINSULA

Known as the land of the sirens, in honour of the mythical maiden-monsters who were said to live on Li Galli (a tiny archipelago off the peninsula's southern coast), the area to the west of Sorrento is among the least developed and most beautiful in the country.

Tortuous roads wind their way through hills covered in olive trees and lemon groves, passing through sleepy villages and tiny fishing ports. There are magnificent views at every turn, the best from the high points overlooking Punta Campanella, the westernmost point of the Sorrento Peninsula. Offshore, Capri looks tantalisingly close.

More developed and less appealing than the coast west of Sorrento, the area to the east of town protects the district's longest sandy beach, Spiaggia di Alimuri, at Meta, and the Roman villas at Castellammare di Stabia. From Castellammare you can catch a cable car to the top of Monte Faito (1092m).

◉ Sights

Baia di Ieranto BEACH

A spectacular beach at the tip of the Punta Penna peninsula south of Sorrento, Ieranto is reached via a walking path that starts in the village of Nerano. The walk takes about 45 minutes one-way and there are several steep downhill sections to negotiate. Wear good shoes. The pebbly beach is sheltered by headlands and perfect for swimming, but can get crowded in summer.

Monte Faito MOUNTAIN

Rising above Castellammare and accessible by an eight-minute **cable-car** (one-way/return €5.50/8; ⊙9.30am-4.30pm Apr-Jun & Sep-Nov, 8.30am-8.30pm Jul & Aug) ride from the town's Circumvesuviana train station is Monte Faito (1131m), one of the highest peaks in the Lattari mountains. Covered in thick beech forests, the summit offers some fine walks with sensational views.

Eating

Gran Caffè Marianiello CAFE €

(☑081 878 62 83; Piazza Cota, Piano di Sorrento; cornetti from €0.90, gelato from €1.50; ⊙6am-midnight; 🛜) Ask any local *buongustaio* (foodie) where to get the best *cornetto* (croissant) and chances are you'll get directed to this modern, piazza-side cafe. In-house *pasticcero* (pastry chef) Vincenzo Malafronte makes them fresh in a style closer to the flaky French version than the brioche-like concoctions usually sold in Italy. Even the heavenly *crema pasticcera* (custard) filling is made from scratch.

The cafe also serves gorgeous, velvety ice cream, including a standout salted caramel flavour. The cappuccinos here are great (soy milk available) and there's usually live jazz on Friday nights. It's in Piano, four minutes from Sorrento by train.

❶ Getting There & Away

The easiest way to access the peninsula is on the Circumvesuviana (p272) train from Naples.

Regular SITA Sud buses run to/from the Amalfi Coast towns and on to Salerno.

Massa Lubrense

☑081 / POP 14,300

The first town you come to following the coast west from Sorrento is Massa Lubrense. Situated 120m above sea level, it's a disjointed place, comprising a small town centre and 17 *frazioni* (fractions or hamlets) joined by an intricate latticework of paths and mule tracks. For those without a donkey, there's a good network of regular SITA buses, but this is excellent walking country with the *due golfi* (the two gulfs of Naples and Salerno) rarely out of sight.

◉ Sights & Activities

Marina della Lobra HARBOUR

From central Largo Vescovado it's a 1.5km descent to this pretty little marina backed by ramshackle houses and verdant slopes. The marina is a good place to rent a boat, the best way of reaching the otherwise difficult-to-get-to bays and inlets along the coast.

Coop Marina della Lobra BOATING

(☑081 808 93 80; www.marinalobra.com; Marina della Lobra; boat hire per hr from €40) A reliable boat-hire outfit, operating out of a kiosk by the car park. It also runs tours of Capri (€60).

Eating

⭐La Torre SEAFOOD €€

(☑081 808 95 66; www.latorreonefire.it; Piazzetta Annunziata 7, Annunziata, Massa Lubrense; meals €30-40; ⊙9am-midnight Mon & Wed-Thu, to 1am Fri-Sun Apr-Feb) 🖉 Not quite in Massa, but almost, La Torre has its berth in Annuziata, an attractive little *borgo* on a hill overlooking the Gulf of Naples. Occupying a handsome old stone building next to a church, it specialises in 'slow' seafood such as amberjack grilled with Sorrento lemons or linguine with anchovies.

Funiculi Funiculá SEAFOOD €€

(☑081 878 93 92; Via Fontanelle 16, Marina della Lobra; meals €32; ⊙noon-3pm Tue-Sun, plus 7-11.30pm Sat & Sun Apr-Oct; 🖶) FF is a jack of all trades overlooking Marina della Lobra's dinky harbor where the parked cars are usually Fiat 500s and the moored boats are equally diminutive. Depending on your mood, choose between a cappuccino in the cafe or a plate of the local catch in the sit-down restaurant. If you're undecided, toss a coin – they're both good.

❶ Information

Tourist Office (☑081 533 90 21; www.massalubrenseturismo.it; Viale Filangieri 11; ⊙9.30am-1pm daily, plus 4.30-8pm Mon, Tue & Thu-Sat) Can provide bus timetables and maps.

❶ Getting There & Away

BUS

SITA Sud (☑199 73 07 49; www.sitabus.it) runs buses to Massa Lubrense (hourly 7am to 9pm), departing from the Circumvesuviana train station in Sorrento (€2.20, 20 minutes).

CAR & MOTORCYCLE

Massa Lubrense is an easy 20-minute drive from Sorrento.

Parking is a matter of trawling the streets; there are some meters in the centre (€2 per hour).

Sant'Agata sui due Golfi

Only 4km from Sorrento via a direct walkable route involving copious steps, the village of Sant'Agata sits atop the crest of the Sorrento Peninsula with sea views over the *due golfi* (the two gulfs of Naples and Salerno). Despite its proximity to numerous holiday havens, the village generates a tangibly different climate to nearby Sorrento, both meteorologically and culturally. It's cooler up here – and quieter too. Walking options are legion. Trails lead off in all directions and it won't take long before you hit a coast. The food is equally legendary, even by Italian standards, with some wonderful *agriturismi* (farm stays) and the peerless Don Alfonso 1890, surely one of the best restaurants in Italy.

DON'T MISS

DON ALFONSO 1890

Food-lover favourite **Ristorante Don Alfonso 1890** (☑ 081 878 00 26; www. donalfonso.com; Corso Sant'Agata 11; meals €80, six-course tasting menu €150; ⊙ 12.30-2.30pm & 7.30-11pm Wed-Sun Aprlate Oct; ℗) is as much an experience as a meal – and a world-class one at that. Not only is the food exquisite, creative and true to its Sorrentino roots; it's also immaculately presented by genuinely friendly staff who treat every guest like they're visiting royalty.

The restaurant itself is a gleaming white, effortlessly elegant space that manages to feel refreshingly unpretentious (children are welcome).

The food is an ever-changing feast with ingredients plucked from the family-run farm nearby. Expect spectacular flavours concocted from their own eggs, olives, honey, aubergines, lemons and herbs. To top it all, they offer a tour of their wine and cheese cellar and busy working kitchen either before or after your meal.

Convento del Deserto MONASTERY, VIEWPOINT

(Monastero di San Paolo; ☑ 081 878 01 99; Via Deserto; ⊙ grounds 8am-7pm, viewpoint 10am-noon & 5-7pm summer, 10am-noon & 3-5pm winter) This hulking convent is located 1.5km uphill from the village centre. It was founded in the 17th century by Carmelite friars, but since 1983 it has been home to a closed community of Benedictine nuns. While the convent is of only moderate interest, the 360-degree views from the *belvedere* (rooftop terrace) really make the knee-wearying hike worthwhile.

If the door to the *belvedere* is closed during opening hours, ring the bell beside it to be let in.

Lo Stuzzichino NEAPOLITAN €

(☑ 081 533 00 10; www.ristorantelostuzzichino. it; Via Deserto 1a; pizzas from €5, meals €20, tasting menu €40; ⊙ Feb-Dec) 🍴 Stuzzichino means 'appetiser', but you get far more than just starters at this Slow Food movement-affiliated restaurant with gregarious host and owner Paolo de Gregorio at the helm. Loosen up with fish rolls stuffed with smoked cheese, or seafood stew with seasonal vegetables, and plunge in with the rare *gamberetti di Crapolla* (prawns).

Bar Pasticceria Fiorentino CAFE €

(☑ 081 878 00 64; Via Nastro Azzurro 7; pastries from €1.50; ⊙ 6am-10pm Wed-Mon) This is where half of Sant'Agata's population seems to come after Sunday Mass – priests, teenagers, farmers and nonagenarian *nonnas* – to down a potpourri of espresso, gelato and flaky pastries. Join 'em.

❶ Information

Tourist Office (☑ 081 533 01 35; Corso Sant'Agata 25; ⊙ 9am-1pm & 5.30-9pm) For information on the village and surrounding countryside, stop by this small office on the main square.

❶ Getting There & Away

BUS

SITA (☑ 199 73 07 49; www.sitabus.it) buses depart hourly from Sorrento's Circumvesuviana train station.

CAR & MOTORCYCLE

Follow the SS145 west from Sorrento for about 7km until you see signs off to the right.

WALKING

It's a 4km walk from Sorrento to Sant'Agata, mostly uphill, on good paths with steps. From

Piazza Tasso in Sorrento, venture south along Viale Caruso and Via Fuorimura to pick up the Circumpiso footpath, marked in green on the walking maps available from tourist offices. The walk should take approximately one hour.

Marina del Cantone

Round the coast from Massa Lubrense, a beautiful hiking trail leads down from **Nerano** to the clear, placid Baia di Ieranto (p172) and Marina del Cantone. This unassuming village with a small pebble beach is not only a lovely, tranquil place to stay but also one of the area's prime dining spots: VIPs regularly sail over from Capri to eat here.

◉ Sights & Activities

Punta Campanella
Marine Reserve   MARINE RESERVE
(www.puntacampanella.org) A popular diving destination, these protected waters are part of an 11-sq-km reserve that supports a healthy marine ecosystem, with flora and marine life flourishing amid underwater grottoes and ancient ruins. To see for yourself, PADI-certified Nettuno Diving runs various underwater activities for all ages and abilities, including snorkelling excursions, beginners' courses, cave dives and immersions off Capri and Li Galli, the islands where the sirens are said to have lived.

Nettuno Diving   DIVING
(☑ 081 808 10 51; www.divingsorrento.com; Via Vespucci 39; 1/2 immersions €65/110; ☺ 8am-7pm; 🚐) One of the Sorrento Peninsula's best diving operators, based at the **Nettuno campground** (☑ 081 808 10 51; www.villaggio nettuno.it; Via A Vespucci 39; camping 2 people, car & tent €41.50; bungalows €110-130, apt from €150; ☺ Mar–early Nov; 🅿 ❄ @ 🛜 🏊) 🐾. Instructors are authorised to access the Punta Campanella protected marine park on designated days. There are 20 dive sites within 20 minutes of the centre and the friendly team can also organise night dives (€10 supplement), open-water courses (€395) and snorkelling trips to Capri (€35).

✕ Eating

For a tiny place, Marina del Cantone has a clutch of very good sea-facing restaurants perched on stilts above the water. Don't neglect trying the local speciality, *spaghetti alla Nerano*.

Lo Scoglio   SEAFOOD €€€
(☑ 081 808 10 26; www.hotelloscoglio.com; Piazza delle Sirene 15, Marina del Cantone; meals €60; ☺ 12.30-5pm & 7.30-11pm) The only marina restaurant directly accessible from the sea, Lo Scoglio is a favourite of visiting celebs and has been around since the 1950s, when the quickest way to Sant'Agata was on a mule. Come here for Nerano-style spaghetti, although you'd be mad to miss the seafood, especially the raw *tartufi di mare* (sweet clams with a zing of lemon).

❶ Getting There & Away

SITA Sud (☑ 199 73 07 49; www.sitabus. it) runs regular buses between Sorrento and Marina del Cantone from the Circumvesuviana train station in Sorrento.

AMALFI COAST TOWNS

Positano

☑ 089 / POP 3915
Dramatic, deluxe and more than a little dashing, Positano is the Amalfi Coast's front-cover splash, with vertiginous houses tumbling down to the sea in a cascade of sun-bleached peach, pink and terracotta. No less photo-worthy are its steep streets and steps, flanked by wisteria-draped hotels, smart restaurants and fashionable retailers.

Look beyond the facades and the fashion, however, and you will find reassuring signs of everyday reality: crumbling stucco, streaked paintwork and even, on occasion, a faint whiff of drains. There's still a southern-Italian-holiday feel about the place, with sunbathers eating pizza on the beach, kids pestering parents for gelato and chic *signore* browsing from Milan browsing the boutiques. The fashionista history runs deep – *moda Positano* was born here in the '60s and the town was the first in Italy to import bikinis from France.

◉ Sights

Positano's most memorable sight is its pyramidal townscape, with pastel-coloured houses stacked up on the hillsides.

Getting around town is largely a matter of walking. If your knees can take the slopes, dozens of narrow alleys and stairways make strolling around relatively straightforward and joyously traffic-free. The easy option is

Positano

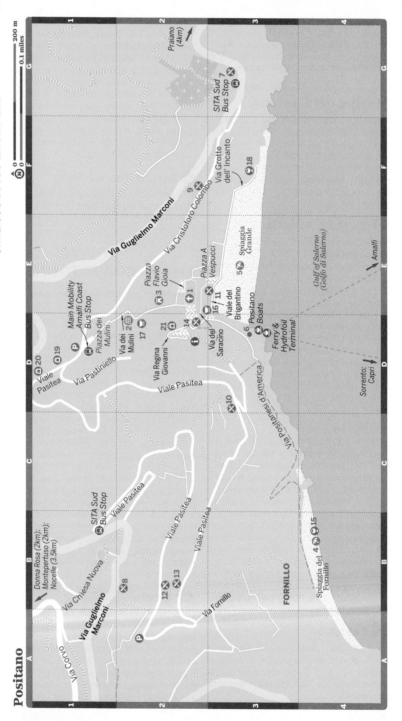

200 m
0.1 miles

Praiano (4km)

SITA Sud Bus Stop 7

Via Grotte dell'Incanto

18

Via Guglielmo Marconi

9

Via Cristoforo Colombo

Piazza Flavio Gioia

3

1

Piazza A. Vespucci

5

Spiaggia Grande

Gulf of Salerno (Golfo di Salerno)

Amalfi

Main Mobility Amalfi Coast Bus Stop

Piazza dei Mulini

Via dei Mulini

17

21

14

16 11

Viale del Brigantino

Positano Boats

6

Via del Saracino

Ferry & Hydrofoil Terminal

Sorrento; Capri

20

19

Viale Pasitea

Via Pastiniello

Via Regina Giovanni

Viale Pasitea

10

Via Positanesi d'America

Donna Rosa (2km); Montepertuso (2km); Nocelle (3.5km)

SITA Sud Bus Stop

Viale Pasitea

Viale Pasitea

Viale Pasitea

Viale Pasitea

Via Chiesa Nuova

Via Guglielmo Marconi

Via Corvo

8

12 13

Via Fornillo

FORNILLO

Spiaggia del Fornillo

4 15

Positano

to take the local bus to the top of the town and wind your way down on foot.

Spiaggia Grande   BEACH
Spiaggia Grande probably isn't anyone's idea of a dream beach, with greyish sand covered by legions of bright umbrellas lined up like parked cars – and expensive cars at that. Hiring a chair and umbrella in the fenced-off areas costs around €20 per person per day (plus extra for showers). Fortunately, the crowded public areas are free and the toilets are spotlessly clean – as is the seawater.

Spiaggia del Fornillo   BEACH
From Positano's main beach, it's a gentle walk west, with an acceptable number of steps (hooray!) to Spiaggia del Fornillo. Toss off your stilettos and lace up your trainers: Fornillo is more laid-back than its swanky neighbour and it's also home to a handful of summer beach bars, which can get quite spirited after sunset.

To reach Fornillo, head for the western end of Spiaggia Grande, by the ferry harbour, and climb the steps. Walk past the Torre Trasita and continue on as the path passes dramatic rock formations and a verdant gully until you reach the appealing beach.

Chiesa di Santa Maria Assunta   CHURCH
(☎089 87 54 80; Piazza Flavio Gioia; ⊙9am-noon & 4-7pm Mon-Sat) Omnipresent in most Positano photos is the colourful majolica-tiled dome of its main church (and the town's only real sight). If you are visiting at a weekend you will probably have the added perk of seeing a wedding; it's one of the most popular churches in southern Italy for exchanging vows.

The church is known for a 13th-century Byzantine *Black Madonna and Child* above the main altar. The icon was supposedly stolen from Constantinople by pirates and smuggled west.

Palazzo Murat   PALACE
(☎089 875 51 77; www.palazzomurat.it; Via dei Mulini 23) Just west of the Chiesa di Santa Maria Assunta, this *palazzo* is now a luxury hotel. It may be beyond your budget to stay here, but you can still visit the balmy flower-filled courtyard, have a drink on the vine-draped patio and contemplate the short, tragic life of flamboyant Joachim Murat, the 18th-century French king of Naples who had the palace built as a summer residence for himself and his wife, Caroline Bonaparte.

Franco Senesi   GALLERY
(☎089 87 52 57; www.francosenesifineart.com; Via dei Mulini 16; ⊙10am-midnight Apr-Nov) Nestled between trendy boutiques and lemon-themed ceramics shops, Franco Senesi is a bold, uncluttered exhibition space with rooms showcasing work by over 20 Italian modern artists and sculptors. You can walk around without being hassled, admiring (and even buying) artworks varied enough to suit most tastes, spanning exquisite life drawings, colourful surrealistic landscapes and edgy abstract sculptures. Shipping can be arranged.

☞ Tours

L'Uomo e il Mare   BOATING
(☎089 81 16 13; www.escursioniluomoeilmare.it; ⊙9am-8pm Easter-Oct) Offers a range of tours, including Capri and Amalfi day trips (from

VICO EQUENSE & HISTORIC HAMLETS

Known to the Romans as Aequa, Vico Equense (Vico) is a small clifftop town about 10km east of Sorrento and just five stops away via the Circumvesuviana train. Largely bypassed by international tourists, it's a laid-back, authentic place worth a quick stop-over, if only to sample some of the famous pizza by the metre. One top spot to do so is **Ristorante & Pizzeria da Gigino** (🖉 081 879 83 09; www.pizzametro.it; Via Nicotera 15; pizza per metre €28-38; ⊙ noon-1.30am; 🕿 🏚), a place run by the five sons of pizza king Gigino Dell'Amura, who introduced pizza by the metre to the world.

Dotted around Vico's surrounding hills are a number of ancient hamlets, known as *casali*. Untouched by mass tourism, they offer a glimpse into a rural way of life that has changed little over the centuries. You will, however, need wheels to get to them. From Vico, take Via Roma and follow Via Rafaelle Bosco, which passes through the *casali* before circling back to town. Highlights include **Massaquano** and the Capella di Santa Lucia (open on request), famous for its 14th-century frescoes from the school of Giotto di Bondone (recognised as the forerunner of modern Western painting). **Moiano** is also worth checking out; an ancient path from here leads to the summit of Monte Faito. And then there is **Santa Maria del Castello**, with its fabulous views towards the southeast.

Three kilometres to the west of Vico, **Marina di Equa** stands on the site of the Roman settlement of Aequa. Among the bars and restaurants lining the popular pebble beaches you can still see the remains of the 1st-century-AD Villa Pezzolo, as well as a defensive tower, the Torre di Caporivo, and the Gothic ruins of a medieval limestone quarry.

€65 to €80), out of a kiosk near the ferry terminal. It also organises private sunset tours to Li Galli, complete with champagne (from €200 for up to 12 people). Private tours should be organised at least a day in advance.

🍴 Eating

Positano excels in deluxe restaurants with fine food and romantic settings, but you can also get by on a budget if you know where to look. Generally, the nearer you get to the seafront, the more expensive everything becomes. Many places close over winter, making a brief reappearance for Christmas and New Year.

★C'era Una Volta   TRATTORIA, PIZZA €

(🖉 089 81 19 30; Via Marconi 127; meals €20-30; ⊙ noon-3pm Wed-Mon, 6-11pm daily) Calling like a siren to any cash-poor budget traveller who thought Positano was for celebs only, this heroically authentic trattoria at the top of town specialises in honest, down-to-earth Italian grub. No need to look further than the *gnocchi alla sorrentina* (gnocchi in a tomato and basil sauce) and Caprese salad. Pizzas start at €4.50; beer €2. In Positano, no less!

It also runs a free shuttle to/from anywhere in Positano in the summer.

La Cambusa   SEAFOOD €€

(🖉 089 87 54 32; www.lacambusapositano.com; Piazza Vespucci 4; meals €40; ⊙ noon-11pm, closed Nov-mid-Dec; 🕿) Sporting summery pastel hues and a seafront terrace, La Cambusa is on the front line, which, given the number of cash-rich tourists in these parts, could equal high prices for less-than-average food. Happily, that is not the case. Ingredients are top-notch and shine brightly in dishes such as homemade crab-filled ravioli and seafood risotto.

Da Vincenzo   ITALIAN €€

(🖉 089 87 51 28; www.davincenzo.it; Viale Pasitea 172-178; meals €40-45; ⊙ noon-2.45pm & 6.15-10.45pm) Superbly prepared dishes are served here by the third generation of restaurateurs. The emphasis is on fish dishes, which range from the adventurous, like grilled octopus tentacles skewered with deep-fried artichokes, to seasonal pasta dishes such as spaghetti with broad beans and fresh ricotta. Be sure to try co-owner Marcella's legendary desserts, considered the best in town. Reservations recommended.

Da Bruno   NEAPOLITAN €€

(🖉 089 87 53 92; www.brunopositano.it; Via Cristoforo Colombo 157; meals €30-45; ⊙ noon-11pm Apr-Oct) With a row of pavement tables overlooking the town and its umbrella-lined

Spiaggia Grande, easy-going, cliff-side Da Bruno serves up beautiful southern Italian flavours made using quality produce. The *antipasto misto* (mixed antipasto platter) usually includes less-common morsels, from local fish served with orange and rocket to rich, sultry *polpo alla Luciana* (tender octopus with cherry tomatoes, olives and capers).

Wine Dark House ITALIAN €€
(☑ 089 81 19 25; Via del Saracino 6/8; meals €25-30; ⊗ noon-3pm & 7-10pm Wed-Mon) This small wine-coloured restaurant bang in the centre spills out into a lovely enclosed piazza and hides a hip little bar in its interior. The emphasis is on neatly presented old standards (try the *parmigiana di melanzane* or beef rolls). Service is charming and the wine list – unsurprisingly – comprehensive.

Ristorante il Saraceno d'Oro ITALIAN €€
(☑ 089 81 20 50; www.saracenodoro.com; Viale Pasitea 254; pizzas from €5, meals €28; ⊗ 12.30-3pm & 6.30-11pm Mar-Oct) There is something so typically Italian about the set-up of this restaurant, where waiters have to dash to and fro across the road with their dishes. But in the evening the traffic is light and the wacky layout only adds to the joy of eating here. The pizza and pasta choices are good; the *contorni* (vegetables) excellent.

★ Casa Mele ITALIAN €€€
(☑ 089 811 13 64; www.casamele.com; Via Guglielmo Marconi 76; tasting menus €75-100; ⊗ 7pm-midnight Tue-Sun Apr-Nov; 🐾) Something of a rarity in this land of traditional trattorias, Casa Mele is one of those cool contemporary restaurants with a lengthy tasting menu and food presented as art – and theatre. The slick open kitchen is a window into the high-powered food laboratory from which emerge whimsical pastas, delicate fish in subtle sauces, and outstanding desserts. Service is equally sublime.

The restaurant's manifesto is inscribed on one wall in English: 'to eat is a necessity, but to eat intelligently is an art'. These people love food, and it shows.

Casa Mele also runs three-hour cooking courses (€120), which include a meal and wine; see the website for more details.

Next2 ITALIAN €€€
(☑ 089 812 35 16; www.next2.it; Viale Pasitea 242; meals €65, 6-course menu €80; ⊗ 6.30-11pm Apr-Oct; 🐾) Local produce and polished takes on tradition underscore sophisticat-

ed Next2. Standouts include the signature *conchiglioni ripieni di ragù alla bolognese e stracciatella*, shell-shaped pasta served with pork-mince *ragù* and *stracciatella* cheese. The kitchen boasts a top-range charcoal oven, put to fine use in dishes like tender octopus and mackerel with chickpea purée and cherry tomatoes. In summer, reserve a table on the terrace.

Drinking & Nightlife

La Zagara CAFE
(☑ 089 87 59 64; www.lazagara.com; Via dei Mulini 8; ⊗ 8am-10pm Apr–mid-Nov) Dating back to 1950, this is the quintessential Italian terrace, draped with foliage and flowers. Flanking the terrace is La Zagara's superb *pasticceria* (pastry shop; cakes from €3), serving both sweet and savoury bites, and especially famed for its *tiramisù al limone*.

Order something indulgent, kick back and indulge in a little Positano people-watching. DJs spin tunes on Friday and Saturday nights.

Music on the Rocks CLUB
(☑ 089 87 58 74; www.musicontherocks.it; Via Grotte dell'Incanto 51; cover charge €10-30; ⊗ 10pm-4am Apr-Oct; 🐾) This is one of the town's few genuine nightspots and one of the best clubs on the coast. The venue is dramatically carved into the tower at the eastern end of Spiaggia Grande. Join a lively crowd and some of the region's top DJs spinning anything from mainstream house to retro disco.

Da Ferdinando BAR
(☑ 089 87 53 65; Spiaggia dei Fornillo; ⊗ 10am-3am May-Oct) Caribbean-style bamboo beach bar that springs up every summer on

---

AT A SNAIL'S PACE

Positano is one of more than 85 towns in Italy, and over 235 worldwide, to have gained Slow City status (an extension of the Slow Food movement, established in northern Italy in 1986). In order to be considered, certain criteria must be met: towns need to have fewer than 55,000 inhabitants, no fast-food outlets or neon-lit hoardings, plenty of cycling and walking paths, and neighbourhood restaurants serving traditional cuisine with locally sourced ingredients. For more information, check www.cittaslow.org.

Positano's smaller Fornillo beach. It rents out sunloungers and serves drinks and light snacks. Rock 'n' roll music creates a party mood after sunset.

La Brezza Net Art Cafe   CAFE

(📱 089 87 58 11; www.labrezzapositano.it; Via Regina Giovanna 2; ⊙ 9am-1am; 🛜) Sporting a steely grey-and-white interior, regular art exhibitions and a terrace with sea views, this is a fine spot for a pit stop. While it serves coffee, *panini*, salads and snacks throughout the day, it's best to head here from 6pm onwards, when the kitchen prepares creative fish tapas, ideally accompanied by a glass of reasonably priced (for Positano) wine.

🛍 Shopping

La Bottega di Brunella   FASHION & ACCESSORIES

(📱 089 87 52 28; www.brunella.it; Viale Pasitea 72; ⊙ 9am-9pm) This shop is one of the reasons local women always look so effortlessly chic. It's one of just a handful of boutiques where the clothes are designed and made in Positano (most boutiques import their stock, despite the sometimes deceptive labelling). The garments here are made from pure linen and silk; the colours are earthy shades of cream, ochre, brown and yellow.

There are two other branches in town, including one opposite Palazzo Murat.

DON'T MISS

DONNA ROSA

Once a humble trattoria, **Donna Rosa** (📱 089 81 18 06; www.drpositano.com; Via Montepertuso 97-99, Montepertuso; meals €45-65; ⊙ 11am-2pm & 5.30-10pm Wed-Mon Apr-Oct, closed lunch Aug) is now considered an Amalfi Coast classic despite its out-of-the-way location in the village of **Montepertuso**. The reason? Jolly good food served by three generations of the original Rosa's family and an nod of admiration from that well-known food-campaigning Italophile, Jamie Oliver. Dinner reservations are highly recommended and obligatory at lunch.

While Donna Rosa's menu changes frequently, you can be guaranteed some of the finest food – and views – on the coast. If it's on offer, don't miss the hot chocolate soufflé. The restaurant also runs excellent daytime cooking courses. Check the website for details.

La Botteguccia de Giovanni   SHOES

(📱 089 81 18 24; www.labottegucciapositano.it; Via Regina Giovanni 19; ⊙ 9.30am-9pm May-Oct) Come here for leather sandals handmade by craftsman Giovanni in his small workroom at the back of the shop. Choose your colour and any decorative flourishes you want (shells are somehow particularly well-suited to Positano...), tell him your size and then nip round the corner for a cappuccino while he makes your shoes. Prices start at around €50.

Ceramiche Maria Grazia   CERAMICS

(📱 089 812 34 81; Viale Pasitea 8; ⊙ 9.30am-8.30pm May-Oct) Browse a sumptuous display of locally produced ceramics with the potential to cause you stress at check-in time; a better bet is to go for the shipping option. The colours and designs are subtle and classy with lots of lemons emblazoned onto urns, plates, tables and even egg cups.

ℹ Information

Positanos' **Tourist Office** (📱 089 87 50 67; www.aziendaturismopositano.it; Via Regina Giovanna 13; ⊙ 8.30am-5pm Mon-Sat, to 3pm Sun) provides lots of information, from tours and sightseeing to transport details. Also supplies a free hiking map.

ℹ Getting There & Away

BOAT

Positano has excellent ferry connections to the coastal towns and islands between April and October from its **ferry and hydrofoil terminal**.

TraVelMar (📱 089 87 29 50; www.travelmar.it) Sails to numerous coastal destinations between April and October, including Amalfi (€8, 25 minutes, six daily) and Salerno (€12, 70 minutes, six daily). To reach Minori (€11), Maiori (€11) and Cetara (€12), transfer in Amalfi.

Lucibello Positano (📱 089 87 50 32; www.lucibello.it) Operates three daily services to Capri (€22, 30 minutes) from mid-April to mid-October.

BUS

About 16km west of Amalfi and 18km from Sorrento, Positano is on the main SS163 coastal road. There are two Sita Sud main bus stops: coming from Sorrento and the west, the first stop you come to is opposite Bar Internazionale; arriving from Amalfi and the east, the stop is at the top of Via Cristoforo Colombo. To get into town from the former, follow Viale Pasitea; from the latter (a far shorter route), take Via Cristoforo Colombo. When departing, buy bus tickets at **Bar Internazionale** (Via Guglielmo Marconi

NOCELLE

A tiny, still relatively isolated mountain village, located 2km southeast of Montepertuso, Nocelle (450m) commands some of the most spectacular views on the entire coast. A world apart from touristy Positano, it's a sleepy, silent place where not much ever happens and where the small population of residents are happy to keep it that way. It's also where the Sentiero degli Dei officially ends.

If you want to stay, **Villa della Quercia** (☑089 812 34 97; www.villalaquercia.com; Via Nocelle 5; d €80-90; ☺Apr–mid-Oct; 🛜) is a delightful B&B in a former hilltop monastery in Nocelle. It comes armed with a tranquil garden and goat's-eye views of the coast. For food, **Trattoria Santa Croce** (☑089 81 12 60; www.ristorantesantacrocepositano.com; Via Nocelle 19; meals €22; ☺noon-3.30pm & 7-9.30pm Apr-Oct) is a modest low-key restaurant in the main part of the village.

Small minibuses run by Mobility Amalfi Coast connect Nocelle to Positano (€1.30, 30 mintues) via Montepertuso 10 times a day. A taxi to/from Positano costs an extortionate €35 to €40: avoid. If you're driving, follow the signs from Positano.

306; ☺7am-1am) or from the **tabaccheria** (☑089 81 21 33; Via Cristoforo Colombo 5; ☺9.30am-9pm) at the bottom of Via Cristoforo Colombo.

SITA Sud (☑342 6256442; www.sitasud trasporti.it) runs up to 28 daily buses to Sorrento (€2, one hour). It also runs up to 25 daily services to Amalfi (€2, 50 minutes), from where buses continue east to Salerno.

CAR & MOTORCYLE

Take the A3 autostrada to Vietri sul Mare and then follow the SS163 coastal road. To hire a scooter, try **Positano Rent a Scooter** (☑089 812 20 77; www.positanorentascooter.it; Viale Pasitea 99; per day from €70; ☺9am-9pm). Don't forget that you will need to produce a driver's licence and passport.

Parking here is no fun in summer. There are some blue-zone parking areas (€3 per hour) and a handful of expensive private car parks. **Parcheggio da Anna** (Viale Pasitea 173; €5 per hour) is located just before the Pensione Maria Luisa, at the top of town. Closer to the beach and town centre, **Di Gennaro** (Via Pasitea 1; €25 per day) is near the bottom of Via Cristoforo Colombo.

ⓘ Getting Around

Mobility Amalfi Coast (☑089 81 30 77) runs local buses following the lower ring road every half hour between 8am and midnight. Stops are clearly marked and you can buy your ticket at tobacconists (€1.30) or on board. The **main bus stop** (Piazza dei Mulini) in central Positano is on the corner of Viale Pasitea and Via dei Mulini. Mobility Amalfi Coast buses also pass by both SITA Sud bus stops. Additionally, the company runs around 10 daily buses up to Montepertuso and Nocelle.

Praiano

☑089 / POP 2020

An ancient fishing village, a low-key summer resort and, increasingly, a popular centre for the arts, Praiano is a delight. With no centre as such, its whitewashed houses pepper the verdant ridge of Monte Sant'Angelo as it slopes towards Capo Sottile. Formerly an important silk-production centre, it was a favourite of the Amalfi *doges* (dukes) who made it their summer residence.

⊙ Sights & Activities

Praiano is glued to a steep bluff 120m above sea level and exploring it inevitably involves lots of steps. There are also several trails that start from town, including a dreamy walk – particularly romantic at sunset – that leaves from beside the San Gennaro church, descending due west to the **Spiaggia della Gavitelli** (via 300 steps), and carrying on to the medieval defensive Torre di Grado. The town also acts as an alternative starting point for the **Sentiero degli Dei** (Path of the Gods; p158).

Torre a Mare   GALLERY
(☑339 4401008; www.paolosandulli.com; Marina di Praia; ☺9am-1pm & 3.30-7pm) Defensive towers sit all along the Amalfi Coast; ironically, they are generally known as Saracen towers, named after the very invaders they were erected to thwart. Although most lie empty, some are privately owned. At Marina di Praia you can combine a visit to one such tower with enjoying the original sculptures and artwork of contemporary artist Paolo

Sandulli. Most distinctive are his 'heads' with colourful sea-sponge hairdos. A spiral staircase leads to further works upstairs, including paintings.

La Boa DIVING
(089 81 30 34; www.laboa.com; Marina di Praia; 1 dive without/with equipment €60/100) Diving operator tucked beneath the cliffs of Marina di Praia, offering dives all along the Amalfi coast up to and including Punta Campanella. Also offers SSI courses for €450.

✕ Eating

Fish and seafood dominate the menus in this old fishing town. Its most famous traditional dish is *totani e patate alla praianese*, a soulful combination of soft calamari rings, sliced potato, *datterini* tomatoes, garlic, croutons, *peperoncino* (chilli) and parsley.

Da Armandino SEAFOOD €€
(089 87 40 87; Via Praia 1, Marina di Praia; meals €35; ⊙1-4pm & 7pm-midnight Apr-Nov) Seafood-lovers should head for this widely acclaimed, no-frills restaurant located in a former boatyard on the beach at Marina di Praia. Da Armandino is great for fish fresh off the boat. There's no menu; just opt for the dish of the day – it's all excellent.

Onda Verde ITALIAN €€
(089 87 41 43; www.ondaverde.it; Via Terramare 3; meals €38; ⊙12.30-9.30pm Apr-Nov) Part of a **hotel** (089 87 41 43; www.hotelondaverde. com; d from €250; ⊙Apr-Oct; P✼⊡🐾) with the same name, this restaurant is located halfway down the steep steps leading to the marina (just beyond the defensive tower). Sit outside for the best views of the bay. The food here reflects an innovative take on traditional cuisine and includes a plentiful choice of salads – just the thing on a sizzling summer's day.

🍷 Drinking & Nightlife

★**Africana Famous Club** CLUB
(089 81 11 71; www.africanafamousclub.com; Via Terramare 2; €10-35; ⊙10pm-late May-Sep, bar opens 8pm; 📶) All Amalfi nightlife converges in the unlikely setting of Marina di Praia. But this is no run-of-the-mill nightclub: Africana's been going since the '60s, when Jackie Kennedy was a regular guest. It has an extraordinary cave setting (complete with natural blowholes), a mix of DJs and live music, plus a glass dance floor with fish swimming beneath your feet.

Music ranges from disco to techno and hip-hop, drinks are pricey and the dress code is relaxed.

Shuttle buses run regularly from Positano, Amalfi and Maiori during summer. You can also catch a Positano Boats water taxi (€15 return per person) on Saturday nights.

🛍 Shopping

Alimentari Rispoli FOOD & DRINKS
(089 87 40 18; Via Nazionale 82; ⊙8am-1pm & 4-9pm, closed Sun Nov-Mar) Sells cheese and cold cuts, as well as fruit and drinks; a useful place to stock up before embarking on the Sentiero degli Dei (p158) hiking trail.

❶ Information

Tourist Office (089 87 45 57; www.praiano. org; Via G Capriglione 116b; ⊙9am-1pm & 4.30-8.30pm Mon-Sat) Can provide maps and information for the area's hiking trails.

❶ Getting There & Away

SITA Sud (p181) runs up to 27 daily buses to Sorrento (€2.40, 1¼ hours). It also runs up to 25 daily services to Amalfi (€1.30, 25 minutes) from where buses continue east to Salerno. Reduced services on Sunday.

❶ Getting Around

Positano Boats (338 1539207; www. positanoboats.info; Spiaggia Grande) runs a water-taxi service to Africana nightclub near Marina di Praia on Saturday nights (€15 return per person).

Furore

089 / POP 840

Marina di Furore, a tiny fishing village, was once a busy little commercial centre, although it's difficult to believe that today. In medieval times, its unique natural position freed it from the threat of foreign raids and provided a ready source of water for its flour and paper mills.

Originally founded by Romans fleeing barbarian incursions, it sits at the bottom of what's known as the fjord of Furore, a giant cleft that cuts through the Lattari mountains. The main village, however, stands 300m above, in the upper Vallone del Furore. A one-horse place that sees few tourists at any time of the year, it exudes a distinctly rural air despite the colourful murals and unlikely modern sculpture.

THE SITA BUS EXPERIENCE

The spectacular road that traces the Amalfi Coast is called Strada Statale 163, aka the *Nastro Azzurro* (Blue Ribbon). Commissioned by Bourbon king Ferdinand II and completed in 1853, it wends its way along the Amalfi Coast between Vietri sul Mare and Sant'Agata sui due Golfi, near Sorrento, snaking round impossibly tight curves, over deep ravines and through tunnels gouged out of sheer rock. It's a magnificent feat of civil engineering, although, as John Steinbeck pointed out in his 1953 essay, *My Positano*, the road is also 'carefully designed to be a little narrower than two cars side by side...'.

You haven't really experienced the Amalfi Coast until you've sat through the animated theatre of a SITA bus ride, squeezing past backed-up lines of cars where motorists exchange impatient hand gestures, or screeching around hairpin bends where waist-high barriers are all that exist between you and oblivion. With a liberal use of their loud klaxons (a familiar sound on the Amalfi), Amalfi Coast bus drivers seem to take the latent dangers in their stride, sitting confidently at their wheels like Formula One racing drivers blessed with super-human peripheral vision.

SITA buses stop at numerous places along the coast with Amalfi town acting as the main nexus. Buy a ticket beforehand in a tobacconist shop or a bar, validate it as you climb on board, and enjoy the ride. Popular bus routes get crowded in July and August, so be prepared to stand.

Fiordo di Furore NATURAL FEATURE
(Fjord of Furore; SS163) The Fiordo di Furore, a deep and narrow cleft in the coastline 6km west of Amalfi, is a misnomer. Fjords are formed by glaciers, whereas the Furore 'fjord' is a drowned river valley carved by the Schiato stream. The mouth of the *fiordo* is crossed by an arched stone bridge, the site of an international high-diving tournament in July. A tiny beach at the bottom of the cleft, accessible by a stone staircase, is backed by a few abandoned houses.

Despite the lack of sun, this is a popular sheltered bathing and boating spot in the summer. There's a also simple, seasonal bar-restaurant.

❶ Getting There & Away

To get to upper Furore by car, follow the SS163 and then the SS366 signposts to Agerola. Otherwise, regular SITA Sud (p181) buses depart from the bus terminus in Amalfi (€1.30, 25 minutes). Buses run up to 10 times daily, with three services on Sunday.

Amalfi

📱 089 / POP 5100

It is hard to grasp that pretty little Amalfi, with its sun-filled piazzas and small beach, was once a maritime superpower with a population of more than 70,000. For one thing, it's not a big place – you can easily walk from one end to the other in about 20 minutes. For another, there are very few

historical buildings of note. The explanation is chilling: most of the old city, and its inhabitants, simply slid into the sea during an earthquake in 1343.

Despite this, the town exudes history and culture, most notably in its over-sized Byzantine-influenced cathedral and diminutive Paper Museum. And while the permanent population is now a fairly modest 5000 or so, the numbers swell significantly during summer.

Just around the headland, neighbouring **Atrani** is a dense tangle of whitewashed alleys and arches centred on an agreeably lived-in piazza and small scimitar of beach; don't miss it.

◉ Sights

First stop is Piazza del Duomo, the town's focal-point square, with its majestic cathedral. To glean a sense of the town's medieval history, explore the narrow alleys parallel to the main street, with their steep stairways, covered porticos and historic shrine niches. Amalfi also has a beautiful seaside setting; it's the perfect spot for long, lingering lunches.

★ **Cattedrale di Sant'Andrea** CATHEDRAL
(📱 089 87 35 58; Piazza del Duomo; adult/reduced €3/1 between 10am-5pm; ⊙ 7.30am-8.30pm, closed Nov-Mar) A melange of architectural styles, Amalfi's cathedral is a bricks-and-mortar reflection of the town's past as an 11th-century maritime superpower. It

Amalfi

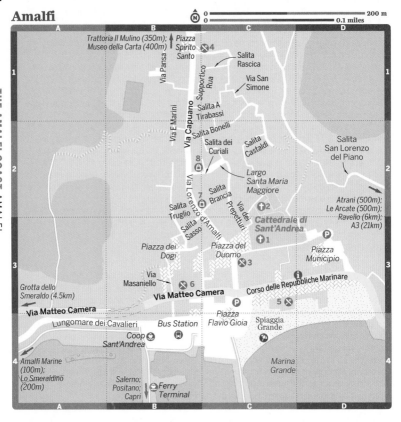

makes a striking impression at the top of a sweeping 62-step staircase. Between 10am and 5pm, the cathedral is only accessible through the adjacent Chiostro del Paradiso, part of a four-section museum, incorporating the cloisters, the 9th-century Basilica del Crocefisso, the crypt of St Andrew and the cathedral itself. Outside these times, you can enter the cathedral for free.

The cathedral dates in part from the early 13th century. Its striped facade has been rebuilt twice, most recently at the end of the 19th century. It was constructed next to an older cathedral, the Basilica del Crocefisso, to which it long remained interconnected. The still-standing basilica now serves as a museum.

The cathedral was originally built to house the relics of St Andrew the Apostle, which arrived here from Constantinople in 1208. Architecturally the building is a hybrid. The Sicilian Arabic-Norman style predominates outside, particularly in the two-tone masonry, mosaics and 13th-century bell tower. The huge bronze doors, the first of their type in Italy, were commissioned by a local noble and made in Syria before being shipped to Amalfi. The interior is primarily baroque with some fine statues at the altar, along with some interesting 12th- and 13th-century mosaics.

Chiostro del Paradiso   CHURCH
(☑089 87 13 24; Piazza del Duomo; adult/reduced €3/1; ⊙9am-7.45pm Jul & Aug, shorter hours Sep-early Jan & Mar-Jun, closed early Jan & Feb) To the left of Amalfi's cathedral porch, these magnificent Moorish-style cloisters, complete with the remnants of 13th-century frescoes, were built in 1266 to house the tombs of Amalfi's prominent citizens; 120 marble columns support a series of tall, slender Arabic arches around a central garden. Entered from the cloisters, the **Basilica del Crocefisso** functions as a museum housing more frescoes and religious artefacts, including silver-embossed, 13th-century reliquary heads. Down below, the crypt contains the relics of St Andrew the Apostle.

Grotta dello Smeraldo   CAVE
(admission €5; ⊙9am-4pm) Four kilometres west of Amalfi, this grotto is named after the eerie emerald colour that emanates from the water. Stalactites hang down from the 24m-high ceiling, while stalagmites grow up to 10m tall. Buses regularly pass the car park above the cave entrance (from where you take a lift or stairs down to the rowing boats). Alternatively, Coop Sant'Andrea (p187) runs boats from Amalfi (€10 return, plus cave admission). Allow 1½ hours for the return trip.

A curiosity of the Grotta is an underwater *presepe* (nativity scene) submerged 4m beneath the water. The objects made from local Vietri ceramics were put there in 1956. Each year, on 24 December and 6 January, skin-divers from all over Italy make a traditional pilgrimage to the site.

Museo della Carta   MUSEUM
(Paper Museum; ☑089 830 45 61; www.museodellacarta.it; Via delle Cartiere 23; adult/reduced €4/2.50; ⊙10am-6.30pm daily Mar-Oct, to 4pm Tue-Sun Nov-late Jan) Amalfi's Paper Museum is housed in a rugged, cave-like 13th-century paper mill (the oldest in Europe). It lovingly preserves the original paper presses, which are still in full working order, as you'll see during the 30-minute guided tour (in English). The tour explains the original cotton-based paper production and the subsequent wood-pulp manufacturing. Afterwards you might be inspired to pick up some of the stationery sold in the gift shop, including calligraphy sets and paper pressed with flowers.

☞ Tours

If you're intent on going for a swim, you're better off hiring a boat and heading out to sea. You'll find a number of operators along Lungomare dei Cavalieri.

Amalfi has great walking trails leading in all directions including into the cool, shady Valle delle Ferriere (p160).

Amalfi Marine   BOATING
(☑338 3076125; www.amalfiboatrental.com; Spiaggia del Porto, Lungomare dei Cavalieri 7) Amalfi Marine hires out boats (without a skipper from €220 per day per boat excluding petrol; maximum six passengers). Private day-long tours with a skipper start from €600.

✖ Eating

La Pansa   CAFE €
(☑089 87 10 65; www.pasticceriapansa.it; Piazza del Duomo 40; cornetti from €1, pastries from €1.80; ⊙7.30am-midnight Wed-Mon, closed early Jan-early Feb) A marbled and mirrored fifth-generation cafe on Piazza del Duomo where black-bow-tied waiters serve minimalist Italian breakfasts: freshly made *cornetti* (croissants), full-bodied espresso and deliciously frothy cappuccino. Standout pastries include the crisp, flaky *coda di aragosta con crema di limone*, a lobster-tail-shaped concoction filled with a rich yet light lemon-custard cream.

Trattoria Il Mulino   TRATTORIA, PIZZA €
(☑089 87 22 23; Via delle Cartiere 36; pizzas €6-11, meals €20-30; ⊙11.30am-4pm & 6.30pm-midnight Tue-Sun) A TV-in-the-corner, kids-running-between-the-tables sort of place, this is about as authentic an eatery as you'll find in Amalfi. There are few surprises on the menu, just hearty, honest pastas, grilled meats and fish. For a taste of local seafood, try the octopus cake or pasta with swordfish. It's right at the top of the town under a simple plastic awning.

Lo Smeraldino   SEAFOOD €€
(☑089 87 10 70; www.ristorantelosmeraldino.it; Piazzale dei Protontini 1, Lungomare dei Cavalieri; pizzas €9, meals €30-45; ⊙11.45am-3pm & 6.45-11.15pm daily Jul & Aug, closed Tue Sep-Jun) Situated west of the centre, on the waterfront overlooking the fishing boats, this inviting blue-and-white beachside restaurant was founded in 1949. As well as crisp-based pizzas, this is a good place for fancy risottos, such as smoked salmon and caviar, or

simple classics including grilled or poached local fish.

Despite the location, this is not a place where you come wrapped in a sarong and wearing flip-flops; the atmosphere is one of understated elegance. Book ahead at weekends.

La Taverna del Duca SEAFOOD €€
(☑089 87 27 55; www.amalfilatavernadelduca. it; Piazza Spirito Santo 26; pizzas from €7, meals €30-42; ⊗noon-3pm & 7-11.30pm Fri-Wed) Grab a chair on the square at this popular fish restaurant. Specials vary according to the catch of the day but might include *carpaccio di baccalà* (thin strips of raw salted cod) or the Campania-esque *scialatielli allo scoglio* (mixed seafood with a short, thick fettucine-like pasta).

Marina Grande SEAFOOD €€€
(☑089 87 11 29; www.ristorantemarinagrande.com; Viale della Regione 4; meals €40-55; ⊗noon-3pm & 6.30-10.30pm Wed-Mon Mar-Oct; 🐾) 🍴 Run by the third generation of the same family, this savvy beachfront favourite serves fish so fresh it's almost flapping. It prides itself on the use of locally sourced organic produce, which, in Amalfi, means superlative amberjack, cuttlefish, prawns and mussels. Reservations recommended.

DON'T MISS

RISTORANTE LA CARAVELLA

A restaurant of artists, art and artistry, **La Caravella** (☑089 87 10 29; www. ristorantelacaravella.it; Via Matteo Camera 12; meals €50-90, tasting menus €50-135; ⊗noon-2.30pm & 7-11pm Wed-Mon; 🕱) once hosted Andy Warhol. No surprise that it doubles up as a de-facto gallery with frescoes, creative canvases and a ceramics collection. And then there's the food on the seven-course tasting menu, prepared by some of the finest culinary Caravaggios in Italy.

Despite its fame, Michelin-starred Caravella, in business since 1959, remains an unpretentious and discreet place that's true to its seafood roots.

Not to be missed are the anchovy croquettes, fish with fennel and sun-dried tomatoes and – the *Mona Lisa* on the menu – a fine lemon *soufflé*. The wine list is, arguably, the best on the Amalfi Coast. Reservations essential.

 Shopping

You'll have no difficulty loading up on souvenirs here – Via Lorenzo d'Amalfi is lined with garish shops selling local ceramic work, artisanal paper gifts and *limoncello*. Prices are set for tourists, so don't expect many bargains.

Il Ninfeo CERAMICS
(☑089 873 63 53; www.amalficoastceramics.com; Via Lorenzo d'Amalfi 28; ⊗9am-9pm) Unabashedly tourist-geared, Il Ninfeo has a vast showroom displaying an excellent selection of ceramics, ranging from giant urns to fridge magnets. If they're not too busy, ask whether you can see the fascinating remains of a Roman villa under the showroom. It makes you realise just how much is hidden under this town.

L'Arco Antico D'Artuono GIFTS & SOUVENIRS
(☑089 873 63 54; Via Capuano 4; ⊗9.30am-8.30pm) Amalfi's connection with papermaking dates back to the 12th century, when the first mills were set up to supply the republic's small army of bureaucrats. Although little paper is made here now, you can still buy it and the quality is high. This attractive shop sells a range of products, including beautiful writing paper, leather-bound notebooks and photo albums.

❶ Information

Tourist Office (☑089 87 11 07; www.amalfi touristoffice.it; Corso delle Repubbliche Marinare 27; ⊗8.30am-1pm & 2-6pm Mon-Sat Apr-Oct, 8.30am-1pm Mon-Sat Nov-Mar; 🕱) Just off the main seafront road in a small courtyard.

❶ Getting There & Away

BUS

Amalfi's **bus station** (Lungomare dei Cavalieri) in Piazza Flavio Gioia is little more than a car park, but it is the main transport nexus on the coast.

SITA Sud (p181) runs up to 27 buses daily to Ravello (€1.30, 25 minutes). Eastbound, it runs up to 20 buses daily to Salerno (€2.40, 1¼ hours) via Maiori (20 minutes). Westbound, it runs up to 25 buses daily to Positano (€2, 40 minutes) via Praiano (€1.30, 25 minutes). Many continue to Sorrento (€2.90, 1¾ hours).

You can buy tickets from the *tabacchi* (tobacconist) on the corner of Piazza Flavio Gioia and Via Duca Mansone I (the side street that leads to Piazza del Duomo).

ATRANI

Atrani is Amalfi town's smaller, shyer sibling, a tiny compact village (the smallest in southern Italy by area) locked into a narrow steep-sided valley where it's been left to develop in splendid isolation. While ostensibly there are similarities between the two settlements (both have unusual churches, small but popular beaches, and milling legacies), Atrani is distinctly quieter, cheaper, more authentic and humming with a sense of community. Part of its charm stems from its lack of traffic: the SS163 coastal road carries the honking SITA buses high above the town centre on a stone bridge. But, the real appeal of Atrani is that it doesn't seem to be bothered about putting on a show. If you are peckish, tuck into fresh fish and pizzas at reputable Le Arcate (☑ 089 87 13 67; www.learcateatrani.it; Largo Orlando Buonocore; pizzas from €6, meals €30; ☺ 12-3.30pm & 7-11pm daily Jul & Aug, closed Mon Sep-Jun; ☎), located right on the seafront.

Atrani is a 10-minute walk east of Amalfi. Take the tunnel through the Luna Rosso underground car park and then cut in front of the Nostromo restaurant and along the seafront.

CAR & MOTORCYCLE

Driving from the north, exit the A3 autostrada at Vietri sul Mare and follow the SS163. From the south, leave the A3 at Salerno and head for Vietri sul Mare and the SS163.

Parking is a problem in Amalfi, although there are some parking places on Piazza Flavio Gioia near the ferry terminal (€3 per hour), as well as at the underground car park Garage Luna Rossa (€2 to €4 per hour). The latter is accessed from the main seafront road between Amalfi and Atrani. From the car park, a pedestrian tunnel leads directly into the town.

BOAT

The **ferry terminal** is a simple affair with several ticket offices located a short hop from the bus station on the seafront.

TraVelMar (☑ 089 87 29 50; www.travelmar.it) Runs a reliable April to October water taxi to/from Positano (€8, 25 minutes, daily), Minori (€3, 10 minutes, seven daily), Cetara (€5, 40 minutes, six daily) and Salerno (€8, 35 minutes, up to 12 daily).

Alilauro (☑ 081 497 22 38; www.alilauro.it) Runs ferries to Sorrento (€21, one hour, two daily) via Positano, and to Capri (€24, 1¼ hours, one daily) from around April to October.

⊙ Getting Around

Coop Sant'Andrea (☑ 089 87 31 90; www.coopsantandrea.com; Lungomare dei Cavalieri 1) runs boats from Amalfi to the Grotta dello Smeraldo (€10 return, plus cave admission).

Ravello

☑ 089 / POP 2490

It cured Richard Wagner's writer's block, provided inspiration for DH Lawrence as he nurtured the plot of *Lady Chatterley's Lover*, and impressed American writer Gore Vidal so much that he stayed for 30 years and became an honorary local. Ravello has a metamorphic effect on people.

Founded in the 5th century as a sanctuary from barbarian invaders fresh from sacking Rome, this lofty Amalfi town was built, in contrast to other Amalfi settlements, up on a hill rather than down on the coast. It's second only to Positano in its style and glamour.

Ravello's refinement is exemplified in the town's polished main piazza, where debonair diners relax under the canopies of al-fresco cafes. It's also reflected in its lush villas (many now turned into palatial hotels), manicured gardens and one of Italy's finest musical festivals (thank Wagner's wife for that).

⊙ Sights

Even if you have absolutely no sense of direction and a penchant for going round in circles, it's difficult to get lost in this town; everything is clearly signposted from the main Piazza Duomo. Explore the narrow backstreets, however, and you will discover glimpses of a quieter, traditional lifestyle: dry-stone walls fronting simple homes surrounded by overgrown gardens, neatly planted vegetable plots and basking cats.

★ **Villa Rufolo** GARDENS
(☑ 089 85 76 21; www.villarufolo.it; Piazza Duomo; adult/reduced €7/5; ☺ 9am-9pm summer, reduced hours winter, tower museum 10am-7pm summer, reduced hours winter) To the south of Ravello's cathedral, a 14th-century tower marks the entrance to this villa, famed for its beautiful cascading gardens. Created by a Scotsman,

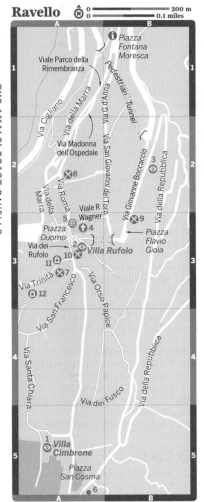

Ravello

The 13th-century Torre Maggiore (Main Tower) now houses the **Torre-Museo**, an interactive museum that sheds light on the villa's history and characters. Among the latter is Reid, the Scottish botanist who purchased and extensively restored the property in the 19th century. The museum also showcases art, archaeological finds and ceramics linked to the villa. Stairs inside the tower lead up to an outdoor viewing platform, affording knockout views of the villa and the Amalfi Coast.

Today Villa Rufolo's gardens stage world-class concerts during the town's annual arts festival.

★ **Villa Cimbrone**   GARDENS
(☑089 85 74 59; www.hotelvillacimbrone.com/gardens; Via Santa Chiara 26; adult/reduced €7/4; ☺9am-sunset) If you could bottle up a take-away image of the Amalfi, it might be the view from the **Belvedere of Infinity**, classical busts in the foreground, craggy coast splashed with pastel-shaded villages in the background. It's yours to admire at this refashioned 11th-century villa (now an upmarket hotel) with sublime gardens. Open to the public, the gardens were mainly created by a British peer, Ernest Beckett, who reconfigured them with rose-beds, temples and a Moorish pavilion in the early 1900s.

The villa (also owned by Beckett) was something of a bohemian retreat in its early days; it was frequented by Greta Garbo and her lover Leopold Stokowski as a secret

Sir Francis Neville Reid, in 1853, they are truly magnificent, commanding divine panoramic views packed with exotic colours, artistically crumbling towers and luxurious blooms. Note that the gardens are at their best from May till October; they don't merit the entrance fee outside those times.

The villa was built in the 13th century for the wealthy Rufolo dynasty and was home to several popes as well as King Robert of Anjou. Wagner was so inspired by the gardens when he visited in 1880 that he modelled the garden of Klingsor (the setting for the second act of the opera *Parsifal*) on them.

hideaway. Other illustrious former guests include Virginia Woolf, Winston Churchill, DH Lawrence and Salvador Dalí. The house and gardens sit atop a crag that's a 10-minute walk south of Piazza Duomo.

Museo del Corallo Camo   MUSEUM
(☑ 089 85 74 61; www.museodelcorallo.com; Piazza Duomo 9; ☺ 10am-noon & 3-4pm Mon-Sat) Hidden away at the back of this cameo shop is a small museum with some magnificent pieces, including a mid-16th-century Madonna, Roman amphorae, early 19th-century tortoiseshell combs and some exquisite oil paintings. While Giorgio's cameos are beautiful (and popular with all kinds of well-known folk), you may think twice about the ethics of buying coral, especially the valuable red coral used locally. An intrinsic part of Mediterranean ecosystems, it is currently endangered due to commercial over-harvesting.

Cathedral   CATHEDRAL
(www.chiesaravello.com; Piazza Duomo; museum adult/reduced €3/1.50; ☺ 8am-9pm) Forming the eastern flank of Piazza Duomo, Ravello's cathedral was built in 1086. Since that time it has undergone various makeovers. The facade is 16th century, but the central bronze door, one of only about two dozen in the country, dates from 1179. The interior is a late-20th-century interpretation of what the original must have once looked like.

Drawing it above the rank of a run-of-the-mill church is the striking pulpit, supported by six twisting columns set on marble lions and decorated with flamboyant mosaics of peacocks and other birds. Note also how the floor is tilted towards the square – a deliberate measure to enhance the perspective effect. The cathedral museum claims a modest collection of religious artefacts.

🐦 Courses

★ Mamma Agata   COOKING
(☑ 089 85 70 19; www.mammaagata.com; Piazza San Cosma 9; courses €250) The mamma of all cooking classes, this congenial family affair is famed for its private classes in the Agata home, producing simple, exceptional food using primarily organic ingredients. A one-day demonstration class culminates in an interlude on a lovely sea-view terrace, tasting what you've been taught to make and enjoying homemade *limoncello*. There is also a cookbook available for purchase.

🎆 Festivals & Events

★ Ravello Festival   PERFORMING ARTS
(☑ 089 85 84 22; www.ravellofestival.com; ☺ Jul-Aug) In July and August, the Ravello Festival – established in 1953 – turns much of the town centre into a stage. Events range from orchestral concerts and chamber music to ballet performances, film screenings and exhibitions. The festival's most celebrated (and impressive) venue is the overhanging terrace in the Villa Rufolo gardens.

🍴 Eating

Surprisingly, Ravello doesn't offer many exceptional eating options. It's easy enough to find a cafe selling overpriced *panini* but not so simple to find a decent restaurant or trattoria. There are a few good hotel restaurants, most of which are open to non-guests, and a couple of deluxe independents, but not much else. Places get very busy in summer, particularly at lunchtime. Book ahead.

Babel   CAFE €
(☑ 089 858 62 15; Via Trinità 13; meals €20; ☺ 11.30am-5pm & 6.30-10.30pm daily May-Sep, closed Wed late Mar, Apr & Oct, closed Nov-late Mar; 📶) A cool little deli-cafe with a compact menu of what you could call 'Italian tapas', affordable bites including Italian *gazpacho* (cold soup), bruschetta, dry polenta and creative salads with combos such as lemon and orange with goat's cheese and chestnut honey. It offers an excellent range of local wines, and Vietri-school ceramics for sale.

Da Salvatore   ITALIAN €€
(☑ 089 85 72 27; Via della Repubblica 2; meals €38-45, pizzas from €5; ☺ 12.30-3pm & 7.30-10pm Tue-Sun Easter-Nov) Located just before the bus stop, Da Salvatore doesn't merely rest on the laurels of its spectacular terrace views. This is one of the coast's best restaurants, serving arresting dishes that showcase local produce with creativity, flair and whimsy;

ⓘ WHERE'S THE PARTY?

Nightlife in Ravello is a sedate affair. Most people spend their evening nursing an *aperitivo* (pre-dinner drink) in one of the handful of bars on Piazza Duomo. For a more lively evening scene, you'll need to hit Salerno or, in the summer, Praiano, which is home to one of the coast's most celebrated nightclubs.

OFF THE BEATEN TRACK

RAVELLO RAMBLES

Ravello is the starting point for numerous walks – some of which follow ancient paths through the surrounding Lattari mountains. If you've got the legs for it, you can walk down to **Minori** via an attractive route of steps, hidden alleys and olive groves, passing the picturesque hamlet of Torello en route. This 2.5km walk kicks off just to the left of Villa Rufolo and takes around 45 minutes. Alternatively, you can head the other way, to Amalfi, via the ancient village of **Scala**. Once a flourishing religious centre with more than a hundred churches, and the oldest settlement on the Amalfi Coast, Scala (2km from Ravello) is now a pocket-sized, sleepy place where the wind whistles through empty streets. In the central square, the Romanesque **duomo** (Piazza Municipio; ⊗8am-noon & 5-7pm) retains some of its 12th-century solemnity. Ask at the Ravello tourist office for more information on local walks.

your premeal *benvenuto* (welcome) may include an *aperitivo* of Negroni encased in a white-chocolate ball.

Wines by the glass include knockout super-reds such as Amarone and Barolo. In the evening, part of the restaurant is transformed into an informal pizzeria, serving some of the best wood-fired pizza you will taste anywhere this side of Naples.

Ristorante Pizzeria Vittoria   PIZZA **€€**
(☑089 85 79 47; www.ristorantepizzeriavittoria.it; Via dei Rufolo 3; pizza from €5, meals €30; ⊗12.15-3pm & 7.15-11pm; 🖼) Come here for exceptional pizza, with some 16 choices on the menu, including the Ravellese, with cherry tomatoes, mozzarella, basil and courgettes. Other dishes include grouper fish with creamed fennel and an innovative stuffed courgette-flower *antipasto*. The atmosphere is one of subdued elegance, with a small outside terrace and grainy historical pictures of Ravello on the walls.

Cumpà Cosimo   CAMPANIAN **€€**
(☑089 85 71 56; Via Roma 44-46; pizzas €7-12, meals €30-35; ⊗12.30-3pm & 7.30pm-midnight) This wonderfully dated trattoria serves down-to-earth Italian grub in a unfussy, celeb-free environment. An informal family affair – meat comes from the family butcher, vegetables and fruit are homegrown, and the house wine is homemade – it serves excellent pasta, hearty gnocchi and some fine main courses. House favourites include rabbit with tomatoes and grilled crayfish.

🛍 Shopping

Profumi della Costiera   DRINKS
(☑089 85 81 67; www.profumidellacostiera.it; Via Trinità 37; ⊗9am-8pm) The *limoncello* produced here is made with local lemons;

known to experts as *sfusato amalfitano*, they're enormous – about double the size of a standard lemon. The tot is made according to traditional recipes, so there are no preservatives and no colouring. All bottles carry the IGP (Indicazione Geografica Proteta; Protected Geographical Indication) quality mark.

Filo d'Autore   CLOTHING
(☑089 85 84 67; www.filodautoreravello.it; Via Trinità 8; scarves from €35; ⊗9.30am-9pm) Although you may associate cashmere with more northern climes, this tiny shop in the Ravello backstreets is worth a visit to view the exceptional quality of the locally produced clothing, made primarily from pure cashmere, as well as linen.

ℹ Information

Tourist Office (☑089 85 70 96; www.ravello time.it; Piazza Fontana Moresca 10; ⊗9am-7pm summer, to 5pm rest of yr) Shares digs with the police station. Provides brochures and maps, and can also assist with accommodation.

ℹ Getting There & Away

BUS

From the bus stop on the eastern side of Amalfi's Piazza Flavio Gioia, SITA Sud (p181) runs up to 27 buses daily to Ravello (€1.30, 25 minutes).

CAR & MOTORCYCLE

From central Amalfi, continue east on the main coastal road (SS163) for 1.4km before doing a hairpin turn onto SS373; street signs indicate Ravello. Vehicles are not permitted in Ravello's town centre.

Consider taking a bus (or walking) from Amalfi to Ravello instead of driving, as parking can be painful. If you do drive up, there is a central car park under Piazza Duomo (€2.50 to €3.50 per hour). Alternatively, head for the underground car park at the **Auditorium Oscar Niemeyer** (☑ 346 7378561; Via della Repubblica 12; per 1/8hr €2/10).

A taxi from Ravello to Amalfi costs around €31. Always agree on the price with the driver before getting in the taxi.

Minori

☑ 089 / POP 2750

About 3.5km east of Amalfi, or a steep 45-minute walk down from Ravello, Minori is a small, workaday town, popular with holidaying Italians. Much scruffier than its refined coastal cousins Amalfi and Positano, it's no less dependent on tourism yet seems more genuine, with its festive seafront, pleasant beach, atmospheric pedestrian shopping streets and noisy traffic jams. The town is also known for its history of pasta making, dating back to medieval times; its speciality is *scialatielli* (thick ribbons of fresh pasta), featured on many local restaurant menus.

⦿ Sights & Activities

Villa Roma Antiquarium   HISTORIC BUILDING
(☑ 089 85 28 93; Via Capodipiazza 28; ⊙ 8am-7pm) FREE Rediscovered in the 1930s, the 1st-century Villa Roma Antiquarium is a typical example of the splendid homes that Roman nobles built as holiday retreats in the period before Mt Vesuvius' AD 79 eruption. The best-preserved rooms surround the garden on the lower level, the highlight being a floor mosaic depicting a bull. There's also a slightly tatty museum exhibiting various artefacts, including a collection of 6th-century-BC to 6th-century-AD amphorae.

Valle del Sambuco   HIKING
This 10.5km circuit explores the hills and valleys behind Minori, circumnavigating lemon groves and the ruins of old paper mills. Its peak is the 13th-century **Convento di San Nicola**, perched high atop the coastline amid pine and oak trees.

Leave the seafront town of Maiori on the well-marked Via dei Limoni before cutting sharply uphill (yes, more of those infamous Amalfi steps) in the hamlet of **Torre**. Oak and pine trees provide shade as the path ascends steeply to the San Nicola convent located 483m above sea level and accessed via a short spur-trail. The main path then hangs left at a rocky mountain pass and heads down to the small agricultural hamlet of **Sambuco**. From here, another path descends onto the opposite (western) side of the river valley past a scattering of old paper mills into Minori. For an alternative ending, you can follow the paved road south out of Sambuco and finish in Ravello.

⭐ Festivals & Events

Gusta Minori   FOOD & DRINK
(www.gustaminori.it; ⊙ early Sep) Food lovers on the coast gather in Minori for the town's

A MAZE OF TRAILS

The Amalfi Coast is laced with ancient footpaths, many of them dating back to the 10th and 11th centuries and the era of the *ducato* (independent city state). Until the coastal road was built in the 1850s, the trails were the primary means of getting around. Today, they're still frequented by a mix of hikers on holiday and locals who use them to access their terraced lemon groves and outlying farm buildings.

Italy's main hiking body, the CAI (Club Alpino Italiano) maintains a list of 124 numbered walking trails in the region, all marked with distinctive red-and-white paint. Between them, they measure out a total distance of 530km. While the Sentiero degli Dei (#327; p158) may be the most popular trail, the longest is the arterial Via dei Monti Lattari (#300), a 70km west–east romp that's rarely done in its entirety. Other well-trodden courses include the Valle del Sambuco behind Minori, which takes in lemon groves, pine forests, a 13th-century convent and old paper mills.

With the coastline mainly made up of plunging cliffs and craggy mountains, the paths are notorious for their steps (there is little flat ground in these parts). Additionally, some of the narrower, higher trails are mildly exposed. If you're out of shape and/or acrophobic, plan your route carefully before setting out.

Spring and autumn are the best times to go walking in the Amalfi, with wildflowers blooming and mild daytime temperatures.

annual food jamboree, with pasta stalls (and the like) as well as live music and other cultural events.

Eating

★ **Sal de Riso** DESSERTS €
(☑089 87 79 41; www.salderiso.it; Via Roma 80; desserts from €4.50; ☺7am-1am) *Pasticceria*? Yes. Cafe? Yes. Gelateria? Yes. Sal de Riso is all these things and more: an emporium of edible sweetness that will make your eyes pop out and your blood sugar shoot up in the same bite. The ample glass display cases are like an art gallery of avant-garde desserts crammed with delicate cheesecakes, eclairs, sponges and pastries.

Il Giardiniello ITALIAN €€
(☑089 87 70 50; www.ristorantegiardiniello.com; Corso Vittorio Emanuele 17; pizza from €8, meals €35-48; ☺12.20-2.30pm & 6.30-11.30pm Thu-Tue) The old sage of Minori restaurants has been around as long as the Fiat Cinquecento and is arguably just as good. Sit on the terrace underneath a canopy of fragrant jasmine and enjoy highbrow, art-on-a-plate dishes that revolve around seafood, with a surprise inclusion of rabbit served with bacon and black truffles.

❶ Information

Tourist Office (☑089 87 70 87; www.proloco. minori.sa.it; Via Roma 32; ☺8.30am-1pm & 4-8pm Mon-Sat, 8.30am-1pm Sun) Head to this small office on the seafront for general information and walking maps.

❶ Getting There & Away

BOAT
From April to October, TraVelMar (p180) sails to Amalfi (€3, 10 minutes, eight daily), Maiori (€3, five minutes, eight daily), Cetara (€5, 25 minutes, around six daily) and Salerno (€3, 40 minutes, six daily). To sail to Positano (€11), transfer in Amalfi.

BUS
SITA Sud (p181) runs up to 19 buses daily to Salerno (€2, one hour) Monday to Saturday, stopping in Maiori (€1.30, five minutes) and Cetara (€2, 30 minutes) en route. Buses run around eight times on Sunday. Westbound, buses run to Amalfi (€1.30, 15 minutes) up to 21 times a day from Monday to Saturday, with services running around eight times daily on Sunday. From Amalfi, buses continue west to Positano and Sorrento.

Cetara
☑089 / POP 2140

Guarding the less-overrun eastern end of the Amalfi, Cetara is a fiercely traditional fishing village with a reputation as a gastronomic hotspot. It has been an important fishing centre since medieval times and today its deep-sea-tuna fleet is considered one of the Mediterranean's most important. At night, fishers set out in small boats armed with powerful lamps to fish for anchovies. Recently, locals have resurrected the production of what is known as *colatura di alici,* a strong anchovy essence believed to be the descendant of *garum,* the Roman fish seasoning.

✪ Festivals & Events

Sagra del Tonno FOOD & DRINK
(☺late Jul/early Aug) Each year the village celebrates *sagra del tonno,* a festival dedicated to tuna and anchovies. If you can time your visit accordingly, there are plenty of opportunities for tasting, as well as music and other general festivities. Further details are available from the tourist office.

Eating

Gourmands across Italy know Cetara for its anchovies, the star ingredient in the town's *colatura di alici,* a strong, amber-coloured essence that is basically the town's answer to fish sauce. There's a good half-dozen fish-orientated restaurants lining Corso Garibaldi leading down to the port.

Cetara Punto e Pasta CAMPANIAN €€
(☑089 26 11 09; Corso Garibaldi 14; meals €25; ☺noon-4pm & 7-11.30pm Mon, Wed, Thu & Sun, 11.30am-midnight Fri & Sat) This tiny eating joint in salt-of-the-earth Cetara is barely larger than a studio flat, with six tables and an open kitchen from which the industrious owner-chef performs minor miracles with local fish and homemade pasta. The menu is scrawled on a blackboard. Don't leave before tasting the fresh-off-the-boat *alici* (anchovies) ground deliciously into a fishy pesto.

The place usually also opens on Tuesdays in high summer (from around mid-July); call ahead to confirm.

Ristorante Da Spadone CAMPANIAN €€
(☑089 26 12 46; Corso Garibaldi 5; meals €23-28; ☺noon-3.30pm & 7pm-midnight) A new player in Cetara's rigidly traditional dining scene,

Spadone is the kind of place where the head chef stands ingratiatingly at the front door at 7pm, smudges of pizza flour still stuck to his apron. Come here for simple renditions of age-old recipes done well – the *linguine alla vongole,* pizza and fried anchovies are all good.

Shopping

Cetarii FOOD
(☑ 089 26 18 63; www.cetarii.it; Via Largo Marina 48-50; ⊙ 9am-1.30pm & 4-8.30pm) Duck into this artistically presented local shop on the port-side to acquire some of the typical fish products that have made Cetara famous, namely jars of red and white *tonno* (tuna) and bottles of the potent *colatura di alici* (a fish sauce made from anchovies).

❶ Information

Tourist Office (☑ 089 26 17 01; Piazza San Francesco 15; ⊙ 9am-1pm & 5pm-midnight) The local Pro Loco has a good town map with walking trails. Staff might only speak Italian.

❶ Getting There & Away

BOAT

From around April to October, TraVelMar (p180) sails to Amalfi (€5, 40 minutes, around six daily), Maiori (€5, 15 minutes, around six daily), Minori (€5, 25 minutes, around six daily) and Salerno (€5, 15 minutes, around six daily). To sail to Positano (€12), you need to transfer in Amalfi.

Buy tickets at the kiosk on the dock.

BUS

SITA Sud (p181) runs up to 20 buses daily to Salerno (€1.10, 30 minutes) Monday to Saturday, with around eight services on Sunday. It runs up to 21 times daily to Amalfi (€2.20, 45 minutes) via Maiori (€1.30, 25 minutes) and Minori (€2.20, 30 minutes). Services are reduced to around eight daily on a Sunday. From Amalfi, buses head west to Positano and Sorrento.

Vietri sul Mare

☑ 089 / POP 7900

Marking the end of Amalfi's coastal road, Vietri sul Mare is the ceramics capital of Campania. Production dates back to Roman times, but it took off on an industrial scale in the 16th and 17th centuries with the development of high, three-level furnaces. The unmistakable local style – bold brush strokes and strong Mediterranean colours

– found favour in the royal court of Naples, which became one of Vietri's major clients. Later, in the 1920s and '30s, the arrival of international artists (mainly Germans) led to a shake-up of traditional designs. These days, the *centro storico* is packed with decorative tiled-front shops selling ceramic wares of every description.

Museo della Ceramica MUSEUM
(☑ 089 21 18 35; Villa Guariglia, Via Nuova Raito; ⊙ 9am-3pm Tue-Sat, 9.30am-1pm Sun) FREE For a primer on Vietri's ceramics past, head to this museum in the nearby village of Raito. Housed in a mildewed villa surrounded by a park, the museum has a comprehensive collection, including pieces from the 'German period' (1929–47), when the town attracted an influx of artists, mainly from Germany.

Ceramica Artistica Solimene CERAMICS
(☑ 089 21 02 43; www.ceramicasolimene.it; Via Madonna degli Angeli 7; ⊙ 9am-8pm Mon-Fri, 9am-1.30pm & 4-8pm Sat, 9am-1.30pm & 4-7pm Sun) This vast factory outlet, which looks like something Gaudí might have built, is the most famous ceramics shop in town. It sells everything from egg cups to ornamental mermaids. Even if you don't go in, it's worth having a look at the shop's extraordinary glass-and-ceramic facade. It was designed by Italian architect Paolo Soleri, who studied under Frank Lloyd Wright.

❶ Information

Tourist Office (☑ 089 21 12 85; www.proloco vietrisulmare.it; Via San Giovanni; ⊙ 9.30am-12.30pm Mon, Wed & Fri) This moderately helpful office with limited hours is next to the *duomo*.

❶ Getting There & Away

BUS

SITA Sud (p181) runs up to 20 buses daily to Salerno (€1.10, 15 minutes). Frequency is reduced to around eight buses on Sunday. Up to 21 buses run daily to Cetara (€1.10, 15 minutes), with around eight running on Sunday. Most of these continue west to Minori (€2, 45 minutes) and Amalfi (€2, one hour). From Amalfi, buses travel to Positano and Sorrento.

TRAIN

Vietri sul Mare is the only Amalfi town with a **train station** (Corso Umberto I). Trains run every 30 minutes to Salerno (€1.20, 10 minutes) and Naples (€4.70, 1¼ hours).

THE AMALFI COAST VIETRI SUL MARE

AT A GLANCE

★

LARGEST CITY
Salerno 133,970

**AREA PROTECTED
BY NATIONAL PARK**
1810 sq km

BEST BEACH
Spiaggia Palinuro
(p208)

**BEST
RUSTIC MEAL**
Osteria del Borgo
(p208)

**BEST
MOSAICS**
Salerno's Duomo
(p199)

📅

WHEN TO GO
Jul & Aug Coast
crowded with Italian
holidaymakers; hotel
rooms hard to find.

May, Jun, Sep & Oct
Temperatures are
pleasant and there's
more towel space on
the sand. Springtime
is best in the Parco
Nazionale del Cilento.

Nov-Apr Services
are more limited,
especially on the
coast.

Duomo crypt (p199), Salerno
STEFANO_VALERI/SHUTTERSTOCK ©

Salerno & the Cilento

S alerno may not have the glamorous looks of the Amalfi Coast resorts, but its gritty historic centre is a kind of mini Naples. Anchoring proceedings is an enthralling archaeological museum and a Norman cathedral worthy of a city twice the size.

Head half an hour south to Paestum where you'll find some of the world's best-preserved Greek temples standing proudly among meadows scattered with wildflowers.

Looming on the horizon is the Cilento region, with its largely undeveloped coastal strip and its mountainous interior famed for its orchids. Both are protected within a little-visited national park where villages have a tangible time-warp feel and rough trails lure intrepid walkers who don't mind getting lost.

CILENTO COASTAL TRAIL ROAD TRIP

Following the wild and rugged coastline of the Cilento peninsula, this trip takes in pristine coastline, atmospheric fishing villages, fascinating hilltop towns and glorious ruins hailing from the region's ancient Greek past.

❶ Paestum

The temples at Paestum are among the best preserved in Magna Graecia.

The Drive > Heading 10km south down the SP430 from Paestum, you start winding into the foothills of the Cilento. Follow signs to Agropoli's 'Centro Storico'.

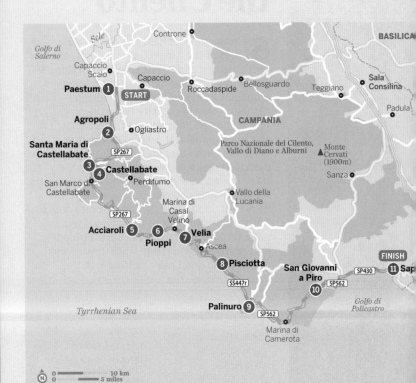

4–5 Days 142km / 88 miles
Great for... Food & Drink; Outdoors
Best Time to Go Spring and autumn for hikers;
high summer for beach types

• •

② Agropoli

An intriguing historic kernel, plus views across to the Amalfi Coast.

The Drive > South of Agropoli, the 13km stretch of the SR ex SS267 turns inland, giving a taste of Cilento's rugged interior, but you'll quickly head west and to the sea.

③ Santa Maria di Castellabate

Four kilometres of golden sand and a charming little harbour.

The Drive > Just past Santa Maria di Castellabate along the SR ex SS267 is the turn-off to Castellabate. The road then winds through orchards and olive groves for 8km.

④ Castellabate

Narrow streets punctuated by ancient archways and small piazzas.

The Drive > Head back down to the SR ex SS267 and follow for 21km.

⑤ Acciaroli

Hemmimgway's old haunt; some say he based *The Old Man and the Sea* on a village fisherman.

The Drive > After Acciaroli, the coastal highway climbs quickly for 8km to Pioppi, proffering stunning views down to Capo Palinuro.

⑥ Pioppi

Join Pioppi's long-living locals on the hamlet's pristine pebble beach.

The Drive > It's practically a straight shot for 8km along the coastal highway to Velia. Some 6km further southeast is Ascea, where coastal mountains make way for the small, rich plains.

⑦ Velia

Former home of philosophers Parmenides and Zeno, Velia's archaeological ruins echo its Greek past.

The Drive > The most hair-raising stretch of the Cilento's coastal highway, with spectacular views as your reward. The total distance is about 10km.

⑧ Pisciotta

The Cilento's liveliest town, with a steeply pitched maze of medieval streets.

The Drive > The 11km trip begins with a steep descent from Pisciotta, then it's a straight road to Palinuro.

⑨ Palinuro

Extending past Palinuro's postcard-pretty harbour, Capo Palinuro offers its own version of Capri's Grotta Azzurra.

The Drive > Begin the 27km drive with a jaunt along the water before heading inland at Marina di Camerota. Expect sharp turns as you wind up the stunning SR ex SS562.

⑩ San Giovanni a Piro

An agricultural town with views to the mountains of Basilicata and Calabria.

The Drive > The final 20km of this trip begins with a winding descent from San Giovanni a Piro to pretty Scario; the road flattens out around the Golfo di Policastro.

⑪ Sapri

Set on an almost perfectly round natural harbour, Sapri is the ideal place to bid the Cilento *arrivederci*.

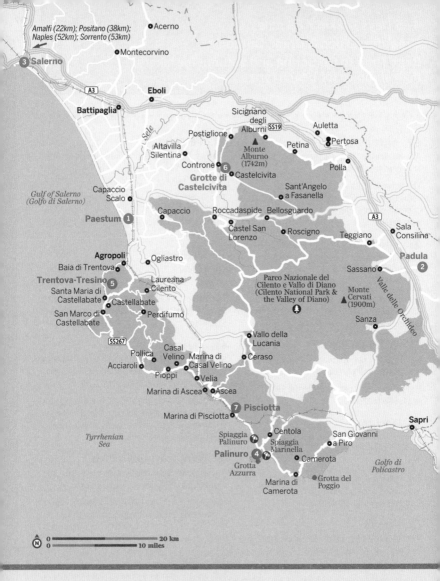

Amalfi (22km); Positano (38km); Naples (52km); Sorrento (53km)

Acerno
Montecorvino
Salerno
Eboli
Battipaglia
Sicignano degli Alburni
SS19
Auletta
Petina
Pertosa
Postiglione
Altavilla Silentina
▲ Monte Alburno (1742m)
Polla
Controne
Grotte di Castelcivita
Castelcivita
Sant'Angelo a Fasanella
Capaccio Scalo
Paestum
Capaccio
Roccadaspide
Bellosguardo
Roscigno
A3
Sala Consilina
Padula
Castel San Lorenzo
Teggiano
Agropoli
Baia di Trentova
Ogliastro
Sassano
Valle delle Orchidee
Trentova-Tresino
Laureana Cilento
Parco Nazionale del Cilento e Vallo di Diano (Cilento National Park & the Valley of Diano)
▲ Monte Cervati (1900m)
Santa Maria di Castellabate
Castellabate
San Marco di Castellabate
Perdifumo
Sanza
SS267
Vallo della Lucania
Pollica
Casal Velino
Marina di Casal Velino
Ceraso
Acciaroli
Pioppi
Velia
Marina di Ascea
Ascea
Pisciotta
Marina di Pisciotta
Sapri
Spiaggia Palinuro
Centola
San Giovanni a Piro
Spiaggia Marinella
Palinuro
Camerota
Golfo di Policastro
Grotta Azzurra
Marina di Camerota
Grotta del Poggio

Gulf of Salerno (Golfo di Salerno)
A3
Sele

Tyrrhenian Sea

N 0 ——— 20 km
0 ——— 10 miles

Salerno & the Cilento Highlights

① **Paestum** (p203) Taking a journey back to Magna Graecia at one of Europe's most majestic archeological sites.

② **Certosa di San Lorenzo** (p211) Counting the multitude of patios, rooms, arches and columns in this gigantic monastery in Padula.

③ **Salerno** (p199) Strolling along the tree-lined promenade in Campania's most authentic southern city.

④ **Palinuro** (p208) Enjoying a sandy Blue Flag beach in this tiny coastal town.

⑤ **Trentova-Tresino** (p205) Tracking the coast on well-marked paths past medieval

towers and sandy beaches south of Agropoli.

⑥ **Grotte di Castelcivita** (p210) Walking through the haunting caverns of this surreal cave.

⑦ **Pisciotta** (p207) Lunching at a simple trattoria amid the twisting streets of a tiny hilltop village.

SALERNO

🗺 089 / POP 133,970

Salerno may initially seem like a bland big city, but the place has a charming, if gritty, individuality, especially around its ostensibly tatty *centro storico* (historic centre), where medieval churches and neighbourhood trattorias echo with the addictive bustle of southern Italy. The city has invested in various urban-regeneration programs centred on this historic neighbourhood, which features a tree-lined seafront promenade widely considered to be one of the cheeriest and most attractive in Italy.

⊙ Sights

Although Salerno is a sprawling town, you can easily visit it in one day and on foot, as the main sights (castle aside) are concentrated in and around the historic centre. Don't miss having a walk along the seafront promenade.

★ **Duomo** CATHEDRAL
(Map p200; 🗺 089 23 13 87; www.cattedraledi salerno.it; Piazza Alfano; ⊙8.30am-8pm Mon-Sat, 8.30am-1pm & 4-8pm Sun) One of Campania's strangely under-the-radar sights, Salerno's impressive cathedral is considered by aficionados to be the most beautiful medieval

church in Italy. Built by the Normans in the 11th century and later aesthetically remodelled in the 18th century, it sustained severe damage in a 1980 earthquake. It is dedicated to San Matteo (St Matthew), whose remains were reputedly brought to the city in 954 and now lie beneath the main altar in the vaulted crypt.

Take special note of the magnificent main entrance, the 12th-century **Porta dei Leoni**, named after the marble lions at the foot of the stairway. It leads through to a beautiful, harmonious courtyard, surrounded by graceful arches and overlooked by a 12th-century bell tower. Carry on through the huge bronze doors (similarly guarded by lions), which were cast in Constantinople in the 11th century. When you come to the three-aisled interior, you will see that it is largely baroque, with only a few traces of the original church. These include parts of the transept and choir floor and the two raised pulpits in front of the choir stalls. Throughout the church you can see highly detailed 13th-century mosaic work redolent of the extraordinary early-Christian mosaics in Ravenna.

In the right-hand apse, don't miss the **Cappella delle Crociate** (Chapel of the Crusades), containing powerful frescoes and more wonderful mosaics. It was so named

SALERNO & THE CILENTO SALERNO

SALERNO & THE CILENTO IN...

One Day

Start off in Salerno by checking out the magnificent cathedral, followed by an atmospheric wander around the narrow backstreets of the city's densely packed *centro storico*. Take a cappuccino break in a typical hung-with-washing piazza, buy some deli fodder, then hop on a train to Paestum for a picnic lunch and an afternoon visiting its magical temples (p203). In the evening continue south to Agropoli for an ocean-front dinner.

Two Days

Stretch your legs with a morning stroll along Agropoli's sweeping promenade. Visit the castle (p205) and historic quarter before continuing south along this dramatic coastline of hidden coves and high cliffs. Stop for a swim, a snack or a walk at small traditional Italian resorts like Acciaroli, a favourite of Ernest Hemingway's; Pioppi, with its pale pebble beach; and medieval Pisciotta, home to a lovely traditional piazza. Carry on along this unspoilt coastline before ending the day in pretty Palinuro.

Three Days

It's not half as famous as its Capri cousin, but Palinuro's Grotta Azzurra (Blue Grotto; p208) is just as spectacular. Next, head inland into the Parco Nazionale del Cilento and the otherworldly caves at Grotte di Castelcivita (p210), one of the largest cave complexes in Europe. Travel over the hills to Padula for some historical immersion at the Certosa di San Lorenzo (p211), a giant among monasteries. Consider staying overnight at one of the park's superb *agriturismi* (farm-stay accommodation).

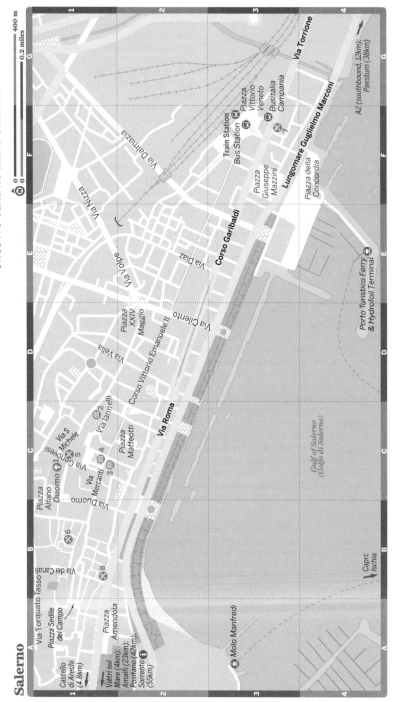

Salerno

Map key

Piazza Sedile del Campo

Castello di Arechi (4.8km)

Via Torquato Tasso

Piazza Alfano

Duomo

Via S Michele

Via Genovesi

Via Mercanti

Piazza Matteotti

Via Iannelli

Via Vella

Piazza XXIV Maggio

Via Volpe

Corso Vittorio Emanuele II

Via Cilento

Via Diaz

Corso Garibaldi

Via Nizza

Via Dalmazia

Piazza Amendola

Via del Canali

Vietri sul Mare (4km); Amalfi (23km); Positano (42km); Sorrento (55km)

Molo Manfredi

Capri; Ischia

Gulf of Salerno
(Golfo di Salerno)

Via Roma

Porto Turistico Ferry & Hydrofoil Terminal

Piazza della Concordia

Lungomare Guglielmo Marconi

Piazza Giuseppe Mazzini

Train Station

Bus Station

Piazza Vittorio Veneto

Busitalia Campania

Via Torrione

A2 (southbound, 12km); Paestum (38km)

N

0   400 m
0   0.2 miles

Salerno

because crusaders' weapons were blessed here. Under the altar stands the tomb of 11th-century pope Gregory VII.

Museo Archeologico Provinciale   MUSEUM
(Map p200; ☑ 089 23 11 35; www.museoarcheo logicosalerno.it; Via San Benedetto 28; adult/reduced €4/2; ⊙9am-7.30pm Tue-Sun) The province's restored and revitalised main archaeological museum is an excellent showcase for the excavated history of the surrounding area, dating back to cave dwellers and the colonising Greeks. The pièce de résistance is the 1st-century BC *Testa bronzea di Apollo* (bronze head of Apollo). Showcased in its own small room upstairs, the head is thought to have been part of a larger statue; it was found by a fisherman in the Gulf of Salerno in 1930.

The upper floor also houses centuries' worth of findings from the nearby necropolis of Fratte (dating from the 6th century BC), including a little vase engraved with salacious gossip describing gay and straight relations between the Greek, Roman and indigenous populations.

Castello di Arechi   CASTLE
(☑089 296 40 15; www.ilcastellodiarechi.it; Via Benedetto Croce; adult/reduced €4/2; ⊙9am-5pm Tue-Sat, to 3.30pm Sun) Hop on bus 19 from Piazza XXIV Maggio to visit Salerno's most famous landmark, the forbidding Castello di Arechi, dramatically positioned 263m above the city. Originally a Byzantine fort, it was built by the Lombard duke of Benevento, Arechi II, in the 8th century and subsequently modified by the Normans and Aragonese, most recently in the 16th century.

Museo Pinacoteca Provinciale   MUSEUM
(Map p200; ☑089 258 30 73; Via Mercanti 63; ⊙9am-7.45pm Tue-Sun) **FREE** Spread through-

out six small galleries, Salerno's multi-era art museum houses a collection dating from the Renaissance right up to the first half of the 20th century.

**Museo Virtuale della
Scuola Medica Salernitana**   MUSEUM
(Map p200; ☑089 257 32 13; www.museovirtuale scuolamedicasalernitana.beniculturali.it; Via Mercanti 74; adult/reduced €3/2; ⊙9am-1.30pm Tue-Sun mid-Oct–Jun, 9am-1.30pm Mon-Sat Jul–mid-Oct; ⏢) In Salerno's historic centre, this small, slightly forlorn museum deploys videos and touch-screen technology to explore the teachings and wince-inducing procedures of Salerno's once-famous, now-defunct medical institute. Established around the 9th century, the school was the most important centre of medical knowledge in medieval Europe, reaching the height of its prestige in the 11th century. It was closed in the early 19th century.

✗ Eating

Pasticceria Romolo   PASTRIES €
(Map p200; ☑089 23 26 13; www.pasticceria romolo.it; Corso Garibaldi 33; cakes from €1.50; ⊙8am-2pm & 3.30-8.30pm Wed-Mon) This sprawling *pasticceria* (pastry shop) across from the station dates from 1966 and the decor has changed little since. The cakes are legendary, and include *frollini* (fruit and chocolate tarts), *amaretti* (macaroons) and the most irresistible treat, *sfogliatelle* (flaky pastry filled with ricotta; warmed and dusted with sugar if you eat in). Fancy chocolates and wine are also available.

Ristorante Santa Lucia   SEAFOOD €
(Map p200; ☑089 22 56 96; Via Roma 182; pizzas from €5, meals €22; ⊙noon-2.30pm & 7-11.30pm Tue-Sun) The surrounding Via Roma area may be one of the city's trendiest, but there's nothing remotely flash about the seafood served up in this old stalwart. Dishes such as *linguine ai frutti di mare* (flat spaghetti

---

DON'T MISS

SWEET TREAT

Look for *torta ricotta e pera* (ricotta and pear tart), a speciality in Salerno and sold throughout the Cilento region. Just about every *pasticceria* (pastry shop) sells this delicious sweet and fruity delicacy – although it's the locals' favourite as well, so it tends to sell out fast.

LOCAL KNOWLEDGE

THE SALERNO MUTINY

On 9 September 1943 in the midst of WWII, the Allies, fresh from victories in North Africa, invaded Italy in an operation codenamed Avalanche, which also became known as the Battle of Salerno. Pitting Allied troops, including Lieutenant General Mark Clark's US Fifth Army, against the German occupiers, its goal was to gain control of Naples and thus force Italy out of the war, smashing the Axis coalition.

Following the flawed invasion, which resulted in terrible casualties, 600 men staged the biggest mutiny in British military history, refusing to form part of the Fifth Army. They had sailed from Tripoli, many having fought with distinction against Rommel's troops in the desert campaign, and had been informed they were to rejoin comrades in Sicily. It was only on board ship that they were told they were in fact en route to the Battle of Salerno. Once in Salerno, the men were taken to a field by the beach and held for three days; the rebellion continued despite the punishments notoriously meted out to wartime mutineers.

Of the hard-core of 300 remaining mutineers, 108 capitulated and 192 continued their refusal to fight. All were then charged with mutiny under the Army Act and sent to Algeria for court martial. The men had only been sent to Salerno in the first place due to clerical error, but the army refused to back down.

All of the men were found guilty, and three sergeants were sentenced to death, commuted to 12 years of forced labour. In time, all the sentences were suspended, but the men had to surrender their war medals and live on reduced pensions.

The battle itself was technically a victory for the Allies, though it was far from the swift surgical attack intended, and left them entrenched in a long and difficult fight to conquer Italy. While part of Salerno's historic centre was miraculously spared, the somewhat featureless wide boulevards elsewhere are a result of postwar reconstruction.

with seafood) and chargrilled cuttlefish may not be original but they hit the spot – as do the wood-fired pizzas.

★ **Mariterraneo**   MEDITERRANEAN €€
(Map p200; ☑ 089 943 31 38; Vico Grimoaldo 12; meals €35-40; ☺ 6-11pm Tue-Sat, also 11.30am-2.30pm Sun) Hard to find, this new purveyor of Slow Food shines brightly amid the grubby graffiti, drying washing and overflowing bins of the *centro storico*. The artistically presented food will have you unashamedly reaching for your camera – if you can put off eating it for that long. Try the delicately baked fish nestled on a bed of vegetables.

Cicirinella   ITALIAN €€
(Map p200; ☑ 089 22 65 61; Via Genovesi 28; meals €25; ☺ 8pm-midnight daily, 1-3pm Sat & Sun; ☎) This place, tucked behind the cathedral, has that winning combination of an earthy and inviting atmosphere and unfailingly good, delicately composed dishes. Exposed stone, shelves of wine and an open-plan kitchen set the scene for traditional Campanian cuisine like pasta with seafood and chickpeas, or a mussel soup that tastes satisfyingly of the sea.

❶ Information

Tourist Office (Map p200; ☑ 089 23 14 32; Lungomare Trieste 7; ☺ 9am-7pm Mon-Sat) Has limited information.

❶ Getting There & Away

BOAT

TraVelMar (www.travelmar.it) Sails seasonally to Amalfi (€8, 35 minutes, 12 daily) and Positano (€12, 70 minutes, eight daily), as well as to Cetara (€5, 15 minutes, six daily), Maiori (€7, 30 minutes, six daily) and Minori (€7, 40 minutes, six daily).

Alicost (☑ Mon-Fri 089 87 14 83, Sat & Sun 089 948 36 71; www.alicost.it) Runs one daily seasonal ferry service to Capri (€25.40, 2¼ hours) via Minori (€7), Amalfi (€8) and Positano (€12).

Navigazione Libera del Golfo (www.navlib.it) Runs one daily hydrofoil service to Capri (€26) from Easter to mid-October.

TraVelMar services depart from the **Porto Turistico** (Map p200), 200m down the pier from Piazza della Concordia. You can buy tickets from the booths by the embarkation point. Alicost and Navigazione Libera del Golfo services depart from **Molo Manfredi** (Map p200), 1.8km further west.

BUS

SITA Sud (www.sitasudtrasporti.it) buses for Amalfi depart at least hourly from the **bus station** (Map p200) on Piazza Vittorio Veneto, beside the train station, stopping en route at Vietri sul Mare, Cetara, Maiori and Minori. For Pompeii, take **Busitalia Campania** (Map p200; ☑ 089 984 72 86; www.fsbusitaliacampania. it) bus 4 from nearby Corso Garibaldi (at the corner of Via Luigi Barrella). For the south coast and Paestum, take bus 34 from Piazza della Concordia near the Porto Turistico ferry terminal. Bus 34 runs roughly every one to two hours from Monday to Saturday, with no service on Sunday.

CAR & MOTORCYCLE

Salerno is on the A3 between Naples and Reggio di Calabria; the A3 is toll-free from Salerno south. Take the Salerno exit and follow signs to the *centro* (city centre).

TRAIN

Salerno is a major stop on southbound routes to Calabria, and the Ionian and Adriatic coasts. From the train station on Piazza Vittorio Veneto there are regular services to Naples (from €4.70, 35 to 45 minutes), Rome (Intercity from €30.50, three hours) and Agropoli (€3.40, 40 minutes).

❶ Getting Around

CAR & MOTORCYCLE

If you want to hire a car, there's a Europcar agency not far from the train station.

Salerno has a reasonable number of car parks. Follow the distinctive blue P sign as you approach the centre of the city. The most convenient car park for the *centro storico* is on Piazza Amendola. Near the train station (and tourist office), other convenient locations are the large car parks on Piazza della Concordia and the adjacent Piazza Giuseppe Mazzini. You can expect to pay around €2 an hour for Salerno car parks.

CILENTO COAST

The Cilento stretch of coastline may lack the sophistication of the Amalfi Coast, but it too has a string of craggy, sun-bleached towns, among them popular Agropoli, gleaming white Palinuro, charming Castellabate and the evocative ruined temples of Paestum. The Cilento can even afford to have a slight air of superiority when it comes to its beaches: a combination of secluded coves and long stretches of golden sand with fewer overpriced ice creams and sunbeds. Yet

Campania's southern bookend is about more than its waterside appeal. It's here that you'll find the ancient Greek temples of Paestum and a large coastal tract of the Parco Nazionale del Cilento, Vallo di Diano e Alburni, also a Unesco World Heritage site.

❶ Getting There & Away

BUS

Busitalia Campania operates regular buses from Salerno and Paestum to several Cilento coastal resorts, including Santa Maria di Castellabate, San Marco di Castellabate and Acciaroli.

Infante Viaggi (p212) runs buses between Palinuro and Naples/Rome.

TRAIN

Some destinations on the Cilento coast – notably Paestum and Agropoli – are served by the main rail route from Naples to Reggio di Calabria. Consult Trenitalia (www.trenitalia.com) for fares and information.

Paestum

Paestum is home to one of Europe's most glorious archaeological zones. Deemed a World Heritage site by Unesco, it includes three of the world's best-preserved ancient Greek temples, as well as an engrossing museum crammed with millennia-old frescoes, ceramics and daily artefacts. Among these is the iconic *Tomba del tuffatore* (Tomb of the Diver) funerary fresco.

Paestum – or Poseidonia as the city was originally called, in honour of Poseidon, the Greek god of the sea – was founded in the 6th century BC by Greek settlers and fell under Roman control in 273 BC. Decline set in following the demise of the Roman Empire. Savage raids by the Saracens and periodic outbreaks of malaria forced the steadily dwindling population to abandon the city altogether.

Today, Paestum offers visitors a vivid, to-scale glimpse of the grandeur and sophistication of the area's past life.

◉ Sights

★**Paestum's Temples** ARCHAEOLOGICAL SITE (Area Archeologica di Paestum; ☑ 0828 81 10 23; www.museopaestum.beniculturali.it; adult/reduced incl museum €12/2, ruins only €8/2; ⊗ 8.30am-7.30pm daily, last entry 6.50pm, museum closed Mon) Very different to Pompeii, Paestum's ruins are smaller, older, more Greek and –

ⓘ GETTING AROUND THE REGION

Salerno is on the ferry route from Naples, Sorrento and (in summer) the Amalfi Coast resorts and islands. It is also on the main train line between Naples and Reggio di Calabria.

The main Cilento coastal towns can be reached by bus or train. Agropoli and Paestum have hourly trains to Salerno with connections on to Naples and Rome.

Transport options are tougher in the inland sections of the Parco Nazionale del Cilento, where there are no trains and bus services can be sporadic. Some smaller villages are only accessible by car.

Overall, the roads are good throughout the Cilento region, with well-signposted towns and resorts within easy reach of each other.

crucially – a lot less overrun. Consequently, it is possible to steal some reflective moments here as the sun slants across the giant Doric columns of this once great city of Magna Graecia (the Greek colony that once covered much of southern Italy). Take the train to Paestum station. Buy your tickets in the museum, just east of the site, before entering from the main entrance at the northern end.

Paestum was probably founded by Greeks from Sybaris in the 6th century BC. It later became a Roman city, but was abandoned in the Middle Ages. The ruins were rediscovered in the 1760s, but not fully unearthed and excavated until the 1950s.

The first structure is the 6th-century-BC **Tempio di Cerere** (Temple of Ceres); originally dedicated to Athena, it served as a Christian church in medieval times.

As you head south, you can pick out the basic outline of the large rectangular forum, the heart of the ancient city. Among the partially standing buildings are the vast domestic housing area and, further south, the amphitheatre. Both provide evocative glimpses of daily life here in Roman times. In the former houses you'll see mosaic floors, and a marble *impluvium* (cistern) that stood in the atrium and collected rainwater.

The **Tempio di Nettuno** (Temple of Neptune), dating from about 450 BC, is the largest and best preserved of the three

temples at Paestum; only parts of its inside walls and roof are missing. The two rows of double-storied columns originally divided the outer colonnade from the *cella,* or inner chamber, where a statue of the temple deity would have been displayed. Despite its commonly used name, many scholars believe that the temple was actually dedicated to the Greek goddess Hera, sister and wife of Greek god Zeus.

Almost next door, the so-called **basilica** (a temple to the goddess Hera) is Paestum's oldest surviving monument. Dating from the middle of the 6th century BC, it's a magnificent sight, with nine columns across and 18 along the sides. Ask someone to take your photo next to one of the columns: it's a good way to appreciate the scale.

Save time for the museum, which covers two floors and houses a collection of interesting bas-relief friezes, plus numerous frescoes dating back to the 5th century BC.

The archaeological site and adjoining museum are particularly evocative in spring when they are surrounded by scarlet poppies.

Museo di Paestum   MUSEUM
(☑0828 81 10 23; adult/reduced incl temples €9.50/4.75; ☉8.30am-7.30pm, last entry 6.50pm, closes 1.40pm 1st & 3rd Mon of month) Facing the east side of the ruins, the Museo di Paestum houses a collection of much-weathered metopes (bas-relief friezes). Among these are originals from the Tempio di Argiva Hera (Temple of Argive Hera), 9km north of Paestum, of which virtually nothing else remains. The most famous of the museum's numerous frescoes is the 5th-century-BC *Tomba del tuffatore* (Tomb of the Diver), thought to represent the passage from life to death with its frescoed depiction of a diver in mid-air.

Tenuta Vannulo   FARM
(☑0828 72 78 94; www.vannulo.it; Via G Galilei 101, Capaccio Scalo; 1hr group tour €5; ☉9.30am-5pm daily, tours 9am-noon Mon-Sat) The first organic producer of *bufala* (water-buffalo) milk, Tenuta Vannulo is a 10-minute drive from Paestum. It makes its mozzarella exclusively from buffalo milk, unlike most producers who combine it with cows' milk. Farm tours (also in English; cash payment only) are available and should be booked two to three days in advance. Visits proceed through the cheese-processing area, stable, agricultural museum and culminate in that all-important mozzarella tasting.

Tenuta Vannulo produces around 400kg of unpasteurised *mozzarella di bufala* per day. It also makes wonderful yogurt, ice cream and *budini* (puddings). Lunch is available with advance reservations.

Eating

There are various restaurants in close proximity to the ruins at Paestum, most serving mediocre food at inflated prices.

Nonna Sceppa   ITALIAN €€
(☑ 0828 85 10 64; Via Laura 53; meals €35; ⊙ 12.30-3pm & 7.30-11pm Fri-Wed; 🛜🐶) Seek out the superbly prepared, robust dishes at Nonna Sceppa, a family-friendly restaurant that's gaining a reputation throughout the region for excellence. Dishes are firmly seasonal and, during summer, concentrate on fresh seafood, like the refreshingly simple grilled fish with lemon. Other popular choices include risotto with zucchini and artichokes, and spaghetti with lobster.

ℹ Information

Tourist Office (☑ 0828 81 10 16; www.info paestum.it; Via Magna Grecia 887; ⊙ 9am-1pm & 2-4pm) Across the street from the archaeological site, Paestum's helpful tourist office offers a map of the archaeological site, plus information on the greater Cilento region.

ℹ Getting There & Away

Trains run around 16 times daily from Salerno to Paestum (€2.90, 30 minutes). The temples (p203) are a pleasant 10-minute stroll from the station.

Busitalia Campania (p203) bus 34 goes to Paestum from Piazza della Concordia in Salerno (€2.70, one hour). Bus 34 runs roughly every one to two hours from Monday to Saturday, with no service on Sunday.

Agropoli

☑ 0974 / POP 21.500

Located just south of Paestum, Agropoli is a busy summer resort but otherwise a pleasant, tranquil town that is a good base for exploring Cilento's coastline and national park. While the shell is a fairly faceless grid of shop-lined streets, the kernel – the historic city centre – is a fascinating tangle of narrow cobbled streets with ancient churches, venerable residents and a castle with superb views.

The town has been inhabited since Neolithic times, with later inhabitants including the Greeks, the Romans, the Byzantines and the Saracens. In 915 Agropoli fell under the jurisdiction of the bishops and was subsequently ruled by feudal lords. It was a target of raids from North Africa in the 16th and 17th centuries, when the population dwindled to just a few hundred. Today it's the largest and most vibrant town along the Cilento coast.

◎ Sights & Activities

To reach the *centro storico* (historic centre), head for Piazza Veneto Victoria, the pedestrian-only part of the modern town, where cafes and gelaterie are interspersed with plenty of shopping choice. Head up Corso Garibaldi and take the wide Ennio Balbo Scaloni steps until you reach the fortified medieval *borgo*. Follow the signs to the castle.

The town has a long, if slightly grubby, sandy beach backed by the Lungomare San Marco that extends for 1km to the north.

Trentova-Tresino   NATURE RESERVE
(Via Fontana dei Monaci; 🅿) Those frustrated by the dearth of well-marked hiking trails in the Parco Nazionale del Cilento, Vallo di Diano e Alburni should pay a visit to this mini park-within-a-park 1km south of Agropoli. A variety of well-documented routes meander through an attractive but relatively untrammelled tract of Mediterranean coast.

A visitor centre acts as trailhead for four named paths, the most popular of which – the 7.2km Sentiero Trezeni – parallels the coast all the way to Santa Maria di Castellabate. Quiet beaches, old military towers (dating from the Middle Ages to WWII) and wild headlands characterise the routes. The area is also good for bird watching.

Some of the trails are popular with local mountain-bikers and horse-riders.

Il Castello   CASTLE
(☑ 0974 82 74 07; ⊙ 8am-10pm Jul-Sep) FREE
Built by the Byzantines in the 5th century, the castle was strengthened during the Angevin period, the time of the War of the Vespers, which was initially sparked by an uprising in Sicily during evening prayers. Agropoli's castle continued to be modified, and only part of the original defensive wall remains. It's an enjoyable walk here from Agropoli's historic centre, and you can wander the ramparts and drink in magnificent views of the coastline and town.

**Associazione Kayak
Agropoli 'I Trezeni'** KAYAKING
(☑320 7531673; Spiaggia Marina; kayak hire per hour €5) Rents kayaks from the port in Agropoli. Can also organise guided tours.

Cilento Sub Diving Center DIVING
(☑338 2374603; Via San Francesco 30; dives from €50) Indulge in your favourite watery pursuit here. Courses include snorkelling for beginners, open-water junior dives (from 12 years) and wreck diving; the latter includes the harrowing viewing of the hulks of ships, tanks and planes that were famously destroyed in the region during WWII.

✕ Eating & Drinking

★ Pecora Nera PIZZA €
(☑320 6115112; Piazza della Mercanzia; pizzas €5-12; ⊙7:30pm-1am) Agropoli's self-proclaimed 'black sheep', Pecora Nera has emerged as a new challenger for the title of the town's 'best pizza' and they might just be on to something. The small but slickly furnished pizzeria in a piazza by the port is run by a hip team of *ragazzi* whose uncluttered pizzas use a light chewy dough and carefully sourced DOP ingredients.

La Brace ITALIAN €
(☑0974 82 16 05; Via A De Gasperi 60; meals €15, pizzas from €3; ⊙noon-2.30pm & 7-11.30pm Sat-Thu) There's no sea or historic-centre view from this ristorante-pizzeria on the main drag to and from the station, but who cares? This is the kind of simple homespun trattoria every Italian town has: green and orange furnishings, a crooner on the keyboards, boisterous families at the weekends and – this being Agropoli – damn good seafood.

Il Gambero SEAFOOD €€
(☑0974 82 28 94; www.gambero.it; Via San Marco 234; meals from €25; ⊙12.15-3.30pm & 7pm-midnight, closed Tue winter) Il Gambero is located across from Agropoli's beach – get here early to grab a table out front and enjoy the sunset over the Lungomare. Specialities include seafood mixed salad, pasta with clams and pumpkin, and fried mixed fish. Although there are some non-seafood dishes, fish has star billing. Reservations recommended.

★ Nero Café BAR
(☑0974 82 33 19; Via Petrarca 8; ⊙7am-midnight; ☏) The best place for an afternoon *pausa* (break) in Agropoli is the leather-seated, art deco-tinged Nero Café, although the intended 'pause' could turn into a longer intermission should your attention be diverted by the veritable feast of bar snacks laid out on the counter in the late afternoon for *apericena* (dinner-sized appetisers).

ℹ Information

Tourist Office (☑0974 82 74 71; Viale Europa 34; ⊙9.30am-2pm) Dispatching basic information out of a small kiosk in the town centre.

ℹ Getting There & Away

Busitalia Campania (p203) bus route 34 runs to Paestum (€2, 15 to 20 minutes) and Salerno (€3.40, 1¼ to 1¾ hours). Buses run roughly every one to two hours Monday to Saturday and four to five times on Sunday.

Trains (www.trenitalia.com) run around 14 times daily to Paestum (€2, five minutes) and around 17 times daily to Salerno (€3.40, 45 minutes). Agropoli-Castellabate Station is on the east side of town, a 1km walk from the centre.

There's a **car-rental outfit** (☑0974 82 63 01; www.agropolirent.it/en/; Via A De Gasperi 75; per day from €50; ⊙9am-1pm & 3.30-8pm) opposite the train station.

Castellabate & Around

Castellabate, 10km south of Agropoli, has multiple appeals: a classic Italian hilltop village, close proximity to Campania's backbone mountains and a string of broad municipal beaches.

Medieval Castellabate clings to the side of a mountain 280m above sea level and is one of the most endearing and historic towns on the Cilento coast.

Glued to the coast below and gifted with a luscious 4km-long beach is the former fishing village of Santa Maria di Castellabate. Head for the southernmost point, which still has a palpable southern Italian feel, with dusky pink-and-ochre sunbaked houses blinkered by traditional green shutters.

Heading south from Castellabate, the next stop is the pretty harbour at San Marco di Castellabate. This was once an important Greek and Roman port, and tombs and other relics are on view in the museum at Paestum.

All three settlements lie inside the Parco Nazionale del Cilento, Vallo di Diano e Alburni.

◉ Sights

Castellabate's labyrinth of narrow pedestrian streets is punctuated by ancient archways, small piazzas and the occasional *palazzo*. The animated heart and soul of the town is the numerological mouthful Piazza 10 Ottobre 1123, with its panoramic views of the Valle dell'Annunziata.

Castellabate Beach   BEACH
Santa Maria's golden sandy beach stretches for around 4km, which equals plenty of towel space on the sand, even in midsummer.

San Marco's Blue Flag beach is the natural continuation to the south. Here you'll find the esteemed Spiaggia del Pozzillo, populated with several *lidi* (beach establishments renting loungers and umbrellas).

Castello dell'Abate   CASTLE
(Castellabate; €1; ⊙9:30am-12:30pm & 4-8pm) Approached from its coastal sidekick, Santa Maria di Castellabate, the summit of Castellabate is marked by the broad **Belvedere di San Costabile**, from where there are sweeping coastal views. Flanking this is the shell of a 12th-century castle. Commissioned in 1123 by Saint Costabile, the abbot who founded the town and remains its patron saint, the castle retains its original defensive walls. The interior has been significantly remodelled and now serves as a very basic art gallery.

✗ Eating

The widest selection of good eating places is in the older part of Santa Maria di Castellabate, close to the beach. There are a handful of atmospheric places in the small hilltop town of Castellabate proper. One of them, **Cantina Belvedere** (☑0974 96 70 30; www.cantinabelvedere.it; meals €30-35; ⊙noon-2.30pm & 7-11.30pm Wed-Mon), backs up a good menu with equally sublime views.

Il Capriccio   ITALIAN €
(☑0974 84 52 41; Corso da Spiafriddo, Castellabate; meals €20-25; ⊙noon-3pm & 7-11pm) On the road to Perdifumo, this is a favourite local choice. An unassuming place with a terrace, Il Capriccio has a gracious host in owner Enxo. The menu runs the gamut from seafood classics such as *zuppa di cozze* (mussel soup) and *polipetti affogati* (poached octopus) to less fishy options such as *zuppa di ceci* (chickpea soup).

Arlecchino   SEAFOOD €€
(☑0974 96 18 89; Via Gugliemini, Santa Maria di Castellabate; meals €22-40, pizzas from €4; ⊙noon-2.30pm & 7-11pm Mar-Nov; ☜) Located across from the beach in the pretty southernmost part of Santa Maria, popular Arlecchino has picture windows overlooking the small sweep of sand. Packed to the gills at weekends, the restaurant primarily offers seafood, although the *ravioli salsa di noci* (ravioli in walnut sauce) gives the tuna and sea urchins a run for their money.

Divino   ITALIAN €€
(☑339 8080457; Piazza 10 Ottobre 1123, Castellabate; menus €28-35, meals from €25; ⊙noon-3pm & 8.30pm-1.30am) Follow the signs to La Piazzetta from the castle, via a short tunnel, and blink hard when you emerge at this movie-set marvel of a piazza, its terraced restaurants, pastel-coloured houses and overflowing flower-boxes. Divino's menu has local favourites like *pasta e fagioli* (pasta and white beans) and grilled swordfish, plus well-priced daily menus.

❶ Getting There & Away

Busitalia Campania (p203) bus 34 runs a least six times a day (less on weekends) from Santa Maria di Castellabate to Agropoli (€2, 20 minutes) in the north and Acciaroli (€2.70, 30 minutes) in the south. The bus also stops in San Marco di Castellabate.

It's possible to walk between Agropoli and Santa Maria di Castellabate through the very pleasant Trentova-Tresino (p205) nature reserve. Total distance is just over 7km.

Acciaroli to Pisciotta

The coastal road heading south of Castellabate is prettily panoramic, despite lacking the drama (and traffic) of its Amalfi counterpart. This is a land of well-tended sandy beaches and tiny unsung coastal towns epitomised by diminutive Acciaroli. With its charming centre and shady piazzas tastefully restored using local stone and traditional architecture, Acciaroli is a good place to grow old. Few places in the world have such a high proportion of residents aged over 100.

A short 10km hop south of Acciaroli is equally tiny **Pioppi**, with its pristine, pale pebble beach and handful of shops and restaurants, followed by **Marina di Casal Velino**, featuring a small, pretty harbour and a stretch of sand favoured by families.

Ascea, best known as the home of philosophers Parmenides and Zeno, is characterised by its mildewed Greek ruins, while lovely Pisciotta is a medieval town piled high above a ridge.

⊙ Sights

Spiaggia Grande di Acciaroli BEACH

Another Cilento stunner, Acciaroli's main beach has sand, space, a Blue Flag rating and easy access to the historic town at its southern end. Water and sand are kept ruthlessly clean. If you couldn't hack the Amalfi's rocky, crowded 'beaches', this will be a gulp of fresh air.

Parco Archeologico di Elea Velia ARCHAEOLOGICAL SITE

(☑ 0974 97 23 96; Contrada Piana di Velia; adult/reduced €3/1.50; ⊙ 9am-90min before sunset, Wed-Mon) Founded by the Greeks in the mid-6th century BC, Velia subsequently became a popular resort with wealthy Romans. You can wander around the evocative ruins, including parts of the city walls – with traces of one gate and several towers – as well as the remains of thermal baths, an Ionic temple, a theatre and parts of the original Greek streets, paved in limestone blocks and with the gutters intact.

✕ Eating

Pizza in Piazza PIZZA €

(☑ 320 0966325; Piazza Vittorio Emanuele, Acciaroli; pizza from €4; ⊙ noon-3pm & 7-11pm Apr-Nov; 🐾) An upper-crust pizza place on a pretty piazza with magnificent rubber trees and wisteria-draped walls. Sit outside or eat on the go. The pizzas include all the standard choices but are excellent, with a crispy base and garden-fresh ingredients. The *caprese* comes particularly recommended, with its simple topping of cherry tomatoes, *mozzarella di bufala* and basil leaves.

★ Osteria del Borgo CAMPANIAN €€

(☑ 0974 97 01 13; Via Roma 17, Pisciotta; meals €20-35; ⊙ noon-3pm & 7-11pm) From your perch on the stone terrace, you'll hear your order loudly repeated to the chef (ie Mamma), followed by the requisite banging of pots and pans. In a land of simple food, this *osteria* is an expert in making things uncomplicated, from the rustic bread to the scalding espresso via stalwart *primi* (first courses) where the prices rarely stray north of €10.

ⓘ Getting There & Away

BUS

Busitalia Campania (p203) bus 34 runs between Salerno and Acciaroli several times a day, also calling at Paestum, Agropoli and Santa Maria di Castellabate.

TRAIN

Trenitalia (www.trenitalia.com) has hourly trains to Agropoli-Castellabate station in Agropoli (€4, 30 minutes) and Salerno (€5.70, 1¼ hours). Beware! Pisciotta-Palinuro station is 4.5km from Pisciotta proper which sits atop a steep hill.

Palinuro & Around

☑ 0974 / POP 4800

Despite being hailed as the Cilento coast's main resort, Palinuro remains relatively low-key (and low-rise), with a tangible fishing-village feel. Located in a crystal-clear bay sheltered by a promontory, and with superb beaches (considered to be among the cleanest and best-kept in Italy), it gets crowded with Italian holidaymakers in August.

⊙ Sights

Spiaggia Palinuro BEACH

The town's main beach stretches for around 4km north of the centre. There is another more sheltered curve of sand abutting Palinuro's postcard-pretty harbour in the south, replete with colourful fishing boats, several bars and a rocky headland standing sentinel. You can hire kayaks and arrange boat trips here.

Spiaggia Marinella BEACH

For a slightly quieter scene than you might find in Palinuro, head southeast of town to Spiaggia Marinella, surrounded by lush banks of greenery. The beach is approached via steep steps, and there's a small car park at the top. The shoreline here is protected by two breakwaters and is excellent for swimming and pedal-boating (rentals available in the summer).

Grotta Azzurra CAVE

Although it doesn't have the hype of its Capri counterpart, Palinuro's Grotta Azzurra is similarly spectacular, with a brilliant play of light and hue. It owes its name to the extraordinary effect created by the sunlight that filters inside from an underground passage lying at a depth of about 8m. Da Alessandro runs trips to this and other caves from €15.

The best time to visit is the afternoon, due to the position of the sun.

🏃 Activities

Palinuro is known for its boat excursions, including trips out to the Grotta Azzurra and other coves and caves around Capo Palinuro.

Boats depart from the little port, 1km south of the town centre.

Da Alessandro BOATING
(☑ 347 6540931; www.costieradelcilento.it; Spiaggia del Porto di Palinuro; trips from €15; ☺ mid-Mar–mid-Nov) Located at a kiosk at the harbour, Da Alessandro runs boat trips to Palinuro's Grotta Azzurra as well as to Grotta Sulfurea, Grotta delle Ossa and Arco Naturale. Excursions also allow for a dip in the beautiful Baia del Buon Dormire. Kayak hire is available on the beach for €5 an hour.

Capo Palinuro HIKING
This rocky cape just south of Palinuro is punctuated with ruined towers, natural arches, caves and a lighthouse. It's a good place to get some sea air into your lungs and some miles in your legs during a relatively easy 7km hike.

Take the trail (called the Sentiero della Primula) that forks off to the left just past Palinuro's small port and follow it to a ruined fort at **Punta del Fortino**. After admiring the view, retrace your steps 100m to a fork, turn right and climb up through the blustery brush of the headland. The path joins a dirt road that leads to a lighthouse (a military zone, but worth a diversion for the views). Retrace your steps again and take the road downhill, entering a pine forest. When you hit a paved road, turn right and navigate through the small hamlet of Faracchino with the Spiaggia Marinella below. Look out for the famous **Archetiello**, a natural hole in the rocky coast. From here, you can saunter slowly back to Palinuro along Via Capozzoli.

 Eating

O Guarracino SEAFOOD €
(☑ 0974 93 83 09; www.oguarracino.it; Via Porto; meals €20-25; ☺ noon-3pm & 7pm-midnight May-Aug, noon-3pm Mar & Apr, Sep & Oct) This humble beachside eatery is run by a fishing family that still plies the waters in winter. Expect the freshest grilled fish: sea bream, sea bass, yellowtail, swordfish, tuna – it's a long list.

Ristorante Core a Core ITALIAN €€
(☑ 0974 93 16 91; www.coreacorepalinuro.it; Via Piano Faracchio 13; meals €30-40; ☺ 12.45-2.45pm & 8pm-midnight; 🐾) Ignore the cheesy heart-shaped sign: with its glorious garden setting and great reputation for seafood, Core a Core is your best bet in Palinuro. The *antipasti al*

mare (€19.50) is superb, and there's a menu of proper kids' food. Book in advance – it's popular. The restaurant is a 15-minute uphill walk from the centre of Palinuro.

ℹ Information

Tourist Office (☑ 0974 93 81 44; Piazza Virgilio; ☺ 10am-12.30pm & 5-7pm Mon-Sat, 10am-12.30pm Sun) In the main square, the Pro Loco can provide a town map and general information.

ℹ Getting There & Away

BUS
Infante Viaggi (p212) runs buses to and from Rome's Tiburtina station (€21, five hours, three weekly), Naples (€12, three hours, two to three daily) and Salerno (€10, 1¾ hours, two to three daily).

TRAIN
The nearest train station, the deceptively named Pisciotta-Palinuro station, is 8km north of the town proper. Minibuses run between town and station four times a day. If you miss one, it's a not unpleasant walk along a relatively quiet beach road to Palinuro. Alternatively, phone your accommodation to arrange a pick-up.

PARCO NAZIONALE DEL CILENTO, VALLO DI DIANO E ALBURNI

Proving the perfect antidote to the holiday mayhem further north, the Parco Nazionale del Cilento, Vallo di Diano e Alburni combines dense woods and flowering meadows, with dramatic mountains, rivers and waterfalls. It is the second-largest national park in Italy, covering 1810 sq km, including 80 towns and villages. To get the best out of the park, you will probably need a car, although the coastal strip from Castellabate down to Palinuro has reasonable pubic transport. The Cilento is known for its orchids, vast underground cave complexes and handsome hilltop villages. Sitting on the cusp of the park proper are the ruins of Paestum and the Certosa di San Lorenzo, both crucial to it gaining Unesco World Heritage status in 1998.

Compared to the Amalfi, the Cilento is not so well set up for tourism and the network of walking trails is less well marked. If in doubt, join a guided excursion.

Parco Nazionale del Cilento, Vallo di Diano e Alburni

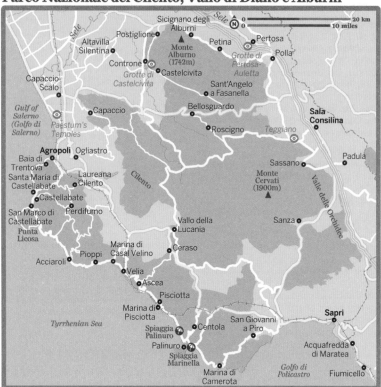

◉ Sights

★ **Teggiano**   OLD TOWN

The ancient coil of streets that makes up Teggiano (population 8,100) comprise what is arguably the most dashing of park's 80 villages. Grafted onto a rise with nary a modern edifice to blemish its beauty, the settlement has Roman antecedents, although most of what you see today – including the Norman Sanseverino castle (privately owned) – is medieval. The town presents itself like a mini Rome complete with half-a-dozen churches, shady cobbled streets and four small museums hidden amid its tangled streets.

★ **Grotte di Castelcivita**   CAVE

(☏ 0828 77 23 97; www.grottedicastelcivita.com; Piazzale N Zonzi, Castelcivita; adult/reduced €10/8; ⊙ standard tours 10.30am, noon, 1.30pm & 3pm, 4.30pm & 6pm Apr-Sep, 10.30am, noon, 1.30pm & 3pm Mar & Oct; ℗♿) The grottoes are

fascinating, otherworldly caves that date from prehistoric times: excavations have revealed that they were inhabited 42,000 years ago, making them the oldest known settlement in Europe. Don't forget a jacket, and leave the high heels at home, as paths are wet and slippery. Hard hats (provided) and a certain level of fitness and mobility are required. Located 40km southeast of Salerno on the northwest cusp of the national park, the complex is refreshingly noncommercial.

Although it extends over 4800m, only around half of the complex is open to the public. The one-hour tour winds through a route surrounded by extraordinary stalagmites and stalactites, and a mesmerising play of colours, caused by algae, calcium and iron, which tint the naturally sculpted rock shapes.

The tour culminates in a cavernous lunar landscape – think California's Death Valley in miniature – called the Caverna di Bertarelli. The caves are still inhabited – by bats – and visitors are instructed not to take flash photos for fear of disturbing them.

Certosa di San Lorenzo
MONASTERY

(☑ 0975 7 77 45; www.polomusealecampania.beni culturali.it; Viale Certosa, Padula; adult/reduced €6/3; ⊙ 9am-7pm Wed-Mon) A giant among monasteries, even by Italian standards, the Certosa di San Lorenzo dates from 1306 and covers 250,000 sq metres. Numerologists can get a kick out of ticking off the supposed 320 rooms and halls, 2500m of corridors, galleries and hallways, 300 columns, 500 doors, 550 windows, 13 courtyards, 100 fireplaces, 52 stairways and 41 fountains – in other words, it is *huge*. The monastery is just outside the hillside town of Padula.

As it is unlikely that you will have time to see everything, be sure to visit the highlights, including the vast central courtyard (a venue for summer classical-music concerts), the magnificent wood-panelled library, frescoed chapels, and the kitchen with its grandiose fireplace and famous tale: apparently this is where the legendary 1000-egg omelette was made in 1534 for Charles V's passing army. Unfortunately, the historic frying pan is not on view – just how big was it, one wonders.

Within the monastery you can also peruse the modest collection of ancient artefacts at the free **Museo Archeologico Provinciale della Lucania Occidentale** (☑ 0975 7 71 17; ⊙ 9am-7pm Wed-Mon; ⌖).

Grotte di Pertosa-Auletta
CAVE

(☑ 0975 39 70 37; www.grottedipertosa-auletta. it; Pertosa; guided visits adult/reduced 100min €20/15, 60min €13/10; ⊙ tour times vary, see website; P ⌖) (Re)discovered in 1932, the Grotte di Pertosa-Auletta date back 35 million years. Used by the Greeks and Romans as places of worship, the caves burrow for some 2500m, with long underground passages and lofty grottoes filled with stalagmites and stalactites. The first part of the tour is a boat (or raft) ride on the river; you disembark just before the waterfall (phew!) and continue on foot for around 800m, surrounded by marvellous rock formations and luminous crystal accretions.

This grotto complex is quite commercial, with souvenir shops, bars and a €3 parking fee. It is located 6km north of Polla just outside the northeastern corner of the national park.

 Eating

Trattoria degli Ulivi
ITALIAN €

(☑ 334 2595091; www.tavolacaldadegliulivi.it; Viale Certosa, Padula; set menus €10-16; ⊙ 11am-4pm Wed-Mon; ⌖) After your marathon walk through the endless corridors of the Certoza di San Lorenzo, head to this uncomplicated restaurant, a short 50m stumble from the main entrance. The decor is canteen-like, but the daily specials are affordable, fresh, flavour-filled and generously proportioned. It serves snacks as well as four-course blow-out lunches.

Vecchia Pizzeria Margaret
PIZZA €

(☑ 0975 33 00 00; Via Luigi Curto, Polla; pizza from €3.50; ⊙ 7.30pm-midnight Tue-Sun; ⌖) Dull building on outskirts of Polla serving notably less dull wheels of pizza, cooked in a wood-fired oven; it also dishes up antipasti and pasta dishes. Service is fast and friendly, and prices are low. You'll find the restaurant just east of the river, near the hospital.

Taverna degli Antichi Sapori
ITALIAN €

(☑ 0828 77 25 00; www.tavernadegliantichi sapori.it; Via Nazionale 27, Controne; meals from €18; ⊙ 12.30-3pm & 7-11pm) Easy to find on the main road through town, this bright, spacious restaurant with exposed stone walls has a small front terrace flanked by scarlet geraniums and a firmly traditional menu, which is great if you like *fagioli* (white beans). Think *gnocchi e fagioli, pasta e fagioli, lasagne e fagioli, riso* (rice) *e fagioli* and a few grilled-meat dishes.

Antichi Feudi
ITALIAN €€

(☑ 0975 58 73 29; www.antichifeudi.com; Via San Francesco 2, Teggiano; meals €25, pizzas from €4; ⊙ noon-3pm & 7-11pm) This gracious restaurant is located within a swish boutique hotel (d/ste from €75/135; ⊙ year-round; ✸⌖) just off Teggiano's elegant main piazza. The menu varies according to what's in season, but typical dishes include juicy chargrilled meat, grilled mussels with lemon, and seafood soup. The hotel bar-cafe is good for pizza, including the *antichi feudi* with mushrooms, fresh cheese and grilled aubergines (€10). Reservations recommended.

ⓘ Information

Alpine Rescue (☑ 118) For emergencies.
Parks.it (www.parks.it/parco.nazionale. cilento/Eindex.php) Useful online information about the national park.

HIKING IN THE CILENTO

The Parco Nazionale del Cilento, Vallo di Diano e Alburni has 15 listed **nature trails** that vary from 1km to 8km in length. But this isn't the Amalf, so don't expect abundant signage, well-trodden paths and an surfeit of trail-side cafes selling cappuccino.

The countryside in the park can be dramatic and, in spring, you'll experience real flower power: delicate narcissi, wild orchids and tulips hold their own among blowsier summer drifts of yellow ox-eye daisies and scarlet poppies.

Thickets of silver firs, wild chestnuts and beech trees add to the sumptuous landscape, as do the dramatic cliffs, pine-clad mountains and fauna, including wild boars, badgers and wolves, and, for bird watchers, the increasingly rare golden eagle.

The sheer size of the park means that hikers are unlikely to meet others on the trail – so getting lost could become a lonely, not to mention dangerous, experience if you haven't done some essential planning before striding out. In theory, the tourist offices should be able to supply you with a guide to the trails. In reality, they frequently seem to have run out of copies. Failing this, you can buy the *Parco Nazionale del Cilento, Vallo di Diano e Alburni: Carta Turistica e dei Sentieri* (Tourist and Footpath Map; €7) or the excellent *Monte Stella: Walks & Rambles in Ancient Cilento* published by the Comunita' Montana Alento Monte Stella (€3). Most of the *agriturismi* in the park can also organise guided treks.

A popular self-guided hike is a climb of **Monte Alburno** (1742m). There's a choice of two trails, both of which are clearly marked from the centre of the small town of Sicignano degli Alburni and finish at the mountain's peak. Allow approximately four hours for either route. The less experienced may prefer to opt for a guide. Reputable organisations that arrange guided hikes of the park include **Gruppo Escursionistico Trekking** (📞0975 7 25 86; www.getvallodidiano.it; Via Provinciale 29, Silla di Sassano), **Associazione Trekking Cilento** (📞338 3576805; www.facebook.com/trekkingcilento; Via Cannetiello 6, Agropoli), **Trekking Campania** (📞339 7456795; www.trekkingcampania.it; Via Amendola 23, Pellezzano) and **Associazione Naturalistica Culturale** (📞0974 82 38 52; www.noitour.it; Via Ianni 16, Agropoli; hikes from €10 per person). Note that some hikes may be in Italian only.

Sicignano degli Alburni Pro Loco (📞0828 97 37 55; www.scoprisicignano.it; Piazza Plebiscito 13, Sicignano degli Alburni; ⊙9am-1.30pm & 2.30-5pm Mon-Sat) Tourist information office with very basic info on the national park.

Tourist Office (p205) The office in Paestum has info on the Parco Nazionale del Cilento.

🛈 Getting There & Away

Transport by bus is relatively easy along the park's coastal strip from Agropoli down to Palinuro. There are also daily buses between Salerno and the Valle di Diano on the park's eastern side. The interior of the park is more difficult to penetrate unless you hire a car, bicycle or taxi to help you get around.

BUS

SITA Sud (p203) runs three daily services between Salerno and Pertosa (Monday to Saturday), two of which continue to Polla. It also runs one daily bus between Salerno and Castelcivita (weekdays only).

Busitalia Campania (p203) runs daily buses between Salerno, Agropoli, Castellabate and Acciaroli.

Infante Viaggi (📞089 82 57 65; www.agenzia infanteviaggi.it) A twice-weekly bus runs to/from Rome stopping in Salerno, Sicignano degli Alburni, Padula and Palinuro.

CAR & MOTORCYCLE

The park is easy to navigate by car, provided you have a detailed map. Car rental is available in Salerno and Agropoli.

Il Leone d'Oro (📞339 5069536) in Agropoli offers a decent taxi service with driver from around €0.50 per kilometre – a good way of getting around the park if you don't want to drive. Reserve by phone several days in advance.

TRAIN

The only train stations in the park itself are Valle della Lucania and Pisciotta-Palinuro. Train stations with bus connections close to the park include Paestum and Agropoli-Castellabate.

Understand Naples, Pompeii & the Amalfi Coast

History

Naples has almost 3000 candles on its birthday cake, and in this time the city and its sparkling coastline have seen it all, from pleasure-seeking Roman emperors and Spanish conquests to devastating plagues, eruptions, revolutions and even uninvited Nazis. History is written large here, with anecdotes seeping out of every church, palace, square and stubborn, weathered ruin. Whoever said history was boring has clearly never known this region.

The Early Years

Ancient Sites

....

Pompeii

....

Herculaneum

....

Museo Archeologico Nazionale, Naples

....

Paestum

....

Anfiteatro Flavio, Pozzuoli

The ancient Greeks were the first major players on the scene, setting up a trading post on Ischia and another settlement at Cumae (Cuma) in the 8th century BCE. As their main foothold in Italy, Cumae became the most important city in the Italian peninsula's southwest during the next 200 years, a rich commercial centre whose sibyl was said to be Apollo's mouthpiece.

According to legend, the traders also established Naples on the island of Megaris, current home of the Castel dell'Ovo, in about 680 BCE. Christened Parthenope, its namesake was a suicidal siren. Unable to lure the cunning Ulysses with her songs, she drowned herself, washing up on shore.

Failure also stalked the Tuscany-based Etruscans, who twice invaded Cumae and were twice repelled. After the second of these clashes, in 474 BCE, the Cumaeans founded Neapolis (New Town) where Naples' *centro storico* (historic centre) now stands.

Despite the Cumaeans' resilience, the Etruscan battles had taken a toll, and in 421 BCE the Greeks fell to the Samnites. They, in turn, proved no match for the Romans, who took Neapolis in 326 BCE. Not long after, in 273 BCE, the Romans conquered Paestum, a Greek city dating back to the 5th century BCE.

Togas, Triumph & Terror

Under the Romans, the Bay of Naples sparkled with lavish villas, thermal spas and cashed-up out-of-towners. Farmland and forests covered Vesuvius' lower slopes, while VIPs indulged by the coast. Notables holidayed

TIMELINE	c 750 BCE	680 BCE	474 BCE
	Greeks establish a colony at Cuma (Cumae) in the Campi Flegrei. The area becomes the most important Greek settlement on the Italian mainland and a strategic part of Magna Graecia.	The Cuman Greeks establish Parthenope on the island of Megaris, naming it in honour of a suicidal siren whose song failed to seduce the cunning Ulysses.	The Cumans found Neapolis on the site of Naples' *centro storico*. The original Greek street plan can still be seen today.

in Stabiae (Castellammare di Stabia), Nero's second wife, Poppea, entertained in upmarket Oplontis and Julius Caesar's father-in-law kept a home at Herculaneum. West of Naples, Puteoli (Pozzuoli) became a major international port, docking everything from Alexandrian grain ships to St Paul, who reputedly stepped ashore in 61 CE. Further west, Misenum (Miseno) boasted the ancient world's largest naval fleet.

Despite the Romans' stranglehold on the region, the citizens of Neapolis never completely gave in to their foreign occupiers, refusing (among other things) to relinquish their language. While the Romans may have tolerated the linguistic snub, the Neapolitans' opposition to Rome during the Roman Civil War (88–82 BCE) was another story, prompting Cornelius Sulla to take the city and slaughter thousands. Equally catastrophic was the unexpected eruption of Mt Vesuvius in 79 CE, which drowned nearby Pompeii and Herculaneum in molten lava, mud and ash. Coming just 17 years after a massive earthquake, it was a devastating blow for the region's already-struggling rural inhabitants.

Inside the city walls, Neapolis was booming: General Lucullus built an enviable villa where the Castel dell'Ovo now stands, and even Virgil moved to town. Offshore, Capri became the centre of Emperor Tiberius' famously debauched operations.

For hundreds of years, Neapolis' welfare was tied to that of the Roman Empire, but the ousting of the last Roman emperor, Romulus Augustulus, in 476 CE saw the city pass into barbarian hands.

Get to grips with southern Italy's ancient Hellenic influence by logging on to www.ancientgreece.com, where you'll find compact histories of all the influential peoples and wars of ancient Greece. It also has an online bookstore.

Normans & Angevins

By the beginning of the 11th century, Naples was a prospering duchy. Industry and culture were thriving and Christianity was the dominant religion. Outside the city, however, the situation was more volatile, as

---

AMALFI: THE GOLDEN DAYS

Musing on the fabled town of Amalfi, 19th-century scribe Renato Fucini declared that when the town's inhabitants reach heaven on Judgement Day, it will be just like any other day for them. It must have been a view shared by the Roman patricians shipwrecked on its coast in 337 CE. Seduced by the area's beauty, they decided to ditch their long-haul trip to Constantinople and stay put.

Despite these early fans, Amalfi's true golden era would arrive in the 9th century, when centuries of Byzantine rule were ditched for Marine Republic status. Between this time and the ruinous Pisan raids of 1135 and 1137, its ever-expanding fleet brought a little bit of Amalfi to the far reaches of the Mediterranean, from churches named in honour of Sant'Andrea (Amalfi's patron saint) to a 'Little Amalfi' quarter in 10th-century Constantinople, complete with expat shops and schools.

---

326 BCE	79 CE	305	536
The Romans conquer Neapolis and the city is absorbed into the Roman Empire. Despite this, locals cling to their Greek heritage and language.	At 10am on 24 August, Mt Vesuvius erupts after centuries of slumber, startling the Neapolitans and burying Pompeii, Herculaneum and other towns on the mountain's slopes.	San Gennaro, patron saint of Naples, becomes a victim of Emperor Diocletian's anti-Christian campaign. The martyr is arrested and beheaded at Solfatara Crater in Pozzuoli.	Byzantine general Belisarius and his fighters sneak into the city through its ancient aqueduct and lay siege. Conquered, Naples becomes a Byzantine duchy.

the Normans were beginning to eye up the Lombard principalities of Salerno, Benevento, Capua and Amalfi.

The Normans had arrived in southern Italy in the 10th century, initially as pilgrims en route from Jerusalem, later as mercenaries attracted by the money to be made fighting for the rival principalities and against the Arab Muslims in Sicily. And it was to just such a mercenary, Rainulf Drengot, that the duke of Naples, Sergio IV, gave the contract to drive the Lombards out of Capua. The principality duly fell in 1062, followed by Amalfi in 1073 and Salerno four years later. By 1130 most of southern Italy, including Sicily, was in Norman hands and, inevitably, Naples joined them in 1139. The Kingdom of the Two Sicilies was thus complete.

The Normans maintained their capital in Sicily, and Palermo began to outshine Naples. The Neapolitans seemed happy with their lot, but when the last of the Norman kings, Tancred, was succeeded by his enemy Henry Hohenstaufen of Swabia in 1194, the mood turned ugly. The Neapolitans

JOAN II: QUEEN OF LUST

Had tabloids existed in the middle ages, Joan II (1373–1435) would have been a fixture. Six centuries after her reign as queen of Naples, Neapolitans still point out the various settings for her 'man-eating' antics. It was at the Castel Nuovo (p71) that she apparently threw her lovers to a hungry crocodile and at the **Palazzo Donn'Anna** (Map p56; Largo Donn'Anna 9; 🚌140 to Via Posillipo) that she threw them straight off a cliff. One can only assume they had underperformed at the queen's infamous orgies.

While the line separating fact and fiction is a very fine one indeed, it is widely accepted that the daughter of Charles III and Margherita di Durazzo was no stranger to the company of men, many of them power brokers. At the time of her coronation in 1414, she was already the widow of William, Duke of Austria, the rejected fiancé of her cousin, Hedwig of Poland. As queen, Joan wasted little time appointing her lover Pandolfello Alopo grand chamberlain, and she was briefly engaged to John of Aragon in 1415.

That same year she married James II of Bourbon, but the honeymoon was short-lived: refused the title of Prince of Taranto, jealous James had Alopo murdered and forced Joan to bestow on him the title of King of Naples. As king, James was determined to assume complete power, imprisoning Joan in the royal household. The king's behaviour provoked rioting in Naples in 1416, forcing him to hang up his crown.

If Joan needed any consolation, she found it in the arms of nobleman Giovanni Caracciolo. Yet the position of prime minister of Naples wasn't enough for Caracciolo, whose increasingly ruthless ambition drove his royal lover to plot his assassination in 1432. His tomb lies in the Chiesa San Giovanni a Carbonara (p62), not far from cunning Joan's own resting place, the **Basilica della Santissima Annunziata** (Map p58; 📞081 28 30 17; Via dell'Annunziata 34; ⏰church 8am-noon & 5.30-7.30pm Mon-Sat, 7.30am-1pm Sun; 🚌R2 to Corso Umberto I).

1139	1265	1343	1414
Naples joins the Norman-ruled Kingdom of the Two Sicilies after the Norman conquest of Capua, Amalfi and Salerno. The city plays second fiddle to the kingdom's capital, Palermo.	Charles I of Anjou beats Naples' hated Swabian rulers, heralding the city's tenure as the capital of the French Anjou dynasty. The port is expanded and Castel Nuovo is built in 1279.	On 25 November, a major earthquake in the Tyrrhenian Sea triggers a tsunami. Ports along the Amalfi Coast, including the town of Amalfi, suffer heavy damage and loss of life.	Joan II is crowned queen of Naples. In 1432, faced with the growing ambitions of her lover, Giovanni Caracciolo, Joan plots his murder; on 19 August Caracciolo is fatally stabbed at Naples' Castel Capuano.

despised their new Swabian rulers and were delighted when Charles I of Anjou routed them at the battle of Benevento in February 1265.

Under the French Angevins, Naples' artistic and intellectual credentials grew. Charles built the Castel Nuovo (p71) in 1279, the port was enlarged, and in the early 14th century Robert of Anjou constructed Castel Sant'Elmo (p77). Alas, nasty politicking between family factions marked the last century of Angevin rule. Queen Joan I was suspected of murdering her husband and fled the city between 1348 and 1352, leaving her vengeful Hungarian in-laws to occupy Naples. Some 70-odd years later, her namesake, Queen Joan II, only stopped her husband from stealing the crown thanks to substantial popular support.

With the royals tangled up in soap-style angst, the time was ripe for the Spanish Aragonese to launch their attack.

History of the Italian People (1970), by Giuliano Procacci, is one of the best general histories of the country in any language. It covers the period from the early Middle Ages until 1948.

Aragonese Angst

Taking control of Naples in 1442, Alfonso of Aragon – dubbed Il Magnanimo (The Magnanimous) – did much for the city, promoting art and science, and introducing institutional reforms. What he couldn't do was live down the fact that he'd overthrown the popular Angevins.

In 1485 the city's barons took up arms against Alfonso's successor, Ferdinand I. Within a year, however, the ringleaders had been executed (in the Sala dei Baroni inside Castel Nuovo) and peace restored. In 1495 Charles VIII of France invaded. Fiercely opposed by the Neapolitan masses, the French monarch was forced out four months later and replaced by the Aragonese Ferdinand II.

After Ferdinand's death in 1496, the mutinous barons crowned his uncle, Frederick, as king. This angered everyone; the Neapolitans, the French and the Spanish had all wanted Ferdinand II's widow, Joan, to succeed him. The upshot was the joint Franco-Spanish invasion of 1501. Frederick tried to hang on to power, but, facing almost total opposition, he skulked off, leaving Naples to the Spanish. Thus Ferdinand of Spain became Ferdinand III of Naples.

Don Pedro & the Spanish Years

As part of the cashed-up Spanish empire, 16th-century Naples prospered. By 1600 it was Europe's largest city, with a population of 300,000. The boom heralded urban expansion, with viceroy Don Pedro de Toledo moving the city walls westward and creating the Quartieri Spagnoli (Spanish Quarter). Hundreds of new churches and monasteries sprang up, giving artistic greats like Caravaggio, Jusepe de Ribera and Luca Giordano the chance to show off their skills. The most prolific of all Naples' architects was Cosimo Fanzago (1591–1678), whose work on the Certosa di San Martino (p76) is a highlight of Neapolitan baroque.

1442	1503	1532–53	1600
Alfonso of Aragon drives out René of Anjou to become Naples' new king; a long period of Spanish control begins.	Two years after a Franco-Spanish invasion of Naples, Spanish general Consalvo di Cordoba enters the city and Ferdinand of Spain becomes Ferdinand III of Naples.	Don Pedro de Toledo rules as Spanish viceroy, moving the city walls westwards and constructing the Quartieri Spagnoli.	Naples is the biggest city in Europe, boasting a population of more than 300,000. Among its growing number of residents is renegade artist Caravaggio, who arrives in 1606.

Less welcome were the ever-increasing tax hikes, resulting from the economic depression that descended in the early 17th century. When the Spanish introduced a levy on fresh fruit in January 1647, it was one tax too many, and on 7 July violence broke out on Piazza del Mercato. Nine days later, the rebellion's illiterate leader – Amalfi fisherman Tommaso Aniello (aka Masaniello) – was murdered in the Chiesa di Santa Maria del Carmine (p65). The culprits were extremists from within his own camp: they wanted to drive out the Spanish, but their leader had been happy with cheaper fruit. Local lore has it that Masaniello lies buried in an unmarked tomb in the church.

The French then tried to cash in by sending the duke of Guise to take the city; the duke failed and on 6 April 1648 was captured by the new Spanish viceroy, the count of Oñate. Order was soon re-established, the rebel leaders were executed and life in Naples returned to a semblance of normality.

Putting a spanner in the works was the plague of 1656, which wiped out more than half of Naples' population and much of the economy. The horror that infected the city's squalid streets is graphically depicted in the paintings that hang in room 37 of the Certosa di San Martino.

Between January and August 1656, the bubonic plague wiped out more than half of Naples' 300,000-plus inhabitants. The city would take almost two centuries to return to its pre-plague population.

Bourbon Brilliance & Habsburg Cunning

With the death of the childless Charles V of Naples (Charles II of Spain) in 1700, Spain's European possessions were up for grabs. Despite Philip, grandson of Charles V's brother-in-law, taking the Spanish throne (and therefore the Neapolitan throne) as Philip V, Austrian troops nabbed Naples in 1707. Waiting in the wings, however, was Philip's Bourbon son Charles, who followed his ambitious mother Elisabetta Farnese's advice to take the city. Between his ascension to the Neapolitan throne in 1734 and Italian unification in 1860, Naples was transformed into Europe's showpiece metropolis. The Palazzo Reale di Capodimonte (p54) hit the skyline, central Palazzo Reale (p66) was enlarged and the Teatro San Carlo (p69) became Europe's grandest opera house.

In 1759 Charles returned to Spain to succeed his father as Charles III. As European law prohibited the simultaneous holding of three crowns (in this case it would have been Naples, Sicily and Spain), Naples was left to Charles' eight-year-old son, Ferdinand, though, in effect, power was held by Charles' conscientious prime minister, Bernardo Tanucci.

When in 1768 Austrian Maria Carolina arrived in town to marry Ferdinand, Tanucci's days were numbered. Maria was one of the 16 children of the Habsburg empress of Austria (the very person whom Tanucci had opposed in the 1740 crisis of Austrian succession). She was beautiful, clever and ruthless – a ready match for Tanucci and an unlikely partner for the famously dim, dialect-speaking Ferdinand.

1656	1707	1734	1737
A devastating plague hits Naples. Within six months, more than half of the city's population is dead and buried in mass graves.	Austrian viceroys begin their 27-year rule of Naples. Tax and university reforms are introduced and coastal roads connecting the city to the slopes of Mt Vesuvius are built.	Encouraged by his ambitious mother and backed by his army, Spanish king Philip V's son Charles takes control from the Austrians and becomes the first Bourbon king of Naples.	The original Teatro San Carlo is built in a swift eight months. Designed by Giovanni Medrano, it is rebuilt in 1816 after a devastating fire.

In accordance with her marriage agreement, Maria Carolina joined the Council of State on the birth of her first son in 1777. It was the position she'd been waiting for to oust Tanucci, and into his shoes stepped a French-born English aristocrat, John Acton. Acton had won Maria over with his anti-Bourbon politics and wish to forge closer links with Austria and Britain. But just as things began to go smoothly with the English, France erupted in revolution.

The Parthenopean Republic

While the Neapolitan court naturally disapproved of the 1789 French Revolution, it would take the beheading of Maria Carolina's sister, Marie Antoinette, to prompt Naples to join the anti-French coalition.

Troops from Naples and revolutionary France clashed in French-occupied Rome in 1798. The Neapolitans claimed the city but within 11 days were scurrying back south with the French in hot pursuit. Panicked, Ferdinand and Maria Carolina headed for Palermo, leaving Naples to its own devices.

Bitterly opposed by most of the population, the French were welcomed by the Neapolitan nobility and bourgeoisie, many of whom had adopted fashionable republican ideas. And it was with the full backing of the French that the Parthenopean Republic was declared on 23 January 1799.

But it wasn't a success. The leaders were an ideologically rather than practically minded lot, and they were soon in dire financial straits. Their efforts to democratise the city failed and the army was a shambles.

Over the water in Palermo, the royal exiles had not been sitting idle. Ferdinand and Maria Carolina dispatched Cardinal Fabrizio Ruffo to Calabria to organise an uprising. On 13 June he entered Naples and all hell broke loose as his men turned the city into a slaughterhouse. With a score to settle, Ferdinand and Maria Carolina returned from Sicily on 8 July and embarked on a systematic extermination of republican sympathisers. More than 200 were executed. Among them was poet and revolutionary Eleonora de Fonseca Pimentel, whose biweekly Republic newspaper *Monitore napoletano* gave birth to political journalism in Italy. The Portuguese-Italian noblewoman would go down in history as a heroine of the Neapolitan revolution.

Bourbon Decline & Nationalist Fervour

Despite the Parthenopean Republic's failure, French forces marched again into Naples in 1806. The royal family once more fled to Sicily, and in 1808 Joachim Murat, Napoleon's brother-in-law, became king of Naples. Despite his abolition of feudalism and kick-starting of local industry, Murat could do no right in the eyes of the royalist masses.

In his *Italian Journey (1786–1788)*, Goethe wrote of Naples, 'I can't begin to tell you of the glory of a night by full moon when we strolled through the streets and squares to the endless promenade of the Chiaia...I was quite overwhelmed by a feeling of infinite space.'

For a wide-ranging general site on Italian history, check out www.arcaini.com. It covers, in potted form, everything from prehistory to the post–WWII period, and includes a brief chronology.

1768	1799	1806	1848
Marie Antoinette's sister, Maria Carolina, marries the uncouth Ferdinand IV. Nine years later she enters the Council of State and ousts prime minister and enemy Bernardo Tanucci.	The Parthenopean Republic is proclaimed on 23 January. It quickly fails, royal rule is reinstalled and more than 200 republican sympathisers are executed.	Joseph Bonaparte occupies the city and declares himself king of Naples. Two years later, Bonaparte is crowned king of Spain.	Pressured by rebellions across Europe, Ferdinand II of the Two Sicilies reintroduces a constitution in January. A dispute with the parliament, however, sees the king dissolve parliament altogether in March 1849.

With Murat finally ousted in 1815, Ferdinand returned to claim his throne. But the French Revolution had stirred up too many ideas for a return to the age of absolutism, and the ruthless Carbonari – a secret political society opposed to absolutism – forced Ferdinand to grant the city a constitution in 1820. A year later, however, it was abandoned as Ferdinand called in Austrian troops.

Pressured by rising rebellion across Europe, another King Ferdinand (this one the son of Francesco I, who had succeeded the previous Ferdinand) reintroduced a constitution in 1848, only to dissolve the parliament altogether. He was as blind to the changing times as his equally obstinate son, who succeeded him in 1859.

More popular was nationalist fighter Giuseppe Garibaldi, whose goal was a united Italy. Buoyed by the victory of Piedmontese rebels against the Austrian army, he set sail for Sicily in May 1860 with a volunteer army of 1000 Red Shirts. Although Ferdinand's 25,000-strong Neapolitan army was waiting in Sicily, the Bourbons' repression of liberalism was beginning to cost it goodwill. With an army that had swelled to 5000 men, Garibaldi defeated the half-hearted Bourbon forces, declaring himself dictator in the name of King Vittorio Emanuele II.

In a case of too little too late, Ferdinand's son and successor, Francesco II, agreed to a constitution in June 1860, but Garibaldi had crossed over to the Italian mainland and was bound for Naples. True to tradition, Francesco fled the city, taking refuge with 4000 loyalists behind the River Volturno, north of Naples. On 7 September Garibaldi marched unopposed into Naples, welcomed as a hero.

After a series of last-ditch attacks on the rebels, the Bourbon loyalists were defeated at the Battle of Volturno and on 21 October the city voted overwhelmingly to join a united Italy under the Savoy monarchy.

A seasoned royal city, Naples was a serious contender for capital of Italy. But when Rome was wrested from the French in 1870, the newly formed Italian parliament transferred from its temporary home in Florence to the Eternal City. From being the grand capital of a Bourbon kingdom, Naples suddenly became a lowly regional centre – something the city has never forgotten.

War & Peace

A poorer shadow of its former self, post-unification Naples suffered two major blows: mass emigration and a cholera outbreak in 1884. In response to the cholera epidemic, a citywide clean-up was launched. The worst slums near the port were razed, Corso Umberto I was bulldozed through the city centre, and a sparkling new residential quarter appeared on the Vomero.

> Between 1876 and 1913, 11.1 million Italians left their homeland in search of a better life in the New World. Of these, at least four million are believed to have come from Naples and the surrounding area. By 1927, 20% of the Italian population had emigrated.

1860	1884	1889	1943
Garibaldi enters the city to a hero's welcome and Naples votes overwhelmingly to join a united Italy under the Savoy monarchy.	A cholera epidemic strikes the city, prompting the closure of Naples' ancient aqueduct system and the launch of a major urban-redevelopment project.	Raffaele Esposito invents pizza margherita in honour of Queen Margherita, who takes her first bite of the Neapolitan staple on a royal visit to the city.	Allied bombing raids wreak havoc on the city, destroying the 14th-century Basilica di Santa Chiara. A year later, Mt Vesuvius erupts.

The Fascists continued the building spree: an airport was built in 1936, railway and metro lines were laid, and the Vomero funicular opened for business. No sooner had many of these projects been completed than the strategic port city was hit by the full force of WWII. Savage aerial bombing by the Allies left over 20,000 people dead and much of the city in tatters.

Although the Nazis took Naples in 1943, they were quickly forced out by a series of popular uprisings between 26 and 30 September, famously known as the Quattro Giornate di Napoli (Four Days of Naples). Led by locals, especially by young *scugnizzi* (Neapolitan for 'street urchins') and ex-soldiers, the street battles paved the way for the Allied 'liberators' to enter the city on 1 October.

Despite setting up a provisional government in Naples, the Allies were confronted with an anarchic mass of troops, German prisoners of war and bands of Italian Fascists all competing with the city's starving population for food. Then, to make matters worse, in 1944 Mt Vesuvius erupted.

Overwhelmed, Allied authorities turned to the underworld for assistance. As long as the Allies agreed to turn a blind eye to their black-market activities, the Mafia was willing to help. And so the Camorra (Neapolitan Mafia) began to flourish.

Seismic & Political Shockwaves

On 23 November 1980, an earthquake registering 6.9 on the Richter scale struck the mountainous Irpinia region east of Naples, shaking vast areas of Campania and neighbouring Basilicata, including Naples itself. The disaster left over 2700 people dead and thousands more homeless, with much of the destruction centred in the province of Avellino. The opportunistic Camorra made the most of the disaster, siphoning off billions of lire poured into the devastated area.

In the decade that followed, *abusivismo* (illegal construction) flourished, profiteering mobsters partied publicly with the city's football icon, Argentine Diego Maradona, and public services virtually ceased to exist. The situation was not unique to Naples – corruption and cronyism were rife across Italy.

It couldn't go on, and in 1992 the 'Mani pulite' (Clean Hands) campaign kicked into gear. What had started as an investigation into bribery at a retirement home in Milan quickly grew into a nationwide crusade against corruption. Industry bosses and politicians were investigated, some were imprisoned, and former prime minister Bettino Craxi fled Italy to avoid prosecution.

In Naples, the city indicated its approval by electing as mayor former communist Antonio Bassolino, whose promises to kick-start the city and fight corruption were music to weary Neapolitan ears. In the seven years that followed, a burst of urban regeneration gave Naples a refreshing

Naples endured its largest WWII air raid on 4 August 1943, when 400 planes of the US Mediterranean Bomber Command dropped bombs for around 90 minutes. The attack destroyed the city's iconic Basilica di Santa Chiara, later rebuilt according to its original Gothic plan.

1980	1982	1987	1992
At 7.34pm on 23 November, a powerful earthquake rocks Campania, causing widespread damage and killing over 2700 people.	A bout of bradyseism – the upward and downward movement of the earth's crust – sees Pozzuoli's seabed rise 1.85m between 1982 and 1984, rendering its harbour too shallow for large vessels.	Under Maradona, Napoli wins both the Serie A championship (lo scudetto) and the Coppa Italia. Mass elation sweeps across the city.	The anticorruption campaign known as 'Mani pulite' (Clean Hands) is launched. The following year, Antonio Bassolino is voted mayor and a major city clean-up begins.

sense of hope and pride, one that included the commissioning of world-renowned artists to design new metro stations, and the G7 summit in 1994.

Despite winning a second term in 1997, Bassolino couldn't keep up the impressive momentum and in 2000 he was elected president of the Campania region, which meant that he was no longer involved in the day-to-day running of the city. Into his shoes stepped Rosa Russo Iervolino, a former interior minister and Naples' first female mayor. Elected on a centre-left ticket first in 2001 and then for a second term in May 2006, her time in office was not free of controversy. In April 2002 political chaos ensued after eight police officers were arrested on charges of torturing antiglobalisation protestors arrested at a 2001 government conference. Even more damaging were the waste-disposal crises of 2003, 2006 and 2008, which saw numerous city streets and squares reduced to festering rubbish tips. The 2008 crisis prompted the EU to take legal action against Italy for its ineffective management of the issue.

> Although much has happened since it was updated in 2003, Paul Ginsborg's *A History of Contemporary Italy: Society and Politics 1943–1988* remains one of the single most readable and insightful books on postwar Italy.

De Magistris & the Starchitects

Beleaguered by years of humiliating headlines involving litter-strewn streets and *camorristi* (Camorra members), voters elected the city's current mayor, Luigi de Magistris, in 2011. For many disillusioned Neapolitans, the youthful former public prosecutor represented a glimmer of hope in a city deeply tarnished and abused.

De Magistris' vision for a cleaner, greener city saw the introduction of a ZTL (limited-traffic zone) in Naples' *centro storico* in September 2011, designed to slash carbon emissions, improve traffic flow and curb the illegal use of lanes reserved for public transport. A stretch of Naples' Lungomare (seafront) was pedestrianised in time for the city's hosting of the World Series of the America's Cup in spring 2012. The waterfront strip has since become a favourite meeting place for locals and tourists. While De Magistris is not without his critics, his progressive anti-corruption agenda has hit the right note with many Neapolitans. In 2016, the Gen X independent was re-elected city mayor, beating rival Gianni Lettieri of the centre-right Forza Italia party with 66.8% of the total vote.

The 2010s also saw the addition of some impressive new architecture in Naples and the greater Naples region. In 2012, the ribbon was cut on the city's Toledo metro station. Designed by Spanish architect Oscar Tusquets Blanca, the Line 1 stop would win 'Public Building of the Year' at the 2013 LEAF (Leading European Architects Forum) Awards. The station is one of Naples' 'Metro Art Stations', designed by leading Italian and international architects and artists. In 2017, the attention of architecture fans was also drawn to the nearby city of Afragola with the opening of its own slithering train station, designed by the late Iraqi-British architect Zaha Hadid.

2004–05	2015	2018	2020
Tension between rival Camorra (Neapolitan Mafia) clans explodes on the streets of suburban Scampia and Secondigliano. In only four months almost 50 people are gunned down in retributive attacks.	After lengthy delays, Naples' showcase Municipio metro station opens to the public, featuring uncovered ancient ruins and a specially commissioned video painting by Israeli artist Michal Rovner.	A severe February cold snap sees Naples blanketed in its heaviest snowfall in half a century. The unusual snowstorm forces the city's Capodichino airport to close for 90 minutes.	The COVID-19 pandemic hits Italy early and hard, although Campania manages to avoid the high death rates recorded in Lombardy and other northern regions.

The Arts

Dramatic, surprising and deliciously contradictory, Naples and its coast have long been a fertile ground for creativity. Caravaggio, Ribera, Scarlatti, Totò, De Sica: the region's list of homegrown and adopted talent spans some of the world's finest painters, composers, playwrights and filmmakers. Indeed, some of Italy's most internationally recognisable cultural icons hail from Campanian soil, among them commedia dell'arte protagonist Pulcinella, the disconcertingly catchy tune 'Funiculì, Funiculà' and celluloid goddess Sophia Loren. Welcome to southern Italy's cultural powerhouse.

Brush-Clutching Greats

While Naples has produced great paintings throughout the centuries, none compare to the works created in the golden 17th and 18th centuries. High on wealth and power, the booming city had become the New York of its time, a magnet for talented, ambitious artists desperate to put their stamp on Naples' grand new churches and palaces.

The main influence on 17th-century Neapolitan art was Milan-born Michelangelo Merisi da Caravaggio (1573–1610), who fled to the city in 1606 after killing a man in Rome. Although he only stayed for a year, his naturalist style and dramatic depiction of light and shade (termed *chiaroscuro*) in paintings like *The Seven Acts of Mercy* (inside Pio Monte della Misericordia; p57) and *Flagellation* (inside the Palazzo Reale di Capodimonte; p54) had an electrifying effect on Naples' younger artists.

Among these was Jusepe (or Giuseppe, locally) de Ribera (1591–1652), an aggressive, bullying Spaniard who arrived in Naples in 1616 after a seven-year stint in Rome. Ribera's combination of shadow, colour and gloomy naturalism proved hugely popular, best captured in his *capo lavoro* (masterpiece), the *Pietà* inside the Certosa di San Martino (p76).

A fledgling apprentice to Ribera, Naples-born Luca Giordano (1632–1705) found great inspiration in the luminous brushstrokes of Mattia Preti (1613–99), not to mention the pomp of Venetian artist Paolo Veronese and the flounce of Rome-based artist and architect Pietro da Cortona. By the second half of the 17th century, Giordano would become the single-most-prolific baroque artist in Naples, his many commissions including wall frescoes in the Duomo's nave (p51) and a ceiling painting in the adjacent Basilica di Santa Restituta. The Chiesa del Gesù Nuovo (p57) boasts several Giordano creations, including vault and wall frescoes in the Cappella della Visitazione and canvases in the Cappella di San Francesco Saverio. Upstaging them all is his *Triumph of Judith,* a ceiling fresco in the treasury of the church of the Certosa di San Martino.

Giordano's contemporary Francesco Solimena (1657–1747) was also influenced by Ribera, although his use of shadow and solid form showed a clearer link with Caravaggio. Solimena would also become an icon of Neapolitan baroque, and his lavish compositions – among them the operatic fresco *Expulsion of Eliodoro from the Temple* in the Chiesa

Culture-Vulture Musts

Teatro San Carlo, Naples

Ravello Festival

Napoli Teatro Festival Italia

Centro di Musica Antica Pietà de' Turchini, Naples

La Mortella, Ischia

del Gesù Nuovo – represented an accumulation of more than half a century of experimentation and trends, spanning Preti and Giordano himself.

The Neapolitan Score

In the 1700s, Naples was the world's opera capital, with industry heavyweights flocking south to perform at the Teatro San Carlo (p69). Locally trained greats like Francesco Durante (1684–1755), Leonardo Vinci (1690–1730) and Tommaso Traetta (1727–79) wowed conservatories across Europe. Naples' greatest composer, Alessandro Scarlatti (1660–1725), trained at the esteemed conservatory at the Chiesa della Pietà dei Turchini on Via Medina, which also gave birth to the renowned music group Pietà de' Turchini (p92).

Creator of around 100 operatic works, Scarlatti also played a leading role in the development of *opera seria* (serious opera), giving the world the three-part overture and the *aria de capo*.

Running parallel to the high-brow *opera seria* was *opera buffa* (comic opera). Inspired by the Neapolitan *commedia dell'arte,* the genre began life as light-hearted, farcical interludes – *intermezzi* – performed between scenes of heavier classical operas. Kick-started by Scarlatti's *Il trionfe dell'onore* (The Triumph of Honour) in 1718, the contemporary interludes soon developed into a major, crowd-pleasing genre, with homegrown favourites including Giovanni Battista Pergolesi's *La serva padrona* (The Maid Mistress) and Domenico Cimarosa's *Il matrimonio segreto* (The Clandestine Marriage).

The following century saw the rise of the *la canzone napoletana* (Neapolitan song), its roots firmly planted in the annual Festa di Piedigrotta folk-song festival. Some tunes celebrated the city – among them the world-famous 'Funiculì, Funiculà', an ode to the funicular that once scaled Mt Vesuvius – and others lamented one's distance from it. Either way, the songs deeply resonated with the locals, especially the millions who boarded ships in search of a better life abroad.

The arrival of the American Allies in 1943 sparked another Neapolitan musical predilection: jazz, rhythm and blues. As music journalist Francesco Calazzo puts it: 'As a port city, Naples has always absorbed foreign influences. Musically, the result is a fusion of styles, from Arab laments and Spanish folk to African percussion and American blues'.

This fusion came to the fore in the late 1970s. A defining moment for Neapolitan music, it saw new-wave pioneers like Eugenio Bennato, Enzo Avitabile and Pino Daniele revive Neapolitan folk and cross it with rock, roots and hypnotic African beats. Singing many of his songs in Neapolitan, Daniele wrote bittersweet lyrics about his beloved hometown. Epitomised by songs like 'Napule è' (Naples Is), his work struck a particularly deep chord with the public. The singer-songwriter's fatal

The region's diaspora turned Neapolitan tunes into the most internationally recognisable form of Italian music. When the sheet music to the Italian national anthem was lost at the 1920 Olympic Games in Antwerp, the orchestra broke into 'O Sole Mio' instead. It was the only Italian melody that everyone knew.

RIBERA: THE RUTHLESS SPANIARD

Even though he was the leading light of Naples' mid-17th-century art scene, success did little to brighten Jusepe de Ribera's dark side. Along with the Greek artist Belisario Corenzio and local painter Giambattista Caracciolo, Lo Spagnoletto (The Little Spaniard, as Ribera was known) formed a cabal to stamp out any potential competition. Merciless in the extreme, they stopped at nothing to get their way. Ribera reputedly won a commission for the Cappella di San Gennaro in the Duomo by poisoning his rival Domenichino (1581–1641) and wounding the assistant of a second competitor, Guido Reni (1575–1642). Much to the relief of other nerve-wracked artists, the cabal eventually broke up when Caracciolo died in 1642.

heart attack in January 2015 prompted widespread grief and camaraderie, with commuters even joining together in song on the metro. Even though he's taken his final bow, Daniele's music lives on as an indelible part of Naples' rich musical heritage, one that forms the focus of John Turturro's documentary *Passione* (2010), a self-proclaimed 'cinematic love letter' to the city and its sounds.

Theatrical Legacies

Naples' theatrical tradition is considered one of Italy's oldest. Its most famous contribution to the world stage is the *commedia dell'arte*, dating back to the 16th century and rooted in the earthy ancient-Roman comedy theatre of *fabula Atellana* (Atellan farce). Like its ancient inspiration, this highly animated genre featured a set of stock characters in masks acting out a series of semistandard situations. Performances were often used to satirise local situations and were based on a tried-and-tested recipe of adultery, jealousy, old age and love.

Not only did *commedia dell'arte* give birth to a number of legendary characters, including the Harlequin and Pulcinella, it provided fertile ground for the development of popular theatre in Naples and was a tradition in which the great dramatist Raffaele Viviani (1888–1950) was firmly rooted. Viviani's focus on the regional dialect and the Neapolitan working class won him local success and the enmity of the Mussolini regime.

The most important figure in modern Neapolitan theatre remains Eduardo De Filippo (1900–84). The son of a famous Neapolitan actor, Eduardo Scarpetta (1853–1925), De Filippo made his stage debut at the age of four and over the next 80 years became a hugely successful actor, impresario and playwright. His body of often bittersweet work, which includes the classics *Il sìndaco del Rione Sanità* (The Mayor of the Sanità Quarter) and *Sabato, domenica e lunedì* (Saturday, Sunday and Monday), encapsulated struggles well known to Neapolitans, from the injustice of being forced to live beyond the law to the fight for dignity in the face of adversity.

The *furbizia* (cunning) for which Neapolitans are famous is celebrated in De Filippo's play *Filumena Marturano*, in which a clever ex-prostitute gets her common-law husband to marry her by declaring him to be the father of one of her three *bambini*. The film adaptation, *Marriage Italian Style* (1964), stars homegrown Sophia Loren (1934–) alongside Marcello Mastroianni (1924–96).

Roberto De Simone (1933–) is another great Neapolitan playwright, not to mention a renowned composer and musicologist. While he is lesser known abroad than De Filippo, his theatrical masterpiece *La gatta cenerentola* (The Cat Cinderella) enjoyed a successful run in London in 1999 before being made into an animated feature in 2017.

The Silver Screen

In Campania, locations read like a red-carpet roll call: 'La Loren' wiggled her booty through Naples' Sanità district in *Yesterday, Today, Tomorrow* (1963), Julia Roberts did a little soul-searching in its historic centre in *Eat Pray Love* (2010), and Jude Law, Gwyneth Paltrow and Matt Damon tanned on Ischia and Procida in *The Talented Mr Ripley* (1999).

Naples' homemade offerings have often held a mirror to the city's harsh realities. Feted for his 1948 neo-realist masterpiece *The Bicycle Thieves*, Vittorio De Sica (1901–74) was a master at depicting the bittersweet struggle at the heart of so much Neapolitan humour. His two

Enzo Moscato (1948–) is a leading figure in contemporary Neapolitan theatre, known for fusing a vibrant physicality with skilful use of dialect and music. His works include 1991 multiple-award-winning *Rasoi* (Razors) and 2017 *Raccogliere e bruciare* (Collect and Burn), a Neapolitan adaptation of Edgar Lee Masters' *Spoon River Anthology* poems.

THE ARTS THEATRICAL LEGACIES

A PUPPET WITH PUNCH

His aliases are many, from Punchinello or Mr Punch in Britain to Petruska in Russia. In his home town of Naples, however, he's simply Pulcinella: the best-known character of the *commedia dell'arte*.

In his white costume and black hook-nosed mask, this squeaky-voiced clown is equally exuberant and lazy, optimistic and cynical, melancholic and witty. As a street philosopher, he is anti-authoritarian and is often seen beating the local copper with a stick (hence the term 'slapstick'). At home, however, his wife's the beater and he's the victim.

While some trace his creation to a 16th-century actor in the town of Capua, others believe he has been dancing and stirring since the days of togas...or even longer. In fact, his iconic hook-nosed mask appears on frescoed Etruscan tombs in Tarquinia, north of Rome. The mask belongs to Phersu, a vicious Etruscan demon known as the Queen of Hell's servant.

Neapolitan classics, *L'oro di Napoli* (The Gold of Naples; 1954) and *Yesterday, Today, Tomorrow* delighted audiences across the world.

Appearing with Loren in *L'oro di Napoli* and the slapstick farce *Miseria e nobiltà* (Misery and Nobility; 1954) was the city's other screen deity, Antonio De Curtis (1898–1967), aka Totò. Dubbed the Neapolitan Buster Keaton, Totò depicted Neapolitan cunning like no other. He appeared in over 100 films, typically playing the part of a hustler living on nothing but his quick wits.

Inheriting Totò's mantle, Massimo Troisi (1953–94) was best known internationally for his role in *Il postino* (The Postman). In his 1980 debut film, *Ricomincio da tre* (I'm Starting from Three), he humorously tackled the problems faced by Neapolitans forced to head north for work. Troisi's cameo in the schlock murder mystery *No grazie, il caffè mi rende nervoso* (No Thanks, Coffee Makes Me Nervous; 1982) – arguably one of his funniest – saw a rambling, pyjama-clad Troisi hopelessly attempting to convince Funiculì, Funiculà (an unseen, helium-pitched psychopath set on sabotaging Naples' new jazz festival) that he is loyal only to the city's traditional cultural offerings.

A newer wave of Neapolitan directors, including Antonio Capuano (1940–), Pappi Corsicato (1960–) and Antonietta De Lillo (1960–), have also turned their cameras on the city in films such as Capuano's critically acclaimed *Luna rossa* (Red Moon) of 2001. While Corsicato's queer-centric classics *Libera* (Free; 1993) and *I buchi neri* (The Black Holes; 1995) evoke the ever-present link between the ancient and modern sides of Naples, De Lillo's *Il resto di niente* (The Remains of Nothing; 2004) explores the psychological complexities of revolutionary Eleonora de Fonseca Pimentel; it's also the inspiration for De Simone's oratorio.

More recent offerings include *E poi c'è Napoli* (And Then There Is Naples; 2014), a documentary film directed by Gianluca Migliarotti (1974–). An ode to classic Neapolitan style and tailoring, its depiction of an elegant, cultured metropolis is a refreshing counterpoint to the blood-stained Naples portrayed in the multi-award-winning feature film *Gomorrah* (2008). Directed by Rome's Matteo Garrone (1968–), but based on the book by Neapolitan Roberto Saviano, *Gomorrah* intertwines five stories of characters affected by the Neapolitan Mafia, the Camorra. Directors Marco Manetti (1968–) and Antonio Manetti (1970–) offer a lighter take on the Mafia in *Ammore e malavita* (Love and Bullets; 2017), an award-winning musical comedy about a Camorra hitman ordered to kill a woman he discovers is a long-lost flame.

Writing under a pseudonym, Elena Ferrante has established herself as Italy's most important writer today. In 2012, she released *My Brilliant Friend*, the first of four novels depicting the intense relationship between two Neapolitan childhood friends. Dubbed the Neapolitan Novels, the quartet has sold almost six million copies internationally.

The Neapolitan Way of Life

There is nowhere more theatrical than Naples, a city in which everyday transactions become minor performances and traffic jams give rise to impromptu car-horn concerts. Neapolitans often wear their hearts on their sleeves, and the streets and squares are a stage on which to play out quotidian dramas. Indeed, nowhere else in Italy are the people so conscious of their role in the theatre of everyday life and so addicted to its intensity.

Language & Identity

Neapolitans have a very strong sense of their own identity, one which includes their very particular dialect. Though not recognised as an official minority language by the Italian government, the Neapolitan dialect (known locally as *napulitano*) is considered one of the world's

Above Quartieri Spagnoli (p66), Naples

endangered languages by Unesco. Influenced by centuries of foreign domination (there are an estimated 400 Spanish loanwords alone), it features its own distinct vocabulary, grammar, orthography and pronunciation. The official language of the Kingdom of Naples between 1442 and 1458, Neapolitan lives on in the region's streets, as well as in a bounty of literature and music written in the language, from Giovanni Boccaccio's 14th-century 'Epistola napoletana' (Neapolitan Epistle) to the contemporary folk-rock anthems of the late singer-songwriter Pino Daniele. You'll even hear the occasional Neapolitan quip from Sophia Loren in classic Italian films like *L'oro di Napoli* (The Gold of Naples; 1954) and *Marriage Italian Style* (1964). As the homegrown actor once famously declared, 'I'm not Italian, I am Neapolitan! It's another thing.'

Neapolitans know that many of the stereotypes foreigners hold of Italians – noisy, theatrical, food-loving, passionate and proud – refer to them. And many revel in it. Everyone has an opinion to give, a line to deliver or a sigh to perform. Eavesdropping is a popular pastime and knowing everyone else's business is a veritable sport. Neapolitans joke that if you were to collapse on the street a local would first want to know all the juicy details, and only after that would they think of calling an ambulance. In a city with a population density of 2653 people per sq km (the highest in Italy), this penchant for curiosity is understandable.

And yet, Neapolitans are far more complex than any earthy, street-wise hallmark can convey. After all, theirs is a city of aristocratic palaces and art collections, a world-renowned opera house, and one of Europe's oldest universities. Naples gave the world pizza and Pulcinella, but it has also given it composer Alessandro Scarlatti, playwright Roberto De Simone and contemporary artist Francesco Clemente. To the world's fashion elite, Neapolitan tradition means meticulous tailoring and inimitable male elegance. This is the hometown of hand-stitched Kiton suits and handcrafted Talarico umbrellas. It's an oft-overlooked side of the city beautifully captured in Gianluca Migliarotti's *E poi c'è Napoli* (And Then There Is Naples; 2014), which portrays an erudite, elegant metropolis.

> Neapolitans' fierce and famous individuality goes back to ancient times. Despite Roman conquest, Neapolis held fast to its Greek language and Hellenic customs.

THE NORTH–SOUTH DIVIDE

While countless *meridionali* (southern Italians) have headed abroad in search of greener pastures, just as many have settled in Italy's wealthier north – a situation comically captured in *Ricomincio da tre* (I'm Starting from Three; 1980), a film starring late Neapolitan actor Massimo Troisi. Punchlines aside, the film reveals Italy's very real north–south divide.

From the Industrial Revolution to the 1960s, millions fled to the industrialised northern cities for factory jobs. As the saying goes, *Ogni vero milanese ha un nonno pugliese* (Every true Milanese has a Pugliese grandparent). For most of these homegrown migrants, the welcome they received north of Rome was anything but warm. Disparagingly nicknamed *terroni* (peasants), many faced daily discrimination from everyone from landlords to baristas.

Although such overt discrimination is now rare, historical prejudices linger. Many northerners resent their taxes being used to 'subsidise' the 'lazy', 'corrupt' south – a sentiment that fuelled the establishment of the right-wing Lega Nord (Northern League) party. At a party event in June 2009, Lega Nord leader and Italian deputy prime minister Matteo Salvini was filmed singing '*Senti che puzza, scappano anche i cani: stanno arrivando i napoletani*' (Smell that stench, even the dogs are fleeing: the Neapolitans are coming). The chant also referred to Neapolitans as *colerosi* (sick with cholera). As might be expected, footage of Salvini campaigning in Campania in the lead-up to the 2018 Italian general election was met with indignation from many Neapolitans, despite his pre-election apology for the comment.

Street-food stall, Naples

Wanted: Opportunity

While Neapolitans may be rightly passionate about their city, a scarcity of jobs sees many forced to bid it a bittersweet *arrivederci*. Campania's unemployment rate is one of the highest in Italy. Figures released by Istat (Italy's Bureau of Statistics) in 2018 revealed that while the national unemployment rate had fallen between 2016 and 2017, the percentage of jobless Neapolitans had increased from 26.6% to 30.5%. Between 2007 and 2017, the city's unemployment rate had increased by 20%, with almost 80,000 more locals without work. The city's youth-unemployment rate is even more disconcerting. Reaching 56% in 2014, the rate enjoyed a modest (albeit unstable) reduction before creeping over 50% once again in 2017.

These figures do little to help the country's ongoing *fuga dei cervelli* (brain drain), which has seen thousands of young Italians head abroad in search of better education and employment prospects. According to a 2018 report by Confindustria, the main association representing the manufacturing and service industries in Italy, half a million Italians moved abroad between 2008 and 2015. The report also claimed that the ongoing *fuga* cost the country €14 billion annually.

For many young, educated and ambitious Campanians wanting to develop their careers, there is little incentive to remain in Italy. Relatively low government investment in research and development (about 1.3% of GDP, compared to around 3% in Austria and Germany) has stunted economic innovation and opportunity. The country's ingrained culture of nepotism prevents many of the country's brightest, most promising talent from obtaining positions they truly deserve. It's a problem well documented in *La fuga dei talenti* (Flight of the Talented; www.fugadei talenti.wordpress.com), a book-turned-blog by Italian journalist Sergio

Focus on the positives. Although Neapolitans regularly lament their city's short-comings, jibes from a *straniero* (foreigner) can cause offence.

Street scene in Naples' *centro storico* (p51)

Nava, which is aimed at reversing the country's loss of human capital. According to Nava, Italy commonly disregards the value of merit, placing family and other personal relations above an impressive CV or an international profile. Indeed, over 60% of Italian companies recruit through personal introductions and recommendations. In a landscape so riddled with nepotism, putting in a good word is not simply a thoughtful gesture, it's essential to help someone get ahead.

Family Life & Gender Battles

While Neapolitans pride themselves on their spontaneity and flexibility, Sunday *pranzo* (lunch) with the family is usually non-negotiable. Rain, hail or shine, this time of the week is sacred to Neapolitan families – a time to catch up on each others' lives, pick over the latest news about politicians, footballers and celebrities, and eat like royalty. The sacred status of Sunday lunch is a reminder that family remains the bedrock of Neapolitan life. Indeed, loyalty to family and friends is deeply engraved in the Neapolitan psyche. As Luigi Barzini (1908–84), author of *The Italians,* claimed: a happy private life helps Italians cope with an appalling public life. This chasm between the private arena and the public one is a noticeable aspect of the southern mentality, and has evolved over years of intrusive foreign domination. Some locals mightn't think twice about littering in the street, but step inside their home and you'll find floors clean enough to eat off. After all, you'd never want someone dropping in and thinking you're a *barbone* (tramp), right?

Maintaining *la bella figura* (beautiful image) is also very important to the average Neapolitan, and how you and your family appear to the outside world is a matter of honour, respectability and pride. To many

Over 60% of Neapolitans aged 18 to 34 live at home. This is not because Naples is a city of *mammoni* (mama's boys) and *figlie di papà* (daddy's girls) – at least, not entirely. High rents make independent living prohibitively expensive for many young locals.

southern Italians, you are better than your neighbour if you own more and better things. This mentality is rooted in the past, when you really did need to own lots of things to attain certain social roles, and ultimately sustain your family. Yet *fare bella figura* (making a good impression) goes beyond a well-kept house, extending to dressing well, behaving modestly, performing religious and social duties, and fulfilling all essential family obligations. In the context of the extended family, where gossip is rife, a good image protects one's privacy.

Families in Campania remain among the country's largest, with an average household size of 2.69 compared to 2.23 in Lazio, 2.26 in Lombardy and 2.18 in Piedmont. It's still the norm to live at home until you marry, and one third of husbands still visit their mothers every day. While many of these will have a bowl of their favourite pasta waiting for them, some will also have their laundry freshly washed and ironed. OECD figures reveal that Italian men spend 130 minutes per day cooking, cleaning or caring, significantly less than Italian women, who spend an average of 306 minutes per day on what the OECD labels 'unpaid work'.

According to Eurostat, Italy's pay gap – at just over 5% – is the second lowest in the European Union. While this may sound promising, it partly reflects the fact that Italy has fewer women participating in the workforce than most other developed nations. According to the OECD, fewer than half of working-age Italian women are in employment. As a result, those women who are employed are more likely to be highly educated and in higher-paying positions. Numerous employers continue to view female candidates as a risk, likely to give up their jobs to raise a family. Add a largely ineffective childcare system, and the juggling of work and motherhood becomes a rather stressful act for many women, both in Campania and other Italian regions.

Steer clear of chrysanthemums when buying flowers for a local. In Italy they're only used to decorate graves.

THE NEAPOLITAN WAY OF LIFE FAMILY LIFE & GENDER BATTLES

Saints & Superstitions

Naples is Europe's esoteric metropolis par excellence: a Mediterranean New Orleans with less voodoo and more Catholic guilt. Here, miracles pack out cathedrals, dreams channel lottery numbers, and horn-shaped charms ward off the dreaded *malocchio* (evil eye). Despite the contemporary feel of blaring pop and ring tones, Neapolitan streets are littered with well-worn myths and legends, from Santa Maria Francesca's miraculous chair in the Quartieri Spagnoli to an alchemist prince's bizarre anatomical models deep in the centro storico (historic centre).

Friends in High Places

Headlining the city's supernatural scene are the saints, who are veritable celebrities. Fireworks explode in their honour, fans flock to kiss their marble feet and newborn *bambini* (children) take their names. That Gennaro is the most common male name in Naples is no coincidence: San Gennaro is the city's best-loved patron saint. As in much of southern Italy, Neapolitans celebrate their *giorno onomastico* (name day) with as much gusto as they do their birthday. Forgetting a friend's name day is a bigger faux pas than forgetting their birthday, because everyone knows (or should know) the most important saints' days.

The Virgin Mary's status as maternal protector strikes a deep chord in a society where mothers have always fiercely defended the rights of their precious sons. Festival days in honour of the Madonna are known to whip up mass hysteria, best exemplified by the annual Feast of the Madonna dell'Arco. Held on Easter Monday, it sees thousands of pilgrims called *fujenti* (Neapolitan for 'those who run') walk barefoot to the Santuario della Madonna dell'Arco, located near the village of Sant'Anastasia at the foot of Mt Vesuvius. The focus of their devotion is an unusual image of the Virgin Mary, in which her cheek is wounded. According to legend, the wound's origins go back to Easter Monday in 1500, when a disgruntled mallet player hit the Virgin's image with a wooden ball. Miraculously, the image began to bleed, leading to the spoilsport's hanging and the construction of the sanctuary on the site of the event. As they approach the sanctuary, the *fujenti* run towards it. Some fall into a trance, with many more shouting, crying and walking on their knees towards the image in what can be best described as a collective purging of guilt and pain.

In Naples, the lead-up to the festival is an event in itself. From the week following the Epiphany (6 January) to Easter Monday, hundreds of neighbourhood *congreghe* (instrument-playing congregations) parade through the streets, carrying a statue of the Madonna, collecting offerings for the big day and playing an incongruous medley of tunes (think 'Ave Maria' followed by a 1970s Raffaella Carrà pop hit).

Exactly which saint you consult can depend on what you're after. If it's an addition to the family, chances are you'll head straight to the former home of Santa Maria Francesca delle Cinque Piaghe (p71) to sit on the saint's miraculous chair. It's the closest thing to a free fertility treatment in Naples. On the opposite side of Via Toledo, in

For centuries, locals believed that a crocodile lurked below the Castel Nuovo. Some said the reptile lunched on Queen Joan II's ex-lovers. Others swore that political prisoners were on the menu. According to writer and intellectual Benedetto Croce, the crocodile was eventually caught using a horse's thigh as bait.

the Chiesa del Gesù Nuovo (p57), entire rooms are dedicated to Dr Giuseppe Moscati (1880–1927), a much-loved local medic canonised in 1987. Here, *ex-voti* decorate the walls, each one testament to the doctor's celestial intervention.

Despite the Madonna's popularity, the city's ultimate holy superhero is San Gennaro. Every year in May, September and December thousands of Neapolitans cram themselves into the Duomo (p51) to pray for a miracle: that the blood of Naples' patron saint, kept here in two phials, will liquefy and save Naples from any potential disaster.

According to scientists, the so-called miracle has a logical explanation. Apparently, it's all to do with thixotropy, the tendency of certain compounds to liquefy when shaken and then to return to their original form when left to stand. To verify this, however, scientists would have to analyse the blood, something the Church has effectively blocked by refusing permission to open the phials.

Beware the Evil Eye

The concept of luck plays a prominent role in the Neapolitan mindset. Curse-deterring amulets are as plentiful as crucifix pendants, and the same Neapolitan who makes the sign of the cross when passing a church will make the sign of the horns (by extending their thumb, index finger and little finger and shaking their hand to the ground) to keep the *malocchio* (evil eye) at bay.

A common belief throughout Italy, though particularly strong in the country's south, *malocchio* refers to misfortune cast upon an individual by a malevolent or envious person. In fact, Neapolitans often refer to this bad luck as *jettatura,* a derivative of the Italian verb *gettare* (to throw or cast).

Ready to deflect the negative energy is the city's most iconic amulet-souvenir: the *corno*. Usually red and shaped liked a single curved horn, its evil-busting powers are said to lie in its representation of the bull and its sexual vigour.

Another traditional, though rare, deflector of bad luck is the *'o Scartellat.* Usually an elderly man, he can occasionally be spotted burning incense through the city's older neighbourhoods, clearing the streets of bad vibes and inviting good fortune. The title itself is Neapolitan for those suffering from kyphosis (over-curvature of the upper back), as the task was once the domain of the posture challenged. According to Neapolitan lore, touching a hunchback's hump brings good luck, as does stepping in dog poop and having wine spilt on you accidentally.

Scandalous Souls

One figure who could have used some good luck was Donna Maria d'Avalos, who in October 1590 met a gruesome end in the Palazzo dei Di Sangro on Piazza San Domenico Maggiore. Her murderer was Carlo Gesualdo, Prince of Venosa and one of the late Renaissance's most esteemed composers, not to mention d'Avalos' husband. Suspecting her of infidelity, Gesualdo tricked his wife into thinking that he was away on a hunting trip. Instead, Gesualdo was waiting in the wings, ready to catch d'Avalos and her lover, Don Fabrizio Carafa, red-handed. According to eyewitnesses, Gesualdo entered the apartment with three men, shouting, 'Kill the scoundrel, along with this harlot!' Officials investigating the crime scene described finding a mortally wounded Carafa lying on the floor, covered in blood and wearing a woman's nightgown adorned with ruffs of black silk. On the bed was d'Avalos, nightgown drenched in blood and throat slit.

**Mystical
Hot Spots**

*Casa e Chiesa
di Santa Maria
Francesca delle
Cinque Piaghe*

*Cimitero delle
Fontanelle*

*Complesso
Museale di Santa
Maria delle Anime
del Purgatorio ad
Arco*

VICTORY OF THE SHRINES

It only takes a quick stroll through the *centro storico*, Quartieri Spagnoli or Sanità district to work out that small shrines are a big hit in Naples. A kitschy combo of electric votive candles, Catholic iconography and fresh or plastic flowers, they adorn everything from *palazzo* facades to courtyards and staircases. Most come with an inscription, confirming the shrine as a tribute *per grazie ricevute* (for graces received) or *ex-voto* (in fulfilment of a vow).

The popularity of the shrines can be traced back to the days of Dominican friar Gregorio Maria Rocco (1700–82). Determined to make the city's dark, crime-ridden laneways safer, he convinced the Bourbon monarch to light them up with oil lamps. The lamps were promptly trashed by the city's petty thieves, who relied on darkness to trip up their victims with rope. Thankfully, the quick-thinking friar had a better idea. Banking on the city's respect for its saints, he encouraged locals to erect illuminated shrines. The idea worked and the streets became safer, for even the toughest of petty thieves wouldn't dare upset an adored celestial idol.

Gesualdo's jealous rage would not have been helped by Carafa's enviable good looks – it's said that the younger nobleman was so devastatingly handsome that he was known around town as l'Angelo (the Angel). As a nobleman himself, Gesualdo was immune from prosecution, though a fear of retribution for the murders saw him flee to his hometown, Venosa.

In the decades that followed Gesualdo's own death, the Prince of Venosa became a semi-mythical figure, his name associated with ever-more lurid tales of bloody revenge. Some say that the Angel's death wasn't enough for the betrayed husband, who subsequently murdered his own infant son for fear that he really belonged to Carafa. According to other accounts, Gesualdo's victims included his father-in-law, who had come seeking his own revenge.

And then there is the beautiful Maria d'Avalos herself, whose scantily dressed ghost is said to haunt Piazza San Domenico Maggiore when the moon is full, desperately searching for her slaughtered sweetheart.

A later historical figure, Raimondo Di Sangro (1710–71) – a member of the noble Di Sangro family, for which the Palazzo dei Di Sangro was built – remains one of Naples' most rumour-ridden characters. Inventor, scientist, soldier and alchemist, the Prince of Sansevero came up with some nifty inventions, among them a waterproof cape for Charles III of Bourbon and a mechanical land-and-water carriage 'drawn' by life-size cork horses. He also introduced freemasonry into the Kingdom of Naples, resulting in a temporary excommunication from the Catholic Church.

Yet even a papal rethink couldn't quell the salacious stories surrounding Raimondo, which included castrating promising boy sopranos and knocking off seven cardinals to make furniture with their skin and bones. For centuries, rumours surrounded the two perfect anatomical models in the crypt of the Di Sangro funerary chapel, the Cappella Sansevero. One popular legend suggested that the bodies were those of his domestics. Even taller was the tale that the servants were far from dead when the Prince got started on the embalming. It's cruel fiction, undoubtedly, but even today the models' realistic detail leaves many questions unanswered.

So popular was the cult of the *anime pezzentelle* (poor souls) that a special tram – packed with flower-laden locals each Monday, the day dedicated to visiting souls in limbo – ran to the Cimitero delle Fontanelle. Involving the veneration of skulls (each representing a soul trapped in purgatory), the cult was banned by the Church in 1969.

The Campanian Table

Sampling Campania's larder is a mouthwatering experience. Everything seems to taste that little bit better here – the tomatoes are sweeter, the mozzarella is silkier and the *caffè* is richer and stronger. Some put it down to the rich volcanic soil, others to the region's sun and water. Complementing these natural perks is the advantage of well-honed traditions, passed down through the generations and still faithfully venerated. Here, food, identity and pride are inseparable.

A Historical Melting Pot

The region's culinary line-up is an exotic culmination of foreign influence and local resourcefulness. In its 3000-year history, Naples has played countless roles, from Roman holiday resort and medieval cultural hotspot to glittering European capital. As the foreign rulers have come and gone, they've left their mark – on the art and architecture, on the

Above *Insalata caprese* (Caprese salad)

local dialect and on the food. The ancient Greeks turned up with the olive trees, grapevines and durum wheat. Centuries later, the Byzantines and Arab traders from nearby Sicily brought in the pine nuts, almonds, raisins and honey that they used to stuff their vegetables. They also brought what was to become the mainstay of the Neapolitan diet and, in time, Italy's most famous food – pasta.

Although it was first introduced in the 12th century, pasta really took off in the 17th century when it established itself as the poor's food of choice. Requiring only a few simple ingredients – just flour and water at its most basic – pasta proved a lifesaver as the city's population exploded. The nobility, however, continued to shun pasta until Gennaro Spadaccini invented the four-pronged fork in the early 18th century.

During Naples' Bourbon period (1734–1860), two parallel gastronomic cultures developed: that of the opulent Spanish monarchy; and that of the streets, the *cucina povera* (cuisine of the poor). As much as the former was elaborate and rich, the latter was simple and healthy.

The food of the poor, the so-called *mangiafoglie* (leaf eaters), was largely based on pasta, and vegetables grown on the fertile volcanic plains around Naples. Aubergines (eggplants), artichokes, courgettes (zucchini), tomatoes and capsicum (peppers) were among the staples, while milk from sheep, cows and goats was used to make cheese. Flat breads imported from Greek and Arab lands, the forebears of pizza, were also popular. Meat and fish were expensive and reserved for special occasions.

Meanwhile, in the court kitchens, the top French cooks of the day were working to feed the insatiable appetites of the Bourbon monarchy. The headstrong queen Maria Carolina, wife of King Ferdinand I, was so impressed by her sister Marie Antoinette's court in Versailles that she asked to borrow some chefs. These Gallic imports obviously took to the Neapolitan air, creating among other things highly elaborate *timballi di pasta* (pasta pies), the *gattò di patate* (potato tart) and the iconic *babà,* a mushroom-shaped sponge cake soaked in rum and sugar.

More contentious are the origins of Naples' most famous pastry: the flaky, seashell-shaped *sfogliatella.* Filled with cinnamon-infused ricotta and candied fruit, it was created, some say, by French chefs for the king of Poland in the 18th century. Others say that it was invented by 18th-century nuns in Conca dei Marini, a small village on the Amalfi Coast. Nowadays its two most popular forms are the soft and doughy shortcrust *frolla* and the crispy, filo-style *riccia* version.

LA DOLCE VITA

Fragrant *sfogliatelle* and trickling *babà* aren't the only *pasticceria* staples you'll find on a Campanian table. Savour the sweet life with the following local favourites:

Cassatina The Neapolitan version of the Sicilian *cassata,* this minicake is made with *pan di Spagna* (sponge), ricotta and candied fruit, and covered in glazed sugar.

Pastiera Traditionally baked at Easter (but available year-round), this latticed tart is made of shortcrust pastry and filled with ricotta, candied fruit and cereals flavoured with orange-blossom water.

Torta caprese A flourless almond-and-chocolate torte from Capri. Naples *pasticceria* Scaturchio offers a twist with its lemon version.

Torta di ricotta e pera A light, tangy ricotta-and-pear torte.

Delizia al limone A light, tangy lemon cake made with *limoncello.*

Paste reali Cleverly crafted miniatures of fruit and vegetables, these sweets are made of almond paste and sugar (marzipan), and are gobbled up at Christmas.

Raffioli A yuletide biscuit made with sponge and marzipan, sprinkled with icing sugar.

Campanian Culinary Icons

Pizza

Despite the Bourbons' lavish legacy, Campania's no-nonsense attitude to food – keep it simple, keep it local and keep it coming – remains deeply rooted in the traditions of the poor. This is especially true in its predilection for pizza, a mainstay of *cucina povera* and one of the foundations on which Naples' gastronomic reputation stands.

A derivation of the flat breads of ancient Greece and Egypt, pizza was already a common street snack when the city's 16th-century Spanish occupiers introduced the tomato to Italy. The New World topping cemented pizza's popularity and in 1738 Naples' first pizzeria opened its doors on Port'Alba, where it still stands. Soon after, the city's *pizzaioli* (pizza makers) began to enjoy minor celebrity status.

To this day, the city's most famous dough-kneader remains Raffaelle Esposito, inventor of the classic pizza margherita. As the city's top *pizzaiolo*, Esposito was summoned to fire up a treat for a peckish king Umberto I and his wife, Queen Margherita, on a royal visit in 1889. Determined to impress the Italian royals, Esposito based his creation of tomato, mozzarella and basil on the red, white and green flag of the newly unified Italy. The resulting topping met with the queen's approval and was subsequently named in her honour.

More than a century later, pizza purists claim that you really can't top Esposito's classic combo when it's made by a true Neapolitan *pizzaiolo*. Not everyone is in accordance, and Italians are often split between those who favour the thin-crust Roman variant and those who go for the thicker Neapolitan version.

According to the official Associazione Verace Pizza Napoletana (True Neapolitan Pizza Association), genuine Neapolitan pizza dough must be made using highly refined type 00 wheat flour (a small dash of type 0 flour is permitted), compressed or natural yeast, salt, and water with a pH level between six and seven. While a low-speed mixer can be used for kneading the dough, only hands can be used to form the *disco di pasta* (pizza base), which should not be thicker than 3mm. The pizza itself should be cooked at 485°C (905°F) in a doubled-domed, wood-fired oven using oak, ash, beech or maple timber.

There is no seafood on a Neapolitan pizza marinara – just tomato, garlic, oregano and extra virgin olive oil. The pizza's name stems from its popularity with local fishermen, who'd take it out to sea for lunch.

Pasta

Pizza's bedfellow, pasta, arrived in Naples via Sicily, where it had been introduced by Arab merchants. The windy Campanian climate was later found to be ideal for drying pasta, and production took off in a big way, especially after the 1840 opening of Italy's first pasta plant in Torre Annunziata.

The staple itself is divided into *pasta fresca* (fresh pasta), devoured within a few days of purchase, and *pasta secca* (dried pasta), handy for long-term storage. One of the top varieties of local *pasta fresca* is Amalfi's own *scialatielli*, a flat noodle both longer and thicker than tagliatelle and often 'pinched' in the middle. Its name stems from the Neapolitan term *sciglià* (to tousle), and it's a perfect match for delicate tomato-and-seafood *sughi* (sauces).

This said, Naples is more famous for its *pasta secca,* the most obvious examples of which are spaghetti, macaroni, penne (smallish tubes cut at an angle) and rigatoni (similar to penne but with ridges on them). Made from *grano duro* (durum-wheat) flour and water, it's often served (al dente, of course) with vegetable-based *sughi,* which are generally less rich than the traditional *pasta fresca* varieties.

The best of the region's artisanal pastas comes from the small town of Gragnano, some 30km southeast of Naples. A pasta-producing hub since

THE CAMPANIAN TABLE CAMPANIAN CULINARY ICONS

Parmigiana di melanzane

the 17th century, its main street was specifically built along the sun's axis so that the pasta put out to dry by the town's *pastifici* (pasta factories) would reap a full day's sunshine.

As for the queen of the region's pasta dishes, it's hard to beat the mouth-watering *pasta al forno* (baked pasta), a decadent combination of macaroni, tomato sauce, mozzarella and, depending on the recipe, hard-boiled egg, meatball and sausage. No less than a gastronomic 'event', it's often cooked for Sunday lunch and other special occasions.

Vegetables & Fruit

Poverty and sunshine also helped develop Campania's prowess with vegetables. Dishes like *zucchine fritte* (panfried courgettes), *parmigiana di melanzane* (fried aubergines layered with hard-boiled eggs, mozzarella, onion, tomato sauce and basil) and *peperoni sotto aceto* (marinated peppers) are common features of both antipasto buffets and the domestic kitchen table.

The word *melanzana* (aubergine or eggplant) comes from 'mela insana', meaning crazy apple. In Latin it was called *solanum insanum*, as it was thought to cause madness.

Some of the country's finest produce is grown in the mineral-rich volcanic soil of Mt Vesuvius and its surrounding plain, including tender *carciofi* (artichokes) and *cachi* (persimmons), as well as Campania's unique green *friarielli* – a bitter broccoli-like vegetable *saltata in padella* (pan fried), spiked with *peperoncino* (red chilli) and often served with diced *salsiccia di maiale* (pork sausage).

In June, Slow Food fans should look out for *albicocche vesuviana* (Vesuvian apricots), known locally as *crisommole* and given IGP (Indicazione Geografica Protetta; Protected Denomination of Origin) status.

DOP (Denominazione di Origine Protetta; Protected Designation of Origin) status is granted to another lauded local, the *pomodoro San Marzano* (San Marzano plum tomato). Grown near the small Vesuvian town of the same name, it's Italy's most famous and cultivated tomato, best known for its low acidity and intense, sweet flavour. Its sauce, *conserva di pomodoro,* is made from super-ripe tomatoes, cut and left to dry in the sun for at least two days to concentrate the flavour. This is the sauce that adorns so many of Naples' signature pasta dishes, including *spaghetti alla puttanesca,* a lip-smacking blend of tomatoes, black olives, capers, anchovies and (in some cases) a dash of *peperoncino.*

A richer tomato-based classic with aristocratic origins is the Neapolitan *ragù,* whose name stems from the French *ragoût.* A tomato-and-meat sauce, it is left to simmer for about six hours before being served with macaroni.

Mozzarella di Bufala

So you think the *fior di latte* (cow-milk mozzarella) served in Capri's *insalata caprese* (a salad made of mozzarella, tomatoes, basil and olive oil) is delicious? Taste Campania's *mozzarella di bufala* (buffalo-milk mozzarella) and you'll move on to an entirely different level of deliciousness. Made on the plains surrounding Caserta and Paestum, it's best eaten when freshly made that morning, its rich, sweet flavour and luscious texture nothing short of a revelation. You can find it fresh at *latterie* (dairies), sold lukewarm in a plastic bag filled with a slightly cloudy liquid: the run-off from the mozzarella making. You'll also find it served in trattorias (informal restaurants) and restaurants across the region.You'll even find dedicated mozzarella eateries in Naples and Sorrento; Muu Muuzzarella Lounge (p87) and Inn Bufalito (p168), respectively.

As for that irresistible taste, it's the high fat content and buffalo-milk protein that give the cheese the distinctive, pungent flavour so often absent in the versions sold abroad. Even more luscious is the *burrata,* a mozzarella filled with a wickedly buttery cream. *Burrata* itself was invented in the neighbouring region of Puglia.

Campania's most decadent mozzarella dish is *mozzarella in carrozza.* Literally translating as 'mozzarella in a carriage', it sees fresh mozzarella sliced, sandwiched in white bread, coated in flour and egg yolk, and fried to golden perfection. Although many Italian pizzerias make it using cheaper *fior di latte* these days, the classic Campanian recipe demands the use of *mozzarella di bufala,* whose higher fat and lower water content prevents the cheese from seeping out when fried. The classic recipe also specifies the use of stale bread, bought straight from the *panificio* (bakery).

Although some producers find these official Italian classifications unduly costly and creatively constraining, the DOCG (Denominazione di Origine Controllata e Garantita) and DOC (Denominazione di Origine Controllata) designations are awarded to food and wine that meet regional quality-control standards.

THE CAMPANIAN TABLE CAMPANIAN CULINARY ICONS

APPETISING READS

Pique your appetite with the following insightful guides to Campania's culinary riches:

➡ *Italian Kitchen: Family Recipes from the Old Country* (David Ruggerio; 2000) Filled with the secrets of a Neapolitan kitchen.

➡ *Foods of Naples and Campania* (Giuliano Bugialli; 2003) A culinary journey through the region led by a prolific Italian cookery writer.

➡ *La Pizza: The True Story from Naples* (Nikko Amandonico, Natalia Borri and Ian Thomson; 2001) Sumptuously illustrated history of pizza, set in Naples' kaleidoscopic streets.

➡ *Naples at Table: Cooking in Campania* (Arthur Schwartz; 2013) Local food trivia and 250 recipes.

➡ *The Food and Wine Guide to Naples and Campania* (Carla Capalbo; 2005) An encyclopedic guide to regional food producers and eateries.

The Campanian Vine Revival

Revered by the ancients and snubbed by modern critics, Campanian wine is once again hot property, with a new generation of wine-makers creating some brilliant drops. Lauded producers such as Feudi di San Gregorio, Mastroberardino, Villa Matilde, Pietracupa and Terredora di Paolo have returned to their roots, cultivating ancient grape varieties like the red Aglianico (thought to be the oldest cultivated grape in Italy) and the whites Falanghina, Fiano and Greco (all growing long before Mt Vesuvius erupted in AD 79). Keeping them company is a lengthening list of reputable organic and biodynamic wineries, among them Terre Stregate, I Cacciagalli, Colli di Lapio and Cautiero. It's all a far cry from 1990, when wine critic Burton Anderson humiliatingly wrote that Campania's noteworthy winemakers could be 'counted on one's fingers'.

Campania's three main wine-producing zones are centred on Avellino, Benevento and Caserta. And it's in the high hills east of Avellino that the region's best red is produced. Taurasi – a full-bodied Aglianico wine – is considered one of southern Italy's finest drops. Sometimes called the Barolo of the south, its notes range from dark berries and leather to roasted coffee and Mediterranean herbs. The wine is also one of only four in the region to carry Italy's top quality rating, DOCG (Denominazione di Origine Controllata e Garantita; Controlled and Guaranteed Denomination of Origin). The other three wines to share this honour are Aglianico del Taburno, a full-bodied red from the Benevento area, as well as Fiano di Avellino and Greco di Tufo, both whites and both from the Avellino area. The province of Caserta is well known for producing Falerno del Massico, a DOC-designated wine grown in the very same area as Falernum, the most celebrated wine in ancient Roman times.

Other vino-producing areas include the Campi Flegrei (home to DOC-labelled Piedirosso and Falanghina vines), Ischia (whose wines were the first to receive DOC status) and the Cilento region, home to the DOC Cilento *bianco* (Cilento white) and to the Aglianico Paestum. Mt Vesuvius' most famous drop is the Lacryma Christi (Tears of Christ), a blend of locally grown Falanghina, Piedirosso and Coda di Volpe grapes.

And while vines also lace the Amalfi Coast, the real speciality here are fruit and herbal liqueurs, with flavours spanning mandarin, myrtle and wild fennel, and the ubiquitous *limoncello* – a simple yet potent concoction of lemon peel, water, sugar and alcohol traditionally served in a frozen glass after dinner. *Limoncello* fans take note: the greener the tinge, the better the drop.

During spring, summer and early autumn, towns across southern Italy celebrate *sagre*, the festivals of local foods in season. Scan www.prodottitipici.com/sagre (in Italian) for a lip-smacking list.

TABLE RULES

➡ Make eye contact when toasting and never clink using plastic cups; it's bad luck!

➡ Pasta is eaten with a fork only.

➡ Bread is not eaten with pasta – unless you're cleaning up the sauce afterwards.

➡ It's fine to eat pizza with your hands.

➡ If in doubt, dress smartly.

➡ If invited to someone's home, take a tray of *dolci* (sweets) from a *pasticceria* (pastry shop).

Limoncello

Pick Your Plonk

To help you navigate Campania's ever-growing wine list, here are some of the region's top drops:

Taurasi A DOCG since 1991, this dry, intense red goes well with barbecued meat.

Fiano di Avellino A dry, fresh DOCG white that's one of Campania's historic wines. Ideal with seafood.

Greco di Tufo Another longstanding favourite, this DOCG white comes in both dry and sparkling versions.

Aglianico del Taburno A rich, dense DOCG red that pairs perfectly with succulent cuts of meat.

Falerno del Massico Its red and white versions originate from the volcanic slopes of Mt Massico in the north of the region.

Cult of Caffè

In Naples, velvety, lingering espresso is a birthright. In most cases, it's also a quick, unceremonious swill standing at local bars. But don't be fooled: the speed with which it's consumed does not diminish the importance of its quality.

According to Neapolitans, it's the local water that makes their coffee stronger and better than any other in Italy. To drink it like a local, keep milky options like caffè latte and cappuccino for the morning. After 11am, espresso and *caffè macchiato* (an espresso with a drop of milk) are the norm. For a weaker coffee (shame on you!), ask for a *caffè lungo* (a watered-down espresso in a larger cup) or a *caffè americano* (an even weaker version of the *caffè lungo*).

Don't believe the hype about espresso: one diminutive cup packs less of a caffeine wallop than a large cup of French-pressed or American-brewed coffee. It also leaves drinkers less jittery.

Vineyard of Greco di Tufo vines

Another ritual is the free *bicchiere d'acqua* (glass of water), offered either *liscia* (uncarbonated) or *frizzante* (sparkling) with your coffee. Drink it before your coffee to cleanse your palate. Just don't be surprised if you're not automatically offered one. After all, what would a heathen *straniero* (foreigner) know about coffee? Don't be shy – smile sweetly and ask for *un bicchiere d'acqua, per favore.*

Courses & Tours

The excellent food and travel portal www.deliciousitaly.com lists culinary tours and courses. Another useful website for lovers of Italian food and wine is www.gamberorosso.it, which offers a plethora of information on Italian food, wine, culinary events and courses.

Eating well is a Campanian obsession, and the region's cornucopia of speciality food stores, markets and time-tested eateries may well ignite a desire to delve into local culinary traditions and secrets. If so, the region has an ever-growing number of cooking courses, many of which are single-session courses aimed at visitors. In Naples, Toffini Academy (p82) offers cooking lessons in an intimate, contemporary setting. Courses are available in Italian and English. Across town, sustainability-focused **Centro di Alimentazione Consapevole** (Map p58; ☑338 6269827; www.centrodialimentazioneconsapevole.it; Vico San Pietro 6; private lesson incl meal from €50 per person; ⊙varies; ⓂDante) offers bespoke private courses for groups of five or more, with enlightened themes like gluten-free cooking and vegan pastry making. For gluttons who prefer sampling to stirring, Culinary Backstreets (p82) offers food-themed walking tours of the appetite-whetting *centro storico*. Further afield, a number of highly regarded restaurants also offer cooking courses. Among these is Positano's celebrated Donna Rosa (p180) and Casa Mele (p179), as well as Sant'Agata sui due Golfi's two-starred Michelin hotspot Ristorante Don Alfonso 1890 (p174).

Glossary

Places to Eat & Drink

enoteca	wine bar
friggitoria	fried-food kiosk
osteria	informal restaurant
pasticceria	patisserie; pastry shop
ristorante	restaurant
trattoria	informal restaurant

At the Table

cameriere/a	waiter (m/f)
carta dei vini	wine list
conto	bill/cheque
spuntini	snacks
tovagliolo	napkin/serviette
vegetaliano/a	vegan (m/f)
vegetariano/a	vegetarian (m/f)

Staples

aglio	garlic
fior di latte	cow-milk mozzarella
insalata	salad
limone	lemon
mozzarella di bufala	buffalo-milk mozzarella
oliva	olive
panna	cream
peperoncino	chilli
pizza margherita	pizza topped with tomato, mozzarella and basil
pizza marinara	pizza topped with tomato, garlic, oregano and olive oil
rucola	rocket

Fish & Seafood

acciughe	anchovies
carpaccio	thin slices of raw fish (or meat)
granchio	crab
merluzzo	cod
pesce spada	swordfish
polpi	octopus
sarde	sardines
seppia	cuttlefish
sgombro	mackerel
vongole	clams

Meat

bistecca	steak
capretto	kid (goat)

coniglio	rabbit
fegato	liver
prosciutto cotto	cooked ham
prosciutto crudo	cured ham
salsiccia	sausage
vitello	veal

Cooking Methods

arrosto/a	roasted
bollito/a	boiled
cotto/a	cooked
crudo/a	raw
fritto/a	fried
alla griglia	grilled (broiled)

Fruit

ciliegia	cherry
fragole	strawberries
melone	cantaloupe; musk melon; rock melon
pera	pear

Vegetables

asparagi	asparagus
carciofi	artichokes
fagiolini	green beans
finocchio	fennel
friarielli	Neapolitan broccoletti
melanzane	aubergine; eggplant
peperoni	capsicums; peppers
tartufo	truffle

Gelato

amarena	wild cherry
bacio	chocolate and hazelnut
cioccolata	chocolate
cono	cone
coppa	cup
crema	cream
frutta di bosco	fruit of the forest (wild berries)
nocciola	hazelnut
vaniglia	vanilla
zuppa inglese	'English soup', trifle

Drinks

amaretto	almond-flavoured liqueur
amaro	dark liqueur prepared from herbs
espresso	short black coffee

Above Reggia di Caserta (p70)

Architecture

Campania's architectural cachet is epic and illustrious. Given the region's rich history, that makes perfect sense. Millennia of political conquests and struggles, of human ingenuity, creativity and ambition, have bestowed the place with a built legacy few corners of Europe can match. This is a land of muscular Greek temples and lavish Roman villas, of storybook Angevin castles, medieval Moorish cloisters and oversized Bourbon palaces. It's an overwhelming list, so why not start with the undisputed highlights?

Graeco-Roman Legacies

The breadth and depth of Campania's ancient architecture is superlative, its jumble of temples, towns and engineering feats delivering a crash course in classical aesthetics and talent.

The Greeks invented the Doric architectural order and used it to great effect at the 6th-century-BC temples of Paestum (p203), confirming not only the ancient Greeks' power but also their penchant for harmonious proportion. In Naples, Piazza Bellini (p65) has remnants of the city's 4th-century-BC walls, while traces of Greek fortifications linger at the acropolis of Cuma.

Having learned a few valuable lessons from the Greeks, the Romans refined architecture to such a degree that their building techniques, designs and mastery of harmonious proportion underpin most of the world's architecture and urban design to this day. The Greeks may have created Naples' first aqueduct, but it was the Romans who extended and improved it. The aqueduct led to the glorious Piscina Mirabilis (p107), a cathedral-like cistern once complete with sophisticated hydraulics.

The space below Pozzuoli's Anfiteatro Flavio (p102) is also testament to Roman ingenuity. Here, an elliptical corridor is flanked by a series of low *cellae* set on two floors and capped by trapdoors that open straight to the arena above. The *cellae* on the upper floor held the caged wild animals used in the stadium games. Hoisted up through the trap doors, the animals could then spring immediately from darkness into the bright light of the arena with rock-star effect.

Across the bay, it's a case of *Vogue Ancient Living* in Pompeii, home to many of Italy's best-preserved classical abodes. Here, buildings like the Villa dei Misteri (p113), the Casa del Fauno (p113) and the Casa del Menandro (p113) illustrate the trademarks of classical domestic architecture, from an inward-facing design (for maximum privacy) to the light-filled atrium (the focal point of domestic life) and the ornamental peristyle (colonnaded garden courtyard). The finest villas were adorned with whimsical mythological frescoes, stunningly exemplified at the Villa dei Misteri, as well as Villa Oplontis (p117), located in nearby Torre Annunziata.

Greek geographer, philosopher and historian Strabo (63 BC–AD 24) wrote that the stretch of Italian coast from Capo Miseno (in the Campi Flegrei) to Sorrento resembled a single city, so strewn was it with elegant villas and suburbs sprawling from central Naples.

ARCHITECTURE SPEAK: 101

Do you know your transept from your triclinium? Demystify some common architectural terms with the following bite-size list:

Apse Usually a large recess or niche built on a semicircular or polygonal ground plan and vaulted with a half dome. In a church or temple, it may include an altar.

Baldachin (Baldacchino) A permanent, often elaborately decorated canopy of wood or stone above an altar, throne, pulpit or statue.

Balustrade A stone railing formed of a row of posts (called balusters) topped by a continuous coping, and commonly flanking baroque stairs, balconies and terraces.

Impluvium A small ornamental pool, often used as the centrepiece of atriums in ancient Roman houses.

Latrine A Roman-era public convenience, lined with rows of toilet seats and often adorned with frescoes and marble.

Narthex A portico or lobby at the front of an early Christian church or basilica.

Necropolis Burial ground outside the city walls in antiquity and the early Christian era.

Oratory A small room or chapel in a church reserved for private prayer.

Tablinum The main room of the house in Roman times, used to receive guests and clients.

Transept A section of a church running at right angles to the main body of the church.

Triclinium The dining room in a Roman house.

Anfiteatro Flavio (p102), Pozzuoli

Medieval Icons

Following on from the Byzantine style and its mosaic-encrusted churches was Romanesque, a style that found four regional forms in Italy: Lombard, Pisan, Florentine and Sicilian Norman. All displayed an emphasis on width and the horizontal lines of a building rather than its height, and featured church groups with *campanili* (bell towers) and baptisteries that were separate to the church. Surfacing in the 11th century, the Sicilian Norman style encompassed an exotic mix of Norman, Saracen and Byzantine influences, from marble columns to Islamic-inspired pointed arches to glass tesserae detailing. This style is clearly visible in the two-toned masonry and 13th-century bell tower of the Cattedrale di Sant'Andrea (p183) in Amalfi. It's also echoed in the 12th-century bell tower of Salerno's Duomo (p199), not to mention in its bronze, Byzantine-style doors and Arabesque portico arches.

For Naples, its next defining architectural period would arrive with the rule of the French House of Anjou in the 13th century. As it was the new capital of the Angevin kingdom, suitably ambitious plans were announced for the city. Land was reclaimed, and bold new churches and monasteries built. This was the age of the 'Gothic', a time of flying buttresses and grotesque gargoyles. While enthusiastically embraced by the French, Germans and Spanish, the Italians preferred a more restrained and sombre interpretation of the style, defined by wide walls, a single nave, a trussed ceiling and horizontal bands. One of its finest examples is Naples' Basilica di San Lorenzo Maggiore (p61), its pared-back elegance also echoed in the city's Chiesa di San Pietro a Maiella (p66) and Basilica di Santa Chiara (p57).

In *Medieval Naples: An Architectural & Urban History 400–1400*, Caroline Bruzelius and William Tronzo deliver a thoroughly researched review of Naples' architecture and urban development from late antiquity to the high and late Middle Ages. Topics include the Angevins' ambitious reconfiguration of the city.

Peristyle (courtyard) of Casa del Menandro (p113), Pompeii

That both the facade of the Basilica di San Lorenzo Maggiore and the coffered ceiling of the Chiesa di San Pietro a Maiella are later baroque add-ons reminds us that much of the period's original architecture was altered over successive centuries. A case in point is the Chiesa di San Domenico Maggiore (p60), whose chintzy gilded interior betrays a neo-Gothic makeover. The church's main entrance, in a courtyard off Vico San Domenico, also bears witness to a series of touch-ups. Here, a delicate 14th-century portal is framed by an 18th-century *pronaos* (the space in front of the body of a temple) surmounted by a 19th-century window, and flanked by two Renaissance-era chapels and a baroque bell tower. Indeed, even the Angevins' Castel Nuovo (p71) wasn't spared, with only a few sections of the original structure surviving, among them the Palatina Chapel. The castle's striking white triumphal-arch centrepiece – a 15th-century addition – is considered one of Naples' most notable early-Renaissance creations.

The Baroque

While the Renaissance all but transformed Italy's north, its impact on southern streetscapes was much less dramatic. In Naples, one of the few buildings to page the Florentine style is the Palazzo Cuomo, now home to the Museo Civico Filangieri (p64). Featuring typically Tuscan rusticated walls, the late-15th-century building was created for wealthy Florentine merchant Angelo Como ('Cuomo' in Neapolitan) before finding new life as a monastery in 1587.

Yet, what Naples missed out on during the Renaissance it more than made up for in the baroque of the 17th and 18th centuries. Finally, the city had found an aesthetic to suit its exhibitionist streak: a style that celebrated the bold, the gold and the over-the-top. Neapolitan baroque rose out of heady times. Under 17th-century Spanish rule, the city became one of Europe's biggest. Swelling crowds and counter-Reformation fervour sparked a building boom, with taller-than-ever *palazzi* (mansions) mixing it with glittering showcase churches. Ready to lavish the city with new landmarks was a brash, arrogant and fiery league of architects and artists, who brushed aside tradition and rewrote the rulebooks.

A Neapolitan Twist

Like the Neapolitans themselves, the city's baroque architecture is idiosyncratic and independently minded. Architects working in Naples at the time often ignored the trends sweeping through Rome and northern Italy. Pilasters may have been all the rage in late-17th-century Roman churches, but in Naples, architects like Dionisio Lazzari (1617–89) and Giovanni Battista Nauclerio (1666–1739) went against the grain, reasserting the value of the column and effectively paving the way for Luigi Vanvitelli's columnar architecture and the neoclassicism that would spread across Europe in the mid-18th century.

In domestic Neapolitan architecture, a *palazzo*'s *piano nobile* (principal floor) was often on the 2nd floor (not the 1st floor, as was common), encouraging the creation of the epic *porte-cochères* (coach porticos) that distinguish so many Neapolitan buildings.

Equally grandiose were the city's open staircases, which reached perfection in the hands of Naples-born architect Ferdinando Sanfelice (1675–1748). His double-ramped creations in the Palazzo dello Spagnuolo (p81) and the Palazzo Sanfelice (p81) exemplify his ability to transform humble domestic staircases into operatic statements.

Another star on the building scene was Domenico Antonio Vaccaro (1678–1745), who originally trained as a painter under Francesco Solimena. Vaccaro's architectural legacy includes the redesign of the cloisters at the Basilica di Santa Chiara (p57), the decoration of three chapels of the church inside the Certosa di San Martino (p76), and the design of the soaring *guglia* (obelisk) on Piazza San Domenico Maggiore. With the help of his father, Lorenzo (himself a renowned sculptor), Vaccaro also contributed a bronze monument dedicated to Philip V of Spain, which topped the Guglia dell'Immacolata (p57) on Piazza del Gesù Nuovo. Alas, the work was later toppled by Charles III and replaced with a much less controversial Madonna, which still stands.

Marble Mavericks

The Piazza del Gesù Nuovo is one of the very few sweeping squares in the city, a fact that led many baroque architects to invest less time on show-stopping exteriors and more time on what the people could actually see: the interiors. A case in point is the Chiesa di San Gregorio Armeno (p61), whose facade gives little indication of the opulence glowing inside.

Indoor splendour also defines the on-site church at the Certosa di San Martino, its glorious inlaid marble a common feature of Neapolitan baroque. This mix-and-match marble is the work of Cosimo Fanzago (1591–1678), the undisputed master of the craft. A revered sculptor, decorator and architect, the fiery Fanzago would cut the stone into the most whimsical of forms, producing a luscious, polychromatic spectacle that is one of Italy's true baroque highlights. The church is not Fanzago's only contribution at the Certosa; the artist had previously completed the charterhouse's Chiostro Grande (Great Cloister), adding to Giovanni Antonio Dosio's original design the statues above the portico, the ornate corner portals and the white balustrade around the monks' cemetery.

Fanzago took the art of marble inlay to a whole new level of complexity, as also seen in the Cappella di Sant'Antonio di Padova and the Cappella Cacace, both inside the Basilica di San Lorenzo Maggiore (p61).

ARCHITECTURE THE BAROQUE

Best Baroque Surprises

Church, Certosa e Museo di San Martino, Naples

Farmacia Storica, Ospedale degli Incurabili, Naples

Sacristy, Basilica di San Paolo Maggiore, Naples

Palazzo dello Spagnuolo, Naples

Top Chiesa di San Domenico Maggiore (p60), Naples

Bottom Chiesa del Gesù Nuovo (p57), Naples

THE NOT-SO-BRILLIANT LIFE OF COSIMO FANZAGO

Like many stars of the Neapolitan baroque, Cosimo Fanzago (1591–1678) was not actually Neapolitan by birth. Born in the small town of Clusone in northern Italy, the budding sculptor-decorator-architect ventured to Naples at the tender age of 17 and quickly earned a reputation for his imaginative way with marble. Alas, it wasn't the only reputation he acquired. According to legal documents, Fanzago was partial to the odd violent outburst, attacking his mason Nicola Botti in 1628 and reputedly knocking him off completely two years later. His alleged involvement in the 1647 Masaniello revolt saw him flee to Rome for a decade to avoid the death sentence on his head.

Yet Fanzago's ultimate downfall would come from his notorious workplace practices, which included missing deadlines, disregarding clients' wishes, and using works created for one client for completing other clients' projects. Responsible for giving him his enviable commissions at the Certosa di San Martino (p76), the Carthusian monks would ultimately learn to loathe the man revamping their hilltop home, suing the artist in a long, arduous legal battle that ultimately affected Fanzago's health and the number of his commissions. By the time of his death in 1678, the greatest baroque master Naples had ever seen cut a poor, neglected figure.

The latter chapel is considered to be his most lavish expression of the form. His altarpieces were equally influential. Exemplified by his beautiful high altar in the Chiesa di San Domenico Maggiore (p60), his creations inspired the work of other sculptors, including Bartolomeo and Pietro Ghetti's altar in the Chiesa di San Pietro a Maiella (p66), Bartolomeo Ghetti and siblings Giuseppe and Bartolomeo Gallo's altar in the Chiesa del Gesù Nuovo (p57), and Giuseppe Mozzetti's exquisite choir in the Chiesa di Santa Maria del Carmine (p65).

Another chisel-wielding genius was Giuseppe Sanmartino (1720–93). Arguably the finest sculptor of his time, his ability to turn cold stone into sensual, soul-stirring revelations is exemplified in the baroque **Complesso Monumentale dei Girolamini** (Map p58; Via Duomo 142, Naples; adult/reduced €5/2.50; ⌚8.30am-7pm Mon, Tue, Thu & Fri, to 2pm Sat & Sun). It's in this church that you'll find his celebrated pair of Carrara-marble angels, their curls and robes imbued with extraordinary softness and fluidity. Sanmartino's talent for breathing life into his creations won him a legion of fans, among them the city's Bourbon rulers and alchemist prince Raimondo di Sangro. The latter's family chapel, the Cappella Sansevero (p55), is home to Sanmartino's undisputed masterpiece, the 1753 *Cristo velato* (Veiled Christ). Considered the apogee of his technical brilliance, it's quite possibly the greatest sculpture of 18th-century Europe. Even the great neoclassical sculptor Antonio Canova wished it were his own.

While Greek Doric columns are short, heavy and baseless, with plain, round capitals (tops), Ionic columns are slender and fluted, with a large base and two opposed *volutes* (or scrolls) below the capital. Corinthian columns are fancier still, with ornate capitals featuring scrolls and acanthus leaves.

End of an Era

Canova may have wished the same of the Reggia di Caserta (p70). Officially known as Caserta's Palazzo Reale, the epic royal residence was one of several grand-scale legacies of the Bourbon years. Designed by late-baroque architect Luigi Vanvitelli (1700–73), son of Dutch landscape artist Gaspar van Wittel (1653–1736), the Reggia not only outsized Versailles but would go down in history as Italy's great baroque epilogue.

Ironically, while it does feature many of the genre's theatrical hallmarks, from acres of inlaid marble to allegorical statues set into wall niches, its late-baroque style echoed a classical style more indebted to contemporary French and Spanish models than to the exuberant playfulness of the homegrown brand. According to the Bourbon blue bloods, the over-the-top Neapolitan baroque was *plutôt vulgaire* (rather vulgar). And as the curtain began to fall on Naples' baroque heyday, a more restrained neoclassicism was waiting in the wings.

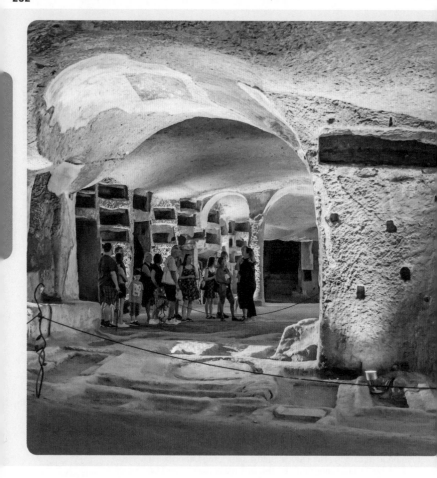

The Subterranean City

Sacred shrines, secret passageways, forgotten burial crypts: it might sound like the set of an Indiana Jones film, but we're actually talking about what lurks beneath Naples' loud and busy streets. Subterranean Naples is one of the world's most thrilling urban other-worlds: a silent, mostly undiscovered sprawl of cathedral-like cisterns, pin-width conduits, catacombs and ancient ruins. Speleologists (cave specialists) estimate that about 60% of Neapolitans live and work above this network, known in Italian as the *sottosuolo* (underground).

An Action-Packed Past

Above Catacombe di San Gennaro (p78), Naples

Since the end of WWII, some 700 cavities have been discovered, from original Greek-era grottoes to palaeo-Christian burial chambers and Bourbon royal escape routes. According to the experts, this is simply a prelude, with another 2 million sq m of troglodytic treats still to unfurl.

Naples' dedicated caving geeks are quick to tell you that their underworld is one of the largest and oldest on earth. Sure, Paris might claim a catacomb or two, but its subterranean offerings don't come close to this giant's 2500-year history.

And what a history it is: from buried martyrs and foreign invaders to wife-snatching spirits and drug-concocting mobsters. Naples' most famous saint, San Gennaro, was interred in the Catacombe di San Gennaro (p78) in the 5th century BC. A millennium later, in AD 536, Belisario and his troops caught Naples by surprise by storming the city through its ancient tunnels. According to legend, Alfonso of Aragon used the same trick in 1442, undermining the city walls by using an underground passageway leading into a tailor's shop and straight into town.

Conversely, the 18th-century Bourbons had an escape route built beneath the Palazzo Reale di Capodimonte (p54). A century later they commissioned a tunnel to connect their central Palazzo Reale (p66) to their barracks in Chiaia: a perfect crowd-free route for troops or a fleeing royal family.

Even the city's underworld has got in on the act. In 1992 Naples' dreaded Stolder clan was busted for running a subterranean drug lab, with escape routes heading straight to the clan boss's pad.

Top Subterranean Sites

....

Catacombe di San Gennaro

....

Napoli Sotterranea

....

Catacombe di San Gaudioso

....

Complesso Monumentale di San Lorenzo Maggiore

....

Galleria Borbonica

From Ancient Aqueduct to Underground Tip

While strategic tunnels and sacred catacombs are important features of Naples' light-deprived other-world, the city's subterranean backbone is its ancient aqueduct system. Naples' first plumbing masterpiece was built by Greek settlers, who channelled water from the slopes of Mt Vesuvius into the city's cisterns. The cisterns themselves were created as builders dug out the pliable *tufo* sandstone on which the city stands. At street level, well shafts allowed citizens to lower their buckets and quench their thirst.

Not to be outdone, the Romans wowed the plebs (abbreviated term for 'plebeians', common Roman citizens) with their new, improved 70km aqueduct, transporting water from the River Serino near Avellino to Naples, Pozzuoli and Baia, where it filled the enormous Piscina Mirabilis.

The next update came in 1629, with the opening of the Spanish-commissioned 'Carmignano' aqueduct. Expanded in 1770, it finally met its Waterloo in the 1880s, when cholera outbreaks heralded the building of a more modern pressurised version.

Dried up and defunct, the ancient cisterns went from glorious feats of ancient engineering to handy in-house rubbish tips. As refuse clogged the well shafts, access to the *sottosuolo* became ever more difficult and, within a few generations, the subterranean system that had nourished the city was left bloated and forgotten.

The WWII Revival

It would take the wail of air-raid sirens to reunite the city's sunlit and subterranean sides once more. With Allied air attacks looming, Mussolini's UMPA (civil-defence program) ordered that the cisterns and former quarries be turned into civilian shelters. The lakes of rubbish were compacted and covered, old passageways were enlarged, toilets were built and new staircases were erected. As bombs showered the city above, tens of thousands took refuge in the dark, damp spaces below.

Underground passage, Naples

The fear, frustration and anger of those days lives on in the historic graffiti that covers some of the old shelters, from hand-drawn caricatures of Hitler and 'Il Duce' to poignant messages like *'Mamma, non piangere'* (Mum, don't cry). Many families spent weeks living underground, often emerging to find their homes and neighbourhoods nothing more than rubble. For the many whose homes were destroyed, these subterranean hideouts became semipermanent dwellings. Entire families cohabited in cisterns, partitioning their makeshift abodes with bedsheets and furnishing them with the odd ramshackle bed. Traces of this rudimentary domestication survive to this day, from tiled 'kitchen' walls and showers, to evidence of DC battery power.

Alas, once rebuilding began, the aqueducts once again became subterranean dumpsters, with everything from wartime rubble to scooters and Fiats thrown down the shafts. And in a case of history repeating itself, the historic labyrinth and its millennia-old secrets faded from the city's collective memory.

Naples' original Graeco-Roman city was covered by a great mudslide in the 6th century. The excavations to open the Roman market beneath the Complesso Monumentale di San Lorenzo Maggiore took 25 years.

Speleological Saviours & Rediscovered Secrets

Thankfully, all is not lost, as a passionate league of professional and volunteer speleologists continues to rediscover and render accessible long-lost sites and secrets – a fact not overlooked by the likes of *National Geographic* and the BBC, both of which have documented the work of these subterranean experts.

Indeed, speleological associations like NUg (Napoli Underground group) play a vital role in uncovering and preserving Naples' heritage.

Archaeological excavation, Complesso Monumentale di San Lorenzo Maggiore (p61), Naples

Each new passageway or cistern discovered unlocks another piece of the city's complex historical puzzle. In one case, an unusual-looking staircase behind an old chicken coop in Arenella led speleologist Fulvio Salvi to discover frescoed depictions of the ancient Egyptian deities Isis, Osiris and Seth. The site is believed to be part of the Secretorum Naturae Accademia, the laboratory used by scholar, alchemist and playwright Giambattista della Porta (c 1535–1615) after the Inquisition ordered an end to his experiments.

Yet even such rare and fascinating finds are not enough to secure the protection and preservation of the city's *sottosuolo*. The golden era of the 1990s, which saw the city council provide generous funding to speleological research, has since been supplanted by standard Italian bureaucracy and political bickering. As a result, many precious sites uncovered by the city's speleologists remain indefinitely abandoned, with little money to salvage and restore them.

The easiest way for visitors to experience the city's buried secrets is on a guided tour at Galleria Borbonica (p73) or Napoli Sotterranea (p66). The latter takes a steady stream of visitors below the *centro storico* for a look at remnants of a Roman theatre frequented by madcap Emperor Nero, as well as to a cistern returned to its original, water-filled splendour. Meanwhile at the Galleria Borbonica, visitors are led on a tour of the Bourbon tunnel running beneath Mt Echia (home to Naples' earliest settlement). Aside from easy walking tours, the Galleria Borbonica also offers thrilling 90-minute speleological tours for adults, which take in unexplored nooks few locals will ever see. The speleological tour can be conducted in English for groups of at least five.

MYTH OF THE LITTLE MONK

It's only natural that a world as old, dark and mysterious as Naples' *sottosuolo* should breed a few fantastical urban myths. The best known and most loved is that of the *municello* (little monk), a Neapolitan leprechaun of sorts known for being both naughty and nice. Said to live in a wine cellar, the hooded sprite was reputedly a regular sight in the 18th and 19th centuries. Some spoke of him as a kindred soul, a bearer of gifts and good fortune. To others, the *municello* spelt trouble, sneaking into homes to misplace objects, steal precious jewels and seduce the odd lonely housewife.

While a handful of Neapolitans still curse the imp whenever the car keys go missing, most now believe that the cheeky *municello* was actually the city's long-gone *pozzari* (aqueduct cleaners). Descending daily down the wells, the small-statured *pozzari* fought off the damp, cool conditions with a heavy, hooded mantel. Naturally, most would pop back up for a breath of fresh air, sometimes finding themselves in people's very homes. For some, the temptation of scouring drawers in search of valuables was all too strong. For others, it was a way of making new acquaintances – or of bringing a little company to the odd neglected homemaker. Regardless, it quickly becomes clear just how the tale of the 'mini monk' began.

Across town is the **Museo del Sottosuolo** (Museum of the Underground; Map p80; ☏081 863 15 81; www.ilmuseodelsottosuolo.it; Piazza Cavour 140; adult/reduced €10/7; ⊘varies; Ⓜ Piazza Cavour, Museo), a DIY ode to speleologists founded by veteran cave crusader Clemente Esposito, lovingly nicknamed il Papa del sottosuolo (the Pope of the Underground) in local speleological circles. Hidden away on Piazza Cavour, between the *centro storico* and the Sanità district, its series of restored underground cisterns can also be explored on a guided tour, booked ahead on the museum website. The space is also an evocative setting for theatrical performances.

To dig even deeper into the region's subterranean scene, check out the information-packed www.napoliunderground.org.

The Camorra

Alongside Calabria's 'Ndrangheta, Sicily's Cosa Nostra and Puglia's Sacra Corona Unita, Campania's Camorra is one of Italy's four main organised-crime syndicates. Its illegal dealings in drug and firearms trafficking, prostitution, waste disposal, racketeering and counterfeiting secure the organisation billions of euros annually. Even more astounding is the human cost: in the past 30 years, the Camorra has claimed more than 3000 lives, more than any other Mafia in the country.

Origins & Evolution

It is widely believed that the Camorra emerged from the criminal gangs operating among the poor in late-18th-century Naples. The organisation would get its first big break after the failed revolution of 1848. Desperate to overthrow Ferdinand II, pro-constitutional liberals turned to *camorristi* (Camorra members) to help garner the support of the masses. The Camorra's political influence was sealed. Given a serious blow by Mussolini, the organisation would get its second wind from the invading Allied forces of 1943, which turned to the flourishing, influential underworld, believing it to be the best way to get things done.

The modern Camorra is a far cry from the days of roguish characters bullying shopkeepers into paying the *pizzo* (protection money). As journalist Roberto Saviano writes in his 2006 Camorra exposé Gomorrah: 'Only beggar Camorra clans inept at business and desperate to survive still practise the kind of monthly extortions seen in Nanni Loy's film *Mi manda Picone* [Where's Picone?]'. While small-time extortion still exists, the Mafia big guns are where the serious bucks lie, from human and arms trafficking, to industries including construction and large-scale waste disposal.

Human Trafficking

In recent years, numerous Camorra clans have forged alliances with foreign crime groups to run lucrative human-trafficking operations. According to the International Organization for Migration (IOM), over 80% of female asylum seekers reaching Europe from Nigeria are unknowingly sponsored by sex-trafficking rings. Once in Italy, the women are provided with fake documents by organised-crime groups and forced into prostitution to pay off their traffickers.

In Campania, this money is usually divided between the recruiter in Nigeria, the smugglers who facilitate the cross-sea journey, the Italian-based Nigerian racketeers who manage the sex trade, and the local Camorra clans who allow the gangs to operate on their turf. Many of the victims are women who find themselves working in Castel Volturno, an infamous Camorra stronghold northwest of Naples. For most, it will take up to six years to pay off their crippling debts.

Naples and Caserta are home to over 100 Camorra clans, with an estimated 4,500 immediate associates, and an even larger number of clients, dependents and supporters.

Drug Trade

The Camorra-ravaged suburbs of Secondigliano and Scampia in northern Naples have the dubious claim of being Europe's largest open-air drug market, supplying addicts from across the country with cheap, low-grade heroin and cocaine. Disputes between rival clans over this lucrative trade have seen the spilling of much blood.

One of the most serious clan battles so far this century was the so-called 'Scampia Feud', ignited by *camorrista* Cosimo Di Lauro in late 2004. As the newly appointed head of the powerful Di Lauro clan, the 30-year-old decided to centralise the area's drug trade, giving himself more power and the clan's long-respected franchisees much less. This did not go down well with many of Di Lauro's associates. Among them were Raffaele Amato and Cesare Pagano, who broke away to form a rival clan dubbed the Scissionisti di Secondigliano (Secessionists of Secondigliano). What followed was a long and ruthless series of murders and retributions between the opposing groups, one that would claim over 50 lives in 2004–5 alone.

Resistance

Over the years, the law has captured many Camorra kingpins, among them Cosimo Di Lauro and his father, Paolo, as well as Giuseppe Dell'Aquila and Pasquale Scotti. The latter – a fugitive Scissionisti boss convicted in absentia of over 20 murders – was arrested in Brazil in 2015 after 30 years on the run.

Despite these victories, the war against the Camorra remains an uphill battle. Its presence in Campanian society spans centuries, and, for many, the Camorra – known locally as *il Sistema* (The System) – has provided everything Italy's official avenues have not, from employment and business loans to a sense of order in local communities.

Although too many Neapolitans shrug their shoulders in resignation, others are determined to loosen the Camorra's grip. In the Sanità district, people like parish priest Don Antonio Loffredo and renowned artist Riccardo Dalisi offer youth the opportunity to learn artistic and artisanal skills, and help restore local heritage sites, including the Catacombe di San Gennaro. Across the city in Ercolano, elderly shopkeeper Raffaella Ottaviano made international headlines for her refusal to pay the *pizzo*. Her courage has influenced other traders to say no, which in turn has led the local council to offer tax breaks to those who report threats of extortion instead of giving in to the Camorra.

The Camorra on Screen

Gomorrah (Matteo Garrone; 2008)

The Professor (Giuseppe Tornatore; 1986)

Where's Picone? (Nanni Loy; 1983)

Luna rossa (Red Moon; Antonio Capuano; 2001)

Survival Guide

Directory A–Z

Accessible Travel

Campania is not an easy destination for travellers with disabilities. Cobbled streets, hair-raising traffic, blocked pavements and tiny lifts make life difficult for travellers with limited mobility, vision or hearing. The steep slopes of many Amalfi Coast towns pose a considerable obstacle.

That said, positive changes are slowly being made. For instance, the ruins of Pompeii now feature a wheelchair-friendly itinerary, while a growing number of city buses (including the R2 in Naples) are set up with ramps and wheelchair space.

Italy's national rail company, Trenitalia (www.trenitalia. com), offers a helpline for passengers with disabilities at ☑199 303060 (7am to 9pm daily). To secure assistance at **Napoli Centrale** (Stazione Centrale; ☑081 554 31 88), you should call 24 hours before departure.

Accessible Italy (www.acces sibleitaly.com) Specialises in holiday services for people with disabilities. This is the best first port of call.

Turismo Accessibile (www. turismoaccessibile.org) Gives a rundown of accessible museums, hotels, restaurants and beaches in Naples.

Moveability.org (https://move ability.org) Offers information on disability-friendly tourism in the Campania region.

Italia.it (www.italia.it/en/ useful-info/accessibility.html) Italy's official tourism website has a handful of useful links for travellers with disabilities.

Sage Traveling (www.sagetrav eling.com) Offers advice and tailor-made tours to assist mobility-impaired travellers in Europe.

Download Lonely Planet's free Accessible Travel guides from https://shop. lonelyplanet.com/products/ accessible-travel-online- resources-2019.

Discount Cards

Free admission to many galleries and cultural sites is available to people under 18 or over 65; in addition, visitors aged between 18 and 25 often qualify for a 50% discount.

For Naples and elsewhere in Campania, consider buying a **Campania Artecard** (☑800 600601; www.campa niartecard.it), which offers free or reduced admission to many museums and archaeological sites and free public transport. .

Electricity

Type C
220V/50Hz

Climate

Naples

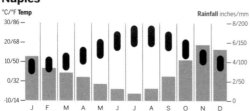

Type L
230V/50Hz

Embassies & Consulates

Rome is home to international embassies (*ambasciate*), with only a handful of consulates (*consolati*) in Naples.

French Consulate (☑081 598 07 11; www.it.ambafrance.org /Consulat-de-Naples; Via Crispi 86, Ⓜ Piazza Amedeo)

German Consulate (☑081 248 85 11; www.facebook. com/ConsoleOnorarioDiGer maniaANapoli; Via Medina 40 ⊙8.30am-noon Mon-Fri; Ⓜ Municipio)

US Consulate (☑081 583 81 11; https://it.usembassy.gov/ embassy-consulates/naples; Piazza della Repubblica 2; Ⓜ Mergellina)

Health

Availability of Health Care

Health care is readily available throughout Campania, but standards can vary significantly. Public hospitals tend to be less impressive than private ones. *Farmacisti* (pharmacists) can give you valuable advice and sell over-the-counter medication for minor illnesses. They can also advise you when more specialised help is required and point you in the right direction. In Naples and major tourist centres you are likely to find English-speaking doctors or a translator service available.

Pharmacies generally keep the same hours as other shops, closing at night and on Sundays. A handful, however, are *farmacie di turno*, which remain open on a rotation basis for emergency purposes. Closed pharmacies display a list of the nearest open ones.

If you need an ambulance anywhere in Italy, call ☑118. For emergency treatment, head straight to the *pronto soccorso* (casualty) section of a public hospital, where you can also get emergency dental treatment.

Health Insurance

If you're an EU citizen (or from Switzerland, Norway or Iceland), a European Health Insurance Card (EHIC) covers you for most medical care in public hospitals free of charge, but not for emergency repatriation home or non-emergencies. Citizens from other countries should find out if there is a reciprocal arrangement for free medical care between their country and Italy (Australia, for instance, has such an agreement; carry your Medicare card).

If you do need health insurance, make sure you get a policy that covers you for the worst possible scenario, such as an accident requiring an emergency flight home. Find out in advance if your insurance plan will make payments directly to providers or reimburse you later for overseas health expenditures.

Recommended Vaccinations

No jabs are required to travel to Italy. The World Health Organization (WHO), however, recommends that all travellers should be vaccinated against diphtheria, tetanus, measles, mumps, rubella, polio and hepatitis B.

Insurance

A travel-insurance policy to cover theft, loss and medical problems is a good idea. It may also cover you for cancellation or delays to your travel arrangements. Paying for your ticket with a credit card can often provide limited travel-accident insurance and you may be able to reclaim the payment if the operator doesn't deliver. Ask your credit-card company what it will cover.

Worldwide travel insurance is available at www. lonelyplanet.com/travel-insurance. You can buy, extend and claim online anytime – even if you're already on the road.

Internet Access

Internet access in southern Italy has improved greatly in the past few years, with most hotels, B&Bs, hostels and even *agriturismi* offering free wi-fi. On the downside, public wi-fi hotspots remain thin on the ground and signal strength is variable.

Legal Matters

Despite its Mafia notoriety, Campania is relatively safe, and the average tourist will only have a brush with the law if robbed by a bag snatcher or pickpocket.

Police

If you run into trouble in Italy, you're likely to end up dealing with the *polizia statale* (state police) or the *carabinieri* (military police). The former wear powder-blue trousers with a fuchsia stripe and a navy-blue jacket; the latter wear black uniforms with a red stripe and drive dark-blue cars with a red stripe.

Italian Police Organisations

Polizia statale (state police) Theft, visa extensions and permits.

Carabinieri (military police) General crime, public order and drug-law enforcement (often overlapping with the *polizia statale*).

Vigili urbani (local traffic police) Parking tickets, towed cars.

Guardia di finanza Tax evasion, drug smuggling.

Guardia forestale (aka Corpo forestale) Environmental protection.

Drugs & Alcohol

Possession of any controlled substances, including cannabis or marijuana, can get you into hot water. Those caught in possession of 5g or more of cannabis can be considered traffickers and prosecuted as such. The same applies to tiny amounts of other drugs. Those caught with amounts below this threshold can be subject to minor penalties.

The legal limit for blood-alcohol levels is 0.05% and random breath tests do occur.

Your Rights

➡ If you're detained, your arresting officers should give you verbal and written notice of the charges laid against you within 24 hours.

➡ You have the right to an interpreter if you do not speak Italian.

➡ You have no right to a phone call upon arrest, though you do have the right to have your relatives and consular authorities informed.

➡ The prosecutor must apply to a magistrate for you to be held in preventative custody awaiting trial (depending on the seriousness of the offence) within 48 hours of your arrest.

➡ You have the right not to respond to questions without the presence of a lawyer.

➡ If the magistrate orders preventative custody, you have the right to contest this within 10 days.

LGBT+ Travellers

Homosexuality is legal in Italy and well tolerated in Naples, perhaps less so in smaller towns on the Amalfi Coast. Resources include the following:

Arcigay Napoli (www.arcigay napoli.org, in Italian) Website for Naples' main LGBT organisation, listing special events as well as gay and gay-friendly venues in town.

Napoli Gay Press (www.napoli gaypress.it, in Italian) Comprehensive coverage of queer current affairs, arts and events in Naples and Campania.

Gay Friendly Italy (www. gayfriendlyitaly.com) English-language site featuring information on everything from gay-friendly hotels to bars.

Money

ATMs at Naples' Capodichino airport and major train stations; widely available in towns and cities. Credit cards accepted in most hotels and restaurants.

Credit & Debit Cards

Bancomats (ATMs)are the best way to obtain local currency. International credit and debit cards can be used in any Bancomat displaying the appropriate sign. Cards are also good for payment in most hotels, restaurants, shops, supermarkets and tollbooths.

Check any charges with your bank. Most banks now build a fee of around 3% into every foreign transaction. In addition, ATM withdrawals can attract a further fee, usually around 1.5%.

If your card is lost, stolen, or swallowed by an ATM, you can telephone toll-free to have an immediate stop put on its use:

Amex ☑800 928 391

MasterCard ☑800 870 866

Visa ☑800 819 014

YOUTH, STUDENT & TEACHER DISCOUNTS

These cards offer thousands of discounts on cultural attractions, restaurants, shops, clubs and courses. See their respective websites for further details.

CARD	WEBSITE	COST	ELIGIBILITY
European Youth Card (Carta Giovani)	www.eyca.org	€14	under 31 years
International Student Identity Card (ISIC)	www.isic.org	US$20, UK£12, AUD$30, €10-15	full-time student
International Teacher Identity Card (ITIC)	www.isic.org	US$20, UK£12, AUD$30, €11-18	full-time teacher
International Youth Travel Card (IYTC)	www.isic.org	US$20, UK£12, AUD$30, €11-15	under 31 years

Currency

The seven euro notes come in denominations of €500, €200, €100, €50, €20, €10 and €5. The eight euro coins are in denominations of €2 and €1, and €0.50, €0.20, €0.10, €0.05, €0.02 and €0.01.

For current exchange rates, see www.xe.com.

Moneychangers

You can change money in banks, at the post office or in a *cambio* (currency-exchange bureau). Post offices and banks tend to offer the best rates; currency-exchange bureaus keep longer hours, but watch out for high commissions and inferior rates.

Tipping

Tipping is generally optional.

Bars Neapolitans usually place a €0.10 coin on the bar when ordering their coffee; if drinks are brought to your table, leave a small tip.

Hotels Tip porters about €5 at high-end hotels.

Restaurants If *servizio* (service) is not included on your bill, leave a euro or two in pizzerias, or 10% of the bill in restaurants.

Taxis Most people round up to the nearest euro.

Taxes & Refunds

A 22% value-added tax known as IVA (Imposta sul Valore Aggiunta) is included in the price of most goods and services. Non-EU residents who spend more than €155 at one shop at a single time can claim a refund when leaving the EU. The refund only applies to purchases from stores that display a 'Tax Free' sign.

When making a purchase at a store that offers tax-free shopping, ask for a tax-refund voucher, to be filled in with the date of the purchase and its value. When leaving the EU, get this voucher stamped at customs and

take it to the nearest tax-refund counter where you'll get an immediate refund, either in cash or charged to your credit card. For more information, see www.tax refund.it.

Opening Hours

Opening hours vary throughout the year. We've provided high-season opening hours; hours will generally decrease in the shoulder and low seasons. Hours can be fickle at some smaller businesses.

Banks 8.30am–1.30pm and 2.45–3.45pm or 4.15pm Monday to Friday

Cafes 7.30am–8pm or later

Clubs 11pm–5am

Post offices 8am–6pm Monday to Friday, 8.30am–1pm Saturday;

smaller branch offices close 1.30pm weekdays

Restaurants Noon–3pm and 7.30–11pm or midnight

Shops 9am–1pm and 3.30–7.30pm (or 4–8pm) Monday to Saturday, some close Monday morning and some open Sunday

➡ The opening hours of museums, galleries and archaeological sites vary enormously. Many museums are closed on Monday or (less commonly) Tuesday or Wednesday.

➡ Currency-exchange offices usually keep longer hours, though these are hard to find outside major cities and tourist areas.

➡ Restaurant kitchens often shut an hour earlier than final closing time. Most places close at least one day a week, often on Monday. Many restaurants are closed for at least two weeks in August, while those in coastal resort towns are usually closed in the low season, between November and Easter.

➡ In larger cities, supermarkets may stay open at lunchtime or on Sunday.

Post

Poste Italiane (www.poste.it), Italy's postal system, is reasonably reliable, though parcels do occasionally go missing.

Francobolli (stamps) are available at *uffici postali* (post offices) and authorised tobacconists (look for the big white-on-black 'T' sign). Since letters often need to be weighed, what you get at the tobacconist for international airmail will occasionally be an approximation of the proper rate. Tobacconists keep regular shop hours.

Postal Service Rates

The cost of sending a letter by *aerea* (airmail) depends on its weight, size and where it is being sent. Most people use *posta prioritaria internazionale* (international priority mail), Italy's most efficient mail service, guaranteed to deliver letters sent to Europe within three working days and to the rest of the world within four to nine working days. Using *posta prioritaria*, mail up to 50g costs €3.50 within Europe, €4.50 to Africa, Asia and the Americas, and €5.50 to Australia and New Zealand. Mail weighing 51g to 100g costs €4.30 within Europe, €5.20 to Africa, Asia and the Americas, and €7.10 to Australia and New Zealand.

Receiving Mail

Poste restante (general delivery) is known as *fermoposta* in Italy. Letters marked thus will be held at the counter of the same name in the main post office in the relevant town.

You'll need to pick up your letters in person and you must present your passport as ID.

Public Holidays

Most Italians take their annual holiday in August, with the busiest period occurring around 15 August, known locally as Ferragosto. As a result, many businesses and shops close for at least part of that month.

National public holidays:

New Year's Day (Capodanno) 1 January

Epiphany (Epifania) 6 January

Easter Monday (Pasquetta) March/April

Liberation Day (Giorno della Liberazione) 25 April

Labour Day (Festa del Lavoro) 1 May

Republic Day (Festa della Repubblica) 2 June

Feast of the Assumption (Assunzione or Ferragosto) 15 August

All Saints' Day (Ognisanti) 1 November

Feast of the Immaculate Conception (Festa della Immacolata Concezione) 8 December

Christmas Day (Natale) 25 December

Boxing Day (Festa di Santo Stefano) 26 December

Safe Travel

Naples has a reputation for being unsafe. The following are some basic safety tips:

➡ Pickpockets are highly active on crowded transport and in crowds. Avoid keeping money, credit cards and other valuables in easy-to-reach pockets, especially coat and back pockets.

➡ Never leave bags unattended on a train. At cafes and bars, loop your

bag's strap around your leg while seated.

➡ Be cautious of strangers who want your attention, especially at train stations and ports.

➡ Wear bags and cameras across your body and away from the road to avoid scooter-riding petty thieves.

➡ At archaeological sites, beware touts posing as legitimate guides.

Scams

Avoid buying mobile phones and other discounted electrical goods from vendors on Piazza Garibaldi in Naples and at street markets. It's not unusual to get home and discover that you've bought a box with a brick in it. At Napoli Centrale, ignore touts offering taxis; use only registered white taxis with a running meter.

On the Road

Car theft is a problem in Naples, so it pays to leave your car in a supervised car park. If you leave your car on the street, you'll often be approached by an unofficial (illegal) parking attendant asking for money. Clearly, you don't have to pay them, but if you refuse you run the risk of returning to a damaged car. In case of theft or loss, always report the incident to the police within 24 hours; ask for a statement, as otherwise your travel-insurance company won't pay out.

Traffic

Neapolitan traffic requires some getting used to. Drivers are not keen to stop for pedestrians, even at pedestrian crossings, and are more likely to swerve. Locals simply step off the footpath and walk through the (swerving) traffic with determination. It is a practice that seems to work, but if you feel uncertain, wait and cross with a local.

In many cities, roads that appear to be for one-way

traffic have lanes for buses travelling in the opposite direction – always look both ways before stepping onto the road.

Telephone

Domestic Calls

➡ Italian telephone area codes all begin with *J* 0 and consist of up to four digits; the Naples area code is *J* 081. The area code is followed by a number of anything from four to eight digits. The area code is an integral part of the telephone number and must always be dialled, even when calling from next door.

➡ Mobile-phone numbers begin with a three-digit prefix such as *J* 330.

➡ Toll-free (free-phone) numbers are known as *numeri verdi* and usually start with *J* 800.

➡ As elsewhere in Europe, Italians choose from a host of phone-plan providers, with a resultant galaxy of price options.

International Calls

➡ To call Italy from abroad, call your international access number, then Italy's country code (*J* 39) and then the area code of the location you want, including the leading 0.

➡ Avoid making international calls from a hotel, as rates are high.The cheapest options are free or low-cost apps such as Skype and Viber, connecting by using the wi-fi at your accommodation or at a cafe or other venue offering free wi-fi.

➡ Another cheap option is to use an international calling card. Note, however, that there are very few public payphones left, so consider a prepaid card that allows you to call from any phone. Cards are available at newsstands and tobacconists.

➡ To call abroad from Italy, dial *J* 00, then the country

and area codes, dropping the first '0', followed by the telephone number.

➡ To make a reverse-charge (collect) international call from a public telephone, dial *J* 170. All phone operators speak English.

Directory Enquiries

National and international phone numbers can be requested on *J* 1254 (or online at www.1254.it).

Mobile Phones

Local SIM cards can be used in European, Australian and some unlocked US phones. Other phones must be set to roaming.

➡ Italian mobile phones operate on the GSM 900/1800 network, which is compatible with the rest of Europe and Australia but not always with the North American GSM or CDMA systems – check with your service provider.

➡ The cheapest way of using your mobile is to buy a *prepagato* (prepaid) Italian SIM card. TIM (www.tim.it), Wind (www.wind.it), Vodafone (www.vodafone.it) and Tre (www.tre.it) all offer SIM cards and have retail outlets in most Italian cities and towns. All SIM cards must be registered in Italy, so make sure you have a passport or ID card with you when you buy one.

➡ You can easily top up your Italian SIM with a *ricarica* (recharge card), available from most tobacconists, some bars, supermarkets and banks.

Payphones & Phonecards

Although public payphones still exist across Campania, their numbers continue to decrease. Those that are still working take *schede telefoniche* (telephone cards), which are available from tobacconists and newsstands.

Time

➡ All of Italy occupies the Central European Time Zone, which is one hour ahead of GMT. When it is noon in London, it is 1pm in Italy.

➡ Daylight-saving time (when clocks move forward one hour) starts on the last Sunday in March and ends on the last Sunday in October.

➡ Italy operates on a 24-hour clock, so 3pm is written as 15:00.

Toilets

➡ Public toilets are rare in Naples.

➡ Bars and cafes usually have toilets, although you may need to buy a coffee before you can use them. Public toilets are readily available at museums, and there are public toilets at the main bus and train stations.

➡ Several public toilets have attendants, who'll expect a small tip – €0.50 should do.

➡ There are free toilets at Pompeii and Herculaneum.

Tourist Information

The quality of tourist offices varies dramatically. Most offer brochures, maps and leaflets, even if staff are uninterested in helping in any other way.

Local & Provincial Tourist Offices

Main tourist offices are generally open Monday to Friday; some also open on weekends, especially in urban areas or during the peak summer season. Affiliated information booths (at train stations and airports, for example) may keep slightly different hours. Be aware that in some popular tourist centres, private tour operators may style their business as a general 'tourist information' point. In reality, they are set up to sell their own tours and offerings.

Tourist Offices Abroad

The Italian National Tourist Office (www.enit.it) maintains offices in 22 cities on five continents. Contact information for all offices can be found on its website.

Visas

Generally not required for stays of up to 90 days (or at all for EU nationals); some nationalities need a Schengen visa. Italy is one of 26 member countries of the Schengen Convention, under which 22 EU countries (all but Bulgaria, Croatia, Cyprus, Ireland and Romania), plus Iceland, Liechtenstein, Norway and Switzerland, have abolished permanent checks at common borders.

Legal residents of one Schengen country do not require a visa for another. Residents of 28 non-EU countries, including Australia, Brazil, Canada, Israel, Japan, New Zealand and the USA, do not require visas for tourist visits of up to 90 days (this list varies for those who want to travel to the UK and Ireland).

All non-EU and non-Schengen nationals entering Italy for more than 90 days, or for any reason other than tourism (such as study or work), may need a specific visa. For details, visit www.esteri.it/mae/en/servizi/stranieri or contact an Italian consulate. You should also have your passport stamped on entry as, without a stamp,

you could encounter problems when trying to obtain a *permesso di soggiorno* (residence permit). If you enter the EU via another member state, get your passport stamped there.

Study Visas

Non-EU citizens who want to study at a university or language school in Italy must have a study visa. These can be obtained from your nearest Italian embassy or consulate. You will normally require confirmation of your enrolment, and proof of payment of fees and adequate funds to support yourself. The visa covers only the period of the enrolment. This type of visa is renewable within Italy but, again, only with confirmation of ongoing enrolment and proof that you are able to support yourself (bank statements are preferred).

Work

➡ Citizens of the European Union (EU), Norway, Iceland, Switzerland and Liechtenstein are legally entitled to work in Italy. Those wanting to stay in the country for more than three months are simply required to register with the local *anagrafe* (register office) in their Italian municipality of residence.

➡ Working longer-term in Italy is trickier if you are a non-EU citizen. Firstly, you will need to secure a job offer. Your prospective employer will then need to complete most of the work-visa application process on your behalf. If your application is successful, your employer will be given your work authorisation.

Your local Italian embassy or consulate will then be informed and should be able to provide you with an entry visa within 30 days. Non-EU citizens planning to stay in Italy for more than 90 days must also apply for a *permesso di soggiorno* (permit to stay) within eight working days of their entry into Italy. Applications for the permit should be made at the nearest *questura* (police station). General information on the permit is available on the Italian state police website (www.poliziadistato.it).

➡ Italy has reciprocal, short-term working-holiday agreements with a handful of countries. These visas are generally limited to young adults aged between 18 and 30 or 35, and allow the visa holder to work a limited number of months over a set period of time. Contact your local Italian embassy (www.esteri.it) for more information.

➡ Popular jobs for those permitted to work in Italy include teaching English. While some language schools do take on teachers without professional language qualifications, the more reputable (and better-paying) establishments will require you to have a TEFL (Teaching of English as a Foreign Language) certificate. One useful job-seeker website for English-language teachers is ESL Employment (www.eslemployment.com). Au pairing is another popular work option; click onto www.aupairworld.com for more information on work opportunities and tips.

Transport

GETTING THERE & AWAY

Several airlines link Italy to the rest of the world, and numerous carriers fly directly to Naples' international airport, Capodichino. Naples is southern Italy's main transport hub, with excellent rail and bus connections to other parts of Campania and beyond. Naples is also a key port, hosting international cruise ships and operating car and passenger ferries to destinations throughout the Mediterranean.

Flights, cars and tours can be booked online at www.lonelyplanet.com/bookings.

Entering Campania

➡ EU and Swiss citizens can travel to Italy with their national identity card alone. All other nationalities must have a passport that is valid for at least six months beyond the length of stay in Italy.

➡ By law you should have your passport or ID card with you at all times. You'll need one of these documents for police registration every time you check into a hotel.

Air

Airports & Airlines

Naples International Airport (Capodichino; ☎081 789 62 59; www.aeroporto dinapoli.it; Viale F Ruffo di Calabria), 7km northeast of the city centre, is southern Italy's main airport. It's served by a number of major airlines and low-cost carriers, including easyJet, which operates flights to Naples from London, Paris, Amsterdam, Vienna, Berlin and several other European cities.

Curreri (Map p153; ☎081 801 54 20; www.curreriviaggi. it) runs ten daily services to Sorrento from Capodichino. Buses depart from outside the departures hall and terminate outside Sorrento train station. Buy tickets (€10) on board for the 75-minute journey.

Tickets

The internet is the easiest way of locating and booking reasonably priced seats. Full-time students may qualify for discounted fares.

ONLINE TICKETS

For reasonably priced airfares, check the following online booking websites:
➡ www.cheapflights.com
➡ www.ebookers.com
➡ www.expedia.com
➡ www.kayak.com
➡ www.lastminute.com
➡ www.orbitz.com
➡ www.priceline.com

CLIMATE CHANGE & TRAVEL

Every form of transport that relies on carbon-based fuel generates CO_2, the main cause of human-induced climate change. Modern travel is dependent on aeroplanes, which might use less fuel per kilometre per person than most cars but travel much greater distances. The altitude at which aircraft emit gases (including CO_2) and particles also contributes to their climate change impact. Many websites offer 'carbon calculators' that allow people to estimate the carbon emissions generated by their journey and, for those who wish to do so, to offset the impact of the greenhouse gases emitted with contributions to portfolios of climate-friendly initiatives throughout the world. Lonely Planet offsets the carbon footprint of all staff and writer travel.

TRANSPORT LAND

DEPARTURE TAX
Departure tax is included in
the price of a ticket.

Land

Reaching Campania overland
involves traversing three-
quarters of the entire length
of Italy, which can either be
a big drain on your time or,
if you have plenty to spare, a
wonderful way of seeing the
country.

Bus

Buses are the cheapest
overland option to Italy, but
services are less frequent
and significantly slower than
the train. Most of the companies below are at Metropark
Napoli Centrale, Corso Arnaldo Lucci.

CLP (☑081 531 17 07; www.
clpbus.it;) Connects Naples
to Foggia.

Eurolines (www.eurolines.com)
Connections from Naples to
cities across Italy and Europe.

FlixBus (https://global.flixbus.
com) Low-cost fares to national
and international destinations
from Naples.

Miccolis (☑080 531 53 34;
www.miccolis-spa.it) Runs several services a day from Naples
to Potenza, Matera, Taranto,
Brindisi, Lecce and Bari.

Marino (☑080 311 23 35;
www.marinobus.it) Runs daily
services from Naples to Bari
and Matera.

SAIS (☑091 617 11 41; www.
saistrasporti.it) Operates long-
haul services to Sicily from
Naples and Rome.

Car & Motorcycle

If you are planning to drive to
Campania, bear in mind the
cost of toll roads and the fact
that fuel prices in Italy are
among the highest in Europe.

In Naples itself, it is unlikely that you will be tempted to
drive, and you will also have
to pay for secure parking.

Although your own car is a
definite bonus when it comes
to visiting more remote areas of Campania, like west
of Sorrento and the Parco
Nazionale del Cilento, Vallo
di Diano e Alburni, given the
cost of driving here, renting a
car is a wiser option.

Train

Regular trains on two western lines connect Italy with
France (one along the coast
and the other from Turin into
the French Alps). Depending
on distances covered, rail
can be highly competitive
with air travel: those travelling from neighbouring
countries to northern Italy
will find it is frequently more
comfortable, less expensive
and only marginally more
time-consuming than flying.

Those travelling longer
distances (say, from the UK,
Spain, northern Germany or
Eastern Europe) will doubt-
less find flying cheaper and
quicker. Bear in mind, however, that the train is a much
greener way to go – a trip by
rail can contribute up to 10
times fewer carbon-dioxide
emissions per person than
the same trip by air.

Naples is served by *re-
gionale* (regional), *diretto*
(direct), Intercity and high-
velocity Frecciarossa trains.
They arrive at and depart
from Napoli Centrale or
Stazione Garibaldi (on the
lower level).

National rail company
Trenitalia (☑892021; www.
trenitalia.com) runs regular direct services between Naples
and Rome (2nd class €12
to €48, 70 minutes to three
hours, around 66 daily), with
many high-velocity services
continuing north to Florence,
Bologna and Milan. High-
speed private rail company
Italo (☑892020; www.italo
treno.it) also runs daily direct
services between Naples
and Rome (2nd class €15 to
€39, 70 minutes, around 20
daily), with onward connections north. From Naples,
Trenitalia trains continue

south to Reggio di Calabria
and to Messina, Sicily.

➡ The comprehensive *European
Rail Timetable* (UK£12), updated monthly online and half-
yearly in print, is available at
www.europeanrailtimetable.eu.

➡ Reservations on international
trains to/from Italy are always
advisable and sometimes compulsory.

➡ Some international services
include transport for private cars.

➡ Consider taking long journeys
overnight, as the supplemental
fare for a sleeper costs sub-
stantially less than a stay in an
Italian hotel.

Sea

Naples is the main seaport
in Campania, serving both
regional ferries and international cruise ships. Year-
round ferry destinations include Capri, Ischia, Procida,
as well as Sicily and Sardinia.
Ferries to Sicily also depart
from Salerno.

For a guide to ferry
services into and out of
Italy, consult **Direct Ferries**
(www.directferries.com).
The website lists routes and
deals, and includes a booking
service.

GETTING AROUND

Air

There are no internal
commercial flights within
Campania.

Bicycle

Cycling is a dangerous option in Naples – a city where
all road rules are seemingly
disregarded. Most drivers
speed, chat on their mobile
phones and ignore traffic
lights. Bicycle and motorcycle theft is rife.

Bicycle hire is costly in Naples (from €20 per day), so if you are staying for some time and are dead-set on taking to the saddle, it may be cheaper to buy a bike. Taking your bicycle to the Amalfi Coast is also a fraught option: think blind corners and sheer, precipitous drops.

Boat

Naples, the bay islands and the Amalfi Coast are served by a comprehensive ferry network. Catch fast ferries and hydrofoils for Capri, Sorrento, Ischia (both Ischia Porto and Forio) and Procida from **Molo Beverello** (Map p50) in front of Castel Nuovo; hydrofoils for Capri, Ischia and Procida also sail from Mergellina.

Ferries for Sicily and Sardinia sail from **Molo Angioino** (Map p50) (right beside Molo Beverello) and neighbouring **Calata Porta di Massa** (Map p50). Slow ferries to Ischia and Procida also depart from Calata Porta di Massa. **SNAV** (☑081 428 55 55; www.snav.it;

Molo Beverollo) ferries for the Aeolian Islands depart from Mergellina.

Fares are for a one-way, high-season deck-class single, unless otherwise stated. Services are pared back considerably in winter, and adverse sea conditions may affect schedules.

Alicost (☑089 23 48 92; www. alicost.it)

Alilauro (☑081 497 22 38; www.alilauro.it; Molo Beverello)

Caremar (☑081 1896 6690; www.caremar.it; Molo Beverello)

Medmar (☑081 333 44 11; www.medmargroup.it; Calata Porta di Massa)

Navigazione Libera del Golfo (NLG;☑081 552 07 63; www. navlib.it; Marina Grande)

Siremar (☑800 627414; www. siremar.it; Calata Porto di Massa)

Tirrenia (☑199 303040; www. tirrenia.it; Calata Porta di Massa)

TraVelMar (☑089 87 29 50; www.travelmar.it)

Bus

Several bus companies service the Campania region. The following are especially useful for travellers:

ANM (☑800 639525; www. anm.it) operates city buses in Naples. There's no central bus station, but most buses pass through Piazza Garibaldi.

City Sightseeing Napoli (Map p50;☑081 551 72 79; www. city-sightseeing.it/en/naples; adult/reduced €23/11.50) runs three hop-on, hop-off tourist routes in Naples. All depart from Largo Castello, beside the Castel Nuovo. Tickets are available on board, and children under five travel free.

EAV (☑800 211388; www. eavsrl.it) Connects Naples to the Campi Flegrei and to Sorrento. It also operates public buses on Ischia and Procida.

Infante Viaggi (☑089 82 57 65; www.agenziainfanteviaggi. it) Runs coaches between Naples and Salerno into the Parco Nazionale del Cilento, Valle di Diano e Alburni.

FERRIES

Tickets for shorter journeys can be bought at the ticket booths on Molo Beverello and at Mergellina. For longer journeys, try the offices of the ferry companies or a travel agent.

DESTINATION (FROM NAPLES)	FERRY COMPANY	PRICE (€)	DURATION (HR)	FREQUENCY (HIGH SEASON)
Aeolian Islands	SNAV (Jun-early Sep only)	from 65	4½-6½	1-2 daily
Aeolian Islands	Siremar	from 58	13¾	2 weekly
Cagliari (Sardinia)	Tirrenia	from 44	14½	2 weekly
Capri	Caremar	from 12.50	80 min	7 daily
Ischia	Caremar	12.50	80 min	8 daily
Ischia	Medmar	13.50	1¼	6 daily
Milazzo (Sicily)	Siremar	from 58	16¼-18¼	2 weekly
Palermo (Sicily)	SNAV	from 40	10¼	1-2 daily
Palermo (Sicily)	Tirrenia	from 41	10¼	1 daily
Pontine Islands	SNAV (Jul-early Sep only)	from 22	3	4 weekly
Procida	Caremar	10.50	1	7 daily

SITA Sud (www.sitasudtras porti.it) Connects Sorrento to the Amalfi Coast. Also runs between Salerno and Naples (including Naples International Airport).

Mobility Amalfi Coast (☑089 81 30 77) Runs local buses in Positano, with connections to Montepertuso, Nocelle and Praiano.

Car & Motorcycle

Much of central Naples is off-limits to nonresident vehicles, and the combo of anarchic traffic and illegal parking attendants demanding tips will quickly ruin your holiday.

Nonresident vehicles are prohibited on Capri for much of the year, and driving is largely discouraged on Ischia and Procida.

Peak-season traffic can make driving along the Amalfi Coast stressful, though having your own vehicle here means ultimate flexibility.

Driving is ideal in the Cilento region, allowing you to discover out-of-the-way towns and beaches.

If driving in Campania, get used to tailgaters; worry about what's in front of you, not so much what's behind you. Also, watch out for scooters and give way to pedestrians no matter where they appear from. Approach all junctions and traffic lights with extreme caution; and keep cool.

Naples is on the north–south Autostrada del Sole, the A1 (north to Rome and Milan) and the A3 (south to Salerno and Reggio di Calabria). The A30 skirts Naples to the northeast, while the A16 heads across to Bari.

When approaching Naples, the motorways meet the Tangenziale di Napoli, a major ring road around the city. The ring road hugs the city's northern fringe, meeting the A1 for Rome and the A2 to Capodichino airport in the east, and continuing towards Campi Flegrei and Pozzuoli in the west.

Automobile Associations

The **Automobile Club d'Italia** (ACI; www.aci.it) is a driver's best resource in Italy. Foreigners do not have to join to get roadside emer-

gency **service** (☑803116; ☉24hr) but instead pay a per-incident fee.

Bringing Your Own Vehicle

If you are determined to bring your own car to Naples, ensure that all the paper-work is in order and that you carry a hazard triangle and a reflective jacket in your car – and don't forget that Italians drive on the right-hand side. Arriving in Naples, you should be prepared for heavy traffic jams, particularly at commuter times and at lunchtime. Familiarise yourself with important road signs like *uscita* (exit) and *raccordo* (ring road surrounding a city).

Car Hire

➡ Pre-booking via the internet often costs less than hiring a car once in Italy. Online booking agency Rentalcars.com (www.rentalcars.com) compares the rates of numerous car-rental companies.

➡ Renters must generally be aged 21 or over, with a credit card and home-country driving licence or IDP.

HYDROFOIL & HIGH-SPEED FERRIES

DESTINATION (FROM NAPLES' MOLO BEVERELLO)	FERRY COMPANY	PRICE (€)	DURATION (MIN)	DAILY FREQUENCY (HIGH SEASON)
Capri	Caremar	18	60	4
Capri	Navigazione Libera del Golfo	from 20.50	45	9
Capri	SNAV	22.50	45	9
Ischia	Caremar	18	55	6
Ischia	Alilauro	from 19	60	10
Ischia (Casamicciola)	SNAV	from 20	60	8
Procida	Caremar	14.50	40	8
Procida	SNAV	from 17.50	30	4
Sorrento	Alilauro	13	45	5
Sorrento	Navigazione Libera del Golfo	13	45	1

➡ Consider hiring a small car, which will reduce your fuel expenses and help you negotiate narrow city lanes and tight parking spaces.

➡ Check with your credit-card company to see if it offers a collision damage waiver, which covers you for additional damage if you use that card to pay for the car.

The following companies have numerous pick-up locations in Campania:

Avis (☏081 28 40 41; www.avisautonoleggio.it; Piazza Garibaldi 92, Starhotels Terminus, Naples; ⊗8am-7.30pm Mon-Fri, 8.30am-4.30pm Sat, 9am-1pm Sun)

Europcar (☏081 780 56 43; www.europcar.it; Naples International Airport)

Hertz (☏081 20 28 60; www.hertz.it; Corso Arnaldo Lucci 171, Naples; ⊗8.30am-1pm & 2.30-7pm Mon-Fri)

Maggiore (☏081 28 78 58; www.maggiore.it; Napoli Centrale; ⊗8.30am-7.30pm Mon-Fri, to 6pm Sat, to 12.30pm Sun)

In Naples, you can hire scooters from **Vespa Sprint** (☏081 764 34 52; http://vespasprint.it/noleggio-vespa-scooter-napoli; Via Santa Lucia 36, Naples; scooter hire per day from €60; ⊗9am-8pm).

Driving Licences

All EU driving licences are recognised in Italy. Travellers from other countries should obtain an International Driving Permit (IDP) through their national automobile association.

Fuel & Spare Parts

Petrol stations located along the main highways are open 24 hours. In smaller towns, the opening hours are generally 7am to 7pm Monday to Saturday, with a lunchtime break. The cost of *benzina*

senza piombo (unleaded petrol) and *gasolio* (diesel) is about €1.56 and €1.41 per litre, respectively.

Spare parts are available at many garages or via the 24-hour **ACI** motorist assistance number 803116 (or 02 6616 5116 if calling with a non-Italian mobile-phone account).

Parking

Parking in Naples is no fun. Blue lines by the side of the road denote pay-and-display parking – buy tickets at the meters or from tobacconists – with rates around €2 per hour. Elsewhere street parking is often overseen by illegal attendants who will expect a €3 to €5 fee for their protection of your car. It's usually easier to bite the bullet and pay them than attempt a moral stance.

You'll find a secure two-level car park beneath Piazza Garibaldi, open from 5am to 1am daily. East of the city centre, there's a 24-hour car park at Via Brin.

Elsewhere in the region, parking can be similarly problematic, especially at the main resorts on the Amalfi Coast and, even more so, in August.

Road Rules

Contrary to appearances, there are road rules in Italy. Here are some of the most essential:

➡ Cars drive on the right side of the road and overtake on the left. Unless otherwise indicated, always give way to cars entering an intersection from a road on your right.

➡ Seatbelt use (front and rear) is required by law; violators are subject to an on-the-spot fine. Helmets are required on all two-wheeled vehicles.

➡ Day and night, it is compulsory to drive with your headlights on outside built-up areas.

➡ It's obligatory to carry a warning triangle and fluorescent

waistcoat in case of breakdown. Recommended accessories include a first-aid kit, spare-bulb kit and fire extinguisher.

➡ A licence is required to ride a scooter – a car licence will do for bikes up to 125cc; for anything over 125cc, you'll need a motorcycle licence.

➡ Motorbikes can enter most restricted traffic areas in Italian cities, and traffic police generally turn a blind eye to motorcycles or scooters parked on footpaths.

➡ The blood alcohol limit is 0.05%; it's zero for drivers under 21 and those who have had their licence for less than three years.

Unless otherwise indicated, speed limits are as follows:
➡ 130km/h on autostradas
➡ 110km/h on all main, non-urban roads
➡ 90km/h on secondary, non-urban roads
➡ 50km/h in built-up areas

Toll Roads

There are tolls on most motorways, payable by cash or credit card as you exit. For information on traffic conditions, tolls and driving distances, see www.autostrade.it.

Local Transport

Funicular

Three services connect central Naples to the city's Vomero district, while a fourth connects the Mergellina district to Posillipo. All operate from 7am to 10pm daily. See the website www.anm.it for more information.

Funicolare Centrale Travels from Piazzetta Augusteo to Piazza Fuga.

Funicolare di Chiaia Travels from Via del Parco Margherita to Via Domenico Cimarosa.

Funicolare di Montesanto

Travels from Piazza Montesanto to Via Raffaele Morghen.

Funicolare di Mergellina

Connects the waterfront at Via Mergellina with Via Manzoni.

Metro

Naples has three metro lines: 1, 2 and 6.

Metro Line 1 (Linea 1; www. anm.it) runs from Garibaldi (Napoli Centrale) to Vomero and the northern suburbs via the city centre. Useful stops include Duomo and Università (southern edge of the *centro storico*), Municipio (hydrofoil and ferry terminals), Toledo (Via Toledo and Quartieri Spagnoli), Dante (western edge of the *centro storico*) and Museo (National Archaeological Museum). Trains run from about 6am to around 11.30pm.

Metro Line 2 (Linea 2; www. trenitalia.com/tcom/Treni -Regionali/Campania) runs from Gianturco to Garibaldi (Napoli Centrale) and on to Pozzuoli. Useful stops include Piazza Cavour (La Sanità and northern edge of *centro storico*), Piazza Amedeo (Chiaia) and Mergellina (Mergellina ferry and hydrofoil terminal). Change for Line 1 at Garibaldi or Piazza Cavour (known as Museo on Line 1). Trains run from about 5.30am to around 11.30pm.

Metro Line 6 is set to re-open in late 2021, when an extension will see it run from Municipio to Chiaia, Mergellina and Mostra.

Both Lines 1 and 6 are operated by **ANM** (☏800 639525; www.anm.it), which also operates the city's buses and funiculars. Line 2 is operated by Italy's state-owned Ferrovie dello Stato (FS).

Taxi

Official taxis are metered; always ensure the meter is running before getting in. In Naples, taxi companies include the following:

Consortaxi (☏081 22 22; www.consortaxi.com)

Taxi Napoli (☏081 88 88; www.taxinapoli.it)

Radio Taxi La Partenope

(☏081 01 01; www.radiotaxi lapartenope.it)

Taxis are available in most major towns and tourist areas in Campania, including Capri, Ischia, Sorrento and Salerno.

Train

Circumvesuviana (☏800 211388; www.eavsrl.it) trains (follow signs from Napoli Centrale station in Naples) run to Sorrento (€3.90) via Ercolano (Herculaneum; €2.20), Pompeii (€2.80) and other towns along the coast.Trains run from about 6am to around 10pm.

Ferrovia Cumana (☏800 21 13 88; www.eavsrl.it) trains run to Pozzuoli (€2.20) and the Campi Flegrei. In Naples, Cumana trains depart from Stazione Cumana di Montesanto on Piazza Montesanto, 500m southwest of Piazza Dante.

Language

Standard Italian is taught and spoken throughout Italy. Dialects are an important part of regional identity, but you'll have no trouble being understood anywhere if you stick to standard Italian, which we've also used in this chapter.

The sounds used in spoken Italian can all be found in English. If you read our coloured pronunciation guides as if they were English, you'll be understood. The stressed syllables are indicated with italics. Note that ai is pronounced as in 'aisle', ay as in 'say', ow as in 'how', dz as the 'ds' in 'lids', and that r is a strong and rolled sound. Keep in mind that Italian consonants can have a stronger, emphatic pronunciation – if the consonant is written as a double letter, it should be pronounced a little stronger, eg *sonno son*·no (sleep) versus *sono so*·no (I am).

BASICS

Italian has two words for 'you' – use the polite form *Lei* lay if you're talking to strangers, officials or people older than you. With people familiar to you or younger than you, you can use the informal form *tu* too.

In Italian, all nouns and adjectives are either masculine or feminine, and so are the articles *il/la* eel/la (the) and *un/una* oon/oo·na (a) that go with the nouns.

In this chapter the polite/informal and masculine/feminine options are included where necessary, separated with a slash and indicated with 'pol/inf' and 'm/f'.

WANT MORE?

For in-depth language information and handy phrases, check out Lonely Planet's *Italian Phrasebook*. You'll find it at **shop.lonelyplanet.com**, or you can buy Lonely Planet's iPhone phrasebooks at the Apple App Store.

Hello.	*Buongiorno.*	bwon·*jor*·no
Goodbye.	*Arrivederci.*	a·ree·ve·*der*·chee
Yes.	*Sì.*	see
No.	*No.*	no
Excuse me.	*Mi scusi.* (pol)	mee *skoo*·zee
	Scusami. (inf)	*skoo*·za·mee
Sorry.	*Mi dispiace.*	mee dees·*pya*·che
Please.	*Per favore.*	per fa·*vo*·re
Thank you.	*Grazie.*	*gra*·tsye
You're welcome.	*Prego.*	*pre*·go

How are you?
Come sta/stai? (pol/inf)   ko·me sta/stai

Fine. And you?
Bene. E Lei/tu? (pol/inf)   be·ne e lay/too

What's your name?
Come si chiama? pol   ko·me see *kya*·ma
Come ti chiami? inf   ko·me tee *kya*·mee

My name is ...
Mi chiamo ...   mee *kya*·mo ...

Do you speak English?
Parla/Parli inglese? (pol/inf)   *par*·la/*par*·lee een·*gle*·ze

I don't understand.
Non capisco.   non ka·*pee*·sko

ACCOMMODATION

Do you have a ... room?	*Avete una camera ...?*	a·*ve*·te oo·na *ka*·me·ra ...
double	*doppia con letto matrimoniale*	*do*·pya kon *le*·to ma·*tree*·mo·*nya*·le
single	*singola*	*seen*·go·la
How much is it per ...?	*Quanto costa per ...?*	*kwan*·to *kos*·ta per ...
night	*una notte*	oo·na *no*·te
person	*persona*	per·*so*·na

Is breakfast included?
La colazione è compresa? — la ko·la·*tsyo*·ne e kom·*pre*·sa

air-con	*aria condizionata*	a·rya kon·dee·tsyo·*na*·ta
bathroom	*bagno*	ba·nyo
campsite	*campeggio*	kam·*pe*·jo
guesthouse	*pensione*	pen·*syo*·ne
hotel	*albergo*	al·*ber*·go
youth hostel	*ostello della gioventù*	os·*te*·lo de·la jo·ven·*too*
window	*finestra*	fee·*nes*·tra

DIRECTIONS

Where's ...?
Dov'è ...? — do·ve ...

What's the address?
Qual'è l'indirizzo? — kwa·*le* leen·dee·*ree*·tso

Could you please write it down?
Può scriverlo, per favore? — pwo *skree*·ver·lo per fa·*vo*·re

Can you show me (on the map)?
Può mostrarmi (sulla pianta)? — pwo mos·*trar*·mee (soo·la *pyan*·ta)

at the corner	*all'angolo*	a·*lan*·go·lo
at the traffic lights	*al semaforo*	al se·*ma*·fo·ro
behind	*dietro*	*dye*·tro
far	*lontano*	lon·*ta*·no
in front of	*davanti a*	da·*van*·tee a
left	*a sinistra*	a see·*nee*·stra
near	*vicino*	vee·*chee*·no
next to	*accanto a*	a·*kan*·to a
opposite	*di fronte a*	dee *fron*·te a
right	*a destra*	a *de*·stra
straight ahead	*sempre diritto*	*sem*·pre dee·*ree*·to

EATING & DRINKING

What would you recommend?
Cosa mi consiglia? — ko·za mee kon·*see*·lya

What's in that dish?
Quali ingredienti ci sono in questo piatto? — kwa·li een·gre·*dyen*·tee chee so·no een kwe·sto pya·to

What's the local speciality?
Qual'è la specialità di questa regione? — kwa·*le* la spe·cha·lee·*ta* dee kwe·sta re·*jo*·ne

KEY PATTERNS

To get by in Italian, mix and match these simple patterns with words of your choice:

When's (the next flight)?
A che ora è (il prossimo volo)? — a ke o·ra e (eel *pro*·see·mo *vo*·lo)

Where's (the station)?
Dov'è (la stazione)? — do·ve (la sta·*tsyo*·ne)

I'm looking for (a hotel).
Sto cercando (un albergo). — sto cher·*kan*·do (oon al·*ber*·go)

Do you have (a map)?
Ha (una pianta)? — a (oo·na *pyan*·ta)

Is there (a toilet)?
C'è (un gabinetto)? — che (oon ga·bee·*ne*·to)

I'd like (a coffee).
Vorrei (un caffè). — vo·*ray* (oon ka·fe)

I'd like (to hire a car).
Vorrei (noleggiare una macchina). — vo·*ray* (no·le·*ja*·re oo·na ma·kee·na)

Can I (enter)?
Posso (entrare)? — po·so (en·*tra*·re)

Could you please (help me)?
Può (aiutarmi), per favore? — pwo (a·yoo·*tar*·mee) per fa·*vo*·re

Do I have to (book a seat)?
Devo (prenotare un posto)? — de·vo (pre·no·*ta*·re oon po·sto)

That was delicious!
Era squisito! — e·ra skwee·*zee*·to

Cheers!
Salute! — sa·*loo*·te

Please bring the bill.
Mi porta il conto, per favore? — mee *por*·ta eel *kon*·to per fa·*vo*·re

I'd like to reserve a table for ...	*Vorrei prenotare un tavolo per ...*	vo·*ray* pre·no·*ta*·re oon *ta*·vo·lo per ...
(two) people	*(due) persone*	(*doo*·e) per·*so*·ne
(eight) o'clock	*le (otto)*	le (o·to)

I don't eat ...	*Non mangio ...*	non *man*·jo ...
eggs	*uova*	*wo*·va
fish	*pesce*	*pe*·she
nuts	*noci*	*no*·chee
(red) meat	*carne (rossa)*	*kar*·ne (*ro*·sa)

SIGNS

Entrata/Ingresso	Entrance
Uscita	Exit
Aperto	Open
Chiuso	Closed
Informazioni	Information
Proibito/Vietato	Prohibited
Gabinetti/Servizi	Toilets
Uomini	Men
Donne	Women

Key Words

bar	locale	lo·ka·le
bottle	bottiglia	bo·tee·lya
breakfast	prima colazione	pree·ma ko·la·tsyo·ne
cafe	bar	bar
cold	freddo	fre·do
dinner	cena	che·na
drink list	lista delle bevande	lee·sta de·le be·van·de
fork	forchetta	for·ke·ta
glass	bicchiere	bee·kye·re
grocery store	alimentari	a·lee·men·ta·ree
hot	caldo	kal·do
knife	coltello	kol·te·lo
lunch	pranzo	pran·dzo
market	mercato	mer·ka·to
menu	menù	me·noo
plate	piatto	pya·to
restaurant	ristorante	ree·sto·ran·te
spicy	piccante	pee·kan·te
spoon	cucchiaio	koo·kya·yo
vegetarian (food)	vegetariano	ve·je·ta·rya·no
with	con	kon
without	senza	sen·tsa

Meat & Fish

beef	manzo	man·dzo
chicken	pollo	po·lo
duck	anatra	a·na·tra
fish	pesce	pe·she
herring	aringa	a·reen·ga
lamb	agnello	a·nye·lo
lobster	aragosta	a·ra·gos·ta
meat	carne	kar·ne
mussels	cozze	ko·tse
oysters	ostriche	o·stree·ke
pork	maiale	ma·ya·le
prawn	gambero	gam·be·ro
salmon	salmone	sal·mo·ne
scallops	capasante	ka·pa·san·te
seafood	frutti di mare	froo·tee dee ma·re
shrimp	gambero	gam·be·ro
squid	calamari	ka·la·ma·ree
trout	trota	tro·ta
tuna	tonno	to·no
turkey	tacchino	ta·kee·no
veal	vitello	vee·te·lo

Fruit & Vegetables

apple	mela	me·la
beans	fagioli	fa·jo·lee
cabbage	cavolo	ka·vo·lo
capsicum	peperone	pe·pe·ro·ne
carrot	carota	ka·ro·ta
cauliflower	cavolfiore	ka·vol·fyo·re
cucumber	cetriolo	che·tree·o·lo
fruit	frutta	froo·ta
grapes	uva	oo·va
lemon	limone	lee·mo·ne
lentils	lenticchie	len·tee·kye
mushroom	funghi	foon·gee
nuts	noci	no·chee
onions	cipolle	chee·po·le
orange	arancia	a·ran·cha
peach	pesca	pe·ska
peas	piselli	pee·ze·lee
pineapple	ananas	a·na·nas
plum	prugna	proo·nya
potatoes	patate	pa·ta·te

QUESTION WORDS

How?	Come?	ko·me
What?	Che cosa?	ke ko·za
When?	Quando?	kwan·do
Where?	Dove?	do·ve
Who?	Chi?	kee
Why?	Perché?	per·ke

spinach	spinaci	spee·*na*·chee
tomatoes	pomodori	po·mo·*do*·ree
vegetables	verdura	ver·*doo*·ra

Other

bread	pane	*pa*·ne
butter	burro	*boo*·ro
cheese	formaggio	for·*ma*·jo
eggs	uova	*wo*·va
honey	miele	*mye*·le

Drinks

beer	birra	*bee*·ra
coffee	caffè	ka·*fe*
(orange) juice	succo (d'arancia)	*soo*·ko (da·*ran*·cha)
milk	latte	*la*·te
red wine	vino rosso	*vee*·no *ro*·so
soft drink	bibita	*bee*·bee·ta
tea	tè	te
(mineral) water	acqua (minerale)	*a*·kwa (mee·ne·*ra*·le)
white wine	vino bianco	*vee*·no *byan*·ko

EMERGENCIES

Help!
Aiuto! a·*yoo*·to

Leave me alone!
Lasciami in pace! la·sha·mee een *pa*·che

I'm lost.
Mi sono perso/a. (m/f) mee *so*·no *per*·so/a

There's been an accident.
C'è stato un incidente. che *sta*·to oon een·chee·*den*·te

Call the police!
Chiami la polizia! *kya*·mee la po·lee·*tsee*·a

Call a doctor!
Chiami un medico! *kya*·mee oon me·*dee*·ko

Where are the toilets?
Dove sono i gabinetti? *do*·ve *so*·no ee ga·bee·*ne*·tee

I'm sick.
Mi sento male. mee *sen*·to *ma*·le

It hurts here.
Mi fa male qui. mee fa *ma*·le kwee

I'm allergic to ...
Sono allergico/a a ... (m/f) *so*·no a·*ler*·jee·ko/a a ...

SHOPPING & SERVICES

I'd like to buy ...
Vorrei comprare ... vo·*ray* kom·*pra*·re ...

I'm just looking.
Sto solo guardando. sto *so*·lo gwar·*dan*·do

Can I look at it?
Posso dare un'occhiata? *po*·so *da*·re oo·no·*kya*·ta

How much is this?
Quanto costa questo? *kwan*·to *kos*·ta *kwe*·sto

It's too expensive.
È troppo caro/a. (m/f) e *tro*·po *ka*·ro/a

Can you lower the price?
Può farmi lo sconto? pwo *far*·mee lo *skon*·to

There's a mistake in the bill.
C'è un errore nel conto. che oo·*ne*·ro·re nel *kon*·to

ATM	Bancomat	*ban*·ko·mat
post office	ufficio postale	oo·*fee*·cho pos·*ta*·le
tourist office	ufficio del turismo	oo·*fee*·cho del too·*reez*·mo

TIME & DATES

What time is it?	*Che ora è?*	ke *o*·ra e
It's one o'clock.	*È l'una.*	e *loo*·na
It's (two) o'clock.	*Sono le (due).*	*so*·no le (*doo*·e)

NUMBERS

1	uno	*oo*·no
2	due	*doo*·e
3	tre	tre
4	quattro	*kwa*·tro
5	cinque	*cheen*·kwe
6	sei	say
7	sette	*se*·te
8	otto	*o*·to
9	nove	*no*·ve
10	dieci	*dye*·chee
20	venti	*ven*·tee
30	trenta	*tren*·ta
40	quaranta	kwa·*ran*·ta
50	cinquanta	cheen·*kwan*·ta
60	sessanta	se·*san*·ta
70	settanta	se·*tan*·ta
80	ottanta	o·*tan*·ta
90	novanta	no·*van*·ta
100	cento	*chen*·to
1000	mille	*mee*·lel

Half past (one).	*(L'una) e mezza.*	*(loo·*na*) e me·*dza
in the morning	*di mattina*	dee ma·*tee·*na
in the afternoon	*di pomeriggio*	dee po·me·*ree·*jo
in the evening	*di sera*	dee se·ra
yesterday	*ieri*	ye·ree
today	*oggi*	o·jee
tomorrow	*domani*	do·*ma·*nee
Monday	*lunedì*	loo·ne·*dee*
Tuesday	*martedì*	mar·te·*dee*
Wednesday	*mercoledì*	mer·ko·le·*dee*
Thursday	*giovedì*	jo·ve·*dee*
Friday	*venerdì*	ve·ner·*dee*
Saturday	*sabato*	sa·ba·to
Sunday	*domenica*	do·*me·*nee·ka
January	*gennaio*	je·*na·*yo
February	*febbraio*	fe·*bra·*yo
March	*marzo*	mar·tso
April	*aprile*	a·*pree·*le
May	*maggio*	ma·jo
June	*giugno*	joo·nyo
July	*luglio*	loo·lyo
August	*agosto*	a·*gos·*to
September	*settembre*	se·*tem·*bre
October	*ottobre*	o·*to·*bre
November	*novembre*	no·*vem·*bre
December	*dicembre*	dee·*chem·*bre

TRANSPORT

Public Transport

At what time does the ... leave/arrive?	*A che ora parte/ arriva ...?*	a ke o·ra par·te/ a·*ree·*va ...
boat	*la nave*	la na·ve
bus	*l'autobus*	low·to·boos
ferry	*il traghetto*	eel tra·ge·to
metro	*la metro- politana*	la me·tro- po·lee·ta·na
plane	*l'aereo*	la·e·re·o
train	*il treno*	eel tre·no
... ticket	*un biglietto ...*	oon bee·*lye·*to
one-way	*di sola andata*	dee so·la an·da·ta
return	*di andata e ritorno*	dee an·da·ta e ree·tor·no

bus stop	*fermata dell'autobus*	fer·*ma·*ta del ow·to·boos
platform	*binario*	bee·*na·*ryo
ticket office	*biglietteria*	bee·lye·te·*ree·*a
timetable	*orario*	o·ra·ryo
train station	*stazione ferroviaria*	sta·*tsyo·*ne fe·ro·vyar·ya

Does it stop at ...?
Si ferma a ...? see *fer·*ma a ...

Please tell me when we get to ...
Mi dica per favore mee dee·ka per fa·*vo·*re
quando arriviamo a ... kwan·do a·ree·vya·mo a ...

I want to get off here.
Voglio scendere qui. vo·lyo shen·de·re kwee

Driving & Cycling

I'd like to hire a/an ...	*Vorrei noleggiare un/una ... (m/f)*	vo·ray no·le·*ja·*re oon/oo·na ...
4WD	*fuoristrada (m)*	fwo·ree·*stra·*da
bicycle	*bicicletta (f)*	bee·chee·*kle·*ta
car	*macchina (f)*	ma·*kee·*na
motorbike	*moto (f)*	mo·to
bicycle pump	*pompa della bicicletta*	pom·pa de·la bee·chee·*kle·*ta
child seat	*seggiolino*	se·jo·*lee·*no
helmet	*casco*	kas·ko
mechanic	*meccanico*	me·*ka·*nee·ko
petrol/gas	*benzina*	ben·*dzee·*na
service station	*stazione di servizio*	sta·*tsyo·*ne dee ser·vee·tsyo

Is this the road to ...?
Questa strada porta a ...? kwe·sta stra·da por·ta a ...

(How long) Can I park here?
(Per quanto tempo) (per kwan·to tem·po)
Posso parcheggiare qui? po·so par·ke·*ja·*re kwee

The car/motorbike has broken down (at ...).
La macchina/moto si è la ma·*kee·*na/mo·to see e
guastata (a ...). gwas·*ta·*ta (a ...)

I have a flat tyre.
Ho una gomma bucata. o oo·na go·ma boo·*ka·*ta

I've run out of petrol.
Ho esaurito la o e·zow·*ree·*to la
benzina. ben·*dzee·*nat

GLOSSARY

Albergo (alberghi) – hotel (hotels)

alimentari – grocery shop

allergia – allergy

archeologica – archaeology

autostrada (autostrade) – motorway, highway (motorways, highways)

bagno – bathroom; also toilet

bancomat – Automated teller machine (ATM)

bassi – one-room, ground-floor apartments mostly found in the traditionally poorer areas of Naples

benzina – petrol

biblioteca (biblioteche) – library (libraries)

biglietto – ticket

biglietto giornaliero – daily ticket

caffettiera – Italian coffee percolator

calcio – football (soccer)

camera – room

cambio – currency-exchange bureau

canzone (canzoni) – song (songs)

cappella – chapel

carabinieri – police with military and civil duties

carta d'identità – identity card

carta telefonica – phone-card

casa – house; home

casareccio – home style

castello – castle

catacomba – underground tomb complex

centro – city centre

centro storico – historic centre; old city

chiesa (chiese) – church (churches)

chiostro – cloister

cimitero – cemetery

colle/collina – hill

colonna – column

commissariato – local police station

comune – equivalent to a municipality or county; town or city

council; historically, a commune (self-governing town or city)

concerto – concert

corso – main street

cripta – crypt

cupola – dome

Dio (Dei) – God (Gods)

faraglione (faraglioni) – rock tower; rock pinnacle (rock towers; rock pinnacles)

farmacia – pharmacy

ferrovia – train station

festa – feast day; holiday

fiume – river

fontana – fountain

forno – bakery

forte/fortezza – fort

forum (fora) – (Latin) public square (public squares)

francobollo (francobolli) – stamp (stamps)

gabinetto – toilet; WC

gasolio – diesel

gelateria – ice-cream parlour

giardino (giardini) – garden (gardens)

golfo – gulf

gratis – free (no cost)

isola – island

lago – lake

largo – small square

lavanderia – laundrette

libreria – bookshop

lido – beach

lungomare – seafront; esplanade

mare – sea

medicina (medicine) – medicine (medicines)

mercato – market

monte – mountain

mura – city wall

museo – museum

nazionale – national

nuovo/a – new (m/f)

orto botanico – botanical gardens

ospedale – hospital

ostello – hostel

palazzo (palazzi) – mansion; palace; large building of any type (including an apartment block)

panetteria – bakery

panino (panini) – sandwich (sandwiches)

parcheggio – car park

parco – park

passeggiata – a stroll

pasticceria – cake shop

pastificio – pasta-making factory

pensione – small hotel or guesthouse, often offering board

pescheria – fish shop

piazza (piazze) – square (squares)

pinacoteca – art gallery

piscina – pool

polizia – police

ponte – bridge

porta – city gate

porto – port

presepe (presepi) – nativity scene (nativity scenes)

questura – police station

reale – royal

ruota – wheel

sala – room in a museum or a gallery

salumeria – delicatessen

santuario – sanctuary

scavi – archaeological ruins

scheda telefonica – phone-card

sedia a rotelle – wheelchair

sentiero – path; trail; track

servizio – service charge in restaurants

sole – sun

sottosuolo – underground

spiaggia – beach

statua – statue

stazione – station

strada – street; road

tabaccheria – tobacconist's shop

teatro – theatre

tempio – temple

terme – baths

torre – tower

treno – train

via – street, road

vecchio – old

vicolo – alley, alleyway

Behind the Scenes

SEND US YOUR FEEDBACK

We love to hear from travellers – your comments keep us on our toes and help make our books better. Our well-travelled team reads every word on what you loved or loathed about this book. Although we cannot reply individually to your submissions, we always guarantee that your feedback goes straight to the appropriate authors, in time for the next edition. Each person who sends us information is thanked in the next edition – the most useful submissions are rewarded with a selection of digital PDF chapters.

Visit **lonelyplanet.com/contact** to submit your updates and suggestions or to ask for help. Our award-winning website also features inspirational travel stories, news and discussions.

Note: We may edit, reproduce and incorporate your comments in Lonely Planet products such as guidebooks, websites and digital products, so let us know if you don't want your comments reproduced or your name acknowledged. For a copy of our privacy policy visit lonelyplanet.com/privacy.

WRITER THANKS

Cristian Bonetto

Grazie infinite to my *Re e Regina di Napoli*, Federica Rispoli and Ivan Palmieri; Igor Milanese; Gabriella De Micco; Valentina Vellusi; Mirella Armiero; Andrea Maglio; Susy Galeone; Enzo Porzio; Marcello De Bossa; Luca Coda; Harriet Driver; Alfredo Cefalo; and Malgorzata Gajo, as well as the many other generous Neapolitans who kindly shared their city insights and secrets. At Lonely Planet, a big thank you to Anna Tyler for the commission and to my co-writer Brendan Sainsbury for his stellar research.

Brendan Sainsbury

Molte grazie to all the skilled Sita bus drivers, helpful tourist information staff, generous B&B owners, expert pizza kneaders and innocent passers-by who helped me, unwittingly or otherwise, during my research trip. Special thanks to Alfonso and Rosalia in Agropoli for their help in the Cilento region. Thanks also to my wife, Elizabeth; my son, Kieran; and my sister, Theresa, for their company on the road.

ACKNOWLEDGEMENTS

Climate map data adapted from Peel MC, Finlayson BL & McMahon TA (2007) 'Updated World Map of the Köppen-Geiger Climate Classification', Hydrology and Earth System Sciences, 11, 163344.

Illustration pp114-15 by Javier Zarracina

Cover photograph: Galleria Umberto I, Naples, Antonio Gravante/Shutterstock ©

THIS BOOK

This 7th edition of Lonely Planet's *Naples, Pompeii & the Amalfi Coast* guidebook was curated by Cristian Bonetto and researched and written by Cristian and Brendan Sainsbury. The previous two editions were written by Cristian and Brendan and Cristian and Helena Smith.

This guidebook was produced by the following:

Senior Product Editors
Elizabeth Jones, Fergus O'Shea

Product Editors
Ronan Abayawickrema, Saralinda Turner

Senior Cartographer
Anthony Phelan

Book Designers Catalina Aragón, Gwen Cotter

Assisting Editors Lucy Cowie, Peter Cruttenden, Barbara Delissen, Emma Gibbs, Kate James, Alexander Knights, Jodie Martire, Angela Tinson

Cover Researcher
Ania Bartoszek

Thanks to Hannah Cartmel, Heather Champion, Gerd Fey, Lino Furci, Sandie Kestell, Claire Naylor, Kirsten Rawlings, Victoria Smith, Anna Tyler

Index

Map Legend

Sights

- Beach
- Bird Sanctuary
- Buddhist
- Castle/Palace
- Christian
- Confucian
- Hindu
- Islamic
- Jain
- Jewish
- Monument
- Museum/Gallery/Historic Building
- Ruin
- Shinto
- Sikh
- Taoist
- Winery/Vineyard
- Zoo/Wildlife Sanctuary
- Other Sight

Activities, Courses & Tours

- Bodysurfing
- Diving
- Canoeing/Kayaking
- Course/Tour
- Sento Hot Baths/Onsen
- Skiing
- Snorkelling
- Surfing
- Swimming/Pool
- Walking
- Windsurfing
- Other Activity

Sleeping

- Sleeping
- Camping
- Hut/Shelter

Eating

- Eating

Drinking & Nightlife

- Drinking & Nightlife
- Cafe

Entertainment

- Entertainment

Shopping

- Shopping

Information

- Bank
- Embassy/Consulate
- Hospital/Medical
- Internet
- Police
- Post Office
- Telephone
- Toilet
- Tourist Information
- Other Information

Geographic

- Beach
- Gate
- Hut/Shelter
- Lighthouse
- Lookout
- Mountain/Volcano
- Oasis
- Park
- Pass
- Picnic Area
- Waterfall

Population

- Capital (National)
- Capital (State/Province)
- City/Large Town
- Town/Village

Transport

- Airport
- Border crossing
- Bus
- Cable car/Funicular
- Cycling
- Ferry
- Metro station
- Monorail
- Parking
- Petrol station
- S-Bahn/Subway station
- Taxi
- T-bane/Tunnelbana station
- Train station/Railway
- Tram
- U-Bahn/Underground station
- Other Transport

Routes

- Tollway
- Freeway
- Primary
- Secondary
- Tertiary
- Lane
- Unsealed road
- Road under construction
- Plaza/Mall
- Steps
- Tunnel
- Pedestrian overpass
- Walking Tour
- Walking Tour detour
- Path/Walking Trail

Boundaries

- International
- State/Province
- Disputed
- Regional/Suburb
- Marine Park
- Cliff
- Wall

Hydrography

- River, Creek
- Intermittent River
- Canal
- Water
- Dry/Salt/Intermittent Lake
- Reef

Areas

- Airport/Runway
- Beach/Desert
- Cemetery (Christian)
- Cemetery (Other)
- Glacier
- Mudflat
- Park/Forest
- Sight (Building)
- Sportsground
- Swamp/Mangrove

Note: Not all symbols displayed above appear on the maps in this book

OUR STORY

A beat-up old car, a few dollars in the pocket and a sense of adventure. In 1972 that's all Tony and Maureen Wheeler needed for the trip of a lifetime – across Europe and Asia overland to Australia. It took several months, and at the end – broke but inspired – they sat at their kitchen table writing and stapling together their first travel guide, *Across Asia on the Cheap*. Within a week they'd sold 1500 copies. Lonely Planet was born.

Today, Lonely Planet has offices in Tennessee, Dublin and Beijing, with a network of over 2000 contributors in every corner of the globe. We share Tony's belief that 'a great guidebook should do three things: inform, educate and amuse'.

OUR WRITERS 914.573 NOV - '21

LON

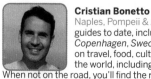

Cristian Bonetto

Naples, Pompeii & Around Cristian has contributed to over 30 Lonely Planet guides to date, including *New York City*, *Italy*, *Venice & the Veneto*, *Denmark*, *Copenhagen*, *Sweden* and *Singapore*. Lonely Planet work aside, his musings on travel, food, culture and design appear in numerous publications around the world, including the *Telegraph* (UK) and *Corriere del Mezzogiorno* (Italy). When not on the road, you'll find the reformed playwright and TV scriptwriter slurping espresso in his beloved hometown, Melbourne. Instagram: rexcat75. Cristian also wrote Plan Your Trip and Understand.

Brendan Sainsbury

The Islands, The Amalfi Coast, Salerno & the Cilento Born and raised in the UK in a town that never merits a mention in any guidebook (Andover, Hampshire), Brendan spent the holidays of his youth caravanning in the English Lake District and didn't leave Blighty until he was 19. Making up for lost time, he has since squeezed 70 countries into a sometimes precarious existence as a writer and professional vagabond. His rocking-chair memories will probably include staging a performance of 'A Comedy of Errors' at a school in war-torn Angola and running 150 miles across the Sahara Desert in the Marathon des Sables. In the last 11 years, he has written over 40 books for Lonely Planet, covering everything from Castro's Cuba to the canyons of Peru. Brendan also wrote the Activities and Travel with Children chapters.

Published by Lonely Planet Global Limited
CRN 554153
7th edition – September 2021
ISBN 978 1 78701 596 8
© Lonely Planet 2021 Photographs © as indicated 2021
10 9 8 7 6 5 4 3 2 1
Printed in China